SH▲
HOTE.

SUPPORTING THE LITERATURES OF THE PACIFIC RIM

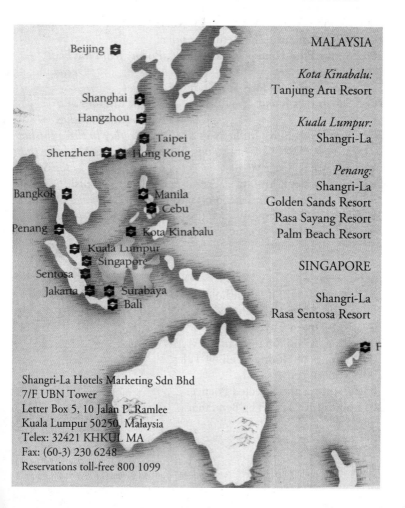

Beijing

Shanghai
Hangzhou
Taipei
Shenzhen Hong Kong

Bangkok Manila
Cebu
Penang Kota Kinabalu
Kuala Lumpur
Singapore
Sentosa
Jakarta Surabaya
Bali

MALAYSIA

Kota Kinabalu:
Tanjung Aru Resort

Kuala Lumpur:
Shangri-La

Penang:
Shangri-La
Golden Sands Resort
Rasa Sayang Resort
Palm Beach Resort

SINGAPORE

Shangri-La
Rasa Sentosa Resort

Shangri-La Hotels Marketing Sdn Bhd
7/F UBN Tower
Letter Box 5, 10 Jalan P. Ramlee
Kuala Lumpur 50250, Malaysia
Telex: 32421 KHKUL MA
Fax: (60-3) 230 6248
Reservations toll-free 800 1099

SKOOB *Pacifica*

Joint Series Editors: C.Y. Loh & I.K. Ong

SKOOB *Pacifica*
No: 2013

SKOOB PACIFICA ANTHOLOGY No.2
The Pen Is
Mightier Than
The Sword

Joint Series Editors:
Ms C.Y. Loh & Mr I. K. Ong

SKOOB BOOKS PUBLISHING
LONDON

Introduction © Prof. J. McRae
Cover Design & Preface © I. K. Ong

First published 1994
SKOOB BOOKS PUBLISHING LTD
Skoob PACIFICA Series
11a-17 Sicilian Avenue
off Southampton Row and
Bloomsbury Square
London WC1A 2QH
Fax: 44-71- 404 4398

ISBN 1 871438 54 3
Agents:
Skoob Books (Malaysia) Sdn Bhd
11 Jalan Telawi Tiga, Bangsar Baru
59100 Kuala Lumpur
Tel/Fax: 603-255 2686

Atrium Publishing Group
11270 Clayton Creek Road
Lower Lake
CA. 95457
Tel: 1-707-995 3906
Fax: 1-707-995 1814

Graham Brash (Pte) Ltd
32 Gul Drive
Singapore 2262
Tel: 65-861 1335, 65-862 0437 Fax: 65-861 4815

Typeset by Pearly Kok. Tel/Fax: 603-255 2686
Printed in Malaysia by POLYGRAPHIC. Fax: 603-905 1553
Colour Separation by Universal Litho Fax: 603-717 7527

SKOOB PACIFICA ANTHOLOGY NO. 2
The Pen Is Mightier Than The Sword

Contents

PART TWO: Malaysian/Singaporean Writings of the 1990s

Preface

by

I.K.ONG

The *Skoob PACIFICA Anthology No.1: S.E.Asia Writes Back!* has been a greater success in the West than it has been in Asia. For an eclectic approach, we have purchased the rights to several literary features and selected Nobel Lectures. The post-modernist/postcolonial approach is to deviate from the tradition and to develop a new direction of thought which leads to a evolution of culture. Geographical boundaries are no longer relevant in literature, economic status of the East is comparable to that of the West and sociological problems are universal. This philosophy has been adopted in the development of the Anthologies. The appearence of Toni Morrison's 1993 Nobel Lecture in this Anthology is a first. The Nobel Lectures for Literature since 1901 will be serialised in future Anthologies.

Literary criticisms in the Anthologies serve to illustrate the availability of literature in the Pacific Rim as well as to promote a greater understanding of the cross-cultural disintegration. During the post-decolonisation era, methods utilised to counter colonial racism is "anti-racist racism" as Jean-Paul Sartre described, "...to announce not just that we are as good as the next man but that we are much better!".

I profusely apologise to Philip Jeyaratnam, Kirpal Singh, Maggie Smith and Prof. Wole Soyinka for the errors in the first Anthology. We welcome contributions from the Pacific Rim. Please send your contributions to the address given on the imprint page. Successful contributors will be notified. All manuscripts will not be returned.

We wish to thank the numerous people who have helped to make *Skoob PACIFICA* a success: Miss Vixie Yong, Edward Yong, M.H.Yong, Jacylyn Chia & Noor of Universal Litho; Anthony Goh, Christopher Wong, Grace Wong & K.S. Boey of Polygraphic; Goh Eck Kheng of Landmark Books; Thor, Geraldine Jeremiah & Edwin Lim of Skoob K.L.; Joan Lau, Lee Jia Ping & Helen Ung of Wordsworth Bookshop, Ampang Point; John S.H. Lee of Sasbadi Publishing, Wan Norhayati Ibrahim of Maybank, Kung Beng Hong of Overseas Union Bank Ltd and the Shangri-la Hotels and Resorts.

sungai mekong

antologi latiff mohidin

wayang pak dalang

latiff mohidin

WA

IDIN

Latiff Mohidin

Serpihan dari Pedalaman

DEDICATED

TO

LATIFF MOHIDIN

poet-painter

The Line from Point to Point
The Art of Latiff Mohidin

As a young art student in Berlin in the 1960s Latiff Mohidin found his imagination returning to his homeland, to images redolent with the smells and texture of South-East Asia, until his canvases and drawings, even in the depths of the Prussian winter, became crowded with visions of thorny mengkuang leaves, fountain-like rumbia palms, extravagantly decorated fishing-boat prows and Balinese stone carving. These images were to become the foundation of his 'Pago Pago' series: totem-like forms that root his work firmly in South-East Asia and the 'Nusantara' ~ the Indonesian archipelago ~ in a way that defies mere national stereotyping.

Whilst his imagination roamed through his childhood memories, his mind was occupied with the compelling arguments of the German aesthetic tradition and expressionism, which were to shape both the way he thought and the way he applied paint to the canvas. Like Beckmann and Schmidt-Rottluff before him, he rejected the immediate perception, the first impression. Instead, he allowed these impressions and mental images to pass through the filter of his emotions until what appears on the canvas is as much the original palm of his memories as it is a reflection of his feelings about that palm and nature in general.

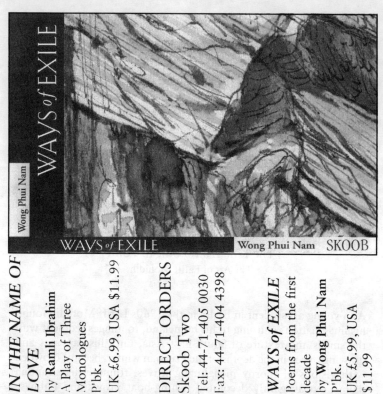

IN THE NAME OF LOVE
by Ramli Ibrahim
A Play of Three
Monologues
P'bk.
UK £6.99, USA $11.99

DIRECT ORDERS
Skoob Two
Tel: 44-71-405 0030
Fax: 44-71-404 4398

WAYS of EXILE
Poems from the first
decade
by **Wong Phui Nam**
P'bk.
UK £5.99, USA
$11.99

The intellectual rigour with which Latiff works infuses his art with a muscularity and rawness which many have found disturbing. Not surprisingly, his works jar against the more decorative aesthetic prevalent in Malaysia and Singapore, and it is rare to find his work in corporate collections. In a sea of pleasing, pastel-coloured, acrylic abstract expressionist canvases churned out by cynical, self-serving artists, his fierce, sexually charged oil paintings stand out as a monument of honesty in art and the supreme importance of emotional truth. As Wong Hoy Cheong, Malaysia's outspoken artist-curator, says: 'Latiff is one of the very few Malaysian artists to have returned from their studies in the West having imbibed both the modern style of painting and the sensibility that underpins it.'

One may have expected the fervency of the expressionist creed to have waned with age and experience, especially now that the artist is in his fifties, but the energy and strength of his latest works ≈ the 'Gelombang' series ≈ dispel such fears. A comparison of the first series, 'Pago Pago' (a title drawn from the word 'pagoda'), with his most recent series the 'Gelombang' (loosely translated from the Malay as waves of energy), would seem to suggest no connections, no artistic exegesis.

It is my intention in this article to present and illustrate the underlying themes and arguments in Latiff's work, themes that link the different series together and at the same time explain his commanding importance for art both within Malaysia and the rest of South-East Asia.

But it would be an injustice both to Latiff and to Malaysia to jump into a discussion of the artist and his work without trying to place the man in his landscape and environment, since one is inconceivable without the other. Latiff's work smacks of the inherent contradictions of Malaysia: a country comprising an eclectic racial mix of Chinese, Indians and indigenous Muslim Malays that is at the same time the most industrialised Islamic nation in the world.

Given Malaysia's enormous diversity of languages, peoples and cultures, and the Malaysian government's advocacy of indigenous Malay rights, Latiff is one of the very few artists ≈ and a Malay at that ≈ whose work has escaped the moral stain of political accommodation. In the true spirit of expressionism he has spurned the government's overtures and stayed quite single-mindedly within

LATIFF MOHIDIN, Preah khan - Angkor, 1966,
ink and watercolour on paper, 26 x 18.5 cm,
private collection.

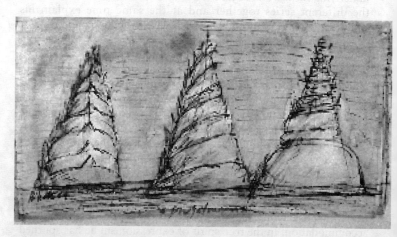

LATIFF MOHIDIN, Penjelman (Transformation),
1964, pencil and watercolour on paper, 12.5 x 23 cm,
private collection.

the plurality of Malaysian life, despite the fact that he is not only the nation's foremost painter but also its most exciting poet writing in Malay. Krishen Jit, the academic turned dramatist, considers Latiff's separateness from the cultural bureaucracy to have been a blessing in disguise: 'Government patronage can be the kiss of death,' he says.

As befits a world-class wordsmith, Latiff's evocation of his youth, both in his poetry and his book *Garis dari Titik ke Titik (The Line from Point to Point)*, is delicate and highly personal, grafting into poetry the expressionist idiom of his painting. As Baha Zain, one of Malaysia's leading literary critics, says of Latiff's poems: 'They do not strive to discuss massive systems of ideas; they flow from a mystical inner source and the personal experience of the poet himself.' An anthology of his poetry is currently being translated into English by Salleh Ben Joned, a renowned poet and critic.

Born in the village of Lenggeng, Negri Sembilan, in 1941 to parents of Minangkabau descent (the Minangkabau are a Sumatran people who practise *adat perpateh*, or matrilineal social customs wherein the property is vested with women), Latiff was one of eleven children brought up in the traditional manner. He was discouraged from frequenting his mother's house and entrusted to the care of his mother's brother.

A hallmark of Minangkabau custom is that the men *merantau*, or wander off in search of fame and fortune, and Latiff was no different. He records in the pages of *Garis* that at an early age, and this is the mid-1950s when the communist Emergency was still simmering in the jungles, he undertook a bicycle tour of the entire peninsula alone, just as in years to come he was to pack his knapsack and head off across Thailand, Indochina, Indonesia and continental Europe.

He had his first one-man show in Singapore at the age of eleven, having spent the year before drawing and painting portraits on the pavement outside Raffles Hotel to earn money to buy paints and materials. At the time, he was hailed as 'the magical boy with the gift in his hands', words that were to become strangely prophetic in the years to come.

After completing his secondary education, he received a German government scholarship which took him to the Hochschule fur Bildende Kunste in Berlin in 1960.

'In retrospect', he says, 'I think I was very lucky to have been sent to Germany and not to London where most Malaysians were sent. It gave me a broader exposure to Europe, in part because I was alone and had to mix with my German contemporaries.' Another benefit was his exposure to the German language which opened up a literary tradition that had been a closed book to Malaysians. This has been an enduring bond which has resulted in him translating the plays of Buchner as well as an on-going project, Goethe's *Faust*.

The 'Pago Pago' painting series is his most famous work, and in this series we can see the way that nature has nurtured his art. In the book *Garis,* illustrated with drawings, etchings and linocuts of the period, there are countless detailed studies of the simplest of natural phenomena, including a raindrop, a snail's shell, a bamboo shoot and a butterfly cocoon. If one looks more closely at the works one begins to see a recurring artistic motif, a product of the fusion of the immediate impression and emotion. In *Kehidupan (Life),* Kepong, 1965, a drawing of a butterfly emerging from a cocoon, the eye is drawn to the triangular shape of the cocoon and the insect's wings. The same shape, the triangle, is repeated in *Penjelmaan (Transformation),* Bangkok, 1964. In this watercolour three forms are shown: a pagoda, a snail's shell and a bamboo shoot. Each appears from the ground, three separate but similar triangular shapes that begin to assume a totemic role in his iconography.

The triangle becomes a building block which enables him to 'see' an object, deconstruct it, and rebuild it again in an amalgam of blocks. Thus the process of 'seeing' becomes active and charged with meaning, a metaphor as it were for the artist's own unburdening and self-examination. Much of the excitement in looking at the 'Pago Pago' series stems from the way it reveals the artist at work, the way he 'sees' an object and then how it is transmuted into art through the prism of his emotions ≈ in short, the 'expressionist' at work.

In *Pago pago nocturno,* 1967, an indigo blue canvas, the familiar triangles have been inverted, combined with one another and turned into a series of unrecognisable organic forms imbued with their own lifeforce. Urgent and rapid brushstrokes suggest the artist's intoxication; darts of black paint appear like the thorns on the nipah palm. One of the most dramatic of these canvases in a public collection, the Singapore National Museum, is his *Two standing figures,* 1968, of which Redza Piyadasa, Malaysia's most prominent art critic, says:

> The painting is a powerful metaphor celebrating nature's exuberance and vitality. The artist has transformed the ordinary and arrived at a symbol of nature's timeless potency. [1]

Latiff's 'Pago Pago' series has a resonance and relevance that extends far beyond the narrow confines of the nation-state, and in a time of growing regional rivalries it is a pleasure to observe the way he has extracted the essence of so much of South-East Asia from his peripatetic years. The drawings of Angkor, the Bayon, Bali and the natural world are infused with the same aesthetic. The same breadth of vision can be seen in his poetry of the time. His most famous poem, 'Sungei Mekong' (The Mekong River), deals with a conflict which for a few years threatened to overwhelm the region in blood.

Latiff is reticent about commenting on his most famous work, though he was drawn to say that he felt the biomorphic forms themselves have rather obscured an equally important aspect of the work: the centrality of the horizontal line, above which the 'Pago Pago' forms have sprouted. To Latiff, the line is the font of creativity and a second universal alongside the triangle.

Latiff has always been interested in the use of *jarak* (distance) in his work and the 'Pago Pago' series is also a play upon the viewer's distance from the objects represented. In certain cases ≈ such as *Ayuthya,* 1965, a charming, naturalistic line drawing of temple roofs ≈ the question of distance is not an issue. In one of his Berlin linocuts, however, a deconstruction and subsequent reconstruction of the visual image leaves one with a disturbing cross between a machine-like building and a monster with its arm raised in defiance.

Other examples of this duality and the play on distance are the two naïf drawings *Kaktus,* Hofheim, 1963, and *Blatter,* Hofheim, 1963. In both works, watercolours have been used to draw what appear to be soft flowers in bloom. On closer inspection, the forms

---

[1] T.K. Sabapathy and Redza Piyadasa, *Modern Artists of Malaysia,* Dewan Bahasa Dan Pustaka, 1983.

become less distinct and amoeba-like. Suddenly, the distance is stretched dramatically and bloom becomes a pulsing amoeba seen through a microscope.

The 'Pago Pago' series was received with almost unanimous praise. Redza Piyadasa says of the series:

> His most important contribution to Malaysian art is his potent imagery which is, perhaps, the nearest thing to a Malaysian art that any artist of the 1960s has arrived at. [2]

Understandably Latiff suffered a degree of artistic 'burn-out' after the draining 'Pago Pago' series. This was also a time of artistic experimentation with performance art, happenings and installations co-ordinated by the Anak Alam (The Sons of Nature). It is a time remembered very fondly by Krishen Jit as being extremely exciting, though he adds that the group, led by Latiff, lost their way when they strayed into more conventional theatre.

This activity was coupled with Latiff's growing interest in poetry. In the 1970s he published four collections of poetry: *Sungei Mekong (Mekong River)*, 1971; *Kembara Malam (Night Travel)*, 1974; and *Wayang Pak Dalang (Puppeteers Wayang)*, 1977; and *Serpihan Dari Pedalaman (Fragments of the Interior)*, 1979. Switching between the two disciplines, Latiff mirrors the artistic development of some of his regional contemporaries and friends such as Angkarn Kalayaanapongse, who also became famous for their success in both fields.

The 'Langkawi' and 'Mindscape' series represent Latiff's break from the past. In these works Latiff explores the relationship between the horizontal line and the superimposed triangular form. In the 'Mindscape' series, he uses different shapes and colours in a manner which remains unconvincing in the end. The 'Langkawi' series was greeted with widespread scepticism, although the wall sculptures have undergone a critical reassessment over the years since they were first shown in the late 1970s, and Wong Hoy Cheong considers them to be among the artist's best work.

---

[2] Redza Piyadasa, *Abdul Latiff, The Artist ≈ An Appreciation*, Retrospective Exhibition Catalogue, A. Latiff, 1973.

The 'Langkawi' series, like the rest of the artist's work, is difficult to appreciate. Carved and sawn wooden forms are painted and then hand-sprayed with more paint. The triangular shapes are placed on the wall in relief. They present an unambiguously atavistic message, their uncompromising formalism demanding a response from the onlooker.

Finally one comes to the 'Gelombang' series. The 'Gelombang' surprised the Malaysian art scene, which was unprepared for Latiff's return to abstract expressionism. The rigidity and hard outline of the earlier works have been lost in broad brushstrokes, swathes of colour and layers of oil paint. Latiff has taken us into the very web and tracery of life, holding up a microscopic view of the world, examining the capillaries and the epidermis of natural forms. Once again the expressionist aesthetic is at work and the artist's emotions are spread across the canvas; it is ironic, perhaps, that it is in the contemplation of the tiniest of details that such resonant and vibrant work should have come forth.

The 'Gelombang' series are like magnified fragments blown up to new dimensions. The strength of the canvases is something that has been remarked upon time and time again by the art dealer Marjorie Chu of *Artforum* in Singapore.

'Latiff's work is very strong. He is the last South-East Asian artist working in the classical tradition of oil on canvas.' If we judge his work according to Clement Greenberg's yardstick of the emotional truth of feeling, there can be little doubt as to its success. Susie Koay, the Curator for Art at the Singapore National Museum, is equally enthusiastic about Latiff's work. 'We have invited Latiff to hold a major retrospective at the Museum in April 1994. His "Gelombang" works are dynamic and full of movement. They possess a kind of energy that is immediate. The paintings are textural and it is exciting to see someone still working in oil, a medium which most younger artists have avoided.' Koay adds: 'We see his motifs as being drawn from the whole of South-East Asia. The diversity of that background and the wealth of these motifs mean that Singaporeans, too, can appreciate the work.'

Latiff's high seriousness of purpose and his quest for what he calls 'the fusion of aesthetics and ethics' sets him apart from the Malaysian and Singaporean art scene in a way that has strengthened

11

his work until it looms over the thin derivative works of his countrymen and so-called peers.

Karim Raslan

This article first appeared in Art & Asia Pacific Quarterly Journal Sample issue September 1993, edited by Dinah Dysart

ART & ASIA QUARTERLY

Annual subscription rates for 4 issues

AUD$54   US$48   SGD$80   HKD$360

Name:

Address:

Postal code

Country

Please make cheques/money orders to FIVE ARTS PRESS, Sydney Australia or STBS (Singapore) Pte. Ltd., or
send Bankcard (Australian), Mastercard or Visa details:
Card no., expiry date and signature.

Please post to:

Art & Asia Pacific	or	Art & Asia Pacific
PO Box 480		c/o STBS Pte.Ltd
Roseville NSW 2069		25 Tannery Road
Sydney, Australia		Singapore 1334

LATIFF MOHIDIN

casuarina

casuarina
in wait
for the dying
of the north wind
at the small stream's edge
of the north wind
at the vanishing point
of day

old decrepit crow
dying
in wait
for the casuarina
at the small stream's edge
for the casuarina
at the vanishing point
of my finger

signs

i see
   these lines
across the mirror's face
suddenly splinter
at my lightest touch

i see
   a lion
   an island

i see
   a sliver of meat
   a coil of hair

i see
   these lines
across the light
suddenly splinter
at my approach

i see
   a bird
   a shred of cloud

i see
   a ball of string
   a bell

i know
   already i have left
   table and window
   lines across clear glass

   lost is the wanderer
   who howls
   into silence

blue bus

a bus
coloured blue
unnumbered
and without driver
moves of itself
slowly
between vehicles
dripping with blood

should it stop
before me
i would then buy
a blue ticket
dead
to humour
dead
to song

friend
the time has come
that i go forth
the ticket i have bought
glows with a live heat
in my hand

the blue bus
presents now an open door
the time has come
that i must endure
a mortal hurt

crete

your white houses
your lightless eyes
are dried out
from crying for your many griefs
incendiaring
in a brittle land
crete
the mules here
fall on their bellies
for deep exhaustion of the world

in the dying olive groves
branches hang shattered in the light

your face still shows you
shrivelled
from sorrowing for ancient griefs
your houses smoking still
from passion of spilt blood

arise now
the waters at iraklion are salt
in the black pits
of your eyes
you may still be moved by hope

leaves are not falling

leaves are not falling
like the leaves that fell
last night
pelting the earth
in a great uproar

rain is not falling
like the rain that came
last night
dissolving the sky
into torrents that swept the earth

only billboards and signs
take root
they stand
imploring expectant
in the day's vacancy left by the wind

who will be there?

who will be there
who will bear the news of dawn
if the night is already out asunder
by the bright keen edge of fear?

who will be there
who will tell the bud's unfolding glory
if the world is burnt to a fine cinder
by the fires of doubt?

who will be there
who will intimate the first stirrings of love
if the heart is already deep
into wallowing in its own deceit?

encounter

beloved
light the way
through the darkness of mountains
where your smile surprises
in a sudden glimpse of sky
light the way
that i may pass
come through to my one true home

well do i know
how difficult the ascent
from dreaming in the gentle valleys
at your breast
into the overshadowing splendour of your hair
to drift traverse
the clear still radiance of your eyes

17

the curve of your cheek
in the wide bay of rippling waters
is fair sign
of weather in which to gain
an inland haven
your lips
to whose approach
i lead across the seas seven armadas
the admiral bearing only a heart
weighed down by longing

i will paint you
(for h.m.)

i will paint you in living moss
i will paint you in clay

in roots beneath the lotus pad
in shooting fingers of rain

in high sibilants of the wind
    i will paint you
in vocables breaking over the crests
    of waves

i will paint you in the clear
    meandering of a stream
    in the queer
    askew forward movement of young fry

in the faint roar of wind in the casuarina
in its dry rasp through a bamboo grove
in whatever else that is gentle
    touched with joy
i will paint you

18

dance fingers dance

dance fingers
dance
our shadow has long been laid out
along the frayed edge of the mat
and the elbows
blackened
dressed in a cloud of flies
gone wild
with the scent

dance fingers
dance
the breast already heavy with thick earth
will want
to have done
with so much frenzy
with so much grasping to hold more pain

dance fingers
dance
the blade has long been poised
waiting

you will never know

you will never know of dawn
flowering from between the hooves
of cattle
cold and small
in a field of black waters
that shine out in the eyes
of our mothers generation to generation

you will never know of any trace
of dream entwining itself
about the wooden rungs
ascending the makeshift ladder to this house
of hope swallowed up
lost between lips
formed of the land's distance and the sky

you will never know of the salt
sweat fallen in small streams into the mud
glistening
soiling sickle and hoe
that have cut
deep into the lallang
wild and bitter in its growth

rise into the wind

i received word
but without the words
i received a rose
but without the colour
i received her
opening my heart to emptiness

rise into the wind
be lifted up
be as nothing in the moving air
like dust

set out then

my heart has caught the song
my eyes the vision of wondrous happenings
my blood the spirit that breathes forth life

set out then through
     heart
         eyes
            blood
                into unknown realms

bring me back reports
after you sight landfall
by these familiar shores
                    (pelayaran)

river mekong

i

river mekong
it is your name
that i have chosen
for it is desolate
in the way
that i am desolate
within your murky depths
i shall have concealed
my warm
my breathing sides
in the moon
immersed
my right foot
and in the sun my left
i shall have set my heart

21

to ride upon your currents
my name to the open sea
and into the mountains
my voice

ii

river mekong
your breath moves lightly
like the wind
over your calm expanse
of water
curving into clear
untroubled day and sky
upon your bank
a mother sorrows
calling out to a lost child
for an answering cry
and when she leans over
to set her face
against your face
you can smile on
your slow undisturbed smile

iii

river mekong
end now your rippling dance
of light
i see upon your silt bed
unfurling blooms of blood
long wounds in stone
out of the north
the storm will come

and your banks go under
as you swell
rage in red coils of water
your undertow
more fearful in its strength
than the flood that breaks
over niagara

(Translated by Wong Phui Nam from the original Malay)

LATIFF MOHIDIN studied art in Berlin from 1960-64, in Paris in 1969 and New York in 1970. Latiff has held numerous solo and group exhibitions both in Malaysia and abroad.

His literary contributions include five books of poems in Malay of which four have been translated into English. *Garis dari ketitik (Lines from point to point)* has been translated by Adibah Amin and was published by Dewan Bahasa dan Pustaka in October, 1993.

LATIFF MOHIDIN
midnight lays

i

tonight
the moon
has pulled aside
her curtain of gold
the waves'
crimson lips
are parted

moon and waves
meet here
along the lower slopes
of your waist
to witness
                    the dance of your desire
                    the dance of my death

ii

look how i rub
your eyebrows
with honey
a column of ants
in trance
are dancing
a drunken dance
along the crescent
of your eyebrows

iii

from the still depths
of your throat
i hear
                    the howling of a wolf

the neighing of a stallion
the roar of a lion
unremitting

and my gullet
vibrates
with ever increasing violence
in answer to the screams
from the depths
of your throat

iv

your thighs:
sharp scissors
of thrilling softness

v

seven seas
a lone mountain
of wave
in the whirling
heart
of your belly
a throbbing
in the bowels
of time
is calling my name
i climb down the hill
i leave the vast open field

and crawling
i return
to the dark secret pool
of your being

Introduction
by
JOHN McRAE

South East Asia, Malaysia and Singapore in particular, is the new powerhouse of materialist progress, the economic miracle of the late twentieth century. A society has emerged where art is Picasso prints and culture the mindless violence of Hong Kong movies. Emulation of American and Japanese success has led to a boom, a lifestyle which has given the area a new identity on the world stage centuries removed from the colonial identity of only forty years ago.

It was Raymond Williams who said, "the making of the literatures is part of the social process itself. The society cannot be said to exist until the literature, like all other activities which are part of what we understand by society, has been written." In these terms the emergence of a rich variety of literature in South East Asia is beginning to give a creative identity to the society that literature is inspired by.

In the process of emerging from colonial, through "post-colonial" to a present-day sense of cultural identity, South East Asia has followed a recognisable pattern. There has been the strong affirmation of nationalism and local identity; there has been the rejection of English as the language of culture, and the virtual exclusion of literature in English from consideration as part of local culture; and there is now a swing back to the recognition of the cultural possibilities of a multi-racial, pluri-lingual society.

English is almost acceptable again, but it is not necessarily the English of the colonisers. And in many ways it is no longer the English of the colonised. It is the natural language of broader scale communication, embodying local tradition and colonial influence, the older English of colonial days and the lively new Englishes which are Malaysian English and Singaporean English.

These new Englishes are not a kind of pidgin regression (although some would like to think of them only on that level), but rich social variants on the world range of Englishes, every bit as valid as American street talk and rap, Caribbean patois, or Glaswegian dialect. For English has always been a language of mixes, a hybrid language reflecting myriad cultural influences: where Early and Middle English absorbed influences from such diverse sources as Norse, Germanic languages, Latin and French, modern English similarly absorbs influences from all over the world.

The process was one of invaders (such as the Normans after the Norman Conquest) allowing their own language and culture to be assimilated into the local culture; then a reverse assimilation began, with later colonised cultures beginning to leave their traces on the colonisers. The post-colonial world has seen the next stage in this process.

The shaking off of colonial influences can only ever be partial. What is conserved will be what is useful in the establishing of the new cultural and social identity. And it will include pre-colonial, colonial, and post-colonial elements. Nationalism is not the simple alternative to colonialism that it might seem: it merely replaces the colonial hierarchy governed from outside the country with a new hierarchy working within the country. Cultural identity goes much deeper than that.

In Edward Said's memorable words "all culture is hybrid." This has been true of every cultural representation using the English language for the past seven centuries. And nowhere is it more true now than in the burgeoning cultural production of South East Asia and the other areas of the world where new literatures in English are being written.

The cultural mix is very complex: old and new, local and foreign, oral and written, verbal and visual, traditional and modern, individual and social. All these elements are necessarily part of any culture. And they are compounded, rendered more complex in South East Asia by the new necessity of getting out from under the labels of "post-colonial" and "emerging" which have recently dogged the literatures of the area.

One of the stock responses to post-colonial labelling has been to affirm nationalistic tendencies in cultural production. But as Aijaz Ahmad reminds us in *In Theory*, nationalism is just as much a strait-jacket as any previous label. The affirmation of local culture has to be part of any move towards identity. But then there arises the question of cultural image: there are cultural arbiters who would rule on what is or is not an acceptable part of a nation's cultural image. What should be conserved, promoted, encouraged? Conversely what is less acceptable, detrimental to the image? This way "official" culture lies. And it is almost inevitable that official culture fixes, embalms, and stultifies the cultural manifestations it approves of. However valid its origins and however valid its permanent value, this culture risks becoming tourist culture, culture in aspic. There is a great deal of this kind of cultural production in South East Asia. It is not to be despised, nor is it to be over-valued. For this kind of culture preserves, albeit selectively, much of the traditional, attractive, presentable cultural history of an area. In that sense it serves an enormously important role in establishing cultural identity and pride in culture: it is a vital step in the building of cultural self-confidence.

This is however not to be confused with the cutting edge of active cultural production, which is a reaction to, rather than an affirmation of "the form and pressure of the time." And it must also be remembered that wherever official culture is proclaimed, whatever is not recognised as official culture risks emargination, if not extinction. South East Asia is living through this double-bind of affirmative cultural awareness and the necessity for innovation and growth. The problem is that the encouragement of new writing, and other forms of innovative cultural experimentation, is practically non-existent. The life of the mind is not part of the materialist ethos. And any society without culture is a sterile society. The greatest sign of cultural self-confidence lies in the recognition that culture is in a constant state of redefinition, of transformation, of assimilation, of ever-growing hybridity. The cutting edge is never comfortable. The most exciting writing challenges the accepted modes, questions, wrestles with the problem areas of experience. Materialism and sexuality are not easy themes to handle in a cultural context where a satirical edge is suspect.

In the 1990s there have been several developments in South East Asian writing. Where, for example, the novels of K.S. Maniam and Lloyd Fernando centred on the 'struggles of becoming' from colonial to post-colonial society, and where the writings of Shahnon Ahmad and Anwar Ridhwan focused on the *kampung* and the clash of the modern (as in Thomas Hardy) between country and city, the new generation of writers which grew up after the end of the colonial era, have new subjects, new emotional and social

28

geographies to explore. The earlier generation is not being left behind, however. Maniam's *In A Far Country,* in its use of dreams and shifting time-schemes experiments, formally as well as thematically, with the move forward and onward from the colonial experience. His short story *Rock Melon* in the present volume tackles themes of female sexuality and adultery in a way that owes nothing to post-colonial preconceptions. The questions it asks are rooted in present-day Malaysia, but are as valid as those of any story of our times, whether it be set in Detroit, Dulwich or Dungun.

There are new questions to be asked, new struggles to be documented, and new forms to be experimented with. Ramli Ibrahim in his play *In the Name of Love* brings new life to theatre in Malaysia, examining the loss of traditional culture and the existential spaces inhabited by some of society's outsiders; Hatta Azad Khan questions religious values in the present-day context of materialism. His play *Corpse (Mayat)* is a subversive and controversial treatment of that most taboo of subjects, death - associated with money and social responsibility in an existential milieu.

The stories of Karim Raslan are disturbing, even shocking, explorations of sexuality, hypocrisy and self-awareness. They are acute observations of present-day "Malaysian-ness," not afraid to mention religion and its conditioning of social mores.

Peculiar Chris is the first major gay novel to be published in Singapore, and it would be a significant publication anywhere. In the context of Singapore's conformity this is something of a breakthrough. All the more remarkable then that it is the work of a twenty-year old who has not published before.

What is particularly impressive is that Lee seems to have gone beyond the seemingly necessary stage of a 'coming out' *Bildungsroman* of the kind which has dominated British and American gay writing since Stonewall, but has gone directly into the greater themes of love and loss, introducing AIDS as the tragic catalyst without any hint of self-pity or righteous anger. It is also clearly not a novel for a restricted readership, as many gay novels self-consciously are - *Peculiar Chris* is an important and entirely successful novel by any standards, and one which deserves to take its place as a significant contribution to all the strands of writing it contains, Singaporean, South East Asian, gay, political writing, and an excellent love story to boot.

Simon Tay made his name as a poet - *Prism* and *5* were significant contributions to the burgeoning output of Singaporean poetry in the 1980s. But with his prose collection *Stand Alone* Tay has touched on a new nerve, and begun to explore the other side of the yuppie success-oriented good-life philosophy which has made Singapore what it is. His theme is the loss of values rather than the gaining of wealth and status, the violence just beneath the surface of a superficially stable society. The story *Drive* is a neat, universally recognisable glimpse into the psyche of the 1990s - the first-person narrator every bit as guilty as the BMW driver who is his antagonist: *Two Lane Blacktop* goes East.

Tay questions at the same time as he gives his reports from the front line. Some lines from the poem 'Moses' which prefaces *Stand Alone* could serve as an epigraph to much of the best recent South East Asian writing:

> What sort of exchanges are these?
> (Of course I love my people
> and my country
> but it's easier from afar).
> Whichever I choose I will regret.
> At the end, it will seem
> I never had the choice, no
> matter what I decide.

To go or to stay, to look forward or back, to accept or reject: each is an aspect of the negotiation between past and present that is the determining theme of all writing about growth. The latest South East Asian writing makes much of the new educated young, the Uni, studying abroad and returning, thus bringing the context of early K.S. Maniam and Lloyd Fernando up to date in the world of BMWs and video games.

There is still, however, a need for writers like Johann S. Lee and Simon Tay to offer a kind of 'author's apology for his work' - excusing the language because it does not "conform to Standard English" or apologising for the subject matter in an atmosphere where "no such liberty exists in our country." Very soon no such apologies will be needed. All that will matter is the quality of the writing and the significance of what is said. Such self-consciousness is all part of a maturing process which, to some extent, needs outside models to refer to, but which very largely must develop its own awareness, its own themes, its own relevance, its own languages, its own voices.

There is no shortage of women's voices, and although there is no figure as yet who can match the achievements of Amy Tan, the writings of Shirley Geok-lin Lim, Hilary Tham, Lee Tzu Pheng, Chin Woon Ping, Siew-Yue Killingley, Catherine Lim and Suchen Christine Lim can take their place on a level with their counterparts in any part of the globe.

Women's voices in Malaysian writing and Singaporean writing, particularly in English, have a distinct note of irony, a touch of humour that is sometimes lacking in male writing in the area. The questioning of patriarchal values and traditional roles is handled by writers who reflect the mix of Malay, Chinese, Indian and other races, and who, writing from their own experience, can give insights which reflect the outside world through an insider's light, and bring the closed world of tradition to outsiders with sympathy and tact.

There is in Shirley Geok-lin Lim a resonant clarity of vision and a pointed naturalness which are as subversive as they are refreshing. How much this depends on distance - Shirley Lim lives and works in California - is an open question.

The influences on these writers are as rich and varied as the individual voices: no longer is English Literature and the canon the basis of creative writing. Local theatre traditions, universal philosophical concerns, personal perceptions and new social awareness combine to give the richest flourishing of new writing the area has ever known.

What is emerging in South East Asian writing in the 1990s is an awareness of what it means to live in a society that is full of contrasts and contradictions at the end of the twentieth century. Complacency is not an appropriate response to the frustrations and challenges of the times: history is continuously evolving, and its processes cannot be ignored or risen above. Every bubble bursts sooner or later - the writing of the area has begun to express the doubts and fears, as well as representing the hopes and aspirations of a society that is more than ever concerned with material success.

There has been a new appropriation of language to come to terms with experience: the refining of language reflecting the ongoing struggle to give expression to the processes of growth, emergence, and maturity. These are exciting times, and the writing they produce is an exciting mirror of the times.

© John McRae, 1993.

JOHN McRAE is Special Lecturer in the English Department at Nottingham University and regular Visiting Professor at the Magistero Faculty in Naples, Italy. He is a leading figure in work on the interface between language and literature, and has published several books in this field. He lives in France and travels widely as a guest lecturer, theatre director, and consultant. He also edited the first critical edition of the suppressed novel *Teleny* by Oscar Wilde and others, and is co-author with Ron Carter of the forthcoming *Penguin History of Literature in English* of which the first volume is to be published in 1994.

The Journal of Commonwealth Literature

The Journal of Commonwealth Literature is published twice annually, usually in August and December each year. The first number of each volume consists of an issue of critical studies and essays; the second is the bibliography issue, providing an annual checklist of publications in each region of the Commonwealth. From 1993 it will be published three times.

All subscription enquiries/orders should be sent to: Bailey Management Services, 127 Sandgate Road, Folkestone, Kent CT20 2BL, U.K.

PART ONE

New Writings

of

the Pacific Rim

Tongue And Root:
Language In Exile

When my husband heard that I had been invited to speak at a symposium on writers in exile, he burst out bitterly, "But you are not in exile!"

Indeed for him, sharing a child and living in domestic quarters with me for over fifteen years, it is intolerable to think of me, his wife, as *someone who is not at home where she is*. The condition of exile is problematic not only for the individual who carries it with her, like a snail with its heavy horned shell, but for the people and country she claims to be exiled from and for the host family which nourishes and supports her in her impoverishment.

Exile immediately presupposes the sense of involuntary removal; it connotes dispossession, displacement, discontentment. As removal from an original and significant place, a homeland, an ancestral plot, it implies movement from inside, with the sense of wholeness, integrity, shelter, belonging, empowerment, to outside, with the multiple negative associations of being outcast, of ostracism, marginalization, estrangement, enfeeblement, rootlessness, disintegration, and loss. The original political use of the term, to punish a citizen by banishment from family, home, and social power to solitary existence among unfriendly strangers, persists today unambiguously, together with a host of new and modern permutations. It persists because the truth of state authoritarianism has not changed. From ancient Greek city-states to recently created African nations, politicians have strategically dispossessed their opposition, stripped them of the rights of citizenship, in order to enforce their own legitimacy and rule. In claiming exile, therefore, the individual is crying foul against a state; is asserting a condition of inequality and injustice at the hand of an oppressing force.

But now one reads of social scientists and historians defining such a thing as voluntary exile. Is voluntary exile the condition by which an individual chooses to remove himself from a centre from which he has already been excluded? If free choice is implied by the modifier, "voluntary," does that freedom extend to those conditions prevailing at the centre which lead inevitably to the hard road of departure? Or do we have in the phrase "voluntary exile" one of those remarkable ironies of the modern political consciousness, where one denies the reality of state aggression by positing the individual's power to escape or circumvent it?

As for me, I have for a long time seen myself as nothing but an individual. This self-image of "an individual" is the bottom of a descent, from nation and community. Growing up as a native-born Chinese Malaysian, I was surrounded by the solid structures of a large extended family, a narrow parochial convent education, a small-town tropical and pluralistic mentality, and the international English language. Nothing about my life was exotic or strange to me; the quiddities of normalcy are the sacred ground from which every writer begins. Nor was it odd that at the age of fifteen and sixteen, we Malacca children were asked to write essays in English on the meaning of democracy, on the topic of Malaysia for the Malaysians. Why should we doubt that our country was for us? We were in no way well-off, but as urbanized and English-educated students we anticipated a future which would include us and in which we were told repeatedly we would be the leaders of tomorrow.

If history were a process whereby expectations came true, perhaps it would have no place for exiles! That sense of destiny so casually instilled into my generation of Malaysians: where is it now? For the country has taken another path, another destination. The process of nation-building is never easy or harmonious, but for those whom it would exclude, it can never be acceptable without a struggle to influence it to larger, more integrative ends.

This struggle is waged by the parties in internal exile, by those whose contributions and services, and in like manner, whose rewards are denied in the present and future of the nation. These are the real heroes, who have not abandoned their vision of their place under the sun, and who daily live in the presence of political absence; their identities to be rendered invisible so as to enable the easier deprivation of their rights. When one group finds it difficult to stand up and say its name; when to say one's identity is already to mark one as lesser than, that is where the boundaries of exile begin.

Many English-language writers in Malaysia have found their foundations shifted in the last twenty years. Poised in 1957 with the attainment of independence to participate in the political fullness of nationhood, they have found instead historical definitions which exclude them. The only national literature, it is promulgated, is literature in the national language. This definition starkly underlines the movement to restrict national identity to a monocultural and monolinguistic position, a constitutional decision which cannot be debated under pain of imprisonment without habeas corpus. Indeed, for many English-language writers brought up to respect their country's constitution, this promulgation is a more effective silencer than tanks and barbed-wire. As a lover of one's country who cannot but wish good for its future, one must cut one's tongue off before one criticizes its law. And indeed I have little wish to criticize, for a newer and younger generation born without that particular sense of destiny that we were imbued with must be free to struggle with its evolution of nationhood. But as a free-floating individual, with my tongue still intact although my roots are cut, I can lament and record.

Andrew Graham-Yooll in an essay made a distinction between the whiners who had given up hope of returning to the homeland and those exiles filled with energy who worked surely towards the day of their return. Between the two groups, I am the whiner. Yet I can always return. The flight from New York where I now live to my home town would take no more than two days of steady travel. More separates me from my original place than distance. Educated to have my talents of service to my society, I know now that my particular linguistic talents are instead viewed as irrelevant to the official line on national development today. Proud of my abilities, I had seen myself when young as belonging to an intellectual and creative elite, helping to shape and create the features of this brave new pluralistic Southeast Asian world. Now the hour for that elite has been taken away, and another had taken up its position.

The unpleasant news about those in exile, whether internal or external, is that unless they overcome paralysis, history will be shaped without them. This exile, after all, has nothing in common with the metaphysical indulgences of individuals who disdain history in the light of existentialist perspectives. "Existence before essence" is all very well for a Frenchman who is so Eurocentrically positioned that from the bosom of his city and his language he dared play with ideas of nothingness and being. But for persons who in their lifetimes have found themselves acted upon so that their sense of selves, the essence of their cultural beings has become progressively denied and marginalized, their deracination is political first rather than philosophical and results from an assault on core identities, whether ethnic, racial, linguistic, or personal.

This assault was clearly formulated under colonial conditions. The suppression of education in the native languages in favour of English-language and British-subject education was a deliberate policy of the British colonial administrators whether in Ghana, India or Malaysia. Simultaneously there was a dismantling of traditional native social and economic structures, replaced by western laws and innovations of agricultural, industrial and mining ventures which would prove most profitable for western economic interests. The destruction and suppression of native customs, languages and economic structures, it is true, occurred together with the instruction in and replacement by western languages, customs, and economic structures. The many positive improvements in living standards (which are real and indisputable, such as better nutrition, improved medical care and water supplies, a more rational and equitable justice system) masked for a long time the many negative consequences of westernization on non-western peoples: the loss in cultural esteem, the empty aping of alien manners which filled in the vacuum after the loss of ancient traditions, the change from culture-production to culture-consumption and the consequent disintegration of social cohesion and communal values, and so on. Any individual coming from a colonial and post-colonial society, as most of the current professionals in Third World countries do, feels the force of these brief historical statements in her life.

Alienation to such an individual is not a philosophical abstraction but a political fact. For many Malaysians of my generation, the language we loved and were most at home in was not our mother tongue, be it Urdu or Hindi or Mandarin or Cantonese, but the tongue of the white man we were educated to fear and admire, English. The Irish nuns who taught me to read Tennyson, themselves children of colonialism, did their jobs well. I not only learned to read, but I also learned to love; I not only learned to imitate, but I wished to belong. For this personal outcome it is not the Irish women I have to thank but the English language itself and its manifestations in literature.

Thus, when the colonial world came to an end in August 1957 in the then Federation of Malaya, I rejoiced in the emergence of my people into their moment of liberation; but I naively expected the sun never to set on the English language. In the quarrel between national identity, as defined by a monocultural and monolingual ideology, and the English language, I recognize that I am not only a whiner but a potential troublemaker. English is to much a part of my identity, confused as it already is ethnically, racially and culturally, that I cannot abandon it for any overriding purpose. Yet I do not believe in the hegemony of English in the international scene; I would always want the wonderful babble of poly-languages about me, for I grew up in a world where I spoke three languages and heard another ten on either hand. And perhaps like a duckling who was hatched in the presence of a cocker-spaniel and waddles in order to wag its non-existent imprinted tail, I waddle rather than romp my way through pages of English prose.

Still, for all that, English is my calling. I make my living teaching it to native speakers, I clean up the grammar of English professors, I dream in its rhythms, and I lose myself for whole hours and days in its words, its syntaxes, its motions and its muscled ideas. Reading it and writing it is the closest experience I have ever had to feeling infinity in my presence.

Idealizing the language, I do not mean to idealize the English-language user. A Filipino writer, explaining why he wrote in English despite the resurgence of Tagalog or Filipino, the national language, after the Philippines won its independence from the United States in 1952, said, "I did not choose the language; it chose me." Another Filipino writer defends his choice of English as a historical accident. Everywhere where colonial masters have left and brown and colored people have entered into the halls of parliaments and universities to rule themselves, English has remained as that accidental stain on a people's intelligence and spirit. Leaders can only hope to purify their tribes by sacrificing whole generations of educated intelligentsia; or they can attempt to contain the linguistic contagion by limiting mastery of it to a few privileged elect. In either case they are also condemning their societies to economically regressive and authoritarian measures. The Third-

World English-language user is no historical anachronism or anomaly but the business man who desires increased profit, the scholar who wishes to increase his learning, the ordinary man or woman who would share in the goodness of freedom and individual liberty.

For while the English-language user may be motivated by subjective or selfish ends, he is grafting himself not only to a tree of language but to a larger history of human development. English is no longer that Anglo-Saxon-based speech of a few million people living on a small northern island off the Atlantic Ocean. English, in fact, has not been a national language of that kind for more than a century. It is, factually, a global language, the first of its kind; serving more than the needs of empire, unlike Latin; more than the prestige of that originating island nation. Right now, it serves the needs of every human whose understanding and imagination would overleap tribal and national boundaries. The student in Beijing who practices her English with tapes imported from Ohio; the Nigerian who studies for his O levels in his village-school; the Indian journalist who writes his copy in English while he interviews in Marathi; to these and many more, the English language is the means by which they communicate as a species. Independent nations today no longer see English as a tool of western imperialism but as a medium for trans-national species communication.

And yes, in the process of our discovering what we share with others, our tribal boundaries can become unstuck, our ancient or recent national identities can be shaken. This is the risk that Third-World English language writers take, the risk that all explorers come up against in travelling too far, the possibility of alienation from their native cultures, of losing one's way home. The child who leaves home, seduced by a stranger's tongue, and never returns is to be mourned for.

But exile presumes that such a child is forbidden to return. The language this child has learned is surrounded by an aura of illegitimacy, danger, and taboo. This rejection of their English-language writers, in India or Nigeria or Southeast Asia, can only damage those societies themselves. In denying a place for writers who have attached themselves to a language tree other than the politically correct one, these societies are seeking to control the act of creativity at its very root. It is an attempt at social control which sets loose the worst tendencies towards cultural paranoia and authoritarianism and which destroys that which should be precious for young nations and ancient communities alike: the lyric voices of their free men and women celebrating their past and inventing their future.

We should all support nationalistic measures to recover and reconstruct that cultural self-esteem a colonial history has almost obliterated. However, to carry on a vendetta against English-language users is a dangerously divisive policy in countries where social cohesion is most necessary. More to the point, it is ultimately futile when ordinary citizens can see how the political elite are educating their children in English.

As for me, choosing to make my future with the language I love, I find, of course, that language is never enough. The whole of a person is of sights, sounds, smells, motions, tastes, a community of sensations we call country. The naming is in English, but now the objects for naming are no longer at hand. I do not wish to be in exile. To remain faithful to my origins, I must be unfaithful to my present. To be constant to my Malaysian identity, I must continue in the United States to be a stranger in a strange land. Still, I have a language in my hand. To me, it is a language where the idea of freedom is broader and stronger than it is in any country.

"Tongue and Root: Language in Exile" was published in Third World Affairs 1988, ed. Raana Gauher, Third World Foundation for Social and Economic Studies, London.

SHIRLEY GEOK-LIN LIM is currently Professor of English and Women's Studies at the University of California, Santa Barbara. Her first book of poems, *Crossing the Peninsula* won the Commonwealth Poetry Prize for 1980. One of her short stories won second prize in the 1982 *Asiaweek* Short Story Competition and appears in her collection of stories, *Another Country*.

She has published another two volumes of poetry, and has edited/co-edited *The Forbidden Stitch* (recipient of the 1990 American Book Award), *Approaches to Teaching Kingston's The Woman Warrior, Reading the Literatures of Asian America,* and *One World of Literature.* Her book *Nationalism and Literature: English Language Writing from the Philippines and Singapore* was published in 1993 by New Day Publishers. *Monsoon History: Selected Poems* and *Writing S.E. Asia in English: Against the Grain* are due out in 1994 by Skoob Books Publishing Ltd., London.

THE CRNLE REVIEWS JOURNAL

The *CRNLE Reviews Journal* aims to provide a critical survey of English-language literary publishing from the post-colonial societies of the Commonwealth and beyond. The *Reviews Journal* is published twice yearly by the *Centre for Research in the New Literatures in English* at the Flinders University of South Australia, GPO Box 2100, Adelaide, 5001.

Subscription rates run per calender year and include postage:

Individuals:	A$25.00
Institutions:	A$30.00
Single copies:	A$ 7.50
	1979-1990 (inclsive)
	A$12.50 1991-

Cheques should be made out in Australian dollars to: "CRNLE Reviews Journal."

THOR KAH HOONG
Crybaby

- GERROUT.

The word was loud, like thunder drumming on the sky, like the quick anger of a father discovering his son smoking.

Balan, who had just lit the bidi, dropped it to the dirt in surprise, flung it to the ground in an Oh-shit-I'm-dead red alert reflex, the smoke going into his lungs instead of the usual holding in the mouth for a jetting of smoke from the nostrils, or for a snorting, fire-breathing Puff the Magic Dragon, for the O-shaped mouth to try and fail at smoke-rings. The smoke went in and the air came choking out, cough, cough, cough.

The gang turned startled, frightened eyes to the outside, to the black figure of a man outlined in the light, bending low because the ashram floor was only three feet off the ground.

– I said GERROUT.

We got out, scrambling on our knees, bursting out into the open. He was not a father, voice too young, outline too thin. Could be an older brother. One of life's many mysteries, older brothers. Many of our elder brothers also smoked, worse, up to six cigarettes a day. We small-fry with 30 cents pocket money a day, blown at the tuck-shop and 10 cents saved for a try at tikam-tikam, oh God, please, please, please let me win that killer ray-gun, we must look for three one-cent coins lost on the road between school and home, three collected cents for a couple of bidis. We became men when we could inhale the smoke of this foul leaf dried to a bitter essence, inhale it and not choke or cough. But our elder brothers will never treat us as men. They tell tales to Pa and Ma, pleasure for them, pain for us. Our stories were never believed. Of course, most of the time we were guilty...of having fun. That meant the cane. That meant crying, screaming, denying, swear I'll never do it again, promise, more screaming. Scream because it may soften Ma with her often-told memory of carrying nine months of hope, nine months of vomitting even at the smell of food, clenching pain on a hot afternoon, me dragged screaming into life finally on an exhausted early morning. Scream because Pa may get fed-up of the noise, what will the neighbours think. Scream because the bloody feather-duster/rotan/slap/stick of firewood hurts like hell. Scream even though all the tears and snot in the world will not move an irrational adult until some vague sense of justice is recovered from the fire of my pain and the ashes of his anger.

- Why you crying?
Whip of cane across the ankle.
- Keep quiet. How many times I told you not to tell lies, to steal rambutans/chikus/papayas/fish in the monsoon drain, you'll fall in and be swept away to Klang River where you'll be eaten by crocodiles/you think I don't know you have been stealing cigarettes from the tin/you think I stupid?
Whack of cane on backside.
- Stop crying. You think your mother and I not have enough problems? Neighbours complaining. Your teachers. Third from the bottom/third in class. Why can't be first? Are you stupid? Want to be rubbish-collector when you grow up?
Lines of fire on calves, back of the thighs, a protective arm that got in the way.
- If you don't stop crying, I'll cane you somemore. Now what must you say?
- Sorry.
- I didn't hear you.
- Sorry, Pa.
- You don't look sorry. Now go, go and do your...

All this fearful possibilities in the couple of minutes it took us to get out and a stranger move into the gloom of the space under the ashram. He lays down a package, settles down in our clubhouse.

The clubhouse of the Secret Six - God bless Enid Blyton - Balan, Suri, brothers, Balan a year older, Mat, Brian, Soon Heng and me, Chong. We had secret passwords and hand-signals, changed after long argument every week. We played with the other kids, we were not stuck-up, but we never let the other kids inside the club-house where we had our secret meetings, where our favourite photos of Cliff Richard and Tarzan and Jerry Lewis, the best one, Burt

Lancaster as the Crimson Pirate, torn from Movie News, were pasted on the walls of propped-up cardboard, where we kept our lasticks and cherry-guns and knives, where on Sundays we peered through cracks in the floorboards above, blinded by falling dust, trying to catch a flash of flesh, up above, Gopal Shetty teaching little Indian girls to dance, a jingle-jangle of bangles and bells, a thunder of stamping feet above our heads, Gopal clapping his hands, tak ka tum tum, tak ka tum, shouting Stop, stop because somebody danced wrong, because mothers, heavily powdered and perfumed, Indian marmees wrapped like Egyptian mummies in yards of cloth, were gossiping and not respectfully silent.

Now all that was lost to us. A stranger had taken over.

- Hoi, you gerrout. That is our secret clubhouse. Nobody is allowed except for the Secret Six.

There was no reply to Brian's shout. Just the sudden light of a match lighting one of our bidis. Bloody fool! Bloody cheek! Bloody bastard!

We waited. We debated. We all had bloodthirsty suggestions, but no one was brave enough. Then we had to go home for dinner.

Next day, school, was a long, long day. We met in the playground during interval.

- Anybody got any ideas?
- Maybe the fella will be gone by the time we get home.
- Ya, maybe.
- But what if he is still there?
- Then we chase him away. There's six of us. We each carry a stick.
- I will sneak out my father's pen-knife.

Six of us edging close to the ashram and the clubhouse.
- Hoi, you in there. This your last chance. Gerrout or we wallup you.
Silence. A couple of steps nearer.
- Hoi, can you hear us?
The stranger appears from under the ashram in a bent-over rush.
We were screams fleeing.

The next afternoon, Suri called us out of our naps, away from homework.

- The fella gone out. I saw him walking towards the coolie lines.

We ran to check the clubhouse. That bugger had torn down one of the walls and was using it to lie on, Cliff Richard on the underside, rubbed into the dirt. He had not touched our weapons. There was a T-shirt, a short-sleeved shirt, half a loaf of bread, that's all he had. We took the shirts and the bread and ground them into the dirt, into the green wet chicken-shit and hard little black goat droppings deposited by the co-tenants of the space under the ashram. That will teach him not to mess with the Secret Six.

That evening we were playing the finals of the Merdeka Tournament. Nineteen kids in screaming chase of a football. Mat was flying with the ball down the left. Suddenly he stopped. Suri caught up and charged into him, bringing Mat down.

- Foul! Free kick.
- You idiot, why did you stop?
- Accident. Not purposely.

Mat sat up and pointed. We looked. We shit in our stomachs. The bugger was there at the side of the field. He was only about 16 or 18, still very older than us. Suri, the tallest among us, only reached to just above his waist, I don't know how to tell weight but whatever, he was Bigger! Somemore he had this fella with him, Ravi, a gangster from the coolie-lines, real gang one, not like ours. He had failed the Standard Six exam. Got sacked from the Indian sundry shop because he shouted at the boss. He gets into fights at the toddy-shop. Sometimes he stops us, after school, even five cents will do for a cigarette, one time I even had to go to the shop to buy him cigarette with my money. They say he always carries a knife.

We were in trouble. Somehow the other kids sensed it, this oh-shit-we-are-in-deep-shit smell, and they started moving away, running when the stranger and Ravi started crossing the field to us. We didn't move. It was not heroism. There was no panic, not on the outside anyway, mustn't be the first to lose face, to lose balls, there was no thought, there was no moving.

46

- Hoi, what are you boys doing?

It was Uncle Ponnaduray, bless his busybody soul.

- I said what are you boys doing?

Ravi takes off, jumps on a bicycle, and is away.
We take off, jumped on the stranger. Why? I don't know. I don't know who charged first or we did it at the same time but whatever the madness, we were on him, thud, thud, not much power but punches finding flesh, the thigh, shoulder, I was hang-ing on to his left leg, flung off, quickly back to grab a leg, his slipper in my face but hanging on, thud, thud, crack of his arm across Brian's face, thud, what are you boys doing? Stop it. I'll tell your fathers, just a heave and heavy huffing of sweaty bodies, a mass, mess of effort and energy.

- Okay, okay, stop, stop.
We slowly stopped our struggle. I thought we were losing.
- Okay, we share the space. You can use the clubhouse when I'm out.
- When we are there and you come back, you don't tell us to gerrout.
- Okay.
- What's your name?
- Venga.

We never thought to ask him where he came from, why he was staying there, under the brick stilts holding up the ashram. We did wonder where he went in the day, how he found food. We were more interested in the fact that when he joined our football side we ended our losing streak. He was faster and when he wasn't he just slapped aside the kootchie-rats.
What was AWWWSOME was one day when he came to the field, stuck his hands inside his trouser pockets and came out with lots and lots and lots of centipedes and millipedes. Yucks. Awesome. Venga stood there, a grin on his face while these hairy, slimy, creepy-crawlies with poison bites which will do unimaginable terrible

47

things, worse than fever, your body will swell up like a pig, your skin turn purple, these things slip-sliding, slithering, gripping with half a million legs, waving another half million, he grips them in his fists, parts twisting and flopping between his fingers, he shoves them at our faces, we were screams fleeing.

It was in the newspapers. We heard it in the streets. Ravi and his gang had gone to Lido to see a show, had spotted two boys from Scott Road, slapped and kicked them and chased them away. The big boys in Scott Road and the coolie lines were always at war, sworn enemies, nobody can really say why, territory, you stare at me I don't like, leave our girls alone, just for the hell of fighting. Often it was just a lot of staring and glaring and bad-words, not too loud unless you really want to fight, fuck you can go on for some time but fuck your mother or sister means must fight, maybe some pushing, but this time the two boys brought back a brother and his gang...with parangs. When Ravi came out from the show, they chopped off his right arm.

Our area was famous. It was in the newspapers. We heard it in the streets. Awesome. They arrested three Scott Road fellas. Ravi went to court but he didn't say anything, he didn't say those were the fellas who chopped off his arm. He just stood up and said, "We in the coolie lines will settle it our way." Crazy brave. We heard the judge got angry and punished him.

- Did he cry, Venga?
- Who?
- Ravi, when they chopped off his arm and it was lying on the road, he must have cried.
- What? You think he's a crybaby? You know what he told the judge. He will never cry. His family is trying to cool him down before he goes to Scott Road to kill someone.
- He can kill someone?
- Ya, even with only one hand.
- Wah.

Once the others ganged up, picked on me, everybody took turns as victim, it was my turn I guess. The bastards ignored me, then called me names, Fatso, Four Eyes, Pig, oink, oink, then they jumped me, stripped me in spite of my struggles and put kerangga, red ants all over me. When they got bored and relaxed, I broke free, charged, Balan flung a fist, smashed my nose, oh God the blood just wouldn't stop. I inhaled blood until I must have filled all my lungs with blood and still it poured, a red Niagara that will soon leave me a bloodless corpse.

I cried.

Venga came by.

- O stop it. Don't be a crybaby.
- But they...
- I know, but what's the use of crying? Here, take my handkerchief and wipe the blood. See, it is stopping.
- It's not.
- Don't be a sissy. Girls cry. Heroes don't. Men don't.

If ever I had a reason to cry, I thought it was then, at that moment when the bites of the red ants were visibly growing, swollen red hills pushing up, my nose didn't feel broken but how to tell and all that blood, but Venga was staring, my only audience, so I stopped crying.

Strange, he talk so much, so big about not crying, yet one hot afternoon when the others were sleeping and I couldn't and Soon Heng's mother won't let him come out to play, I went to the clubhouse in case Venga was back, he wasn't, I lit a bidi but it's no fun smoking by yourself, so I went out to roam and saw Venga near the bathrooms and jambans, shithouses of the ashram. Venga was going in and out of the bathroom, water cupped in his hands, throwing it on the wall, rubbing at it with his bare hands, taking off his T-shirt and rubbing, scrubbing the wall with it. Someone had written, scratched into the wall (because the water was not erasing it): Fuck Venga moter.

Venga was crying. I didn't know what to say. Come to think of it, Venga must have a mother, a father, family, surely he is not an orphan, where are they?

- Who did this? Why they do this? It can't come out. Why say bad about my mother?

I didn't know what to say. I didn't know what to do. I went into the bathroom, cupped water from the tub and three it on the wall, again and again. Venga didn't seem to know I was there. He just cried and cried.

When you are 10 years old, time is always now, the past goes fast, tomorrow is too far away, there is only today, now, so I do not know how long Venga stayed underneath the ashram, how long he was with us, I think at least three months, maybe a year, whatever, but one Saturday morning, a police jeep appeared on the street, drove up to the compound of the ashram, four policemen got out, someone, some father had reported Venga, a bad influence on the children, a samseng, a gangster, we heard later that he had run away from a home for bad boys in Malacca, don't know true or not. The policemen surrounded the ashram. Venga tried to run, but they caught him. He didn't really fight, just seemed to give up suddenly. They didn't allow him to take his things from the clubhouse. They put him in the jeep. He didn't look at us, at all the people who had come out to see what was happening, like he didn't know us.

He didn't cry .

© Thor Kah Hoong, 1993.

THOR KAH HOONG's "Divide and Rue" was published in **Skoob PACIFICA** Anthology One: South East Asia Writes Back!

This is a short story, possibly part of a novel, probably a performance piece for the theatre. It's work in progress. Note to critics: All spelling mistakes and grammatical atrocities are deliberate and not the fault of Skoob's proof-readers.

He holds a Masters from the University of Malaya for his study of Sylvia Plath and Anne Sexton. After thirteen years of journalism-head leader writer,Thor is now the full-time artistic director of a leading Malaysian theatre company KAMIKASIH and the poor man's "I.C.A.", Skoob Books, Bangsar Baru, Kuala Lunpur. His prose work *Telling Tales* is forthcoming ,1995 with Skoob *Pacifica*, London.

K.S. MANIAM
The Rock Melon

My first thought was to expose her. But what was there to say? I had wasted too much of myself on her; given little of my time to my wife. When I think of the ten years I spent with her, I really get angry. What was I doing with her when I had a wife wedded in temple and at the registry?

She has a husky, caressing voice that touches you in unexpected places, like money. You know what I'm talking about. You have, say, fifty dollars, and you go into the supermarket. Suddenly you feel rich. You buy a bottle of red wine, some bars of chocolate and maybe a rock melon. There is that honeyed, musky crawling all over the body; there is that sense everything is opening up like a world split asunder.

That was the feeling she gave when she came to me in the nights. What a resplendent couch the sofa became when we lay on each other, my wife upstairs, sleeping, swathed in her innocence! Was it my wife's trust that compelled this voyeuring into unexpected regions, this surrender to the woman in her sister?

When she put her hands on my body she roused more than blood. She touched those parts in me that couldn't be systematised. (The sun rises and sets but its light shows up a tumbling chaos in the country of man.) Her fingers on my chest broke that Gordian knot of discipline in me and set loose that wavering need to be free. And I was, sometimes for half an hour, an hour, two hours, when the hard cushions of the sofa dissolved away, the light seeping through the window, like a slap of reality, unshawled rich folds of flesh - the landscape of a sensuous horizon.

Discipline worked to perfection: discipline was perfection. My wife went to work two hours before I did. My sister-in-law and I had enough time on our hands. During that hour or so only she existed for me. The children would have been sent to school. The atmosphere in the house changed, subtly or grossly, I can't decide at this point. Viji and I had each other and breakfasted on flesh. What amazes me now is that this went on for close to ten years, undetected.

I'm, by nature, an honest man, even an attractive one. I'm decisive. I've principles which have supported me through a not-so-comfortable life. I could have had more beautiful women, but I didn't. Had this restraint to do with my upbringing? My mother was certainly a severe woman, never allowing me and my brothers out of the house except for school and the odd football game. But I'd little affection for her; perhaps more disregard. I can't say my relationship with Viji was an indirect abuse of all that my mother stood for. None of those pseudo-technical Freudian underpinnings.

It was something more superficial or something that defies understanding. I'm hurt by the idea that I don't understand, humiliated by the recognition that I was drawn into some kind of a trance or enchantment. Did she or did some impersonal agent of chaos seduce me? Had I, over the years, developed a blind spot at the centre of my personality?

These doubts torment me now. But at that time there was no uncertainty as to what could be done and what had to happen. In the mornings or very late at night I made love to Viji. On two nights of the week, my wife and I practised the smooth passage with each other that supported and paced our marriage. We suspected nothing; we expected nothing. Just that rhythm of respectability and confidence which had given us all that air to breathe. In the mornings the breakfast table was always laid out neatly by Viji and my wife was none the wiser. Come to think of it, Viji understood about that sense of space I'm talking about.

She used it with a flair I can't give her credit for. She had dropped out of school; she had dropped out of work. The reason she came to stay with us was to get some kind of practical training: secretarial or manual. She only managed, or managed it in such a way as to take over the chores a servant or a dutiful wife needed to do around the house, or for a family. The house was always set up in its structure of routine so that nothing could be suspected.

For me there were no two ways about conducting myself in life. I remember a Tamil film I saw in my adolescence. It was named after a man, a very strong man and he has continued to be the guiding light in all my relationships with people. It was the way he stuck to his principles that won me over to hero-worship. He didn't struggle through the agony of choice: he carried out what his principle commanded.

The story may sound complex only because of the many incidents but the underlying truth was simple. This man, the son of a wealthy landowner, falls in love with a servant's daughter. The girl and her family stay in the quarters behind the house so that very early in their lives they can't escape from each other. The boy takes the lead role and is always dominating in the games they play in the front compound. They cease to be children and love buds between the two as they reach beyond puberty. The young man tells his rich father that he won't marry anyone else. The father says he will continue to give him an allowance as long as he doesn't marry her. The young man goes away to the city to study law but falls to drinking instead. The young woman is married off to a man old enough to be her father. Drunk and despairingly in love, the former lover visits her. He refuses to allow her to take care of him - love being stronger than marriage on her side - and says he will come to her one day before he dies. He does. He is dying from drink and he makes the long journey, but the train doesn't get to her village. It stops at the nearest town, some distance away. He gets down and sits at a stall to have a drink, then collapses and dies. The woman's husband, who happens to pass by, sees the crowd around the dead man and learning his identity refuses to inform her. But something tells her that her former lover is on a different kind of journey. As she rushes towards the doors - her husband has ordered them padlocked - she strikes her head on a swinging lamp and falls, fatally wounded.

What I liked about the story was that no one made compromises. The man didn't violate his lover's marriage; she didn't offer herself to him as some prostitute. There was a cleanness about their conduct that came close to purity. No one can keep up that kind of discipline. I don't mean by discipline a simple following of rules. It is much more than that. It's a kind of space within which you live with freedom and assurance. It's the space within which nothing irrelevant comes to disturb the peace. The space that allows you to be yourself. The space that allows you to be a husband and father. And a lover?

There was no violation. In fact, the one reinforced the other. I mean the love-making with Viji strengthened the ties with my wife. Take, for instance, the breakfast table. The wife ate there; the children scrambled all over it before going off to school. Then that very table became something else between Viji and me. The children spilled tea and chutney on its smooth surface. Viji and I spilled ourselves across the breadth and width of its yielding region of varnished wood; when our bodies met and flesh slid into rhythm the table didn't exist. Then it was that I was touched by a giddiness, as a swimmer would be if he finds no seabed when he dives for the bottom. The water covers him with an exhilaration not uncoloured by danger.

Viji swabbed the table clean after that and gave it a shine of a deepened respectability. The day began and gradually took me through work, family and finally to my wife's bed, on those appointed nights. At that time when I sank into the soft bed beside my wife, I only experienced the deliciousness of being with a different kind of woman.

She had always kept me stable. I recall the days I met and courted her. I went with my hockey team to her town. The field where we practised - the ball knocking against the sturdy sticks across the uneven ground - was next to her college. She was training to be a teacher. She didn't see me seeing her but I decided then and there that no other woman could be my wife.

I think of the rock melon I mentioned earlier. She was carved out of nature in that way, solid and filled with sap, the dusky, outer peel needing no further exploration to tell me that the pulp and juices were intact, inside. I accepted and trusted her like I did the earth: both possessed that self-contained set of complex forces rousing in a man a reverence, not shoddy digging about.

Where did I figure in all this? I had my brand of self-sufficiency and perfection. My wife didn't know I'd touched another woman not because I hesitated to tell her but because it was unnecessary. With her my behaviour was the same: nothing betrayed me. It even seems irrelevant to talk of betrayal. From the start of our relationship, she placed immense trust in me and in no way had I abused that.

The violation came from Viji. I didn't get to know of it until much later. Who would suspect a woman of having evil designs on her own sister? Almost everyone who knows my wife talks only of her goodness, sense of responsibility and restraint. I've never heard her say a harsh word to Viji. If anything, she did everything to make her, a grown woman, comfortable in a Hindu household. Hindu society is such that even if nothing went on between husband

and sister-in-law, it suspects something is going on just because she is present in the family for too long. (Viji stayed with us for quite some time.)

She returned to us after her first marriage to a man I'd found for her. I hadn't forgotten why my father-in-law sent her to me. He had done so in the hope that I'd put her onto some career or place her within marriage. I tried both but she wanted only to be back with me. Any man could have given her what she got from me, perhaps in a shorter time, but she didn't want that.

I remember when she returned to me after her first marriage. Those people didn't even have the courtesy to send her to our doorstep. They just dumped her a few houses away and drove off. Her face was swollen from their beating; she had on nothing except a house *sari* and a blouse. She looked like a servant who had been brutally assaulted for bad service and then chucked out.

It took only a few days for her to rehabilitate herself.

"When you're with me I feel very strong," she told me the following morning, after my wife had gone to work.

We promised not to touch each other but our word, after her swellings had subsided, lay limp and crumpled like her *sari* on the living room carpet a few days later.

The day and night circles moved within their particular orbits; there were moments when the circling nearly came close or overlapped. But commonsense and the sheer impenetrability of the two systems prevented a collision. There was one occasion when Viji almost let my wife know that the goat had grazed on unmarital pasture. She was in a strange mood and hurled to the kitchen floor, in a fit of temper, a *kuali* and an aluminium ladle.

"They're not your things," my wife said, "that's why you break them."

"They just fell," Viji said.

From the living room I sensed that the signal man had dozed off: two trains had been re-routed onto the same tracks. I went between them. Viji had her back turned to me perhaps not to give away the passion we had for each other when we were alone.

"We allow no carelessness in this house," I said.

She turned round then and for a moment I feared that she weakly hovered between restraint and telling my wife that she, Viji, had as much stake in me as my wife owned.

"You always side your wife!" she shouted and stamped out of the kitchen.

My wife looked at me and shook her head.

"That temper must be bridled," she said.

I'm a harsh disciplinarian. For a week I denied her what she craved: those mornings of irresponsible love-making. At last I yielded and was late for work that Monday. Was it her physical passion or intense desire for me that broke the bunds of normal practice? Why was it that when I was with her, doing all those little, unimaginable flexings, I felt no guilt at all?

She was no rock melon. The more I reached into her, the more I found myself enmeshed in a tangle of sprays. If my wife had complete trust in me, I had complete faith that Viji wouldn't do anything to jeopardise the situation. She didn't. What mystifies me, however, is that she was building a small circle of admirers around herself. Are trust and faith hindrances to knowledge? Do they in some way shut off your awareness to the possibilities that exist in human relationships?

Viji was my dawn and early mornings; my wife was my afternoons, evenings and nights. The children give the marriage a substantial world in which the rituals of providing and fathering were comfortable realities. What did my wife know about my working self or I of hers? What did I know of my children's school selves? They left the house, dressed and reassured by Viji, in the mornings and returned late in the afternoons, after tuition classes, to be undressed, bathed and soothed by Viji.

Some weekends Viji went away to her hometown, mother and brothers - the father had died a few years back - and in the half-emptiness of the mornings I felt stealing upon me a discomforting sense of rest. I never wondered nor questioned what Viji did when she went back to the remnants of her family. I was told, and I couldn't believe it, that she was a quarrelsome bitch who wanted to have everything her way. My experience with her showed me only a subservient, pleasure-loving person.

We were a family, Viji included, and had always enjoyed the reputation of being thought of highly. I was a hero in my in-laws' eyes, somewhat like that man with the principled behaviour, in the film I mentioned. My good looks, height and width of chest added no little weight to the impression. And though we struggled to keep our heads above water we never became submerged by money demands or difficulties. People looked upon us as a kind of model family - sun seemed to add a gloss to the picture we made - and, I fear, with envy in their hearts.

Was it not possible that when Viji went back she began to look at her brothers, mother and relatives out of this picture of quality and attractiveness? The only thing was that she brought into it a bit of dirt - the harsh grating of jealousy. The fascination she had for me, the power she had over me, were after all self-centred. That is how I began to read the situation after my wife and I discovered ourselves becoming increasingly unpopular.

She was using all the tricks she knew from the book of womanhood to get back at her sister. Something in their early relationship as sisters must have drawn the steel wire of tension between them. My wife forgot whatever incident it was that drew so much planning and self-surrender from Viji for a soft, feathery satisfaction. I tried to find out from my wife. She only remembers that being the eldest in the family she had to be an example and an exacting provider. The family was down and out. From the allowance she received as a trainee-teacher she had to stretch frugal resources for the upkeep of family image and dignity. The father had no pension to speak of. Even when I was a visitor to the family, during those courtship days, I saw no signs of struggle with finances, poverty. The talcum powder, after her sisters and brothers had bathed, made luxurious clouds over the meagre but clean furniture in that small living room.

Viji was trying too hard to get into our frame - my wife's and mine. While she acted in such a way as not to threaten any displacement in our household, she was perhaps trying for that breathing space I touched on earlier, in which to be herself. But the problem was that she didn't know she was indirectly causing tremors to the very foundation on which our relationship rose like a sphinx. Nobody knew, not even my wife, the creature that rose in the dark, fed by the sensuous air of the living room. When Viji called me *"athan"* in front of the family or visitors it was not the term of endearment a wife used towards the husband but that of a sister-in-law well-wrapped within the folds of intimate living.

"She's so close to you," a visitor once remarked. "Doesn't your wife mind?"

The reassurance in the innocent smile my wife gave him put an end to further surprise.

On weekends either my wife went out to my in-laws or Viji did. There was always a woman by my side. That weekend I decided in favour of my wife and accompanied her to her mother's house. The long ride was done efficiently. Once I took the wheel my wife and children left everything to me. If there were stops for drinks, we didn't linger over them. I didn't need any stretching of the legs. Besides, I was anxious to see my mother-in-law - twice over, I thought secretly - and my brothers-in-law. They were all working, small jobs in that small town, but the respect with which they welcomed and treated me was worth any sacrifice.

My mother-in-law didn't come out when I parked the car in front of the house. My brothers-in-law were queued up at the bathroom for they had just returned from, apparently, overtime. Vasu, my favourite brother-in-law, had a strange smirk on his face as he turned it away from me. My wife, relieved that the motoring was over, went to the room we had used immediately after our marriage, and changed. Once she came back to her family, she took over whatever work had to be done in the house. Perhaps the routine instilled into her life so long ago had not been in any way tampered with.

My mother-in-law was nowhere to be seen. When bathing time was over, the young men drifted away except for Vasu, who sat across from me and wouldn't take his eyes off my face. That was perhaps the first time in my life when I was scrutinised so closely. At first I didn't feel uncomfortable for I was used to being looked at in a hero-worshipping sort of way. I was a hero to my very young brother-in-law: a tall, dark stranger who suddenly appeared to them one afternoon, a long time ago, from a glamorous city, Kuala Lumpur. They had followed me about, even imitating the way I walked. Of course, by that time their hair was combed back, straight over the nape, like mine. But that evening, Vasu's stare continued to sit on my face longer than was necessary.

When my wife called them in to dinner, the usual conviviality was absent. They usually teased her about her city ways, how she would have lost touch with the ritual of cooking simple, tasty food and how she would have to stoop every time she entered the kitchen because the doors were large, the lintels high and the ceiling even higher up (casting mischievous glances at me) in her husband's house.

But that evening there was no such banter. The meal had the air of being eaten in the way mourners did after they came back from burying the dead and the bereaved host had to make a gesture at hospitality. I had a vague feeling that some part of me had died.

Situations are usually brought back to normality through not resorting to aggravation and only through persistence. My wife may or may not have noticed the way her mother and brothers were behaving. (Later she told me that her mother was too sick to come among people.) She washed up the plates and cups, put them away and hung up the drying rag on its nail. I sat in the kitchen watching her, a strange restlessness playing havoc with my usual sense of order.

The family went to sleep, my brothers-in-law studiously avoiding me and my mother-in-law noticeably absent, and I slept out in the living room as was my practice. Even here, I recall, in the very centre of house and family she had come out fumbling for me in the dark, having left the bathroom light on and banging its door shut. But the quiet that surrounded me that night did nothing to calm me down. I intuitively felt something was wrong and as if on some kind of cueing, I heard a suppressed but trailed sobbing and then snuffled crying. I sat up and hunted for my cigarettes in the dark. I wished Viji had been there for then with her bustling efficiency and showmanship she would have put everything right.

"What have you done to Viji?" my mother-in-law asked in a hollow voice, between sobs. "Why do you come here?"

That was one of the rare times I heard my wife raise her voice.

"What did that good-for-nothing tell you?"

There was another burst of crying and lights went on in the room and in the next one, where the young men slept. Someone switched on the living room light. The brightness dazzled me for a while and threw a kind of shroud over the figures that now gathered around me: my wife pushed my mother-in-law forward and my brother-in-law huddled around her like watch dogs.

"What's all this?" I said.

My mother-in-law thrust her sons away, then stood not more than a few feet from me.

"You should know," she said.

My mind suddenly filled with all kinds of thoughts. Had we, Viji and I, overlooked some detail? Did this woman, who stood before me, know the truth? I vowed then and there to have nothing to do with Viji. I looked up and almost recoiled in surprise, for the familiarity I had read into her face, wasn't there any more. Could this woman have given birth to two girls so entirely different? Now, when she needed most to reassure, she swayed before my eyes like a statue of doubtful origins.

My wife spoke.

"Viji has been telling all kinds of stories. Specially about me. About how I ill-treat her, look on her as a servant. Worse still, she has told them I don't want anyone in our house except you. You tell her the truth."

She went away to the kitchen. At moments of crisis she always made a hot drink for herself.

"You married my daughter but you don't want me in the house," my mother-in-law said. "Even as a visitor for a day or two."

"The house is open to everyone," I said.

"All a show," she said.

There's no need to repeat the rest: they were accusations mainly against my wife. The rock melon hadn't been understood. I saw behind my mother-in-law's shoulder Vasu leering at me. No more that glow of admiration, only an ugly contempt. Was that what I had become?

How can I expose her? She admitted, when I talked to her on returning to K.L., that she too wanted to be honourable, a woman as unspotted as my wife. If I don't play up to her fiction then she will be the one to expose me. Can that happen? Who will believe her? Already the winds of doubt are lifting the veils of fabrication. I might have fallen from the heights of hero-worship only because I let someone like Viji cast suspicion on my wife's character. What am I to do with my own fiction: those nightly and morning trembling pleasures that take hold of me and refuse entry to commonsense?

There is no such thing as absolute discipline or even purity. Somehow our activities and desires get coloured by ambition. That thing, principles, that gets into the nooks and crannies of all my behaviour is of no use. And ambition lies dormant even in sated flesh, like a sensuous snake dreaming of repletion. No, Viji doesn't use her body because it thrills to pleasure but because it suffocates discretion and virtue. She had made of me a thing beyond ordinary ideas of good and evil, right and wrong. I thought nothing could touch the unalloyed passion with which she gave herself to me. I was wrong. How do I now look at the severe, upright, innocent face of my wife? I head now towards a collision in the dark and that rock melon might be split and scattered all about the axis of my anxiety.

K.S. MANIAM graduated from the University of Malaya in 1973 in English, and received an M.A. in 1979. He is associate Professor in English at the University of Malaya.

His short stories were published in *Commentary, Southeast Asian Review of English, Solidarity* and anthologised in *Malaysian Short Stories* (Heinemann Asia, 1981), *Encounters: Selected Indian and Australian Short Stories* (Pointer Pub., Jaipur, 1988) and *Rim of Fire: Stories from the Pacific Rim* (Vintage, New York, 1992). His collection *Plot, The Aborting, Parablames and Other Stories* came out in 1989. His play, *The Cord*, published in 1983, was staged in Kuala Lumpur in 1984 and Singapore 1986. *The Sandpit: Womensis* was staged in Singapore in 1990 and in Kuala Lumpur 1991. *The Third Child* and *A Hundred Years After and Other Stories* will be published by Times Intn., Singapore. His first novel *The Return*, a *Bildungsroman* was republished by **Skoob PACIFICA**, in 1993. His new novel, *In A Far Country* was also published by**Skoob PACIFICA** in 1993. *Sensuous Horizons*, a collection of four stories: *Ratnamuni, The Loved Flaw, The Rock Melon* and *Mala* with four plays: *The Cord, The Cord Playlet, The Sandpit Monologue* and *The Sandpit: Womensis* is available from Skoob *PACIFICA* , London.

BETH YAHP
Before My Mother Became A Christian
An excerpt from
The Crocodile Fury

Before my mother became a Christian she was convinced that her
luck was bad. My mother's bad luck hung on black hooks from her
shoulders, like wings. As she walked it brushed the earth behind
her. My mother picked up this bad luck when she was just a child
and did not know the techniques of bad luck evasion. That morning
she stood at the scene of a murder the night before, watching the
blood spots on the path slowly browning. The spots bunched like
flowers on the path that led through the field from my mother's
house to the river. My mother dropped her bundle of washing. In
the distance she could hear the echoing of shouts of her brothers
and sisters at play. On each side of the clustered blood spots was a
handprint, one faint, the other heavy, holding the spots together.
My mother bent to inspect the handprints more closely. She
touched the tip of an outspread finger with her own. Although she
did not know it then, this was when the bad luck hooked itself
onto her back.

'Was it heavy?' the bully asks, flexing her own broad shoulders
on which, if anything dared to hook itself, she would immediately
know.

'Did it hurt?' I add.

'Can't you see how she is bent over?' Grandmother cries. 'Can't
you see her face. She thinks she's passed her bad on to Jesus, but
see how she's bent!'

My mother carried her bad luck home when she finally ran to
tell about the murder. The body twisted into the undergrowth
reached out its arms to make her run faster. The moment she
entered the house, everything changed. The shadow of the bad luck
coloured the whole front room. My mother tripped on the doorstep, which was raised to prevent demons from entering. Her
outstretched arms broke her fall. Her palms slid to a stop along
the knotted wood, leaving skin, picking up splinters. Her palms
made two marks on either side of her head, one faint, the other
heavy. From that day, everything began to go wrong. Rising with

eyes brimful and palms scraped ragged, my mother felt the unfamiliar weight of the bad luck on her shoulders. As she grew it spread itself more evenly. It bent her knees, making her shuffle, and drooped her head, and hung like lead in her hands so that even the things she touched with the lightest touch spilled, and cracked, and shattered. The bad luck slipped into my mother's blood. It weighed down the corners of her mouth.

Slowly, her reputation spread. When the people of her village saw her coming they spat three times and turned the other way. They sprinkled salt into her footprints and covered the faces of babies when she passed. No-one looked her in the eye. My mother's family, already burdened with too many debts and children and worries, decided to send her to the city with the Auntie who came to recruit servant girls. My mother sat in the back of the taxi listening to the creak of the wheels over the ruts and potholes, under the weight of her luck which tipped the taxi sideways. Other village girls slipped against her, grumbling. Her tears splashed dark spots onto her new red dress. When my mother had been beaten for spoiling the rice, or holding back the rain, or bringing sickness to the family, she had felt the bad luck on her shoulders. She had felt it rise in her throat in lumps of varying sizes. Even, years later, after she became a Christian and no longer believed in this luck, in unguarded moments she sometimes felt its roundness, its black smoothness, at the base of her throat. But try as she might to spit it out, my mother never could.

When Grandmother first saw the bad luck she shook her head with pity. She beckoned my mother over to cup her chin in one hand. 'Does it hurt?' Grandmother asked, tapping the places on my mother's shoulders where the bad luck hooked.

My mother was so startled she dropped the heavy winejar she was carrying, she stood motionless as the puddle of first-quality wine spread round her feet. The brothel keeper leapt cursing from her chair to beat at my mother with her opium pipe, to slap at her head which was already scarred with the brothel keeper's bracelet cuts, already dented in the shapes of her rings. 'Aiya, old friend, leave her,' Grandmother said. 'I'll pay for the wine.'

In those days my grandmother's ghostchasing business was so busy she needed an assistant. So Grandmother looked at my mother closely. Grandmother had noticed my mother, who worked at the local brothel, whom the brothel keeper screamed at from morning till night. My mother was a young girl in those days, but already she walked with her shoulders hunched and her head permanently lowered. Her feet shuffled even when she wasn't lugging groceries or emptying slopbuckets, or moving furniture upstairs and downstairs according to the brothel keeper's latest whim. My mother walked as though carrying a great weight. She neither ducked nor flinched from the blows aimed at her, though once she cried out: 'Auntie!' and Grandmother heard from the other end of the street. My mother's eyes drooped at the corners where heavy tears trembled.

'Take her!' the brothel keeper exclaimed when Grandmother asked. 'Look at that face! I'm sorry I promised her parents I'd look after her, she's brought me nothing but bad luck. I took her from the village, I gave her good clothes and good food, but is she grateful? Does she try to be nice? All she does is mope around the place, turning customers off!'

Grandmother felt my mother's liver, which was stiff to the touch, meaning she could withstand great shocks. She studied her brow, which was low and hairy, meaning she was timid but would not die of fright. She examined her tongue, large and rounded, meaning she wouldn't talk back.

'I'll take her,' Grandmother said.

My mother's large hands were good for carrying ghost-catching equipment: a bucket, some rags, some gunpowder and lamp-oil, a bag of spells and seals, a cloth soaked in menstrual blood. A live chicken, beak tied with string, temple prayer beads, a cross. Since every ghost was different, Grandmother never knew what she would need. Grandmother watched the slope of my mother's back under the weight of the tools. She looked at my mother's hands, which were square-fingered but nimble, which cut and folded paper quickly, neatly. She examined her eye whites, poked her in the ribs. 'Eat more,' Grandmother said. 'Eat slowly. Do eye exercises. Drink this.' At the height of Grandmother's ghostchasing career they were called out on jobs every day. Sometimes they didn't come home for weeks.

At market, at the height of the food shortages, Grandmother shoved my mother into the paths of one-leg-kick servants, the most tenacious and ferocious of shoppers, who had only one leg left for kicking, their other limbs slaving day and night at their endless work. Every market day my mother went for training.

'No good!' Grandmother scolded when she mumbled frantic apologies, when she cowered in fright and ducked away. Grandmother poked the small of her back. 'Bad, bad, bad! Aiya, stand up! Stand straight! Why are you hiding?' One glare from Grandmother sent the servants grumbling away. 'Try again!' Grandmother cried.

My mother wiped her furrowed brow. She filled out her lungs as far as they would go, trying to focus as Grandmother showed her the swirling power of her breath. Her chest swelled out her blouse, her glaring expression, eyebrows drawn in a straight black line, emphasized her ferocity, her don't-mess-about-with-me-ness, her unladylike stance. My mother stood amidst the market bustle looking like a woman warrior, like the legendary Bandit Queen of the jungle, her face unlike her passive mother's face that the bully and I are used to, more like an opera singer's: each feature pronounced. Her expression wild and fierce.

'Good,' Grandmother nodded. 'Remember that face. That will scare anyone, human or ghost.'

When anyone dared to bump into my mother or jostle her or push her out of the way of the best bargains, the choicest vegetables, the least rancid meats, she turned her fierce wild face towards the offender, she unleashed her wild fiery breath. 'Out of my way!' she copied Grandmother's tiger shout. No-one was more surprised than she when even the fiercest matriarch, the wiliest one-leg-kick servant backed away, releasing the chunk of meat or vegetable they were both clutching, removing their elbows from her sides, their nails from her ribs.

'Aiya, what a fuss,' came the outraged mutters to mask their fear, the lopsided grumbles to hide their loss of face. 'Why so fighting-cock!'

'Accident!' they cried, hurrying away.

My mother tilted her radiant face towards Grandmother, lurking like a watchful schoolmistress just beyond the beancurd stall.

'Good!' Grandmother roared, jumping the beancurd seller out of his skin, sending the beancurd watery with fright.

In those days my mother too was always jumping out of her skin. Though just a girl, her skin already bore the first signs of sagging, her bones were watery, her back curled in a stoop that ended with the sag of her head. My mother's bad luck diluted her courage, her blood. With watery bones and blood, she barely filled her skin. She could hardly stand up. My mother's body was thin and delicate, held gingerly, as though it had no right to be there. As though the very air around her would hurt. She slipped through the days, through her daily work, around people and objects, a streethawker, a roadsweeper, lamp posts and bullock carts, even pots and pans, as though each of these had more substance, more of a place in the world than she. Her hands hesitated in the instant before touching anything, her feet every moment before leaving the ground. Her eyes were always shiny with tears about to be shed.

'*Tauhu*,' Grandmother called her. 'Beancurd. Useless!'

Grandmother's method was to scare the timidity, the fright, right out of my mother. Grandmother set her the hardest tasks, the scariest, the ones to stiffen the blood. She pushed her into telephone booths that were ringing at three in the morning, made her listen to the crackly voices cursing from the other side. If the curses were not so bad, my mother was to ask for a lucky lottery number, if they weren't forthcoming, Grandmother made her curse back. My mother shivered uncontrollably, cursing back. Grandmother made her huddle in midnight graveyards to count the number of creepings over the earth, the number of flittings above her head. She rubbed her eyes with dog tears so she could see why they howled. Grandmother filled my mother with herbs and potions that ran riot inside her and sent her racing to the outhouse, or filled her with energy and euphoria, or swelled her gut to grumbling. Every morning my mother woke before the first stirring cock crow, the first whistle summoning the road coolies to work. She woke to see the change of soldiers patrolling the street. On special days she rushed around preparing the offerings for the house gods, the earth gods, the gods guarding the door. She learnt the special days and offerings by heart, and the names of the gods and spirits, the naughty demons and the dangerous ones, and how they could be placated: what they liked to wear and smell and eat. Every evening Grandmother tested her. Grandmother swished her cane to remind her to get her memory right. Every morning they stood side by side in the faint light before sunlight, breathing the difference between day and night. Their movements, flowing one into another, was a dance of heavy shadows.

Before my mother became a Christian she was convinced the bad luck was a winged demon crouching on her back. She was convinced the demon came from deep inside her. Touching her finger to the murdered handprint on the path from her house to the river that long ago childhood morning had merely let it out. The demon was not an unusual demon but one her own mother said every girl child carried inside her, which made her blood dirty and prompted her to mischief, and let loose a smell so potent it made men dizzy, it attracted madness, dishonour, bad luck. This inside demon pressed girl children's faces to the dirt at childbirth, it sold them to strangers for the price of a meal. Good women were girl children who grew up accepting their inside demon, learning to disguise its smell with perfumes and eyes cast downwards, with voices and ways that were soft and malleable. Good women were girl children who learnt to keep their demons still. That day, at the touch of the murdered handprint, my mother's inside demon leapt out. But she snatched her hand away so quickly that instead of tearing off into the world, loose, leaving my mother a mere skin sack on the path to the river, her inside demon only managed to get halfway out. My mother's demon clung to her shoulders, stuck, venting its anger on my mother. It channelled its frustration into her: filled her with aches that crawled all over the body. Prickled her skin with secret longings, flushed her cheeks hot and cold with cravings she could not name. The bad luck demon, stuck, pushed and pulled against her in fury, pressed her further into the earth, almost lifted her into the air. It filled her head with a dizzy sensation of flying.

When she became a Christian the bad luck howled and whimpered, leaping wildly, making my mother howl and whimper at the door of the chapel. At the sight of the cistern glistening full. My mother scampered on all fours, tried to creep under a pew. The Old Priest, frail as he was, held her firmly. The nuns gripped her arms, pushed the hair back from her face. At the first touch of holy water the bad luck shrivelled to a hump on her shoulders which later she could hardly feel. My mother fell against the nuns, faint and reeling. After she became a Christian, she no longer believed the badluck demon ever crouched on her back. To her its tormenting antics became less than dreams. Unlike Grandmother my mother no longer believed in bad luck, in fortune telling by physical sensations, a tic in the right eye at 2 am meaning someone was thinking of her, a ringing in the left ear at 7 p.m. meaning money would soon be lost. She no longer joined in Grandmother's early morning exercises to strengthen the breath and promote balance: she no longer believed in the power of human breathing. My mother's faith was set in a more celestial draught.

Eyes raised to the plaster statues of Jesus and the Virgin nesting among the other figures on our family altar, hands clasped till her knuckles shone white, my mother mouthed fervent prayers of hope and reconciliation. Unlike Grandmother she no longer believed in raising her fists to life. She lived each day as if it was a gift of penance, as if saving for a holiday to be taken once dead. The weight on her shoulders was not a badluck demon but a trial from God, glass shattering at her touch, furniture sliding forwards to trip her, all were a test of patience: punishments sent for her sins. My mother's room is filled with religious icons peering from the tops of cupboards, from window ledges and side tables, even from under her bed. Every extra space in the laundry huddles a nest of saints the bully and I spend hours examining when my mother isn't there. The bully and I turn the heavy plaster in our hands, we push our fingers into saintly orifices, eyes and ears and noses, we colour lips pursed in saintly ecstasy with our crayon purples, yellows and reds. When my mother discovers our handiwork she flies into one of my grandmother's tempers, but being a Christian always calls us back. She quickly returns to calm. She makes us carefully scrub the saints. The bully, my mother and I stand side by side at the laundry basin, singing hymns for penance, scrubbing saints.

© Beth Yahp, 1992.
HarperCollins, Sydney

BETH YAHP, born in Johore, studied communications at the University of Technology, Sydney. Her first short story was published eight years ago and she has since had various works in literary magazines and anthologies.

An Ethnic Affairs Commission grant in 1989 enabled her to write full-time. Her first novel, *The Crocodile Fury,* published by HarperCollins, Australia (1992) and Heinemann Asia (1993) won the 1993 Victorian Premier's Prize for First Fiction and was shortlisted for the New South Wales Literary Prize for Fiction.

KIT LEEE

BLANKLY I stare:

Q stares blankly back. Gradual intensification. We coalesce.

I am Q, Q me.

Everything looks different from the right where re Q really is, not *left* as she appears to be if you aren't Q. But

I am Q and I need you: can't exist meaningfully without you (except

in qintar, qantas, qirone, qoph, and similar foreign non-conformists.) Just you I want, must have to live: but someday I hope they'll let me marry doubleyou. Qwite understandly some will consider this qwixotic; and the qwintessential qwestion will spring forth qwietly in the minds of men and women alike - ? (why) But why? is the pivotpoint, the centre key, and by and by we shall know Why: but as it is we are moving from right to left unless you aren't Q and insist on deluding yourself that left to right is right, and right to left is wrong. (Rong and wong are wrong, only *wrong* is wright: argue all you want. This is an established and accepted wrule.)

The Rules say Loitering is unLawful, so we may not linger as long as we like: the longer we linger the less the likelihood of our getting to know Why. We have outlived ourselves, doubleyou has eloped with Q, and ere Why is known E shall demonstrate his essentiality, having been in existence for eons in every form (Official or Otherwise): typewritten or clearly printed, in bleakblue, blueblack, grey, green, turquoise, turple or purpoise, but *never* in ballpoint or crayon, nor in brown, indigo or pink (so says Officialdom or Otherwisdom)...

but returning to the key under scrutiny, taking into account his especial elasticity: as emphatic as an elephant, as elusive as an eel, as everywhere as in eerie. The emphasis is on elusion, with particular emph on el - el being also essential in the extreme though obviously on a lower level - but remember, Love begins with El, and so doth Life: both of which end with, grimly, E... so grit your teeth, say *eeeee* and easily you will see, still saying *eeeee*, that: elephants and eels may not be executed, never electrocuted, for eels are eclectic and elephants expansive (both eat and everything is edible).

The answer is no if you want to know Why immediately. We are (or is) very close to why?, slightly right of it, or rt. if you are an obsessive abbreviator. But

this is the truth. And soon we shall come to the truth, you and i, and oh, peace/power/purity, nothing prurient/pornographic/or picayune: but before all, to do the rt. thing we are, aren't we, we *are* too. Rrrrrright!

To reason is rong (remember, wrong: sowwy). It is wrong, it being not right to reason - ridiculous to imagine a radical radicle renouncing its right (or left) to ravish the earth! - realise, you who aren't are, to rationalise by ratiocination is redundant and retrogressive, but you know it's *de rigueur* to probe and ponder like roots that rape the radius of their rhizosphere, surrounded, alas! by truth and why? at left, and the everpresent everything and What for? When? Where? Who? Which? well, and related qwestions at right. Lord and Lady and Son and Daughter! Impossible, inconceivable, with parched throat and dehydrated tongue to rrreason rrrightly as do the Irrrish and the Iberrrians. Relent to rapture, lubricate your larynx with *reasonability*, for the tume is come: I am now crucified, and presently shall know why? and Why.

Tea time, tic toc, tok tok, tick, pick pocket times pock picket equals (approximately) tock tock, tic, ticket talk talk: time is a thief. It may steal your life before You get to know Why, so finish your tea and see Me as tee, as tyme with a why?, as truth with a you, as three crosses on calvary and a thaumaturgist aged thirtythree who was seen between a why? and a rogue; for I am, in truth, the terminus, the turnstile before you and why? and the answer to Your qwery which, ultimately, ought to be (if You're thoughtfully thinking) what is this truth. Like tourists who arrive in omnibuses to view the hippopotamuses in the river: three (or four or five) hippos swimming slowly upstream on their broad backs occasionally grinning for the colourful, happy tourists who make bad photographs with good cameras and tell the folks back home about the swimming/grinning/cleanshaven hippos with friendly armpits. And *that*'s the truth (they think). But the truth is there - where, don't ask me, i'm here (at the typewriter - don't ask *them*, they're neither there nor here nor anywhere...

70

Too much! I've had of totem, theology, and transistorised truth. Too little! tyme with a why? to proceed to you and i, and oh, peace...

Why! why?, a man with arms held high above head, an upsidedown person in Chinese: I can't tell You Why when I am why?, but all I need is you and oh and I am not Me but *You*. I am a key (and even keys ask why?) and when depressed I come up with ? a coat hanger, a pearl earring, an inverted fishhook, a contortionist on a ball - don't ask *me*, I am why? Qwery, qwery without the all-important truth; you and i must pray (to whom to what) or merely hope for that eventual final qwerty to end all qweries, before oh (despair/resignation), purity/perpetuity/perfection or putrefaction marks our period - .

What is left is left, the right is done with for now unless You still persistently deny that you are a key or different keys at different moments in different situations. But

let me be you now: I stand apart, i separate you from perfection just as You stand stubbornly between Me and my panacea... you, imperfect ellipse, unconnected unround, uncircle, will your poles touch and discover perpetuity? Again the why? After all, You begin with a qwery and end with an unfulfilment; i stand between you and completion, Your incompletion bars Me from my peak. Surely, for the benefit of You, Me, and Us, we must coalesce, or at least seal the space between our keys - but how, how, how when i am a pillar and you are a You. Though I pretend to be You I cannot, will not accept You as Me, not even if you humbly dot yourself too, and pronounce Yourself i.

Oh, oh, oh. Close to perfection but somehow hollow, somehow empty. Lips pursed for a kiss, mouth open in a scream of supreme orgasm, or uttermost horror. Oh me oh my, forever longing for Om sweet home...

The Prize is precious, pregnant with promise; at tea time it seemed so near, but never, it's impossible for Me to be protoplasm and perfection until I have mastered metempsychosis or some such perversion. Pain, pressure, pain is the only key I play at present; and I don't play it with pride - I hate being a pawn, prawns keep asking why? as they are shelled, masticated, and digested; prawns just don't have It. Neither do I, who knows about You. I hope You do (*know*, I mean). Pelagius was no pessimist, optimism was his peduncle (rhymes with carbuncle): I wonder if he drowned. No, let's not wonder; that would take us back to doubleyou, rrright back to What for? When? Who? Which? well, and related qwestions. And everybody is much too weary by now (I hope). So from oh I gaze longingly at peace, plenty, pleasure, purity, permanence, and other paradisaical platypus eggs.

Many things unaccomplished, sixteen more lives to lead, all on lower levels, different planes. Planes, planes: that is significant. Up, down, below, above, toward, away, play with planes or let them play with You and Me and Everybody. But

that is another story.

Release me now and I shall travel to the end of the page...

KIT LEEE has dedicated this to Joseph F. Martino, Jr. It is concerning a typewriter's self-exploratory travels from right to left on a particular plane.

He is a composer, caricaturist and a freelance writer of numerous genres, currently developing an Arts centre at Kuala Kubu Baru, the "Ubud" of Malaysia.

KIRPAL SINGH
Monologue

I am lying on an old mattress in the living room. All around me is white. White walls. White built-in cupboards. White ceiling. White window panes. White. I don't like white very much. Reminds me too much of death. Or of purity. In my mind purity and death have a similar reference point. Termination. My wife, however, likes white. I wonder what she'll say when we move into another house where my colour - my favourite is black - predominates. Right now she is blissfully sleeping in the bedroom. Blissfully. She does not know what's on my mind. No one does. I am my own master. I keep my own secrets. But white irritates me. Gives me a headache. Takes away my concentration. I get up and turn on the ceiling fan. It is an old-fashioned fan. I like old-fashioned things. I lie again. It is a hot afternoon and the sun is shining brightly outside. Even the day is white. Because of this I have decided not to go to work this afternoon. I am not sure whether it is the white alone which prompted me not to go to work. I am lying down on an old mattress. It is a discarded one. As I lie on it my eyes gaze at the ceiling. I see the fan going round round. Round and round. Regularly. Monotonously. I see the fan. My mind does not see the fan. Outside the birds are chirping away. There are all kinds of birds here. Cockatoos, gelas, wagtails, crows, sparrows. Even an owl. But he is asleep I think. Like me, he too does not like white much. But the other birds are obviously enjoying the sunshine. My house has a white fence around it. Not much of a fence - my neighbour's dog comes through it easily - but white nevertheless. Sometimes when I look up at the trees I see white birdnests on the white tree branches. Eucalyptus. Gum. As I lie down on my mattress I try to concentrate. But I can't. My mind gets too full of things. I hate Descartes. I think therefore I am not. My thoughts take me away from myself. They deny the real me. A fake me takes over. The real me just wants to stare endlessly into the fan as it goes round and round, round and round. The fake me is thinking of all kinds of things. I don't see the connection between the real me and the fake me. I see a little boy being followed by a woman in black. I do not know who she is. I don't think I know the boy either. But my mind is not seeing. My mind is thinking. It is now thinking of a line from Yeats. I think it comes from "The Second Coming." All about me reel shadows. Indignant. Because my mind does not see the little boy or the little woman. When I was young and living in Jalan Eunos our house had a small well at the back. The little boy is walking around this well. The woman in black is following. Nothing else seems to happen. Shadows appear. My mind is still thinking. It now has moved on to Tagore. It recalls the famous line from *Gitanjali*. Where the head is held high and the mind is without fear. I do not know what the line means. The real me is seeing the boy walking around the well. The woman in black is relentlessly following. Am I seeing things? My mind is still trying to fathom the meaning of Tagore's line. Yeats and Tagore knew each other. Can the mind be without fear when there are indignant shadows about? Can the head be held high when the second coming is at hand? I think I'm beginning to feel drowsy. I don't seem to be making sense of the boy going round the well. But this mattress is not the one on which I like to sleep. My wife is sleeping in the bedroom. She does not know about this small boy. She did not see the well of my childhood. And my mind which should remember the well clearly is getting lost in strange and abstruse thoughts. The real me is still just lying down here, staring into the ceiling. Outside the birds are still chirping. I cannot be sure if the birds know what I know. Do they see the small boy around the well? I cannot be sure. When I was eight I wore a pair of white pants to school. I remember the teacher - she was a pretty girl - held my pants and laughed. All the other boys laughed too. Since then I have not liked white underpants. My wife likes them. White. It comes between me and my wife. Now it is coming between me and the ceiling fan. As I see white, my mind is still engrossed on those two buffoons. I call them buffoons because they sang songs which made good melody but which nobody understood. We still await the second coming. We still cannot hold our heads up high. Our minds are still not without fear. I don't know what I am thinking or what I am seeing. It is getting rather confused. When my uncle used to ask me to get water for the dogs I used to be very happy. It gave me a chance to play near the well. I used to run round and round the well. I used to look inside the well. It was all very black inside the well. The woman in black is still going after the little boy round and round the well. I think I

74

know who the little boy is. But I don't know who the woman is. But she is in black. And I love black. Black is the opposite of white. Opposite of purity. Opposite of death. I have never known my mother. I left her when I was a baby. She left me when I was a baby. We left each other. Alone. Alone, alone in a white white room. Coleridge is one of my favourite poets. I read him often. I remember he helped Mill come back to reality. I think Mill was a genius. I do not know if I am a genius. But I think the small boy going round and round the well is a genius. I think the woman in black following him is a genius too. Only geniuses do that sort of a thing. Going round and round, round and round. I think I am repeating myself. But my mind does not seem to be with me. It has finally got away from the literary figures of Yeats and Tagore. Outside my room I cannot hear the birds anymore. But my neighbour is playing on his piano. I like piano music. So I want to listen to him playing on the piano. I don't really know my neighbour. But I know his dog. Our fence is not very good because it allows our neighbour's dog inside our compound. My fan, old-fashioned as it is, is still going round and round. I remember when I was at the University I read a book in which it was said that if one stared at the ceiling for too long one could be hypnotised. Maybe I am being hypnotised by this old-fashioned fan. I love old-fashioned things. The little boy seems to have grown bigger somehow. And the lady older. I think I can now see her wrinkles. She seems to be carrying an umbrella. I wonder why. It is very hot. This is why I have turned on the fan. Outside the sun is shining brightly. My neighbour is still on his piano. I don't know what he is playing. Maybe Mozart. I love Mozart. I think Mozart was a genius. I think the little boy going round the well is a genius. My mind has strayed away from me. My mind is now thinking about writing a story. My real self is not a writer. My fake self is a writer. My mind is my fake self. I hate Descartes. I do not like to be predicated. My mind wants to predicate my senses. It wants to control my thoughts. But I want to keep staring at the fan as it goes round and round, round and round. Monotonously. I think life is like my old-fashioned fan. I think life is a genius like the little boy going round the well. I love life. I never knew who my mother was. When I was small my uncle used to ask me to get water from the well. I used to love painting near the well. One day I wore white underpants to school and my teacher laughed at me. The other boys laughed at me. My wife buys me white underpants. I hate wearing white underpants. I love black. The woman in black is carrying an umbrella. But it is hot. The sun is shining brightly outside. I think my neighbour has changed his tune. He has left Mozart and is now playing a piece by Chopin. I think Chopin was a genius. But I don't like Chopin. He reminds me of white. Purity. Death. I like black. This is why I cannot take my eyes off the woman in black. But my mind is pulling me away. My mind is making it difficult for me to concentrate on the fan. My wife is sleeping blissfully in the next room. She does not know what is in my mind. She does not know what is in store for her. I am my own master. I keep my own secrets. But I love black. I see a young man going round the well now. He is going round and round, round and round. The woman in black is still there. She is pointing her umbrella at the young man. She is very old now. She is not able to walk fast now. But she still holds her umbrella firmly. I don't know why she has an umbrella. It is hot outside. The birds have all gone away. My neighbour has stopped playing his piano. My fan is still going round and round. Weave a circle round it thrice. I love Coleridge. He brought Mill out of insanity. I think Coleridge was a genius. I think the old woman in black chasing the young man round the well is a genius. My mind is seriously making plans about writing a story. It is searching for a subject. I don't like my mind very much. When I was at the University my philosophy professor told me that the mind is a blank tablet. White. I don't like white very much. My long hair is getting sticky all over. I have long hair. I love long hair. Grinding at the mill, eyeless in gaze. I think Milton was a genius. I do not know if I am a genius. When I was small they did an IQ test on me. They never told me the results. Maybe I am a genius. I have long hair. I ask my wife to wash my hair every month. My hair is long and black. I love black. The old woman in black is still pointing her umbrella at the young man going round the well. My wife is sleeping in the next room. Somehow I never got to know my mother. When I was young I used to play near the well. Right now I think about the well in our house in Jalan Eunos. Both well and house are no more. But the little boy still goes round the well and the woman in black still struggles to catch him. I think I know who the boy is. He is a man now. I think my mind has got hold of an idea for a short story. My mind is forcing me to think. I think about the boy and the woman and the well. I think about my uncle and the teacher and the boys and the white underpants. I think about Yeats and Tagore and Coleridge and Milton. I think I am like Samson. Samson had long hair like me. I ask my wife to wash my long hair once a month. She does not like to do this. Now she's sleeping in the next room. She is sleeping on the mattress I like to sleep on. I am lying on this old discarded mattress here. The sun outside is still shining brightly. I love black. I think Mohammed Ali is a genius. Black is beautiful he said. I love black. The woman in black has stopped suddenly. The young man has disappeared. My mind is telling me to concentrate on the story it is thinking of writing. The fan is going round and round. Life is going round and round. I love life. I cannot see the connection between my mind and me. I hate Descartes. My real self wants to lie down and just look at the ceiling fan as it goes round and round. All around me is white. My mind is trying to hold my attention. It is telling me about a story it has thought about. I don't want to listen to my mind. I want to see what the old woman in black is going to do now that the young man is not there. I don't seem to be able to see the old woman clearly now. I think I am getting confused. I think I may be falling asleep. But I know I cannot sleep on this mattress. It is an old mattress and everything around me is white. I don't like white. White is purity. I am not pure. White is death. I don't think I am dead. But the old woman in black seems to be dying. She is beginning to change into white. Everything about me is quiet. My mind is working at top speed now on the story it has thought for itself. My mind is telling me to get up and write it down before it loses the main thread of the story. But I took this afternoon off from work. I want to lie down and watch the fan going round and round. When I first lay down I saw a small boy going round and round the well with a woman in black following. Now the boy has disappeared. And the woman is changing into white. When I was young, in our house at Jalan Eunos, I used to play near the well at the back of the house. My wife seems to have woken up. I hear her calling my name. But I am not listening to her because I am feeling hot and I am busy watching the change in the woman in black. I have lost the small boy. Now I think I am going to lose the woman too. My long hair is really sticky. My wife wants to know if I want my hair washed. It is one month today. She does not know what is on my mind. The fan is going round and round. (Monotonously) My mind is succeeding I think. It is telling me to get up and write a story. The story is about a small boy going round and round a well at the back of a house in Jalan Eunos. The small boy is being followed by a woman in black. All this is too much for me. I have to stop looking at the fan. My mind has taken over. I hate Descartes.

DR KIRPAL SINGH's poems and stories have been published all over the world and he has been invited to read at Arts Festivals in the U.K., Canada, Australia and Germany. *Catwalking* and *Why Make Love Twice* are his two forthcoming publications. Kirpal lectures at the Nanyang Technological University, Singapore.

Span

Articles, interviews, creative writing, and reviews relating to post-colonial literatures in English.

Span is the journal of South Pacific chapter of the Association for Commonwealth Language and Literature Studies (SPACLALS). It appears twice a year for AUD$20.00 ($10.00 students and Pacific Islands).Visa & Master Card acceptable. Foreign currency transaction require an extra A$6.00.

All correspondence to: The Editor, SPACLALS, School of Humanities, Murdoch University, Murdoch, WA 6150, Australia.

FEROZ FAISAL MERICAN
Fireworks

People were standing, not moving, outlines etched in sharp relief by the clear, clean orange light. Murmurs. Everybody, then nobody, murmuring, murmuring, "He was very dejected, very dejected", said with an exasperated sigh, the eyes pleading, the voice wavering and dying. His friend doesn't look at him. In the background, high above and far away from the house, a tower stands black and unlit. Birds sit on the roof uncannily spaced; perfectly, symmetrically, apart. I thought they were pieces of wood sticking out from the roof. Then one flew off.

The sun was creeping out of view behind the tower, as if to say, "I can't help you, I'd like to but my time is up, you'll have to make do". There are two ladies leaning on Mike's car; one has tissue in hand, and a pathetic, quizzical frown on her face, she is silent but her head bobs slowly from side to side.

No car can pass. We are standing all over the road. Standing in a silent, distorted, mutated horse shoe shape, with the open end being the front gate of Sunitra's house; most faces are looking towards it, towards the house. Suddenly a shriek, followed by a long low moan. Sunitra's mother grieves for her son. Other voices join in, soon there is a monotonous, chanted, wail.

So many people are standing outside Sunitra's house motionless, powerless, like pigeons stupidly, silently looking this way and that. That woman leaning on Mike's car feels on her cheek my stare, she turns sideways, but doesn't see me. She dabs the right eye and murmurs to the woman at her side, who makes no sign, save a very slight nod. She speaks again, the other woman finally looks at her and says something. They are both old and experienced. They've probably seen a lot of funerals and their looks and gestures are practised to perfection. A man next to them actually smiles as he relates information that has been passed round and round, uprooted, churned out, dug up and regurgitated, from early that morning when they first heard about it, to probably when the body comes back from the airport, and probably still when his coffin goes up in flames and it will continue on tomorrow and the day after, day and night, unceasing, uncaring, relentless, unstoppable, for the next 45 days, which is the decent minimum specified for mourning, expected by society, with prayers every day in the evenings. Every day for 45 days while stocks last.

And probably then still after.

The light on white walls was a thin, transparent amber. Faces looked more thoughtful, pensive, dignified. The strong blacks of sunless, sheltered spaces softened to damp, deep blue. The sky on my right was pursuing lilac.

And still the people stood, and still we blocked the road. Waiting for the body, waiting for showtime. One Japanese man comes through the crowd. Yvonne turns to us, "that's his boss, I think..." she whispered, not looking, "he worked in Singapore. Japanese boss, I think..." He is quite young, with hair touching collar; he wears a dark blue suit and strides into the house towards the wailing throng, looking only ahead of him. A fair Indian woman blows her nose; the birds have left the rooftop; the bottom of light grey clouds is painted softly red.

The Japanese man comes out, talks to someone, hesitates, then is off. Back to Singapore; to the office where he is boss; where Sunitra's brother used to work. For him, it is a death in the office; for others, that of a friend, for others still, death of all hope and meaning.

And still the people stand; the body is not back yet, "Sunitra has gone to the airport to pick her brother up", said Jessie, a friend, "you're still in shock, I see," for I made no sound, "Bullshit", thought I, "wrong again...so much for bloody woman's intuition", "Selamat Hari Raya, huh?" she continued. I tried not to, but grinned anyway, while replying, "hmmph," which I do often, for it says a lot and is usually, though not often enough, fatal to unwanted and unnecessary conversation. "Yeah, yeah," I thought, "It happens on holidays too," as I remembered a certain Christmas and a certain coffin. She always sounds so earnest and definite but unfortunately, her speech reverberates with twangs of Strine, on account of living in Brisbane. She is tall and graceful and has beautiful brown eyes. She is the kind of woman that I would gladly kiss to make her shut up.

The neighbours, a Chinese family, crane their necks and look like beakless penguins staring over the red brick wall. The mother of the family is cradling a young child; she grips him fast. He is curious and apprehensive, struggling, wriggling, trying to get free. She begins to hold him tighter and then decides to bounce him in her arms. As she does that rapidly, he doesn't bounce so much as shake and nod while she also moves him from side to side from her hips, slowly, gradually, comfortably. And the van arrives, carrying Sunitra and her dead brother's body.

A few days later, it was April Fool's day.

A firework just exploded, and another. A car horn at some distance beeped twice; then another bangclap. Silence. The air-conditioner hums, softly halting, thumming, apologetically endless. A low dark roar and a car has swept away. Impossible you say? no, but really, it was ten, I think, ten little tablets. Eight was supposedly lethal. "What was that?" "Sunitra tried to commit suicide last night," was what the telephone voice said. "Commit suicide?", I said, "My foot", I thought. No, no that wasn't "trying to commit suicide", no sir, she tried to kill herself maybe, but commit suicide?, no, not classy enough, not clever or serious or gutsy enough. Plain fucking stupid. Swallowing 10 pills.

"Ooooohhh...I want to leave this world, I want to die and go to him! I want to join my breder!! I want to be with my breder!! (Her brother burnt to death in a car wreck in Singabloodypore 7 days ago) I want to leave my horrible, terrible parents and join my breder; I'll go to him right now! Waaaaaaaaahhhhhh...!! "

Fucking weak, selfish, thoughtless, ...

But she told me things later, after everything.

When she left for the airport to retrieve her brother's remains, one of her cousins, who travelled with her in the hearse, said, "Hey, Sunitra, you got the car number, ah? your brother's car number, do you know it? do you remember it? huh, Sunitra, hey...the number, girl, the number..."

When the all-white hearse finally came back from the airport, she was sitting in front, wearing big, aviator sunglasses and as soon as the van stopped, she flew at once to her father, who had been called out of the house; her voice was raised and garbled. She said something over and over again to her father, hugging him, holding tight, but I couldn't make out the words. When the coffin was slowly dragged out of the back of the van, the father let out a soft sob and cried, crying like a small stream bubbling; Sunitra rending the air with a crumbling, shattering cry, back to repeating, over and over again, a chant, a phrase, a prayer.

Because of the way he died, the coffin was closed. "Let me see my son, I want to see my son", screamed the mother, each time louder and more resolute, supported and held at each arm by friends of her son, saying in turn, whispering in fact, "Auntie please, auntie, please auntie, don't, don't auntie, you cannot auntie, please understand, please calm down, please auntie...", "my son! I want to see my son, he's my only...", but the coffin was closed and not to be opened.

"He was her only son. He took her side, he looked out for her and he was angry with me and my father for being dismissive of and indifferent to her," said Sunitra before she took the pills next day. After her son's death, Sunitra's mother's state of mind was such that she accused Sunitra of the most heinous crime, of causing the greatest wrong, that of being responsible for her own brother's death. Sunitra's crime was that of bringing bad luck to the family. She'd always been bad luck, she was told. God was punishing them for Sunitra's sins. She was always a bad girl. She never listened. She wasn't married. No one wanted her, she wasn't good, no, she wasn't good like her brother. Sunitra listened in stupefaction. What was there to say in reply? To think...and what do you know, here comes auntie and grandma, sister and mother, sarees trailing, eyes narrowing, hissing between teeth, "yes, yes, she was always a bad girl, she never listened to her poor, dear mother, she always thought she knew everything, showing off, being clever, answering back, always answering back, she caused her poor, dear mother so much pain, that girl..."

And still they continued, (remember, everyday they were there at Sunitra's house and everyday they talked and talked, with stern and sour faces, all the while completely ignoring Sunitra's mother herself, who at this time was given to pacing around the house, talking aloud to walls and pictures and herself), Grandma imparting pearls of wisdom, "look at her...look at her hair...I never see her in a saree...and she acts as though there's nothing wrong with her, at this age [25] and still not married, not even engaged. She's very dark, not fair at all like her mother, not fair like us, you can see why she's not married, of course...no one wants her..."

When Sunitra's mother snapped out of her reverie, she would start on Sunitra again, and auntie and grandmother would reload and fire point blank shots at Sunitra's face; revelling in her abject misery as they did so.

She could not put up with it any longer, her father, her only hope, was not equipped to deal with the knives, barbs and venom of the three women. Indeed, he was not even inclined to stop them. He was not inclined to do anything at all; and so she felt the situation hopeless, she really truly absolutely thought the situation hopeless.

The family doctor was livid. "They are not supposed to give out more than eight pills, how could they give her 10 pills! even 8 is too many, why, for heaven's sake 8 pills are lethal! What was that doctor thinking? a doctor like him should be reported and dealt with...harshly dealt with... oh dear, oh dear, oh dear...".

I don't think they ever got round to busting him or suing him, it was just talk for the moment, performance for the day, hot air from the weak middle-aged, with more, more reason to play one's part, to belong to the circle of sorrow wrung dry.

For 45 days, everybody and his mother would have a shot. A lightning flash, it's going to rain, the sky shows itself to be mother of pearl and dark blue at the sides, and then darker still opposite the set sun. An Indian man with a prodigious, if predictable, paunch steps forth and begins to direct the proceedings. Several rings of flowers are thrust into the hearse. These are yellow, white, pink, peach, salmon and they stand on rickety, fragile, cane legs. The driver of the hearse puts the flowers in with not a trace of solemnity, much less reverence, he is doing his job, and would like to be on his way. A wreath of flowers gets caught in the side door that he has shut impatiently. It sticks out of the white van/hearse choking, entangled, hideously strangled. No one thinks to put that bit of the wreath in and shut the door proper and tight. All of us stand there and ignore it, leaning now on one leg, now on the other, some with gaping mouths, some digging noses.

Sunitra wants to ride in front. She wants to go in the hearse, she wants to go with her brother. For some reason, they won't let her, too many in front. "Please girl, go with uncle, he'll take you there, he'll take you there, you'll be right behind us, go in the car girl, please girl, it's all right you'll be right be- OK, OK, put her in the back, you can go in the back, OK girl? you go in the back, there, there, that's all right, now that's all right, you'll be with your brother." So she sat there amidst the flowers, holding on tight to the coffin.

It starts to drizzle; because of the rain, people sway and shift, things are acting up, the body is going soon, time to get ready, time to hitch rides, "are you going?", "are you going?". "No priests are coming here because it is an unnatural death. They won't come", said Jessie. Unnatural death? a car crash? for this, priests make themselves scarce? "Spare me...", "No, it's true", said Jessie, "the parents have to do everything themselves, do you suppose the crematorium is open?", "Of course, it's open...isn't it?"

No, no she was wrong again, that stupid ..., I don't know why I get so worked up, listening to these people; she wasn't wrong about the priests, though. The rain splashed onto the road splintering, shattering into brilliant points and circles of light, shinily mocking. People were beginning to go. I had decided not to. Mike was going, because he knew the guy, then again maybe he didn't. None of us, Kelvin, Sunny, Yvonne nor me ever met Sunitra's brother. We were there because she was our friend, and at funerals they never refuse anyone admittance, everyone is invited. Unlike weddings. Labels, strings, ties, they mean little or less than usual at death's appearance. Family ties, what an abominable lie in most cases. They've known us from the day we were born, but remain resolute, complete, total, absolute and utter strangers. Oblivious, indifferent, exhausted.

Thank God for friends.

Else I would have gladly died long ago.

Kelvin and Yvonne didn't want to go to the cremation either. Sunny, dependable and right and loyal as ever, thought he should go, at least to save Mike the experience of having to go alone; he would go with Mike.

I walked down the road to Kelvin's car. Kelvin and Yvonne were ahead of me, hurriedly trying to get out of the still strengthening rain. After I had walked 10 or so steps I turned back. I would go also. When I got to Mike's car, Mike was there and ready to go and Sunny was missing. We waited for Sunny; then these Singaporeans came hurtling into our car, "could you give us a lift, could you, there are three of us, are you going? could you give us, you're going aren't you, could you please, three of us, give us a lift? could you, could you, hello..." We said, "no, no, I'm sorry, sorry, we're waiting for someone, there's someone else coming, our friend,

waiting for our friend, sorry, no, we're waiting for a friend, no...".
Then we said, "OK, I guess, yeah we could take, we could yeah,
could take, I guess we could take two of you, could take two of
you, but only two...there's someone else, yeah ok..."

Then Sunny came running, "I go in Kelvin's car, la, we follow
you", while the rain poured around him and the black turbulent
sky paralysed all with the sound of chilling, hostile thunder. "OK,
you sure, ah!", I said as he ran away through the crisscrossing and
disappearing headlights.

And then the Singaporeans erupted, "Aaah, we can take three,
we can take three, we can take, we can take, ...Kenneth, Kenneth,
Ken, Ken, HERE, over here, Hey, KEN, this car, this car, come on,
come on...", the car door is pushed out, a wet body thumps into
the back seat, bringing with it a stinging breeze, the door thuds
shut and there are three Singaporeans sitting in the back seat. The
whole way, they didn't even bother to fucking introduce themselves.
they might have mumbled thanks for something or other. Mike
and I remained silent, we were not exactly chatty, we listened to
the music through his blown out speakers, as the Singaporeans
whispered amongst each other, carrying themselves and their world
with them wherever they go.

We made it to the crematorium but Sunny, Kelvin and Yvonne
never did. In the rain and the glare apparently they followed the
wrong car and got lost.

I was surprised when they set fire to the coffin. I hadn't expected
it. When we got there the coffin was already in place. The enclosure
was long and high, with white surfaces long since etched by grey,
open to the elements, supported by pillars surrounded by a low,
thick concrete wall; rounded and softened by the desperate, fevered,
unconscious, cold hands of mourners through the years. It was still
raining - it wasn't raining, it was roaring. The coffin was placed on
dark, wooden logs, several of them, larger ones below, smaller and
shorter ones on top. As before, all the people remained standing,
this time all eyes facing the coffin, the men of the family, around
the father, a handful of friends, around Sunitra. Her mother had
not come, or rather, she was in no position to attend, perhaps she
was advised not to, in any case, she was left behind, taken care of
and comforted by other middle aged ladies, sedated by a doctor
more than likely.

He must have been a priest, he was responsible for starting things; first this, then that, then the other. Nothing could be heard save the crashing rain and amidst the standing people and the cold, hurrying wind and the bent over, sobbing human that was Sunitra that man began to sing. He sang alone and quickly. The song sounded old (very old) and sad and weary. The voice sliced through the rain not booming nor low nor ominous and neither shrill nor persistent, nor damning. Just higher than usual, rising, falling, quavering, patient, matter of fact, irrevocable.

And then the rice. A mound of rice grain, uncooked, was heaped upon a large, flat, tin dish. It was placed at the side of the coffin, next to the head with the priest standing next to it. You had to climb three steps up to the coffin where the dish and the priest were, then you would release a handful of grains of rice on the coffin. For some reason when they began to implore people to go up the steps, to start it off, as it were, most were slow to react and I found myself the third person in line to sprinkle rice onto his coffin. I had never met Sunitra's brother, didn't even know what he looked like. Slowly a queue formed, waddling, swaying forward with more and more coming out from shadows, treading lightly over steps, glancing eyes flung all over, bouncing off, bouncing back. Cupped hands, cradling rice, would slowly pull themselves apart while moving in a slow arc over the head of the coffin, over the face of a man burnt to death in a car wreck on the way to Changi Airport, Singapore. The rice rained down softly, gently, from under faces of calm, faces of indifference, of patience, of self-righteousness, of tiredness, of shallowness, of dedication and neverending remembrance, of turbulence; faces of turbulence akin to molten lava boiling, a bridge about to buckle, perhaps it was only a quivering jaw; another face and another pair of eyes - a still and stunned deer, lastly, the shattered, crystal eyes under a wrinkled brow and then Sunitra.

She had to be led up there, she was the last to go. No need to describe her face, suffice to say - grief. She raised her cupped hands over her head, speaking to the gods, before releasing the rice, and she took another handful, caressing her brother's coffin this time, and she took another, and another, until there was nothing left. She did not want to go, she had to be led down slowly but forcefully by the silent and understanding priest.

Large, yellow slabs of ghee, the length of a large loaf of bread, were heaped, onto and around the coffin. They torched it from all sides. As the ghee melted and burned, it left shiny, silvery streaks criss-crossing over the top and sides of the coffin. It slid and dropped onto the logs, shrinking, reducing, disappearing. Thus the sound of the crashing rain was overcome and swallowed whole by the crackling flames which threw themselves up, higher, further towards the roof of the enclosure; not reaching it but seemingly determined to lick and catch something, anything, so that it might not burn alone.

It was not the thing to do to hang around until the fire died out, I would've liked to, but the crowd containing friends, co-workers, family and perhaps one or two lovers slipped away, having their last look, stare, glance at the chanting whispers of the ever-circling, eradicating, annihilating flames. The coffin was bright red from the yellow glare, black edges trimming the evanescent, transitory flames, thick grey smoke climbing the eaves, set free into the wet, the dark, the rain. The light danced on the pillars and floors and on the back of heads and on faces, but it was over, it was done.

Sunitra was surrounded and led away, through the corridor, through the wide concrete circle. Stopping, turning around, slowing down, turning round, stopping again, just for another look, another look, and yet another, then again being pulled gently away, whispered words frantically trying to reach from all sides, all directions. Jessie and the other girl had one arm each across her back, and one each near her elbows, not daring to think what would happen if one were to let go. I stopped and turned around, for my last look. The flames must have been nine feet tall, at least. "Let me see...!!," she screamed, "he's my own...brother...why won't you...I must..." she was almost at the car, Jessie and the other girl holding tight, whispering, whispering, Mike was there too, the car door was opened, she said his name over and over, she said goodbye, was gently pushed in and the car door slammed.

I asked Mike what he thought about waiting for the Singaporeans, "Fuck 'em", replied Mike. So we climbed into his dark grey Mazda 323 with the shitty sound system, and drove away, and all of a sudden, I saw my own funeral in my mind, surrounded by a language I do not understand (Arabic - on account of learning the Quran parrot-like when young), surrounded by people I do not know and will never comprehend (my relatives) and I thought of my friends who would not be able to read any eulogy for me, much less act as pall bearers for me (as I had acted once, for my father). As that thought seared through my head, I unfastened the seat belt, wound down the window, could hear the wind in my ears as I pushed my head out, and I screamed.

© Feroz Faisal Merican, 1993.

FEROZ FAISAL MERICAN, 27, is an assistant film director at a commercial production house. He read film studies in Penn State University.

"I don't like the fact that most Malaysian writers are journalists, lecturers and lawyers. For our literature to be vibrant we need criminals, maladjusted youngsters and psychotic housewives to write fiction. Then we'll raise some eyebrows."

DINA ZAMAN
Philippa

I

For once, when the alarm clock rang, Philippa refused to move. She was on her bed, tucking in every part of her blanket tightly around her. She was back in her mother's womb, she was in a cocoon - a cool and safe place from the day ahead of her.

Philippa then sat up on her bed, still wrapped in her blanket. She could feel moist and sticky perspiration beads trailing down her back, like tiny gel-like snails. The streaks of wet stuck to her skin. She had not turned on her air-conditioner. She was already cold inside. Anxious clammy freezing hands were playing putty with her heart.

The weeds in Mr. Hong's garden were reaching astronomical heights, Philippa observed. She looked out and up the window and was struck with wonder there was no wind accompanying the sun to cool your heated thinking, to give you hope. The new sun she was adjusting to offered her smiles. She brushed her brownish-blonde hair away from her eyes. Her hands massaged her navel.

Maybe today will be hopeful.

Philippa had talked to Mam last week about a weekend off from work. Mam was delighted, of course Philippa, go, go! Mam was worried at first, her new *amah* never even ventured to the gates, reserved was she, one of the bridge team asked. Mam was happy too, at last, a weekend without a stranger in her house. She never was comfortable with the idea of a live-in maid but all the British Consulate ladies had them!

So Philippa telephoned Ah Peng, the half-wit grocer's helper for the bus route to Chow Kit Road. She thought about her predicament, gathered all the money she had and decided on the solution. She knew, she just KNEW that somewhere in Chow Kit, her solution will be waiting for her.

Philippa knew it, anticipated it and was not surprised to learn she was carrying it.

Stupid, stupid I!

She knew everything about sex. After all, did she not sell her body back in Jakarta to get money to work here? She also had loved a few men passionately. She had never had a mistake.

Now she was pregnant.

SHAME!

She had no money to pay for the taxi fare when she first arrived at Mam's house two months ago. She had spent all the rupiah she had earned from spreading her legs on her travel fare, her new identity card, registration fees and agency fees at the Foreign Maids' Bureau.

So Philippa sold her physical wares to the taxi driver. She had thought she was safe. She had miscalculated her days. The last ecstatic thrust had made a child.

Hmm.

Philippa decided against having her shower. She would have one after she was empty. She dressed herself in clean underwear, a pink shirt and blue pants. She slipped on her sandals and tucked RM 500 in her left bra cup.

She locked the back door, padlocked the gates, walked to the bus stop and took Bus No. 23 to Chow Kit Road. She rubbed her stomach all the way there. Gas, she lied to comfort herself.

*

Philippa felt nervous when she arrived at Chow Kit. The bustle of the buses, cars and motorcycles hungrily attacking each other frightened her. The smell of sour spit, wet garbage and exhaust fumes made her head throb and stomach churn.

An old fat Chinese woman by the kerb picked at her nose and spat a stream of gray goo. A group of Muslim and Christian missionaries were hawking Qurans and Bibles by the roadside. A middle aged man grabbed Philippa's right arm. Listen to the sky! he implored. She pushed him away. She mused, her new country was strange. One country should have one people, but this place she was in was a stew.

But now, Philippa did not want to think of the strangeness of the new land. She had only the evening and Sunday morning. She sourly smiled to herself.

It will not hurt.

She went to a fruit stall to buy some pickled mangoes. As she munched on the fruit, she noticed a man smiling at her. Or rather, a woman. The person patted the stool next to her or him, indicating to Philippa to sit by him or her.

Hello, my name is Midah. You must excuse my voice. I just had a throat operation.

Midah had curly hair, pencil drawn eyebrows, pink cheeks and lips set on top of a pimpled and dark brown face. She also had stubble on her face and spoke in baritone. Midah, Philippa decided was a real man.

Midah was sipping Coca-Cola, dressed in a tight, short sleeved purple dress, exposing curly and hairy legs. Midah also had tissues crumpled as breasts in his dress; Philippa saw the white of the tissues peeking from his dress' neckline.

Philippa smiled at him.

Do talk, woman, you smile but are silent! My, your hair is yellow, that's not fake! Your skin - hello - are you a half and half?

Philippa nodded.

Oh, oh, oh do tell!

My mother's Indonesian and my father's Dutch. That's why I have a different name. Philippa.

What a lovely name. No wonder...you look like us, your features, but your colour is of the white man's. How come you don't look like the halves in Malaysia? They're usually pretty.

Am I ugly?

No but you can't be a model.

I work for someone. An amah.

Oh, orang gaji!

Cars and buses rushed by fast, honking hellos and insults to each other. Philippa hoped it would be fast, too.

Midah seemed to have lost interest in his new girlfriend. He winked at passing, startled men and cooed at schoolchildren. He sipped daintily on his straw. Then he turned sharply to Philippa.

Is your stomach feeding for two?

Eh?

You keep massaging your navel. And I see a slight bulge. You may be having worms but the bulge is too firm. You are having a baby?

So what if I am?

Astaga...if you are a foreign servant, you cannot afford to be *bunting!* Your mama will disown you! You foreign girls! Always get into problems! Your bureau finds out, bye, bye, Flipah, back to Indonesia! Are you so naive?

Do not insult me, you man in woman's panty! I know more about being a woman than you! And I certainly know how to please a man!

Oh, dear, did you miscalculate your days, Flipah?

Philippa burst out crying.

II

Philippa looked at the old Indian woman. The older lady glared back at her. Philippa sniffed. A mixture of Dettol and blood stung her nostrils, making her anxious.

The room they were in was dark. Philippa could see dust hovering like spirits in the room. The windows had wooden shutters and they were shut loosely. There was a table with a roughly sawn hole at the end of it. Underneath the table's hole was an aluminium basin filled with boiled water. Steam rose very lazily from the basin. A small kerosene lamp giving out very little light stood on the floor. The floor was made out of old splintered wood.

Midah had brought Philippa to a room at the top of a shophouse selling Chinese herbs, at the back of one of the many Chow Kit Road's mazed alleys. After having hushed Philippa's sobs at the door, Midah went into the room for a short while. He came out again, smiling. He held Philippa's hand and led her in.

Midah knew what Philippa wanted. Midah also told Philippa, that if Philippa was not dead at month's end, please come back to see him again, same place and time, he should be there on the last Saturday, around tea time. Midah blew a kiss and trotted down the road.

Philippa took off her pants and underwear and got on the table. She bent her knees and edged her rear nearer to the hole. She laid back, grinding her spine against the table.

The Indian woman put in a betelnut leaf in her mouth. She chewed slowly. Red spittle oozed from the corners of her mouth. She walked to a closet, opened its doors and reached into one of its drawers.

From between her bent legs, Philippa saw what the old woman had in her hands. There was a long lalang, green in the middle and brown at the edges. Its sharp point greeted her. There was also a scalpel blade fastened with wire to a thin stick. The dull glint of the blade slyly winked at Philippa.

She wondered if she would feel anything inside her. A penis was warm, firm and round. The blade looked cold and unfriendly. Would she feel its thinness?

A wizened, age spotted hand pried Philippa's legs wider. With the other hand, the old woman slowly inserted the lalang. She could not feel it, yet.

Are you a prostitute? The old lady at last spoke.

No. A servant. Why?

Your hole is big. Hee, hee.

Will it hurt? Oh!

Philippa felt the grass' point poking at her insides. Then she felt it slide out. The scalpel-stick snaked its way in. She understood then that her wish was about to be granted.

She did her best to remember. The beach she went to when she visited her cousins at Nusa Dua. Her father's laughter. Her cats. Her many boyfriends she had fought with, loved with and talked to. Her mother soothing her tears away.

Haa-aah!

How could something touching a foreign body in her sting so much? That's not her body, it belonged to another.

Zzh, zzh; she swore she heard the scalpel sawing at something inside her. Zzh, zzh.

Aaaw!

Did it cut a leg? Did it poke the stomach?

A huge wooden spatula was placed between her teeth.

The pain seemed like a paper cut at first. She imagined that the blunt saw was molten lead scraping bluntly away at her, as if it could not cut through but was forced on to her again and again. She felt blood as hot as lava pouring out of her and tinkling prettily into the basin below her. The blood boiled and swirled inside her. The scalpel hacked away at the vines in her womb. Bruises drummed orchestras everywhere.

The cutting stopped. She heard herself breathing heavily and saw her chest heaving rapidly. She sensed the scalpel easing out of her slowly. She refused to look at it. She forced her body up to look into the basin.

Where is it? I only see blood mingled with water. Is that all?

When you shit, it'll come, the woman promised as she stuck a sanitary pad between Philippa's legs. The woman pulled her up from the table. She smacked her behind.

Come, girl, come.

Philippa was led to a smaller room. There was a clean mat and pillow on the floor. She sat on the mat and looked around. It was as dark as the former room. The Indian woman caressed Philippa's cheek and smiled, exposing red teeth, stained from years of betelnut leaf chewing. Then she went out of the room.

In less than half an hour, Philippa felt the need to go to the toilet.

The pickled mangoes! I knew I shouldn't have eaten them on an empty stomach!

She went to an even smaller room adjoining to the one she was in. There was a huge clay tub full of water with a small bucket bobbing in it. A white pot with Dettol in it sat next to the tub, like a Buddha.

She crouched over the pot, her behind balancing precariously in the air. She rubbed her stomach inward, hard.

Plop.

She peered down.

Were those legs?

Blob. A small entity, covered in red and black slimy clots.

She looked up to the ceiling and waited.

At last it was over. She looked down again into the pot for the last time. She saw what seemed to be a bloody baby doll, amputated into chopped meat. Just like those broken dolls one saw at a garbage dump.

She cleansed herself with the water from the basin. She threw the soggy pad into the white pot. Her crotch ached and burned. She patted it gingerly. How it hurt. She thought that even if she were able to bend down to see her private parts, she would not. She put on her panty and walked weakly back to the room, blood trickling down her legs.

Once she was on her mat again, she tried to make herself cry. She searched right down to her soul to look for tears. She found them, molded into a ball and would not be persuaded to cry. She moaned and made "waa, waa" sounds so that she would cry.

She leaned her forehead against the wooden wall. She opened her mouth and watched saliva transform into a long, sticky tear-shaped droplet.

Baby. Baby, baby, baby.

She heard herself crying the word out loud but did not know if the word meant her or her lost child.

DINA ZAMAN graduated Cum Laude (Hons) in Mass Communications and Creative Writing from Western Michigan University. "Philippa" is her first published short story and is part of a projected collection of tales about house-maids.

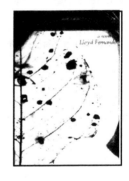

Green is the Colour
a novel by
Lloyd Fernando

Nobody could get May sixty-nine right, she thought. It was hopeless to pretend you could be objective about it. Speaking even to someone close to you, you were careful for fear the person might unwittingly quote you to others. If a third person was present, it was worse, you spoke for that person's benefit. If he was a Malay you spoke one way, Chinese another way, Indian another. Even if he wasn't listening. In the end the spun tissue, like an unsightly scab, became your version of what happened: the wound beneath continued to run pus.

ISBN 981-3002-68-9
Paperback   200 pp

Published by:
Landmark Books Pte Ltd
5001 Beach Road,
#02-74/75,
Singapore 0719

KARIM RASLAN
Neighbours

Datin Sarina prided herself on being well-informed. She was always the first to call her friends, sometimes even her enemies with the latest bit of news. News, mind you, not gossip. There was a difference. The first was confirmed and therefore true whilst the second was unconfirmed and possibly untrue. Untrue at least until it was confirmed and to be quite honest it couldn't be confirmed unless it was repeated a few times.

She was also very proud of her ability to ferret out the truth, however unpleasant. Ignorance and stupidity were insults to Allah: the truth was always worth fighting for. For example, she had been the first to alert the world to Tengku Mizan's second wife, an achievement she regarded as equal to her husband's 'hole-in-one' the year before at the Golf Club. She had seen the girl, Aida, at Habib Jewels. The face was of course familiar to her, Sarina was an avid reader of URTV and FAMILI - she knew her artistes; her Wann's, her Ziela's and her Jee's. She'd sidled over to where the girl was sitting and watched her pick over the expensive trinkets, opening her ears wider as the girl lisped her husband's name.

When she saw the gold supplementary credit card she knew her research was done. She dashed home and called all the ladies in her circle. She spared none of the details: regaling them with the size of the diamond, "don't play the fool: two carat, you know?", her scent "Giorgio **satu** botol - smelly!", the thickness of her make-up "like elephant skin-lah" and the shortness of her skirt, "no shame can see her buttock!" Proud of her sleuthing abilities she relished her nickname, *Radio Sarina*.

Sarina was forty-five years old, romantic by disposition, shortish and a little too plump to be good-looking. As if to compensate for her stoutness, she liked to think she was voluptuous. She wore the loudest colours possible, shocking reds, turquoises and vermillions and tottered around on four-inch heels. She wore make-up at all times, serious jewellery for at least eight hours a day and exercised sparingly. Married to Dato Mus, a civil servant ten years her senior the couple had three children, all of whom were now studying abroad. Her husband's busy schedule and the children's absence had forced her to find other sources of entertainment, if only to stave off boredom.

Which was why it came as such a pleasant surprise when she heard that the house next door had finally found a new owner. It had been deserted for the past three years and she relished having neighbours once again - if only to have someone new to talk to and about. According to the estate agent the people were called the Kassims and they were from Penang.

Patient as always, she waited for the newcomers' arrival. And what a move. Lorryloads of furniture and fittings arrived followed by contractors and their workmen. The next few days were a riot of comings and goings as lorries, vans, cars and motorbikes unloaded all manner of people and goods. It was only when she was making an inventory of the furniture, totting it all up in her mind that she realised how much time she had spent looking at her neighbours. She was suddenly conscious of how wrapped up she had become in the Kassims.

It was all very well to be nosy about people like Tengku Mizan: they deserved all that was coming to them. Besides everyone knew Mizan - his inability to keep his hands off big-breasted women was legendary. However, interest in the Kassims and people like that was a different matter, it was a bit embarrassing really. They were nobodies: it served no purpose - she couldn't talk about them to her friends. After a great deal of thought she decided that her interest in the Kassims had been a little extreme. However, it was educational - she had to learn about everybody. She shouldn't limit her interests.

Hastily then, she decided she should be a little more disciplined about these things. So she ignored the house next door - exercising a noble restraint when the servant girl came running to her one evening to tell her that the family had arrived to look at the house. Instead of rushing off to have a look at her new neighbours, she retired to her bedroom, drew the curtains and went to sleep. Self-control was very important in these matters.

She continued to treat the arrivals, then, as a temporary distraction, one that would be absorbed and made familiar in good time. This she considered was the correct way for a lady in her position to behave. Of course, the occupants of both houses soon made their own introductions. Her broken tailed pariah cat Chomel impregnated one of her neighbour's silvery Persians very noisily late one night. And her own servant girl Amina, who was it must be said irrepressibly flirtatious, had done her utmost to get herself impregnated by the neighbour's surly chauffeur.

It was some time, however before the heads of the respective households actually met. Sarina well understood the trials of house-moving and chose she thought, once again with great restraint not to impose herself. One particularly hot afternoon she did, in breach of her own personal sanction, send cold drinks over to the house when she heard - through Amina - that the electricity had yet to be connected.

Towards the end of the fourth week, and just after the prayers, Isyak, Encik Kassim called at the gate, introduced himself and was invited in to have some coffee.

He was almost six feet tall. Somehow she had known he'd be tall. He was ramrod straight, smooth shaven, golf-tanned and smiling. Such a smile; she was quite disarmed. He couldn't have been more than thirty-five years old and was well dressed - he was wearing a well-tailored pair of pants and a pink polo shirt that set off his healthy colour. Sarina felt a tremor of excitement as well as irritation with herself for not seeing him earlier: her new neighbour was so very good-looking. She was a little lost for words at first. But Kassim smiled again and, as if aware of his effect on her, made himself quite comfortable without troubling her. He was just so athletic, so attractive. She couldn't wait to tell her sisters: they'd die of jealousy.

Mus and Kassim soon dispensed with introductions and started talking about business. He said he was a lawyer and she was even more impressed. She slipped away into the kitchen as they started discussing market capitalisations, PE's, flotations and hot tips, subjects that always bored her. Once in the kitchen she prepared coffee for her husband and her new neighbour.

Arranging the coffee service on a silver tray, she marvelled at the splendour of this, her 'everyday' coffee service. She felt sure that the charming Encik Kassim man would notice the fine quality of the porcelain. She could imagine the expression on his wife's face when he, as she felt sure he was bound to, described the thick gold inlay of the saucers and the delicate transparency of the cups. His wife would be jealous, envious and not a little flattered to be living next door to people of such distinction and quality. There were times when she felt that she was one of a dying breed: a Scarlett O'Hara in a land of pygmies.

Placing the tray down on the small side table between her husband and the visitor, she glanced at Encik Kassim, expecting him to exclaim aloud, 'Allah, what exquisite porcelain you have Datin. Could it..could it be *Noritake*?' But he didn't, at least not initially. She was unsure that the men noticed her departure. As it was the two men had progressed from business to religion.

"..Datuk, these people they say that it's our duty to intervene and direct those that are transgressing the Koran. Well I think that's wrong. Islam brings all men together under the guidance of Allah. We are beholden to Him to live as closely as we can within the dictates of the Koran. That doesn't mean that we should force the unwilling...Oh, two sugars please Datin, thank you very much. What nice coffee cups Datin."

Sarina looked on admiringly as he drank his coffee; she was going to like this young man. He was so observant and such a gentleman. Didn't even slurp as he drank his coffee. Even Mus was beaming: Mus enjoyed a good theological debate and he was pleased to have a similarly inclined neighbour.

"Encik Kassim, you are so right. These preachers would have us living in the desert sands. The spirit of observance is of most importance not mere outward display. There are many ways of serving Allah and it is important to allow each individual his right to chose his own way, and his own time within the dictates, as you say, of the Koran and the Hadiths."

She watched Encik Kassim closely. He had a handsome sculpted head, a large forehead - he was a lawyer after all and brown eyes. Oh, if only she was young again, she thought: only to be shocked by the impropriety of her thought. Kassim nodded politely as Mus made his points. Such nice manners. Observing him so closely, she felt sure she knew him or at least his family. It didn't seem possible that she didn't know him. He was obviously far too polished to be just anybody. She couldn't help liking the way he deferred to her husband and smiled so pleasantly - there just weren't enough nice young men around like this Encik Kassim. If he hadn't been married she would have rushed out and called all her unmarried nieces there and then.

"...it is not of interest to me that you or anyone else might drink alcohol, gamble or commit adultery. There is, of course only one figure to whom we all owe obeisance and that is Allah. I might possess views about your behaviour which I could voice, were I inclined to do so, just as you would be free to reject whatever I have to say. Similarly I am free not to have to act according to your interpretations of the Koran and the Hadiths - because interpretations are all that they are, neither wrong nor right, merely differing views pertaining to the same subject," once Mus started it was often difficult to stop him.

"We are no longer living in small bedouin communities now in the desert. Neither are we personally equipped to act as judge against our fellow man. To be a judge of men's morals, personal or public, is something quite different."

"Datuk, I cannot agree with you more. It may be every Muslim's solemn duty to seek to attain the purest state before the Will of Allah. But that doesn't empower us to be moral arbiters and judges ourselves."

"I'll leave the highest state of grace to those that know better," Mus replied cheekily. He was enjoying the discussion. "I always say," he continued, "that Allah has endowed me with a brain that allows me the liberty of making my own decisions as to how I should lead my life. And I have chosen rightly or wrongly to seek the humblest place in heaven and no more. In short Encik Kassim I am an ordinary mortal using the blessings Allah has given me, to ask the questions that Allah must have expected us to raise.

"Come, come don't let me bore you with my talk. Drink your coffee and I will show you the garden wall that I was telling you about earlier," and with a broad sweep of the hand Mus drew the conversation away from religion to the commonplace.

Having been silent earlier, Sarina spoke up. She was very keen to meet Mrs Kassim now. If the husband was this good-looking and well-brought-up, the wife had to be exquisite.

"Encik Kassim, I do hope that your wife will do me the pleasure of calling on me when the family has settled in. Please don't be afraid to ask for any help. I understand how very tiring it is to be moving house".

"I will tell her," he replied warmly and then added, "actually my mother says she is related to you Datin; her mother is Datin's mother's cousin."

Sarina couldn't contain her excitement.

"Oh really, I should have known - you seemed so familiar. How interesting. Mus we're related! You must be Tok Su's *cucu* then? I remember now!" Mus smiled as well. She knew he was as pleased as her.

"I can assure you that my wife will call around as soon as she can. She would have come with me tonight, but her mother was not feeling well, so she had to go to Damansara Heights."

"Come Encik Kassim, I'll walk you out. We can have a look at this troublesome wall." The two men stood up and walked out into the garden, where the shadows cast from the street lights drew patterns across the damp lawn. Sarina watched as the two figures, both so tall and poised passed through the streaks of light, disappearing and reappearing. And as she watched them growing shadowy and dim in the dark she realised that from a distance it was hard to tell the difference between the two men. 'What a pleasant surprise,' she thought to herself as she cleared away the coffee things in preparation for bed, 'Such a nice young man, and a relative, too.'

The next morning after her prayers, Sarina chose to watch the sunrise - a special luxury that she allowed herself now that her children had left home. As she sat, quiet and composed on the verandah outside her bedroom, she tried to think about the household. But try as she might she couldn't help but think of Encik Kassim; visions of him flashed through her mind. And, if she was honest it was because of Encik Kassim that she was now sitting on her verandah. Her verandah afforded her a view of her neighbour's master bedroom and whilst she tried to pretend to herself that she was enjoying the cool morning air, she couldn't banish entirely the real motive for her early morning vigil. Thoughts of the young man had swirled through her dreams all night long and as soon as it was possible she had arisen and taken her place on the balcony.

Just then, she noticed a light being turned on in the room opposite her verandah. The previous owners, a nice Chinese family called Teh, had known that anyone who had a mind to, could see into their main bedroom if the light was left on. As a consequence they had been scrupulous in their use of curtains when getting changed. Of course, the new occupants were not to know and Sarina, realizing this had waited patiently on the verandah. She knew that she ought not to sit on the verandah now, but the prospect of seeing Encik Kassim again enthralled her too much.

The first streaks of sunlight began to tell upon the lawn, airily slicing the dawn mists. Even without Encik Kassim this was still her favourite time of day, and her reluctance to sit on the verandah drifted away much like the mists hanging over the garden. A delightful bluish tinge clung to the lawns now damp with the morning dew and swallows from the neighbouring trees swooped down to drink from the swimming pool. She had planted her garden with care, tending it lovingly over the years; the beds of heliconias had flourished and flowered showering the garden with their crimson brilliance and dragon-like intensity. She never lost her wonder at their startling voluptuousness and the way they cascaded pod after pod. Alongside them she had planted pale silvery hibiscuses, ferns and more ferns. The garden was looking lovely and she let herself be lost in the play of colours and scents that surrounded her, forgetting for a moment her new neighbours.

Changing her mind once again she made a mental note not to glance over at the house opposite. She would enjoy the morning air and then return inside: deferring to the Kassims' modesty. She felt sure that *nice* Encik Kassim would understand. It was not uncommon for her to make such fine resolutions: not to talk about Raja Karina and not to spend too much of her husband's bonus. Inevitably, over tea at the Hilton or in her sister's house she would find the excitement of the occasion loosening her tongue and then, before she could stop herself, she had imparted to all assembled the truth about Raja Karina's little operation in Geneva or agreed to buy yet another set of diamonds.

Thus it was, that she pledged to herself not to look at the bedroom window of her neighbour's house whilst sitting directly opposite it. As was always the case with such situations Sarina felt defeated by surrounding circumstances. Here she was, trying not to be nosy, minding her own business - enjoying the early morning coolness only to be thwarted by the Kassims next door, who insisted on leaving the lights on in their bedroom for all to see. She tried to feel irritated and annoyed with the Kassims. But try as she might she couldn't help admitting to herself that she was dying to see Encik Kassim again. He had been so attractive, so polite: she felt she had to stay, just had to stay and watch.

'Just this once', she thought, 'just this once I'll watch. I must find out about these people - I must learn about these new people.' She knew it was wrong, but ignorance was wrong too. Anyhow, as long as no one knew what did it matter? It was all quite innocent really. After all, she thought, they must know that people could look in. Maybe it was a deliberate act, some kind of deliberate oversight; maybe they were exhibitionists? Perhaps the young man wasn't as wholesome as he appeared? She laughed to herself: he was as wholesome as ketupat, just a million times better looking, that was all. Maybe he was shameless? And she laughed again. Much relieved to discover that the fault, if indeed there was any, lay with her neighbours, she let her eyes settle on the room.

The room was entirely unadorned, spare and empty. There was a bed and a bedside table, no more. The wife, this Puan Kassim, was obviously not the sort of woman who cherished the small, poignant tokens of love - a family photo or bottle of scent. Having met Encik Kassim, only the night before she tried to create in her mind what she thought the wife would be like. Yes, she thought to herself, the wife must be exquisite but cold and hard.

Then, in the house opposite, the door opened from the bathroom and a woman entered the room. Her sarong was tied casually around her waist, her breasts exposed. Sarina was taken aback and with a jolt she turned her head away to face the garden, now mockingly enrobed in the gathering sunlight. Surprised by the sight, she determined to forget ever having seen it. She wanted to tear herself away from her vantage point, now shorn of any of the gentle, innocent pleasure it had once given her.

But she was unable to do so. Her curiosity had taken hold of her entirely and she felt impelled to look again: if Mrs Kassim was half undressed then maybe her husband would be too? Sarina was half-embarrassed by what she had seen, more angered by the invidious position that it had put her in. She wasn't a voyeur or a pervert. But look she did, and with a terrible avidity.

The woman was tall and slim with small breasts. Sarina felt a pang of jealousy at the woman's slimness - if only she had persevered with her diets. The woman had surprisingly powerful shoulders - shoulders that wouldn't have needed shoulder pads and bedraggled hair that kept falling into her eyes though she tried to push it back. Because of the distance Sarina was unable to make out the woman's face clearly. But she thought her good-looking enough, with striking features and, like her husband, she was tall and erect - she had such bearing. There was a firmness and masculinity about her, emphasized in part by her lack of curves. She, this Mrs Kassim that wandered around her house bare-breasted, had no hips and thighs to speak of. The bearing of the woman, her pencil-slim shape and demeanour served to remind Sarina of the vast gap that separated the two of them. She was a woman of softer, older ways whilst Puan Kassim was stronger and more dynamic.

Mrs Kassim seemed unhappy. Her hands rifled through the bed clothes for some jewellery or underclothes. Sarina smiled to herself as she remembered similar fleeting encounters with Mus, and the men before Mus, meetings that had been snatched in between dances and dinners, baby-sitting and badminton. Those were in the days when sex had been something exciting for her and Mus. Now it was a chore as tiresome as dusting the furniture or washing the car, a chore that one underwent unwillingly with less frequency as the years progressed.

By now the light had reached its most perfect moment, lending a bronzed glow to all that it touched and she turned to her garden once again. The ranks of bougainvillaea in her garden seemed to strain to receive the welcome warmth of the sun, so different from the harsher glare of midday. She had almost forgotten about Mrs Kassim as she watched, charmed and warmed by the steady illumination of her garden. Suddenly she felt the soft delicious cool of the breeze that curled its way through the suburbs kissing her face as it passed by.

Mrs Kassim was sitting on the edge of her bed applying cream between her legs. Sarina winced, both from the sight and from the memory of having had to do the same in the past. Then the woman started rubbing herself with greater vigour, arching her back and cupping her breasts with her free hand. Though Sarina had never herself masturbated, she knew that this was what Mrs Kassim was doing. She had been a little disturbed initially. She knew that she should have been shocked by what she saw but she wasn't and she carried on watching. She wanted to know as much as possible about this woman whose body shuddered with each stroke.

Just then another door opened and a man, Encik Kassim, came into the room. Sarina felt her own breathing quicken and she placed her hand on her chest, squeezing her own breast inadvertently. This was what she was waiting for and she moaned silently. The wife did not notice him as she continued to stroke herself. Her strokes quickened and she shuddered violently. Encik Kassim walked around the bed until he was standing directly in front of her. Undoing his trousers he nursed his penis into her mouth. Sarina pressed her breast again and shivered.

She couldn't believe it! They were making love; this was far more than she had expected, though she couldn't say that she hadn't hoped for it. Even so she wasn't sure if she should be shocked or thrilled. Encik Kassim pulled off his trousers and underwear, throwing them across the room in his hurry. He leapt onto the bed and straddled it on all fours like a dog. She gasped and her hand dropped from her breast: what was he doing? He had a strong muscular back with just a hint of a paunch. His penis was monstrously enlarged.

The wife turned around and grabbed Encik Kassim firmly by the waist. Sarina could almost feel the bruises on his body. They were so violent and animal-like with one another! So, she thought, this was what it was like to make love passionately. She imagined herself for a moment in the place of Mrs Kassim, touching that young man and being touched by him. It was like one of those blue movies she had watched years before, only more real and more fervent. Her head was spinning with the possibilities.

Seductively and slowly the wife let her sarong fall to the floor. It slipped off her slim thighs and gathered in a pile at her ankles. Sarina swallowed hard, her mouth went dry. The woman's belly didn't taper off into a mound as her own did. The woman, or at least what she thought was a woman had a penis of her own, a penis that was also erect. It was a *pondan*. She mouthed the word silently, a *pondan*.

'This can't be the wife!' she thought. 'No, surely not! How *could* he! He was so nice!' She didn't know what to think. He'd been such a polite and charming young man and a relative of her's as well - how could he do *this*...to her? It couldn't be! Her head spun painfully. She felt deflated and angry as if she had been let down. Encik Kassim had disappointed her, cheated her with his charming smile and his grey eyes.

The woman positioned herself behind Encik Kassim...her handsome Encik Kassim. Now she really was shocked, horrified in fact but still she watched, engrossed by the ugliness of it all. She was unable to pull herself away. But as she watched she became aware of the unnaturalness of what she was doing. Why was *she* watching? Why did she feel compelled to watch? Was there something wrong with her? Why couldn't she be like other people and mind her own affairs? Somehow she felt that it was her nosiness, her selfish persistence had brought Encik Kassim to this.

Had she been more respectful of his privacy, none of this would have happened. She would have thought him charming and good-looking. Now he appalled her. It was all her fault, her responsibility. She had pushed him. Just as the thoughts rushed through her head the woman eased herself into him, shaking her head with pleasure.

She pulled herself out suddenly and slapped Encik Kassim hard across the buttocks as if he were a fat *kerbau* and sneered. And as she did Sarina saw that he, *her* despicable Encik Kassim, moaned like a woman. He was no longer the man she had met the night before - sprawled across the bed like an animal he seemed grotesquely subservient and feminine. The woman - she just couldn't call him a man, it was too monstrous, stood up. Encik Kassim moaned again and thrashed his buttocks in the air like a bitch on heat. Sarina wanted to retch. What was going on? She saw that the woman's features were hard and prominent like a man's. Did she have an Adam's apple? How had she missed it earlier? The woman turned the overhead light off.

With the light now off, Sarina realised that it would be possible for the couple to see her on the verandah. So, the blood draining from her face, and terrified lest she be seen she went back to her bedroom. It was a rare moment, a moment of shocking clarity. She could see herself as she was - the pretence and the falsity of how she lived her life had slipped away. Everything around her was sheared of its innocence. It was all a sham. She was a fat, overweight woman, neglected by her husband, whose emotional life was so thin and insubstantial that she could only find satisfaction in the private lives of others, a parasite who fed off the secret lives of others. She had nothing herself: she was nothing herself.

© Karim Raslan, 1993.

KARIM RASLAN graduated from Cambridge with a degree in Law. He is now a writer and has contributed to local, regional and international publications, newspapers and magazines.

---

new literatures review

writing from the post-colonial world.

Individual textual studies, interviews, bibliographies,and reviews, comparative and theoretical work on critical practice and the cultural politics of constructing a 'new' academic field.

<u>Past issues</u> focus on: African, Pacific, Carribean, Indian, Canadian and Australian writing, the canon, non-anglophone writing, drama. Most back issues are available.
<u>Future issues</u> include: New Zealand writing, post-graduate work in the field, post-modernism, popular culture, bio- & autobiography. General issues appear occasionally.

Twice-yearly for A\$15.00; three year-sub. A\$38.00
(Australian currency only, or add your equivalent of A\$6.00 for charges; cheques made out to 'New Literatures Review')

Write to the Editors, *New Literatures Review*, Dept. of English, University of Wollongong, Locked Bag 8844, South Coast Mail Centre, NSW 2521, Australia.

SHIRLEY GEOK-LIN LIM

Tropical Attitudes

I: Jet Lag

Sometimes I wake up and do not remember
where I am. Jet lag is miserably here
and occurs at anytime. I forget
for the briefest moment who I am.
Time and place wait beneath rushed wings;
catch, unexpected, words said ancient nights
ago, ill-assorted sounds that no longer
can be unsaid in memory's sheet,
glare of dead lives, yet with power
to stir as crimson bouganvilleas,
gloriosas, and goldenshowers cannot.
Features given up for solitary search
return, asking recognition.

II: Singapore International Airline-Kuala Lumpur Shuttle

Catching the S.I.A. shuttle
to K.L., alphabet countries grounded
in colonial ironies, steaming
face-towel heat, engorged palms,
all pricks and swells of other lives
rub against self's inner peel like
thighs' tenderest skin chafed.
Nothing hides the toughened malaise
that feeds desire to staleness:
the persistent wintry hum
and thump of machine-purged oxygen
in glass expanse of glittering zircons.

Approaching Subang, grey-ash tin pilings,
leavings of gashed lunar mounds -
and ponds as blue as sky, filled

with inverted cloudy landscapes,
aqua, navy, yellow-grey. Then the new
patterned palm-blossomed checkerboard,
plantation linearities
of postcolonial growth still here;
despite a different history,
different color, still prolific.
We will never stop being overwhelmed
by history and race. That's all I'm allowed.
In the dirty airport: smudged suspicious
exhaustion of racial home-coming.

III: The Singapore-Malacca Bus Express

Mandarin voices way above the edge
of comfort speak from Nippon boxes.
No escaping them even though the leg-room
is fine, air-conditioning blasting,
and sun screened beyond tinted glass.

Singapore seen from a bus seat
at 8 a.m. is full of sullen men
in the back of Toyota trucks, Hondas,
and taxis. You strain to observe raintrees
splaying like trimmed cauliflowers.
Tanjong Bunga blossoms, unattainable
in the fenced centre-dividers
only a suicidal botanist
would consider picking; also,
royal palms, ixoras, thorny bouganvilleas,
unvarying tropic fans. Not nature
but opulence. Avenues of freshly
painted houses on top of others.
Not luxury but order.

                    Above,
the unharnessed clouds, cirrus, cumulus,

striated monsoon underhand of thunder heads.
The sun, swiftly rising, breaks free.

IV: Johore

Across the Causeway, two border checks.
The population coagulates like sick
arterial clots in the Malaysian pulse,
saved by smiles, meekness, never-mind-lahs.
The woman who smuggles her hair
in beige cloth poses on stilletó
heels under a long black sateen skirt,
two peg-a-legs on the Chief
Customs Officer. They are tearing down
the South Seas Chinese shop fronts.
The police station is newly trimmed
in white and blue. It doesn't matter.
Easy once or uneasy now,
the multi-races are everywhere.

V: Malacca

I had forgotten how dense the country.
Layers of vegetation: padi
kangkong ubi sugarcane banana
thickets of mango rambai duku durian
attap groves, the lanky nipa and coconut.
Not mangrove or jungle but settled
habitation, bearing native possession.
Layers of houses - open, planked, pillared,
with tiled steps, behind the pastel
lace curtains of Malay womenfolk.
Or bold red calligraphy of Nanyang;
peeling shacks, facades of rusted zinc,
bald concrete cutouts, and steel accordian
gates.

Clotted thick in old Malacca,
the red roofs of old Malaccans -
neither foreign nor bumi - latecomers
who live in ancient homes, in a country
in their own right. Among shadows
of Dutch Stadthouses in a new order,
school-children struggle with old definitions.

On Muar river, hyacinths drift in rafts;
they need no law to take over the water,
autochthonous creations. Everywhere,
discouraged shophouses, unpainted,
those who had given up, gone off. Everywhere,
bright shop signs - cloth, gold, new teeth,
electronics. Mechanics and engineers,
layers of pipes: the old and new orders
do not shake them out, but hone a will
to make the most of it, of the
god-given day and god-given night.
The boys play in the cool-after-six hour,
thrashing the lallang with bamboo rods.
Proud fathers drive sleepy families
in new cars; the young man takes
his girl behind him on his new bike.

VI: After Malacca

Stern but welcoming my eldest brother
stands before the house. Guardian of the past
he reminds me the future is here
Grandfather's Heeren house crumbles.
Its red roof has buckled. Reclaimed land
stretches for hundreds of wild grass yards.
Straits waves recede. Behind abandoned lots,
beneath back rooms now stranded and propped
on stone pillars, the old Malacca swamp
still silts. Tiger mosquitoes breed, mumble.

Black pythons slide out of the stinking
oily water at evening when tourists,
guards, and rulers are out of sight.

Strange Meeting

Larger than a city block, the Boeing glides
past the viewing glass. Its hollow body
glows with myriad eyes, each eye holding you
gliding into Los Angeles. It is seven years
since we've met, and more than twice seven
before that. Two babies separate us,
brown boys with different mates.
Together we had managed
to pull apart whatever pushed us
together. You come down
the gray industrial carpet,
your rolling shuffle just the same
as the young man's whose American
speech splintered my native ears
I want to take you home
inside myself, a cannibal,
to eat your juicy heart,
mingling blood with blood.
Or like that thick-shelled bird,
to carry you in my glowing body,
howling in the wind-stream,
back to where we both had been.
But the moment passes, baffled
by love and what it cannot do

112

At the Christian Funeral Parlor

"Perhaps the past is a paper house."
Patricia Ikeda

Pastor John in platform shoes walks to the boom
box on the concrete floor, bends over, and turns
the knob till the volume hisses, "WE SHALL
MEET BY THAT BEAUTIFUL SHORE." Sensitive-fingered
chrysanthemums, spotted tiger and spider
orchids, and red-hot fleshy tropical ginger
blossoms gape in dense maiden-hair fern.
Their musk jabs our nostrils like carrion.
You lie embowered, a pale lemon giant worm.
"What honor!" someone whispers, of the calling cards
from the rich brother's corporate connections.
The fall of brown-edged frangipani leis
with your name engraved like gold-rimmed kinfolk.
This moment too is new. Disbelief lies
beside your waxy cheek. Before the sermon
Pastor John invites a prophetic bond with me,
the visitor from New York. I have arrived
decades too late, after the red Singapore-
chopped blue aerogrammes that urged scripture
and held out for attention. Then the Chinese pastor
headed for Los Angeles, greying sisters
and lonely Tamil adolescents, the minor bureaucrats
whose Christ raises the dead and who are looking
for nothing your island can offer ≈ these charismatics ≈
are gone. We leave you beneath more bouquets
than lovers and children have delivered
in your life, to gawk at the Taoist shaman.
In black ceremonial robes he stacks pyramids,
gold and silver paper bricks, on the macadam
before the Chinese funeral room,
pours brandy over this extravagant wealth,

and sets the conflagration with a Cricket
barbecue starter. Electric blue Mercedes models,
shiny skyscrapers papered on bamboo girders,
flash up behind acetate Maytag deep freezers.
The black-hatted paper man in coat-tails
toasts crisply down to a twisted heap.
Casually the Taoist jumps over the fire, once, twice,
three times. Who can guess the import of his actions,
as he lifts his robes above his pants and clears
the flames? The bamboo bones burn slower,
glowing long after the papery ash collapses.
I stand, thinking of you, delivered
to the crematorium tomorrow,
your body the wealth accompanying
Christian smoke and ash into the earth.

© Shirley Geok-lin Lim, 1994

From Skoob Books Publishing Ltd

SHIRLEY GEOK-LIN LIM'S

Writing S.E. Asia in English: Against the Grain

A literary criticism containing ten chapters written
between 1986 and 1993, demonstrating an evolving
reading of South East/Asian cultures and South East/
Asian subjects writing in English, against the grain
of national languages and national canons.

A God Drowns

Out of the eruption of a primal chaos
you came - of a moment, when the sky broke,
dividing into darkness and water.
You were cast out, to wait for return
of life in the disintegration of the shell
that holds the world. But out of your wounds,
a bursting tide of mud destroys our fields.
Our rivers give up their burden of white fish.
All day, you were presence by the kapuk tree,
rousing the crows over the foul mudflats.
Now all night, you keep floating back,
swollen, grey man, rejected by the waters,
caught by wire on the cross-bars of a gate
wrenched upstream, from dusun under violent flood.

A Fire Easter
(for Edwin Thumboo)

The hill looms, leaning so black
out of the shocked sky, I find myself
ascending still an abyss of dreams
into the morning heat. Day ignites
into a furnace upon the ridge,
laterite-lined, fired by the sun.
In its white blast,
the thief, the murderer wait.
Fires that smoulder in my bones
stick now like blue flies
on black skins around their wounds,

eating into eye-balls and parted lips.
The soldiers wait, brittle
in the fires... like coal... In the ascent,
I faint into the fumes
of the three-tonner that bears me
in chains up the hill.
The sixth hour... I become light
as my own flames leaping from blood,
from skin and hair roots turned up
by the crown of barbed-wire
woven round my skull. I am palms, soles,
peeling off onto the metal of the truck.
Where is the help now as I cry out
that I am only flesh in pain?
The ninth hour... Am only a crushed throat,
gurgling and whistling queerly
into the air like these two
who sag from their cross-trees into mid-sky.
I would melt quickly into the sun.
No vinegar... hyssop... bayonet probing
into my sides for life...
Let the howling women fade.
Mariamma, the other Mary, rolling
onto the laterite in such savage grief.
Muthu... John... In the sword-dry lallang,
the others... Upturned faces,
bruised fruit that are much handled.
And the jostling crowd, also of the dead...
There shall be no winding cloth,
no myrrh, no aloes, no deception
this time of me risen in body
that passes through locked door and wall.
Let fire eat me
from genitals, from the bowels

into the tree of flesh caught up in dreams,
in death... Do not wait then
for me at nightfall at any cross-roads,
or morning by rail-track, by mining pool,
or deep into the ferns beyond the estates
where once you had looked for me,
the dishevelled, mild, unattainable
man of miracles
who, by secret, snake-infested streams,
shared with you your rice and fish.
Except you come with me into the fire,
you will not return, with your own eyes
and in the flesh see me raised in glory.

WONG PHUI NAM graduated from the University of Malaya in Economics and has since worked mainly in development finance and merchant banking.

Most of the poems he wrote during the Sixties first appeared in *Bunga Mas,* an anthology of Malaysian Writing published in the United Kingdom in 1963. They were subsequently collected and published as *How the Hills Are Distant* in 1968 (*Tenggara* Supplement) by the Department of English, University of Malaya. In 1989 his second volume *Remembering Grandma and Other Rumours* was published by the English Department, National University of Singapore.

Mr Wong's poems have also appeared in *Seven Poets, The Second Tongue, The Flowering Tree, Young Commonwealth Poets '65, Poems from India, Sri Lanka, Singapore and Malaya.* He was also published by literary journals like *Tenggara, Tumasek, South East Asian Review of English* and *Westerly.* His latest book *Ways of Exile: Poems from the First Decade* has been published by **Skoob PACIFICA,** London in 1993. He also writes a poetry column for a newspaper.

SALLEH BEN JONED
Ria

*'and We know
what his soul whispers within him,
and We are nearer to him than the
jugular vein.'*
- The Quran, L: 15-18(Arberry)

i

Moments that peeled my awareness
were the times I remember you best:
mornings in autumn, your gaiety dissolving
the secret tension of light and air,
lithely lisping the magic of your name
into the smell of each falling leaf
that clung to your hair.

One such morning remains
the clearest of all,
like a thin slant of light
in a dark musty hall.

That morning the current of air
touched your bone.

You were standing on the slope of the path,
your feet anchored to a mass of leaves,
clinging damply to the earth,
You saw me off with a sticky kiss,
sensing your moment in the slant of light,
your bewildered voice lisping a wish
I couldn't hear.

I jumped over the fence
and left your voice to freeze
in the light.

Two hours later,
a casual voice clinically declared:
'Your child is dead.'

ii
Light was everywhere
when I came out of the dark;
so much light slanting so simply,
flooding my eyes, blinding them
with the yesses of my senses,
the noes of my knowledge;
as on the day I buried you,
an unblessed child in blessed earth,
wind blowing dust
round and round the bare hill,
and the noonday autumn light
steadying in its slant
a sweetness of honey in the air.

iii
Now you are dead, I want to dream
your physicality
back into this house
in which you hardly lived.
Defiantly, I filled the rooms
with your laughing faces, defiling
the ritual of denial
I'd been taught to observe.
Discreetness of absence my Ria
cannot be
in the space that was hair
between darkness and light,
in the trace of your breath
that my tongue must retrace.
I can smell your body still
in the thick mohair rug,

my tactile little darling,
you learnt the rub of things
with the feel of fur
on your cheeks.
Your butterfly kisses
on the side of my neck,
on my scarred ageless face,
taught me the joy you felt
in the fact of the senses.
Tauntingly physical
was your being,
testing mine and the world's
with dark trembling lashes;
that queer left eye
(faulty delivery the doctor said)
fluttering more than the other
the lashes of your joy in my joy
in your realness.

You were nearer to me, my Ria
than my own jugular vein.

At times, your alertness
quickened my sense
of futility -
as when, puzzled
by my burning life away,
you made a wild lunge
and singed the lash
of your troubled eye.
At times, your alertness
quickened my sense
of what you meant -
as when, heady
with knowing curiosity
you somersaulted on to our love-

spent bodies,
your crazy nose triumphantly sniffing
the smell of rancid honeyed cheese
through screwed-up sheets.

iv
Joy means your name Ria
in the tongue of your blood.

You were made for us to reaffirm
the wild impulse of adolescence,
to reconcile a past with a past,
an instant with an instant,
and a tongue with a tongue.
You gave a woman reason
for a moment of hard acceptance
of me and my inscrutable lusts,
and would have taught perhaps
my stubborn ancestral liver
the needs of an unfamiliar heart.

I grew to love you with my body love
as you grew to feel me with your needs,
but our mutual growth
was blighted from the start.

You came raw before the light
burdened with all our hopes;
your mind opened to a strange world,
groping for a sense of self
only to let in
early intimations of estrangement.
I came raw in pursuit of light,
from the place of sun and certainties
into a chaos of new sensations;
my mind opened to an alien world,

the blood's blind urgings locked
in the mind's dumb questionings.

v

The night of your burial
was my sinless night of the soul,
the gaiety that was yours
danced the darkness on every tongue,
all the dreams we had in you
burst to a wake in a sudden song:
an unwilled blasphemy
affirming the will.

But the morning after
was a different matter.
And the morning after.
And the morning after.

Each break of day my love
is a break of day:
my body athwart the slant of light
across the emptiness hollowing my bed,
seeing an endless row of other beds,
dreading all the mornings
when I shall darkly awake
to the harsh fullness of sheer light
that knows no season;
dreading the hangover
of my days
on this island of Circe,
I my own Penelope,
weaving and unweaving
an endless moment,
resisting the light
of the hard sun
that forged my existence,

betraying my blood's vow
to the living now.

vi
The scar, the scar's the thing -
as darkly etched on my native flesh
as the sunburnt line
across your pale sewn-up breast;
as clean as the lightning
across the tropic sky
I had forgotten.

vii
The room seemed suspended
in the haze of the sea,
the light a blend of dusk and dawn.
You were sitting on the edge of my bed,
in which so many needs
were hurriedly buried,
in which so many betrayals
were joyfully consummated,
true to the sterile sensuality
of this time, of this place.
It all seemed part of a floating world,
the still silent sea below;
your child face aged,
your legs casually crossed,
the way you crossed them
when you parodied my pretence
of being a man.
Grace was yours, meaning was yours,
as you shook the clipped vines of your hair
over the floating form of another self;
no bitterness, all sweetness,
as you breathed a breath of spring
along the slant of autumn light,

stirring the presence of warmth
in the chilly dullness of the air.
It was a dream so physical
I woke up to the feel of your breath,
your sister kneeling by my side,
her breezy greeting riding the light,
the moment of your name alive
in those honeyed eyes
staring into the sun.

viii

Marking the days before my return
with a burden of knowledge
that doesn't make any sense,
I sit here among my three thousand books;
behind my back another autumn sun,
shining so simply,
rises over a strange familiar hill,
brown and bare among bluish
eucalyptus green.
I sit here, my pen bleeding words,
gripped by fingers bruised
from cutting your name
into sandstone,
feeling again the firmness
of hallowed letters
sharply etched,
following the contours
of the only misery
truly mysterious.

ix

Joy means your name Ria
in the tongue of your blood,
a tongue I must learn again
to sing the mystery of our pain.

Be with me my Ria
in the sheer light
of my old sun.

SALLEH BEN JONED was a lecturer in English Literature at the University of Malaya. He is now a poet and columnist with a newspaper. His first book of poems *Sajak Sajak Saleh: Poems Sacred and Profane* was published in 1987.

Myths, Heroes and Anti-Heroes

Essays on the Literature and
Culture of the Asia-Pacific Region

Edited by

BRUCE BENNETT &
DENNIS HASKELL

Do traditional myths matter in contemporary societies? Is there much difference between a "hero" and a "heroine"? Does anyone believe in heroes any more anyway? Can the "hero" by merely a political creation? Do myths function differently in different countries of the Asia-Pacific region?

Centre for Studies in Australian Literature
The University of Western Australia

PART TWO

Malaysian/Singaporean Writings

of the 1990s

Telling Stories, Expressing Values:
The Singapore Novel in English
Tenggara 25

As more Singaporeans become literate in English, at a pace accelerated by English having become the sole medium of instruction in schools (an official confirmation in 1987, of a virtually accomplished fact by the early eighties), the reading public for the literature in English will correspondingly increase. Two recent national readership surveys of 1980 and 1988 bear this out. Of particular interest is the fact that a large majority of those who do read books, read novels. [1] More of the school-going population are also reaching higher levels of education, especially Junior College and the university, with a probable widening too, of the pool of potential writers in English.

Another factor which seems to augur well for the prospects of novels in English is a growing tide of sentiment for things Singaporean, a pride in a new-found identity resulting from rapid socio-economic and cultural development. With national self-confidence has come a feeling that like its airline, airport and seaport, things Singaporean can be, and are as good, if not better than anything imported from the West, and this sentiment seems to have spilled over into the creation and consumption of cultural products. Lee Tzu Pheng has rightly observed (although she doesn't go into causes) that short fiction and drama

> have not only witnessed an increase in the volume of works produced, but - especially drama - have in the 80s generated and profited by a more widespread public enthusiasm and attention. [2]

Lee is silent on the situation of the novel, perhaps because the immediate beneficiaries of these developments have been the more accessible (or readily consumable) popular forms, short fiction and drama. Certainly, both short stories, plays and their authors have been featured or highlighted in a spate of national celebrations this decade as expressions of and contributors towards a sense of national consciousness. [3]

The signs these past two years indicate that the novels in English are riding the crest of the popularity of the short stories and plays. A recent list of the ten best-selling paperbacks in English sold by one of the two largest local bookchains includes five recent novels in English by local authors, with four of them being among the top five best-sellers.[4] There also appears to be a symbiotic relationship between the recent popular successes. Philip Jeyaratnam's best-selling first novel, *Raffles Place Ragtime* (1988) swiftly followed upon the heels of his first short story collection, *First Loves* (1987) which had broken all records for a local literary work both in sales and number of reprints. Catherine Lim, the best-selling short story writer before him had similarly come out with her first novel, *The Serpent's Tooth* (1982), following upon the success of her two collections of short stories. Lim's short stories moreover, have been staged as plays, while among the playwrights, Ovidia Yu had enjoyed prior success as a short story writer, and another, Robert Yeo, flush after the successful staging of his plays, came out with a first novel, *The Adventures of Holden Heng* (1986), which has sold reasonably well. One kind of success seems to feed the other, the media enthusiastically assisting - just as behind this newfound popularity are socio-economic developments which seem to have fueled a desire among readers for an imaginative celebration of Singaporean experience, particularly in humorous or ironic accents; or more seriously, in the form of self-critical, introspective evaluations of this experience and the conditions which produced it.

None the less, despite these signs in the late eighties, that the novel in English is on its way to popular success (the signs could equally be but a flash in the pan of a youthful national euphoria or mere fashion), the novels in English (at least, up till 1988) have not generally done as well when compared with the other main literary forms in English such as the poetry, short stories and drama. No novel or novelist to date, has achieved the level of critical attention and acclaim paid to poetry and the leading poets; rivalled the combined popular success of the short stories and the plays; or enjoyed the public and corporate financial support of the latter. The plays, especially, in the eighties have acquired an unrivalled glamour and a sense of direction and purpose hitherto associated only with the poetry. Up till recently, too, before the increase in the number literate in English, the local novels that had had a popular success were those in Malay and in Chinese, the English-educated minority (as any number of bookshops' best-selling lists then could testify) preferring imported works from the West.

The for long poor cousin status of the novel in English is as much due to historical and sociological circumstances as to causes inherent in the nature of the novel form itself. Critical acclaim is most often reserved for the 'serious' work of fiction, but a novel has to sell in reasonably large numbers if the novelist is to continue being published; and 'serious' novels have a modern history of not selling as well. These two aspects of the novel, as the history of the novel everywhere amply illustrates, are often difficult to reconcile, for above all, the novel must entertain, must grip the reader's imagination and ideally should be (to use the reviewer's favourite adjective) "unputdownable", with the reader being drawn on inexorably by the need to know "what happens next?" E.M. Forster, who enviably managed to achieve both critical and popular success (the acme of which is to have one's novel made into a "major movie") sums up well the novelist's dilemma when he sighed, "Yes - oh dear yes - the novel tells a story".[5] But in a former colony and immigrant society which moreover, suffered the trauma of a brutal war-time occupation, the real-life experiences of individuals initially provided gripping enough stories, and these, not fictional histories, were the first to be published in English, remaining till today with other biographies and memoirs, steadily popular among readers curious about or nostalgic for a rapidly disappearing past under the assault of rapid modernization.

Thus for a long while, readers in English did not feel the lack of local novels in English, nor did there appear a novelist to kindle a demand for them. Consequently, the Singapore novel in English was a late-comer on the literary scene, with some attendant disadvantages. While poems and some short stories were already being published by members of the tiny English-educated elite at the University of Malaya in Singapore from the colonial, post-war period of the forties onward - albeit in a small, tentative way - and fitfully afterwards, the first novels in English did not appear till 1972, well after Singapore's achievement of self-government in 1959 and independence in 1965. One was Goh Poh Seng's *If We Dream Too Long,* which may be regarded as the first serious attempt to represent critically, contemporary Singaporean experience; the other was *China Affair*, an oriental thriller by the lawyer, Kirpal Singh, featuring high international intrigue set in Singapore and the Far East.

Since then, some 25 novels in English have been published, at the rate of less than two novels a year, with a spurt to six in the past two years. None the less, a Malay novelist such as Ahmad Lutfi alone would already have some 25 novels to his name by the sixties, and in sheer quantity, taken together, the novels in Malay and in Chinese by local authors far outnumber their counterparts in English. However, given current linguistic developments, the situation is changing and the number of novels in English (if recent trends are anything to go by) published since 1965 seem set to outstrip that in the other languages published in Singapore.

But for the moment, the novelists (and the novels) in English have yet to rival the poets, short story writers and playwrights in their impact on the public consciousness. Although novels have the advantage in being more accessible to the general reading public than poems (notorious among most readers for being 'difficult' and too 'literary'), the novels in English had not enjoyed publication opportunities available to the poets, for instance, from the "poetry corners" of the newspapers to the pages of literary magazines such as *Focus* and *Singa* or serious general interest magazines like *Commentary*, the now-defunct *New Directions* and other, albeit short-lived little magazines. The short story writer, too, has had more publication outlets as the history of the short story in Chinese testifies, the great numbers published being due to the traditional support of the Chinese newspapers which down the years (unlike the for too long, colonial English papers) provided generous space and publicity in their literary supplements.

As local publishing history also reveals, both poems and short stories conveniently lend themselves to being collected or anthologised by enterprising authors, compilers and editors, thus enhancing their public visibility and marketability. Moreover, there also existed more little presses which were willing to publish long and short fiction in the so-called "vernaculars" of Malay and Chinese.

There are besides, annual national poetry, short story and playwriting competitions, the best known of which, sponsored by government agencies offer several thousands of dollars worth of cash prizes, consequent publicity in the national media, prestige and publication opportunities. Novelists can, at most, hope for a National Book Development Council of Singapore (NBDCS) award for fiction. But this is only presented biennially, and the novelist is also caught in a bind because only published works are eligible for consideration. Being fictional works, the novels have moreover, to compete in the same category as short stories. [6]

The poem's respectable "literary" status also ensures that if all other avenues are closed, it still gets institutional support. A poet of sufficient worth in Singapore, if spurned by the commercial press, can still turn to private sponsors such as the Shell Literary Fund, administered by the Department of English Language and Literature at the National University of Singapore. Whether by conscious editorial policy or not, the Fund has to date, sponsored only volumes of poetry. Lee Tzu Pheng in the earlier overview mentioned, points out the value of such sponsorship when she notes that "it is conceivable that without this assistance, some volumes might not have found their way into print" [7] The slimness of volumes of poems and their short print-runs probably make sponsorship of their publication more attractive, too.

Lacking therefore the "high art" prestige of poetry which transfers to its authors, sponsors and patrons, the novel, traditionally a popular, "low" literary genre, has to rely almost solely on the commercial publisher. In practical terms, it requires of an author an ability to "sell" his or her product, catering therefore to fashion and the current taste of the mass market. Or, the novelist must at least have a proven track record and public presence, to sell. A novelist with serious literary ambitions such as Goh Poh Seng, for instance, could find no publisher for his pioneering first novel and had to publish *If We Dream Too Long* himself. Even an established publisher such as Heinemann Education Books, seems to have shown an interest in publishing Goh's second novel, *The Immolation* (1977) for its "Writing in Asia" series only after his first novel had won the NBDCS award for fiction. This seems the case, too, when it brought out a revised second edition of Michael Soh's *Son of a Mother* (first published in 1973 by an obscure small press), in 1981, after it had won the award. As mentioned earlier, Catherine Lim and Philip Jeyaratnam, having established themselves as best-selling short story writers certainly had no difficulty getting their first novels published.

Another way to establish a track record is to have your novels published first elsewhere, preferably in the West, which will at least, win you considerable media attention, as happened to Minfong Ho, a Singapore expatriate. Both her *Sing to the Dawn* (1975) and *Rice Without Rain* (1986) were first published in New York and London respectively, with the former moreover, winning an American award for children's books. They were then reprinted in Singapore.

It is common knowledge that what the mass market wants, what sells, are novels of high entertainment value - thrillers, adventure tales, detective novels and the like which provide large doses of action, and better still, crime and sex. Thus while the 1988 National Readership Survey hearteningly noted that the majority (62%) of book readers read novels (compared to only 38.8% in a 1980 survey) and while 70% of the books loaned out by the National Library to adults and young people are novels, predictably, "popular fiction was preferred while literary works...were lowest on the interest scale". A National Library branch survey of 1987/88 found that the most popular categories of novels were suspense/thriller type novels, followed by mystery/crime, horror stories, romances and family stories. Fantasy and Asian/Singaporean fiction and modern classics lagged far behind. [8]

These surveys confirm what the best-selling lists of the two largest book chains, MPH and Times the Bookshop, regularly show - that the best-selling authors are the likes of Sydney Sheldon, Frederick Forsyth, Victoria Holt, Judith Krantz and the latest publishing sensation from the West. (Clearly, another factor limiting the market for local novels in English in Singapore, despite the attested popularity of novels as such, is sheer competition from the overwhelming number of imported books, especially of pulp fiction, in an already relatively small market). A recent local best-selling novel like *Miss Moorthy Investigates* (1989) by Ovidia Yu, for instance, probably owes its success to a combination of local setting and characters presented through the medium of the time-tested genre of the Western crime mystery novel.

Another factor hindering the development of the novel in English is the undeveloped state of local publishing itself. Whereas established firms in the West, supported by long publication lists and far larger book markets, are better situated to take risks, or more prepared to subsidise worthy, but potentially less marketable works, the local publisher either cannot afford or doesn't care to do the same. A spokesman of even a major publisher in Singapore such as Heinemann Education Books (now Heinemann Asia) is on record as saying that since "crime and sex" sell books, and book publishers are in the business to sell books, it is more likely to publish such books. Recent local Singapore publishing successes amply testify to this. The absolute record-breaking bestsellers have in fact been "real life accounts" of crime and sex such as the notorious ritual child-killings by the trio of Adrian Lim, his wife and mistress (which generated not one, but three books, two of them bestsellers) while the title heading the current best-selling list mentioned earlier is *Affairs of a Roving Eye* (1990), a collection of cases of sordid sexual misdemeanours culled from the files of a well-known local private eye. Besides publishing one of the Adrian Lim books, Heinemann also brought out Robert Yeo's *The Adventures of Holden Heng* (1986); that the novel has gone into a second printing owes not a little to the fact that it is about the sexual adventures of a bachelor whom, as the blurb declares, "women are still sampling" and who "goes through a series of affairs" with three women, one a nymphomaniac, every red-blooded male's fantasy sex object who "makes sex sensational for him". In keeping with its nature, the paperback novel's cover is dominated by a pair of provocative, bare female legs (somewhat toned down in colour and reduced in prominence in the second edition, after it had achieved its "come-hither" purpose for the first edition). That the novel earned the ire of a feminist reviewer in a major newspaper abroad, fuelling a small local controversy, could only have added to its piquancy and hence, its sales.

One detects signs that a more open attitude today among the public (especially young adults) in Singapore towards sexual matters and their explicit description, may in part account for the recent spate of best-selling short stories such as Jeyaratnam's *First Loves*, (The second edition of Gopal Baratham's collection of short stories was significantly changed from the original literary and witty *Figments of Experience* to *The Loveletter*) and novels such as Adrian Tan's *The Teenage Textbook* and its sequel, *The Teenage Workbook* which focus heavily on adolescent or teen sexuality. Tan's first novel, *The Teenage Textbook* (1988), marketed as a story "about love, lust and lechery" was reprinted twice the year it appeared and four more times in 1989. Its sequel, *The Teenage Workbook* (1989), described by the blurb as taking "an unexpurgated romp through the home, school and love life" of its teenaged characters, even more amazingly (or not amazingly), had to be reprinted within a mere three *days* of publication and again, only a mere month afterwards.

Certainly, it is the "serious" novel that tends to have difficulty finding a publisher. It is illustrative that whereas Goh had to publish his novel, *If We Dream Too Long* himself, Kirpal Singh's thriller, *China Affair*, found a publisher in the same year, selling moderately well both in Singapore and the region. As far as I am aware, while the local market for Singapore novels in English cannot get enough of books by the young writers mentioned above who cater for young people like them, completed novels by older writers whose published work show them to be committed and serious, are not finding publishers. Goh Poh Seng has a third, completed novel, Christine Su-chen Lim, a second, and Gopal Baratham the short story writer a first novel, still awaiting publication.[9]

But those serious Singapore novels in English that do get published have not either together or singly enjoyed a favourble critical response as literature either. Compare this situation with the considerably higher literary reputation of the Malaysian novels in English which were also latecomers to the literary scene and are far fewer in number. Yet these few - Lloyd Fernando's *Scorpion Orchid* (1976), Lee Kok Liang's *Flowers in the Sky* (1981), and K.S. Maniam's *The Return* (1981) have achieved virtual canonical status and elicit a more favourable and greater critical attention in Singaporean and Australian literary circles than do their Singaporean counterparts (although not much better sales, all three having been pulped by their publisher, Heinemann Educational Books). [10]

The failure of the novelists and their novels to establish a public and critical presence is starkly and materially evident from the fact that it is the poets - Edwin Thumboo, Arthur Yap and Lee Tzu Pheng - who have, to date, between them garnered all the available national and regional literary awards and the occasional international recognition as much as the critical attention. [11] Consequently, they attract a degree of media and public attention rivalled only, since the eighties, by the best-selling short story writers, Catherine Lim and Philip Jeyaratnam. If the novelists, Goh and Yeo are relatively well-known, that is mainly because both are also poets and playwrights, Yeo's plays being among the earliest to enjoy (if not also initiate) the current surge of interest on the drama scene.

Is the relative critical neglect and dismissal of the novel because the achievement of the novels as one local critic has reiterated "is in doubt" and "not up to scratch", lacking in "the stamina and sense of purpose which will lead to the creation of worthwhile prose?" [12] The implicit comparison here is with the poetry in English. In a real sense, through a complex interaction of factors, the poetry in English, produced by an elite minority at the university, practising a hardly popular art, published in little university magazines, anthologies and volumes of small circulation, written in the language of first colonial then administrative power, sedulously cultivating a vocation of high purpose, acquired in time public status and presence and occupied the centre of the literary stage in Singapore among the English-educated Establishment.

The novelists did not have a comparable group identity, a shared programme and that sense of purpose possessed not only by the poets in English, but also by many of the writers and novelists in Malay and in Chinese in the colonial era who were associated with a nationalistic sense of mission and social purpose which gave their work a legitimizing serious edge. Except for Goh Poh Seng, who is also a poet, none of the novelists were similarly fired by questions of national cultural identity, the creation of an indigenous linguistic idiom and expressions of a local sensibility born of the heady years of anti-colonial struggle and subsequent post-independence nationalistic sentiment. [13]

Goh, the only Singaporean novelist who wrote in English that I know of, who has explicitly declared in writing and tacitly shown in his novels a strong sense of serious purpose, has vigorously denied the suspicion of the novelist's lack of "stamina". Rather, he believes (with the poets in English) that

> it has to do with the problem of language...to attain a prose style that is original, that depicts life here, authentically...and which is unmistakably Singaporean.

He also stressed that "a good writer, in whatever language" has almost always been concerned with the central problems confronting his age and place". [14] This seems a good working definition of a "serious" novelist.

But the novel is such a loose, baggy form that it can accommodate a great variety of achievements and purposes, and by the same token, attract a far more varied, less homogenous pool of practitioners of different, even non-literary backgrounds and uneven talent. Nevertheless, it is a valid observation that the Singaporean novels in English seem lacking in comparable literary achievement and ambition. Unlike its Malaysian counterparts (one thinks of *Scorpion Orchid* and *Flowers in the Sky*), the Singaporean novel has not been notably experimental or innovative in form and language. None has managed to interconnect confidently and meaningfully content and form to make a whole that is an expression of a mature novelistic vision of self and society, representing persuasively "the central problems confronting his age and place". Yet, as I have elsewhere argued at length, it may be inappropriate, given the short history of the local novels in English and the lack of a substantial body of work by any individual novelist or collectively, to apply a strictly evaluative criticism to still fledgling work. [15] Furthermore, unless a writer achieves unequivocal success with a first novel, the form's length renders it a longer haul to build up a substantial body of work and to establish or sustain a literary reputation.

A brief run-through of the 25 novels published so far will show what a mixed bag of novels in English that has been produced. The nature of each, even when briefly described, is often capable of being its own comment.

138

Interestingly, perhaps indicating the cosmopolitan tendencies in Singaporean culture, especially among the English-educated middle class which chiefly produces and consumes these novels, about a quarter of the novels are not set in Singapore, but in countries of the surrounding region. Goh's *Immolation* (1977), inspired by the self-immolation of a Buddhist monk, is obviously set in Vietnam, although the country is intentionally unnamed and vaguely described as "Southeast Asian", presumably to make its representation more typical of Southeast Asian sociopolitical realities than merely descriptive of Vietnam; *China Affair* by Kirpal Singh is set largely in Taiwan although the action opens in Singapore; John Tan Chor Yong's *Birds Without Wings* (1977), first published in the Philippines, is a novel of social protest against the exploitation of the Filipino poor by a decadent, exploitative rich class, the "birds without wings" being the young men and women from the villages drawn by grinding poverty to the cities into lives of vice; Tan Kok Seng's *Three Sisters of Sz* (1979) traces the relationships and fortunes of the members of a wealthy Chinese family in Penang, from which there is a brief visit to Singapore; Ewe Paik Leong's *Bandits!* (1980) is set in Ipoh during the Malayan Emergency period; and finally, both Minfong Ho's *Sing to the Dawn* (1975) and *Rice Without Rain* (1986) are set in Thailand, the former about a Thai village girl, who in competition with her brother, wins a scholarship and gets to go for further study in the city, while the latter is about a group of idealistic, middle class Thai University graduates who go to live and work among the poor peasantry in an attempt to alleviate their condition and raise their political consciousness.

Another group of novels (which would include *Bandits!*) seems to have no ambitions beyond entertaining through action-packed, suspenseful thrills and terrors. Such are Peter Manzu's *Naga* (1980) which is about a Singapore village terrorised by a monstrous, vicious snake; Lim Su-Min's *The Ninja of Seletar Reservoir* (1984), a fantasy about some ninjas, left-overs of the war, who resort to kidnapping of school children to swell their ranks; N.G. Kutty's *The Heroin Trail* (1986) which is self-explanatory; and L.H. Tan's *The Russian Pigeon* (1987), a spy mystery of the standard variety about the disappearance of the narrator's friend while doing national service and involves communists and a missing roll of film. The only science-fiction novel, Han May's *Star Sapphire* (1985) with its space adventures, formulaic love story and idealised characters, also falls into this group, despite being a fantasy with serious intentions.

Given the traumatic nature of the Japanese Occupation of Singapore during the War, and the inevitable imprint on the memories of the local population, it is to be expected that there should be some novels set in and about this period. There is Paul Lee's *Tenderly Tolls the Bell* (1973), written originally as a script for a film that didn't materialise; Lim Thean Soo's *Destination Singapore: from Shanghai to Singapore* (1976) and most recently, Goh Sin Tub's *The Nam Mei Su Girls of Emerald Hill* (1989), about a group of girls who were waitresses at a Japanese brothel and their fortunes both during and after the war. These may also be regarded as historical novels as is Stella Kon's *The Scholar and the Dragon*, a semi-fictional account of a poor Chinese immigrant who made good and achieved public prominence.

Kon's novel is obviously written for young people and belongs as well to a growing body of fiction representing a trend towards novels written with a young audience in mind. This group includes some titles which fall also into some of the earlier categories described above - *The Ninja of Seletar Reservoir, Sing to the Dawn, Rice Without Rain, The Russian Pigeon* - and may be expanded to include the recent spate of novels written by young, often first-time authors, recently graduated from or still at university, with a mainly teen audience or young adults like themselves in mind. Among these are the two "Teenage" books by Adrian Tan, a law undergraduate; *The Stolen Child* (1989) by Colin Cheong, a recent Arts graduate; *Miss Moorthy Investigates* (1989) by Ovidia Yu, an English Honours graduate, and now full-time writer; and *Kampung Chicken* (1990) by Ravi Veloo, a journalist with a degree from an Australian university. The first three focus mainly on the adolescent experiences of schoolboy and schoolgirl characters, especially their growing sexual awareness and relationships with the opposite sex or with their peers, parents and teachers, while *Kampung Chicken*, winningly advertised as "an adventure story that captures the flavour of life in the kampung with passion and imagination", turns out to be about the life and emotions of a kampung hen and her "tragic" attempt to save her eggs.

This crop or rather, spate of novels by authors mostly born after Singapore's achievement of independence, can seem to the mature adult reader either too self-consciously humorous, like Tan's two "Teenage" books; too full of claustrophobic, angst-laden adolescent emotion and emerging sexuality as in *The Stolen Child*; or, like *Kampung Chicken*, embarrassingly sentimental: it is quite difficult to get worked up over the excitements of a hen and other farmyard animals through 116 pages of large print. All these new authors are highly literate, and in the case of Adrian Tan and Ovidia Yu, very clever, such that one wonders whether deathless prose such as the following from Tan's *The Teenage Textbook*, opening a chapter called "Lessons in Love" is being parodic or is deliberately catering for a Mills and Boon juvenile reading public, or both:

> The first time he kissed her, Mui could only feel his power. But the second time he kissed her, moments later, she could feel his searching, surging passion. Her lips seem moulded against his, melting in the burning passion like butter in the red heat of a furnace. [16]

And so on, for a few paragraphs more. There is obviously an audience out there for these best-selling books. The writers, too, seem prolific, both Colin Cheong and Ovidia Yu having each already announced a second novel in press. [17]

Ovidia Yu (whose short stories and plays have won a number of literary awards) writes an unusually competent prose, has a gift for characterisation and lively, intelligent observation; but like Adrian Tan, she too often succumbs to the clever undergraduate student's habit of "smart-alec" jokiness and fails to develop the occasional mature seriousness promisingly glimpsed in both *The Teenage Workbook* and *Miss Moorthy Investigates*.

That sort of seriousness in varying degrees characterises the last group of novels to be covered in this overview, novels which were obviously written with serious intention and literary ambition although not always with sufficient novelistic skill. Among these are Goh's *If We Dream Too Long*; Michael Soh's *Son of a Mother* (1973); Lim Thean Soo's *Ricky Star* (1978); Catherine Lim's *The Serpent's Tooth* (1982); Christine Su-chen Lim's *Rice Bowl* (1984); and Philip Jeyaratnam's *Raffles Place Ragtime* (1988). That some, such as *Ricky Star* and *Rice Bowl*, may not be quite as readable as

Miss Moorthy Investigates (the authors not being very skilled at characterisation, handling of plot and point-of-view - and oh dear, yes - telling a story) or as capable of raising as many laughs as Adrian Tan, yet they all touch on some central questions facing the largely English-educated middle-class in a time of rapid change. This gives their attempts at representing important aspects of contemporary Singaporean experience and concerns, an inherent interest. As I have elsewhere explored, a common preoccupation is the relation of the individual with the contemporary socio-economic and political order, with the current attitudes and values about the self, family and society, and how far the individual can go by breaking away (or not, as the case may be) from the various constraints placed on him or her. [18]

The novels of Goh Poh Seng and Philip Jeyaratnam, for instance, are separated by 18 years and their authors a generation apart, but *If We Dream Too Long* and *Raffles Place Ragtime* share a common thematic preoccupation with the adequacy of contemporary social conditions and current values (traditional and otherwise) to meet the aspirations of individuals to self-fulfilment and personal happiness. Goh's novel is the bleaker of the two and ends on a note of trapped despair for its hero whose desire to escape from his Singaporean world is frustrated by circumstances and family obligations. Jeyaratnam's hero, perhaps reflecting the wider options available to youth in eighties Singapore, finds himself able to reject the selfish, stifling, social-climbing, materialistic ethos of the yuppie world he initially had thought would bring him the desired happiness and self-fulfilment, and returns to his own lower social class roots. But in neither novel do we find the possibility of an alternative vision, both novels ending on an unconvincing, and ultimately unsatisfactory note of resolution. Both, like most of the novels in English, can only acquiesce tacitly in the status quo, however claustrophobic. The hero of Colin Cheong's somewhat lugubrious novel, *The Stolen Child,* at the end can only weep bitterly and helplessly over his loss of parents who were divorced, his girlfriend and his childhood. In one of the *The Teenage Workbook's* more serious moments, the two adult characters sum up indecisively, a current dilemma among English-educated professionals. A Junior College teacher, the beautiful, well-groomed and intelligent Miss Debbie Boon has to decide whether to marry her dashing boyfriend, Captain Hari, an RSAF pilot, and emigrate with him to Australia, or end their relationship; and this is their exchange:

"Come on, Deb, you can't fool me. Don't tell me you like living on this island. You hate it. You hate being a teacher. I've heard you complain about everything from the Ministry of Education to the weather - you can't deny that. Just think of what opportunities there are...
"Listen", Miss Boon said very, very softly. "I love being a teacher. I love living in Singapore. It's my home. All my friends are here. My family is here. I'm not about to give all this up to follow you to some strange country and start rebuilding my life all over again. This is my home, you understand? My home. [19] "

Notes and References

1. Hedwig Anuar, "The Reading Habits of Singaporeans", *Mirror,* 25:19, October 1, 1989; pp. 11-12 (*Mirror* is published by the Ministry of Communications and Information, Singapore).
2. "Words in Search of People: a Brief Overview of the Current Poetry in English from Singapore", *Tenggara* 24, 1989; p. 72.
3. Four mile-stone anniversaries fall within the period 1980-90: the 21st and 25th in 1980 and 1984, celebrating self-government since 1959; and the 21st and 25th in 1986 and 1990, celebrating independence since 1965.
4. "Bestsellers", *Sunday Times,* Singapore, February 4, 1990.
5. *Aspects of the Novel* (1927), Pelican Books, Harmondsworth, 1962; p. 34.
6. Since the appearance of this article, the publishing house of EPB (Educational Publications Bureau), with the support of the National Book Development Council of Singapore, launched the Singapore Literature Prize in 1992 for the best unpublished manuscript in English submitted by a Singaporean. Worth S$10,000 and to be rotated annually among the main literary forms, it was won last year by Christine Su-chen Lim for her novel, *A Fistful of Colours,* published in 1993 by EPB. The next award will go to poetry.
7. *Aspects of the Novel* (1927), p. 73.
8. Hedwig Anuar, ibid, p. 12.

9. Baratham has since published two novels, *Sayang* (Singapore: Times International, 1991); *A Candle or the Sun* (London: Serpent's Tail, 1991). Christine Lim's second novel, *Gift from the Gods,* (Singapore: Graham Brash, 1991) and her third, *A Fistful of Colours* (Singapore: EPB, 1993) have also since been published.

10. All three, however, have since been re-issued. *Scorpion Orchid* (Singapore: Times Books International, 1990); *Flowers in the Sky* (Singapore: Federal Publications, 1990) and *The Return* (London: Skoob Books Publishing, 1993).

11. See Arthur Yap, "Survey of the Criticism on Singapore Poetry in English" which lists almost 200 items in contrast to the survey of the prose fiction which mentions less than 10. *Singapore Studies: Critical Surveys of the Humanities and Social Sciences,* Basant K. Kapur, ed. Singapore University Press, 1986; pp. 456-478, 480-486.

12. Kirpal Singh, "An Approach to Singapore Writing in English", *Ariel,* 15:2, April, 1984; p. 11; *Singapore Studies;* p. 481.

13. See Koh Tai Ann, "Singapore Writing in English: the Literary Tradition and Cultural Identity", Tham Seong Chee, ed., *Essays on Literature and Society in Southeast Asia: Political and Sociological Perspectives,* Singapore University Press, 1981; pp. 160-186.

14. "Creative Writing in Singapore: a Historical Background", *Singapore Book World,* 1980; p. 2.

15. "Self, Family and the State: Social Mythology in the Singapore Novel in English", *Journal of Southeast Asian Studies,* XX:2, September, 1989; p. 275.

16. Hotspot Books, Singapore, 1988; p. 51.

17. Cheong has since published two novels, *Poets, Priests and Prostitutes* (Singapore: Times Books International, 1990) and *Life Cycle of Homo Sapiens, Male* (Singapore: Times Books International, 1992).

18. "Self, Family and the State", pp. 273-287.

19. Hotspot Books, Singapore 1989; p. 195.

This article originally appeared in *Tenggara* 25, 1990; pp 96-109, and with regard to published novels, is current only up to January, 1990. While not discussed, novels published since this date are mentioned at relevant points in the "Notes and References". *(Koh Tai Ann, August, 1993)*

© Koh Tai Ann, 1993.

KOH TAI ANN is Associate Professor at the Department of English Language and Literature, National University of Singapore. Her publications cover postcolonial literature, including the writing from Singapore and Malaysia, women's and educational issues, cultural development and the arts in Singapore. She contributed the section on Southeast Asian women's writings in *The Bloomsbury Guide to Women's Literature* (1992), and is currently co-editing a comparative study of the novel in Southeast Asia as well as an Annotated Bibliography of the imaginative writing in English from and set in Malaya/Malaysia, Singapore and Brunei produced by both native and expatriate writers.

Singular Stories

Tales from Singapore, Volume One

Selected by Robert Yeo

Singular Stories presents the finest of these (flowering short fiction in Singapore) efforts, to demonstrate the diversity of themes and styles being employed by Singaporean writers. Volume One looks at the conflict between traditional and modern societies, the role of women, the Japanese occupation, and the lighter side of the Singaporean character; styles range from straight narrative to surreal to experimental.

ISBN 981-00-3939-5
Paperback   152 pp

Yang Publishers,
44 Jalan Sembilang,
Singapore 2057.

SOMETHING ELSE OR MEETING MR LEE

by

Timothy Michael Donnelly

We're not really there to do an interview. We are fine-tuning the text of "Marcus and Elliot", his short story which will appear in the second *PACIFICA* Anthology and, as always, time is short. But he knows that when writer meets writer no quirk of phrase or passing observation is going to be wasted and initially this makes him uneasy. He refers to the *Straits Times*, a Singapore paper that interviewed him in 1992. I've seen the piece and concur that it's not the most insightful profile I've ever read. Still, if I can jot down my impressions, plus a few anecdotes, we may just satisfy my itch to get him on paper, his need for privacy and a demanding publisher. Compromise agreed, we begin.

Given that we know little about each other and he has never worked with an editor before things don't go too badly. I had readily agreed to working at his place as it would be more relaxing for him and anybody's flat has got to be more comfortable than my office! For the Anthology we also need to select an extract from *Peculiar Chris,* his first novel. This is the book that Johann S Lee wrote at nineteen. The book that every major publisher in Singapore rejected. Politely of course; there was no denying the boy had talent, but couldn't he, they suggested, write about "something else"? Nothing doing. This is the book that Mr Lee had wanted to write since realising that none of the western fiction he had come across met his particular needs and by implication, those of his countrymen. Nobody seemed to address the complexities of embracing one's true nature in a milieu where "family values" are the bed-rock of society, not merely cynical government sloganeering. His persistence paid off when Cannon International, known chiefly for school text-books, took a gamble on an unknown author and a taboo subject. There was quite a stir when the book came out. Here was the first Singaporean novel to deal candidly and without apology with homosexuality. A book about young gay men, their relationships, and the prejudice they face in a country whose social and moral codes make England seem like the fount of liberality by comparison. The book was an immediate best seller.

Publication brought the young author a certain profile, a lot of post and a degree of attention that was not altogether welcome. Not that he's a hermit. But he did find it hard to live up to peoples' expectations. It felt as though all those anxious young men circling his stand at the International Book Fair really expected, perhaps wanted, to meet Christopher Han, the book's gay protagonist. Wasn't he going to be something of a disappointment? Personally, I think not, but self-doubt is endemic in late teenagers. This was poignantly evidenced by the story of Ernest, by name as well as nature it turned out, who took several hours to pluck up the courage to ask for an autograph. Next day came a long, touching letter explaining how a confused and unhappy sixteen-year old had finally found life bearable. Contrary to his expectations, none of the reaction from strangers was hostile. It sometimes felt as though a whole generation had been waiting for this book. Perhaps they had. In fact the only openly dissenting voice came from closer to home. A near relative with a certain "profile" of his own offered to buy every copy of the book, not in order to help sales, but to have it destroyed and thus spare the family any embarrassment. There was actually none for them to be spared. The reaction at home had been good. Supportive and ultimately proud. Alright, it might have been nicer if he'd written about "something else", but just how many people have sons who are published authors at nineteen? With characteristic modesty Mr Lee is quick to point out that he does not regard one book as a career, but it's still an achievement. Cue the Straits Times and 'that' interview. Despite the inevitable reservations about the book's 'unusual' er, 'odd' subject, the paper clearly wants to let you know that underneath it all the precocious Mr Lee is just the kind of regular guy anybody would be delighted to take home to mother. The article is packed with reassuringly normal biographical details and describes the author in terms of his good looks, muscular physique, lightening smile etc. Hanging over all of this is the unspoken assertion that he will in future write about "something else".

Well, physically he is all that the ST claimed. He is also shrewd, witty and one of those people who are completely at home in their own skins. His almost excessive politeness goes some way to concealing all of this. He invariably speaks in perfect sentences, one can almost hear the full stops puncturing the air. The next journalist to interview him need have no fear about obtaining good, literate quotes. Content is another matter. If he's satisfied about your credentials, you may get a few personal details like his passion for Barbara Streisand and a fondness for Heagen Dazs ice-cream. But intimate revelation? Forget it. He is often unsure about his writing abilities but show me an author with any talent who isn't. He recognises that *Peculiar Chris* has its faults and knows that promise only becomes real creative talent when nurtured with practice and experience. And practice he certainly does. In addition to *Marcus and Elliot* he is hard at work on a second novel, *One Tree Hill*. He begs me not to describe this as a Singaporean "Tales of the City", asserting that few writers and absolutely not him, could produce anything that good. I suppose comparisons are odious aren't they, so let's just say that so far it is a wry, engaging, episodic account of the lives of the inhabitants of a house in down-town Singapore which demonstrates again his instincts for dialogue, character and plot. Experience? Well, Law Studies have brought him to London and he has settled in the heart of SoHo. Amidst the neon lit bustle of that district Mr Lee feels quite at home. He has the air of a bemused, often amused, observer, casting his writer's eye over the eternal cabaret of dreams and disappointments played out in the streets below his sitting room window. Plenty of experience there. Possibly distractions too. But Mr Lee is in no doubt that this is a time for study and for writing. Attachments? He hasn't the time. London seems to suit him, though privately he will admit to a lingering unease about his undeniable foreignness in a western capital. But don't be duped by the polite manner and the slight frame. Woe betide the sales assistant who tries to treat him like a tourist! Since getting to grips with the labyrinthine complexities of Cockney rhyming slang he is no longer offended by the soubriquet "me old China", which is not as he first suspected a term of racist abuse but a uniquely London term meaning "mate". But he's not prepared to tolerate the crass abuse that the English routinely mete out to anyone who isn't local. You have been warned.

We have effectively finished work by now and I propose a well deserved drink. We are better acquainted than when the day began and he is pleased at the prospect of a change of scene.

He lives a short stroll away from one of the less offensive cafe-bars catering to a determinedly fashionable clientele that litter the West End these days. En route he elaborates on an idea for another novel, set in London this time, set perhaps in SoHo. His talk is often like that, idea upon idea. There are so many things he just has to write and write in his own particular way. Will this be the "something else" I wonder, this London novel. Mr Lee is no longer an absolute beginner and we might benefit from what an outsider has to say about us all. As he continues his theme about a young Singaporean student catapulted into the maelstrom of nineties London I feel an attack of déja vu coming on. Could this be art borrowing from life again? Again? He requires an explanation. I venture to suggest that there are certain similarities between what he is proposing and his own circumstances. Just as there are between him and his previous hero. He patiently points out that Christopher Han is a six-foot teenage athlete, an orphan and gay. To regard the book as some kind of autobiography would be to negate the author's ability to imagine anything or anyone other than himself, would it not? Point taken. He might also have said that even at the conclusion of his rights of passage Chris still faces an uncertain future and has a great deal to resolve. As we proceed along the dusk kissed streets I am intensely aware that Johann S Lee knows exactly who he is and just where he's going.

© Timothy Michael Donnelly, 1994.

JOHANN S. LEE
Marcus and Elliot

"I'm not afraid of dying. I'm not afraid of whatever awaits me. I'm just afraid of what my last breath will do to Elliot."

And upon hearing those words, I learned something. The real victims of death are not those who die, but the close ones who survive them.

"Write about Marcus after he dies. Please. He's so afraid of being forgotten. He doesn't know that I'll never need written words to remember him by. I have my memories."

And in those lines, I found yet another reminder of the strength of human love.

I first met Marcus and Elliot in 1992, sometime after my first novel was published. By then, I had received about forty letters from people who read the book. A handful of them were actually addressed to Chris, the gay protagonist, instead of me. What struck me about these particular letters was that they appeared to have been written to an old friend. In retrospect, I suppose I must have known the moment I started on *Peculiar Chris* that there the line between reality and fiction was an illusionary one. But it was not until I read those letters that I realised I could never escape from the reactions to my work.

I answered every letter, and to those readers who wanted to meet me, I said that they might find me at the World Trade Centre during the Book Fair. Little did I know then that I was destined to meet two people whom I would remember for a long time to come.

Marcus was the one who had written to me, and in his letter he mentioned that he had a lover by the name of Elliot. When they showed up together at the book fair, I knew instinctively that one of them was stricken with Aids. It was Marcus. He appeared pale and gaunt, and wore a faint and slightly trembling smile that belied his resoluteness of character. He had strong features and would have looked rather harsh but not for that enigmatic smile. Elliot, on the other hand, was a benign-looking fellow who stood closely by Marcus, one palm on his lover's back. Even in that slight, apparently casual physical contact, I sensed a deep, unspoken intimacy.

I have been told that my fictional characters are nearly always likeable and good-looking, but there in real life were two tall, slim men in their late twenties whom I found genuinely attractive.

"Hello, Johann. I'm Marcus, and this is Elliot, my significant other."

"Personally, I prefer the word 'lover'," Elliot grinned. "But Marcus makes it a point to be politically correct."

I smiled. The sight of a settled couple always filled me with mixed feelings of envy and gladness. "Thank you for your letter, Marcus. It made me very happy, and I'm pleased to meet both of you."

I excused myself from the autographing session. Minutes later, we were strolling along the stretch of waterfront outside the Harbour Pavilion. It was a cloudy afternoon and the sea was calm. I was strangely at ease with these two people whom I knew little about. But I also felt a sense of expectancy.

"I have Aids," Marcus said after a while.

I nodded.

"I didn't want to mention it in the letter because I was afraid that you might feel obliged to meet me if you knew."

"Why did you think I'd feel obliged?" I asked.

"Because you're a nice person."

"Maybe you're getting me confused with Chris."

"Am I?" he challenged.

Marcus was looking at me earnestly, and I shrugged in response. There is something unnerving about the eyes of a dying man.

"I enjoyed reading your book, Johann," Marcus said. "I found it very honest, and very...very affirming."

"Thank you."

"But why did Samuel have to contract the virus through a blood transfusion? Why not through sex?"

It was a familiar question.

"I guess I was trying too hard to make gays appear like guiltless people," I admitted. "The journalist who reviewed my book said I tried to sanitise homosexuality."

"And she said you weren't brutal enough," Marcus added.

"She was right," I said. "I wasn't brutal enough."

"Do you want to know how I got it?"

I was not sure if I needed to know, but he told me anyway.

"Reckless sex. Unsafe sex. When I was younger. A long time before I met Elliot," he added.

"Any regrets?" I said.

"That's a line from the book."

"What?"

"Chris asked Samuel whether he had any regrets," he pointed out. "Anyway, to answer your question, no. Not anymore. I'm through with all the screaming and hair-pulling. I have other things on my mind now."

Marcus suddenly stopped walking and sat on a bench. "Sorry," he muttered. "We've been out since morning. I get tired easily nowadays."

For some reason, the apology made me shudder.

Elliot and I seated ourselves on either side of him and after a moment of silence, he started speaking again.

"Your novel was moving, and at first I thought the part after Samuel discovered he was HIV positive was pretty convincing. But later on I read another book, *Borrowed Time*, and then I sensed that you've never really experienced the death of a loved one under those circumstances. Am I right?"

I nodded.

"Well," he commented, "soon you'll be able to say that you really knew someone who died of Aids."

Elliot, who had been quiet and expressionless all this while, gave me a wry smile. "Don't worry," he said. "I don't think Marcus expects you to give a whoop of joy."

Marcus laughed. "Maybe if we become good friends fast enough," he said, "you might want to write about us someday."

"Maybe," I responded.

"Johann," Elliot said, "we'd like to invite you to our home for dinner."

Somehow, I forgot that I had resolved not to get too close to my readers. "That sounds like a wonderful idea," I said.

"Great," Elliot said. "And now I think we ought to go. Marcus needs rest."

I turned to look at Marcus and caught a fleeting expression of amazing tenderness cross his face. He ran his fingers lightly across the fringe of Elliot's hair and smiled. "Sometimes," he said barely audibly, "I'm amazed at how lucky I am."

Elliot's eyes reddened. And so did mine.

In time, Marcus and Elliot became my friends. And this is their story.

Once there was a man named Elliot. He was a romantic misplaced in a circle notorious for its promiscuity. Elliot longed for the day when he would discover The One - the person who would rescue him from the suffocating loneliness in those cold dungeons which people called discotheques. The One would find enough in Elliot to want to share his life with him, and abandon, once and for all, bars and back-alleys. Elliot dreamed of the "blessed" day when he would find - Did he dare say the word? - love.

Then there was Marcus, who shied away from that dubious thing called a "relationship". Why did everyone want a relationship? When no one really knew what it was all about? Marcus spent years stumbling from one sexual partner to another, devoid of feeling about his exploits, remaining what some would call an emotional virgin. Love was dead, he thought, and even if it were alive, it would not show its presence in his dark world.

When they met in a disco, Marcus was on the prowl for yet another pick-up, while Elliot was as usual trying to look good. Barely an hour after they began exchanging glances, they were between the sheets in each other's arms, and that was when Marcus felt something new.

Elliot cradled his face in his hands and kissed him with a gentleness that Marcus had never known. It went on for minutes but seemed more like hours. Just kisses - on his lips, his cheeks, his nose, his forehead, his eyes. He's making love to my face, Marcus thought in amazement.

They saw each other regularly after that night, and even this was new to Marcus, whose sex life had been nothing more than a series of brief encounters. Soon they started having conversations, real conversations which went beyond the realm of horoscope and the weather. And with each meeting, they learned more about each other.

Marcus told Elliot he was a flight steward, and that his parents had emigrated to Canada. He was now alone, and he liked it that way. Elliot, a promising young lawyer, was the only child of a wealthy and deeply religious couple. They would be devastated by the knowledge of their son's sexual orientation, so Elliot's life remained a lie.

Marcus and Elliot spent much of their time together in a small apartment left to Marcus by his parents, and one afternoon, as sunlight poured in through the windows and illuminated the flecks of dust in the air, Elliot took a breath and opened his heart.

"I think I love you," he said.

Marcus looked at him, confused.

"I know you don't want to get serious but I just had to say it. Am I making a mistake? Do you want to stop seeing me?" He tried to sound nonchalant but his heartbeat had stopped.

"I can't make any promises," Marcus replied. "But no, I don't want to stop seeing you."

"Marcus," Elliot started falteringly, "are you seeing other people? We've been with each other for more than half a year. I think I have the right to know."

Marcus paused. "You're not the only person I'm sleeping with."

"Fine," Elliot said.

Elliot knew by then that nothing would make him happier than settling down with Marcus. But he was also aware that one committed person, no matter how ardent, did not make a relationship. He overcame the disappointment and controlled his emotions with a somewhat surprising restraint. And his patience eventually paid off. One year after their first meeting, as they were cleaning the dishes together after dinner, Marcus came up behind Elliot and placed his wet, soapy hands on Elliot's hips.

"Elliot," he whispered into his ear. "Will you marry me?"

Elliot nearly dropped a plate. "What?"

"Are you deaf?"

"Are you serious?"

"Elliot, I don't want to lie to myself anymore."

"What do you mean?" Elliot asked.

Marcus sighed. "The truth is, I can't have sex with anyone else without thinking of you. Do you think that's a sign?"

"A sign of what?"

"A sign that it's time to settle down."

"What happened to your fear of commitment?"

"Who said I was afraid of commitment? I just never wanted to commit."

"And now you do?"

Marcus nodded.

"Do you love me, Marcus?"

"Do you ever wonder if anyone really understands the meaning of the word?" Marcus questioned.

"I think that every person is entitled to give the word his own meaning, and use it when he truly means it," Elliot said.

Marcus pondered for a moment. "In that case," he said, "I love you, Elliot."

Elliot was stunned.

"Well?" Marcus said.

He shrugged. "I'm speechless."

"No," Marcus pressed. "Don't just keep quiet. Otherwise, I'll freak out."

"What do you want me to say?"

"Anything."

Elliot laughed. "What took you so long, you nincompoop?"

Chuckling, Marcus turned Elliot around to face him and planted a kiss on his forehead.

And thus began a relationship which would go on to last for another six years.

Shortly after Marcus and Elliot started what they hoped would be a stable and lasting relationship, Elliot decided to leave his parents' house and move in with Marcus to set up a home together. Elliot's parents confronted him, and after some deliberation, he decided to write them a letter.

Dear Mother and Father,

I pen this letter knowing full well that it will cause much pain and grief to the people whom I love most in this world. But "the truth hurts", and there is no other situation more appropriate for the cliché than the one I am facing now.

On this sheet of paper are words that I have been meaning to say to you for what seems like a lifetime, but I have never been able to muster the courage. Perhaps if you had not confronted me, I would have continued to keep you in the dark for God knows how long.

There is little of what I am about to tell you that I expect you to understand, but what you must try to understand is that I never meant to hurt, disobey, or dishonour you.

Mum, Dad, I am gay.

This is not a fad, a phase, or a choice. It is what I am. Asking me when I became a homosexual is like asking a straight man when he became a heterosexual. Do you know what I mean? It is not a question that can be answered.

I have been this way for as long as I can recall. Yes, even as far back as my childhood. You may be angry with me for never calling out for help. But even I have learned to forgive a ten-year-old boy for being too frightened to tell his parents that he was attracted to other boys. Couldn't you forgive him too?

I have been tormented over the years, especially during my adolescence, by why's and how's, and I have learned enough to satisfy myself. Strangely, I know that I can offer no reasons for explanations that will ever satisfy you, especially since you are such devout Christians.

This is not about both of you. Not about what you have done or failed to do as my parents. It is about me. My life. And as much as you would like to think about how this is affecting both of you, please try to understand that ultimately, it is I who must bear the consequences of my actions. Hence it is appropriate that I make my own decisions.

My first sexual experience was actually with cousin Tim when he came from Australia to stay with us for a month. I was twelve then, and Tim was fourteen. Remember that morning, Mother, when you asked me why I looked so dejected? I told you that I was sad because our dog had died. For some strange reasons, Duffie happened to pass away the very night that Tim and I explored each other in bed. But the true reason for my sadness then was the realization - even at that age and in spite of the fear and shame - the realization that the way I had behaved with Tim was what I was destined to be. Believe me, it was a painful discovery.

(Please do not distress Uncle Tom and Auntie Ping by relating to them what I have just told you. I don't think it matters anymore, now that Tim has settled in San Francisco and is living the kind of life that he had never expected his parents to understand. What they don't know can't hurt them, right?)

I shall spare you the "lurid" details of my sex life, but one or two things ought to be said. I have fallen in and out of love (or so I thought) and made attempts to have some kind of meaningful relationship more times than I care to count. It is not something that I am happy about, and some people say that this seemingly pointless and fruitless search is a characteristic of the gay lifestyle. I was just beginning to turn into a cynic when I met a wonderful man about a year ago, and now I believe

156

I am truly in love. The fact that he is in my life at the moment is the only reason I have managed to find the courage to write you this letter. And I cannot imagine life without him.

Last year, one of my friends contracted the HIV virus and died of Aids. I watched him as he fought his life and I watched as his lover stood by him throughout the ordeal. At the risk of sounding perversely self-contradictory, let me tell you what I learned from the experience. I learned that, despite all their foibles, my kind of human beings can become the strongest and most resilient people in times of crisis. It is a unique kind of strength that is developed, tried and tested, because of all the prejudices and resentment that these people are forced to live with all their lives. And I feel it is something to be proud of.

Someone once told me that the strength of love and family ties can enable people to stand up against societal mores and pressures. I do not expect that kind of support from you, but I cannot deny that I hope desperately for it. Meanwhile, I shall find solace in my relationship with Marcus, the man whom I have decided to share my life with. Though his past is far from untainted, Marcus is strong and steadfast, and I believe I have made the right decision. I hope you will give us your blessings.

Mum, Dad, I love you dearly, and I know very well that I face the risk of losing you forever. So perhaps you have some idea of how much pain I am going through even as I write this. My only consolation is that blood-ties can never truly be severed, so I will always, always be your son.

There seems to be so much more to say, but I know that I cannot make up for a lifetime of silence with a few sheets of paper. And because tears always get in the way of my thinking, I feel it is best that I end here. I am sorry I have hurt you, and I hope you will talk to me again.

Your son,
Elliot

To this day, Elliot's parents have not said another word to him.

In September of 1992, I departed for London to embark on my legal studies, and by the time I returned in June of the following year, Marcus had died. I met up with Elliot once again for a walk outside the Harbour Pavilion, and the first thing I noticed was how haggard he looked.

"I should have known," he said softly, "that no book or movie could ever prepare me for his death."

Elliot's voice, though low and quavering, seemed resonant with spiritual strength, and the only tears that were shed that day were mine.

"I've decided to write about you and Marcus," I revealed.

He nodded slowly. "That's good. If Marcus knew, he'd be pleased. But it'd be such a simple story. You should embellish it with dramatic details."

"No, Elliot. Every life is worth a story, and more."

He looked at me searchingly. "Marcus once told me that if he hadn't been in love before he died, his life would have been in vain. Do you think I really made a difference, Johann?"

"I think you already know the answer to that question, Elliot."

He sighed and his lips broadened slightly.

Even though it was humid that day, we knew we had to walk down that stretch of harbour, just the way we had done with Marcus less than a year ago.

After a while, Elliot stopped and rested on a bench. Then a strange radiance appeared on his face, as if a pleasant thought was crossing his mind.

"Sorry," he said with a smile. "I've been out since morning. I get tired easily nowadays."

JOHANN S. LEE studied at Raffles Institution, Raffles Junior College, Singapore and is presently reading Law in London. At the age of twenty, Johann wrote his first novel, *Peculiar Chris*, which was published by Cannon International, Singapore in 1992.

Review of
PECULIAR CHRIS
by
Miles Lanham

A reader of *Peculiar Chris*, especially if they are gay, would be likely to approach the novel with some pre-conceived ideas. A self-proclaimed 'coming of age' novel, with a gay hero, might be expected to fit into the British/American 'coming out' genre. These, often badly written, accounts of coming to terms with homosexuality, are churned out ad infinitum by the niche presses. Often, they are filled with insulting stereotypes of whatever sexuality. *Peculiar Chris* does not fit into this category, largely due to Lee's skill as a writer.

Lee's 'novel' could better be described as an 'account', and despite denials of it being an autobiography, it is written with insight and understanding of very personal events.

Chris of the title, our first person guide through the novel, does not make an amazing discovery about his sexuality; he has known all along, a fact which separates it from the 'coming out' novel. Chris himself falls into no identifiable gay stereotype, and it appears that Lee is at pains to depict an ordinary college boy, albeit 'built like a bull', who just happens to be gay. This is emphasized all the more by some easily categorised gay men: Camp Nick, closet Ken, Lonely Jack and so on. But these are not stereotypes, Lee makes them real people, using descriptive restraint to create the isolated world these people live in.

The reader might expect Lee to describe contemporary Singapore in more detail. Lee's spartan style omits this, which has the effect of giving the persecution of gay men in the novel no concrete context. The events could quite easily have taken place in Britain before the Wolfenden Act of 1967; especially Chris's national service medical, where a special distinction and subsequent classification exists between effeminate and straight-acting gays.

Stylistically, Lee is crisp and clear. His prose stands in stark contrast to many western gay writers, in that it doesn't dwell on overblown interior design details and clichéd appraisals of the male physique, so when Lee does describe events and people, they are all the more powerful, for instance Chris's self-purging in the ocean, or the potential rapist Lieutenant Samuels.

Arguably two of the most outstanding gay novels in Britain are *Maurice* by E.M. Forster and *The Swimming Pool Library* by Alan Hollingshurst. The evidence for this assertion is given by Lee himself frequently throughout the novel.

Maurice is considered to be Forster's worst novel, and it is likely he forbade its publication due to its lack of his usual descriptive panache, than because of its sensitive content. Maurice suffers from the absence of women for whom Forster writes so well. The plot, set in the England of 1911, concerns Maurice, the character, coming to terms with his sexual identity. It contrasts his unhappiness at the Platonic love demanded by his first lover, Clive, who he meets at Cambridge, with the carnal delights of Alec Scudder the gamekeeper. Unfortunately, Forster has little characterization in the work, and unsubtle class stereotypes are in preponderence.

Peculiar Chris is not as well-rounded as *Maurice*; it is not a typical story, but this is made up for by Lee's success at believable characterization, which is in this instance, superior to Forster's. It is interesting that Maurice was given so much attention by the Singaporean men in *Peculiar Chris*, as oppression apart, they have little in common. This reviewer experienced a similar reaction in contemporary Britain; it seems Forster's book endures despite the times, and it is likely Lee's will do so similarly in the Pacific Rim.

As a first novel, *Peculiar Chris* is perhaps best compared to another first, Alan Hollingshurst's, *The Swimming Pool Library*. They are similarly constructed in that neither really finishes. In *The Swimming Pool Library*, William Beckwith, the central character is supposed not to write an autobiography, the task around which the whole novel revolves. This is an unlikely disappointment when reading the work, and Hollingshurst also leaves other subplots unresolved. In *Peculiar Chris*, the hero completes a very distinct phase in his life which is what the novel is about.

Lee portrays relationships more realistically and sympathetically than Hollingshurst, Lee giving each of Chris's partners a three-dimensional reality which allows them to interact successfully with the other characters, and become uniformally believable. Lee's emphasis is clearly on gay relationships as opposed to gay sex

(Hollingshurst), which the late pioneering David Rees describes:

"Hollingshurst's London is rampant with erections all over the place. The author's fantasies...dim his observations of what is real."

Lee never falls into this trap, and the novel is much less distracted and disjointed as a result. This doesn't mean that Lee is being especially moral, merely observing realistically, and giving the plot some pace.

Lee deals with death with the same stylistic detachment as the rest of the novel. Had he wanted to emphasise the death of Chris's lover, he might well have left out the subplot of his parents' death altogether, although this does have the effect of leaving Chris very much alone at the end of the novel. As it is, Samuel contracts HIV through a blood transfusion carried out over the border. Were it clear this was a fictional account the HIV aspect might be considered unnecessary. However, this plot device may well be politically correct in Singapore, despite near global acceptance of AIDS as a universal problem. Denial coupled with lack of education of the young can only exacerbate the problem - don't die of ignorance!

Peculiar Chris is a deftly woven and compelling work. It may well do for Singapore what the film, *Victim* and *Maurice* did in Britain.

© Miles Lanham, 1993.

MILES LANHAM is reading government at the London School of Economics & Political Science. He lives in Camden and in Brixton with his partner Graham.

JOHANN S. LEE

Excerpt from

Peculiar Chris

Foreword

When a twenty-year-old embarks on a venture of this nature, he subjects himself to an immeasurable amount of public scrutiny. Even as I pen these first words, I wonder with some apprehension at how I may soon become a victim of criticism and scepticism.

In the past two years, I have seen a number of young persons, not much older than myself make their attempts at some form of literary expression, only to fall prey to the judgement of a society which seems to have forgotten that it is only as young as its youths. Hence, I am quite sure that by the time I finish this piece of work, I would have placed myself amongst those who dare to try, but must also have the courage to stand up to allegations ranging from the silly to the bizarre.

I make no pretences over the fact that my story revolves around a male homosexual. Despite the narrative style which I am about to adopt, I must emphasize that this is not an autobiographical account. In particular, this tale spans a period that is longer than a mere twenty years. One reason why I have refrained from writing about my life, is that I doubt the strength of my personal convictions against an onslaught of public criticism. Another reason is my reluctance to believe that anyone would want to hear about the life of a young man who is far from a celebrity of any sort. But write I must, because there is so much to say, and so much that people should know.

In western societies, writers who choose to write about gays can now develop plots that explore beyond the predictable and restrictive confines of "coming out" blues or the "growing-up-gay" syndrome. But no such liberty exists in our country. For this reason, what you are about to read is in one sense, extremely new and yet, in another, very passé.

I do not hesitate to point out that this book does not take a sociological viewpoint. Furthermore, it does not aim to represent the entire cross-section of Singapore's gay society. Attempts at a generalization are hardly ever successful, for we all know that life is a diversity of diversities. Homosexuality is by no means an exception.

In its barest form, what follows is but a story, and a very simple one at that. The thoughts and feelings that I hope to evoke are controlled by one thing only - one's state of mind.

Dear Diary,

Samuel died a week ago. Whenever I think about it, I find it really strange. Because if anyone asked me what the whole thing was like, I wouldn't know whether to say that everything was like a dream, or just cold, hard, cruel reality. I guess it's a bit of both.

Those nights when we talked for hours at a stretch, with the lights off, now seem almost hazy. The strength that he showed in the middle of death, I mean, in the middle of life but facing death, was amazing. But then, aren't we all in the middle of life and facing death?

I just wanted to console him, but that wasn't what he wanted or needed. And yet, deep down inside, I too felt a kind of strength that I had never experienced before. I guess you could call it resilience. Anyway, those moments now seem so distant, yet hauntingly unforgettable.

When things worsened, my will almost gave way. His beautiful hair started falling out in clumps, all over the pillowcases. I became so used to waking up because his hair got into my nose or mouth. I remember that day when I caught him standing in the bathroom, in front of the mirror, stark naked. He looked at the hair clogging the holes in the bathtub. He looked at the dark, peeling patches of skin in the reflection with a dazed, dead look. Then he looked at me.

During those days, I prayed to God that he would break down so that I could cry along with him. But I never saw a single tear. I'm not saying that he didn't cry. He just didn't do it in front of me.

Lord, I miss him. I feel so...Oh, why bother? Life goes on.

When Samuel finally passed away, he was only twenty-four years old. But he looked sixty. Come to think of it, he looked like my father.

Just me,
Chris

Chapter I

"When did it all begin?"

I laugh when people ask me that question.

"When did you start feeling...you know..."

And all that awkwardness and embarrassment start to show on their faces. Just trying to think of an answer used to send me into a frenzy. But later, I stopped getting worked up, because if they knew any better, they wouldn't ask me a question like that. It's not as simple as "When did you graduate?" or "When did you start to wear contact lenses?"

So I usually reply that I don't know. Or, if I discover that the inquirer's mind prefers to work in clichés, I'd ask him about the chicken and the egg. I am constantly amazed at how people always insist on starting at the beginning. Try talking to a student of philosophy about beginnings and you will have no peace of mind for the next hour or so.

Anyway, God knows when it all began but I know for a fact that it didn't begin with Samuel. Just as I don't believe in beginnings, I don't believe in an end, and this is one of the reasons why I managed to survive Samuel's death.

In any case, I have to start somewhere and I believe a good place to do so would be junior college. Prior to that, I graduated from a premier boys' school after having spent four years of hectic academic pursuits, and which were otherwise generally uneventful. In that particular institution, students were expected to go beyond just a modest level of scholastic competence. In short, besides slogging behind the books and being the captain of the swim team, there was little time for me to think of anything else.

But at the back of my mind, I always felt that something was wrong. It seemed sinister at that time, but when I look at my life now, I realize that I was as innocent as a boy of sixteen could possibly be. Once in a while, scenes in the boys' changing room after swimming practices would arouse feelings in me, giving myself a clear definition of that sense of distraction that always seemed to pervade my mind and my thoughts. But these responses seldom went beyond being mildly disturbing, and any further curiosity would be promptly arrested by a sense of fear and defensiveness.

It was a time of tests and examinations, and strenuous swimming training, but amidst all these, miraculously, there was time for pop songs, fashion trends and general goodwill and playfulness amongst the boys. We were a talented and energetic bunch of teenagers, people who could memorize the periodic table and the top forty hits with equal ease. And yet, the awkwardness and immaturity of adolescence was always evident: I am still amused when I recall how difficult it was to disguise frenzied attempts at being "hip" and "cool" and "in", with an air of nonchalance.

When I went to junior college, together with almost all of the other boys, a bit of the camaraderie faded away. This, I blamed on the invasion of the female kind. Academic competition was one thing, but this change introduced a social rivalry of a completely different nature. The initial mania brought about by the sudden introduction of a co-ed environment diminished the collective fervour of the male community. Most of the boys I knew became preoccupied with winning the heart of some girl or other. It was then, more than ever, that I began to feel slightly detached from my peers.

Most of my friends began to spend more time with their female counterparts, and for those who continued to stay together during tea-break or lunchtime, conversation topics almost always hovered around a critical assessment of some girl's attributes, physical or otherwise. I tried valiantly not to be a spoil-sport, but simply could not conjure up the type of enthusiasm that was bubbling around me.

"For goodness sake, Chris," a friend once said with a friendly punch in my shoulder. "You're five feet eleven inches tall, good-looking, and the captain of the swim team. What are you brooding about?"

To speak the truth, another friend commented, being a member of the rugby team would be more of a plus-point. The undercurrents of this hidden "teenage flesh market" or "heart-throb exchange" never failed to amaze me. But later in life, I learned that man's preoccupation with physical attributes transcends age and class.

I had heard and read so much about adolescent blues and that perennial question directed at one's sense of identity. (*Who am I?*) I had seen so many "coming-of-age" movies, most of which feature teenage actors or actresses bathed in soft focus, in close-up, appearing deep in thought and fraught with confusion. When I was fifteen, I thought they were silly. When I was sixteen, I found them thought-provoking. When I was seventeen, I wished I was the leading actor.

It was exasperating. Because that sense of being lost and unfulfilled was always felt, but always defied explanation. But life went on, and I found myself taking refuge in work and training.

I was in the Engineering Faculty, and as is consistent with the nature of this course, there were relatively few girls. Within my tutorial group of twenty-five, there were only four. Amongst these, one was particularly attractive, not to mention popular, and exuded a disarming charisma that I found visibly lacking in the other three girls. Her name was Sylvia.

She was witty, eloquent and seemingly indestructible, almost beautiful in a wild and untamed sort of way, with no traces of stereotypical qualities such as long, silky hair or soft oriental features. Her hair was short and chic, and her figure was full but shapely. Unlike most other girls, she always gave the impression that her flair was effortless, and in her own ways and means, she always managed to solicitate favours from the boys without looking as if she had flirted or compromised her principles. As the chairperson of the Debating Society, she was well-known for her oratorical prowess. The account of how one of her opponents had been driven away from the scene, in tears, by her caustic and flawless rebuttal, had travelled far and wide throughout debating circles across the country. Sylvia Heng was reputed to be someone who always got what she wanted; and this, according to some spiteful gossip, was, in a nutshell, everything.

During the first three weeks, I scarcely had any chance to talk to her, but on the other hand, there was no lacking in opportunity to hear her talk. I found it a regular practice to remain motionless and awestruck in my seat during General Paper tutorials as she articulated her views on topics ranging from abortion to terrorism. Mind you, she wasn't self-important or pompous, though a bit intimidating. Sylvia knew just when to speak, what to say and how to say it, and say it she would, in a manner that would make you want to hear all about it.

One day, as I was leaving the classroom after a tutorial had ended, she tapped me on the back and said, "Would you like to partner me for the next GP presentation? It's about sexual stereotyping."

The smile was deceptive, for there was something in the tone of her voice that seemed to suggest that what I had just heard was not a question.

I cannot remember exactly how my reply was worded, but it must have been affirmative, for I was soon spending hours with her in the library. She was a born leader, and I followed. And it became evident to myself that there was something about her which I found extremely pleasing - something in her disposition, her sense of control, her strength. Predictably, the time we spent together went far beyond that which was demanded by the GP presentation.

It was all very natural. By some unspoken word of agreement, some silent exchange of consent, we studied together, ate together, did research together, and what have you. She impressed me; she made me laugh; she made me like her a lot.

Life at junior college being the way it is, the regularity of our physical proximity could not go unnoticed for long and soon sparked off a series of speculation. I guess when the captain of the swim team and the chairperson of the Debating Society start chewing off the same slice of honeydew in the school canteen, you can't expect people to pretend not to see. My buddies began to rally around me, slapping my back and congratulating me for having taken such a successful shot at something that no other guy had had the nerve to try.

Once, in the middle of a quiet lunch-hour in the canteen, as she was sitting across me watching me devour my meal, Sylvia reached out to flick a grain of rice away from the corner of my mouth. "You know, Chris," she started speaking. "You're like a child sometimes. Built like a bull and very intelligent, but so many things you do remind me of a five-year-old. Like the way you wipe your mouth with the back of your hand. Didn't your mother teach you about napkins and handkerchiefs?"

She paused, and I could see her eyes focused on the spoon going into my mouth.

"Some of your friends are real jerks," she continued. "They go about wooing girls with about as much finesse as a vacuum cleaner. I realize that you never really wooed me. But I don't mind. You're so...different."

Then she took my spoon, gathered the scattered contents of my plate neatly towards me, put it back in my hand, and smiled.

As the days went by, I discovered that beneath that tough exterior, was a person who was capable of the warmest feelings and noblest intentions. Most of this I witnessed in the out-pouring of conviction and emotion, not without logic, from her arguments on euthanasia, religion, surrogate motherhood and juvenile delinquency, amongst other things. And most of all, I was charmed by the way she managed to add her special touch to the lives of those for whom she really cared.

Three months after I entered junior college, the results of the GCE 'O' level examinations were released, and based on these qualifications, a second intake of students from other colleges was absorbed into this institution. It was at this point in time that Kenneth came into my life.

*

I was enthralled.

His hair was long and slightly wavy, concealing most of his forehead. But the sheer masculinity of his features was undeniable. The bridge of his nose was prominent, his cheeks well-defined and his chin well-formed. So there I sat, four canteen tables away, feeling childlike and helpless as I let my gaze wander along his strong jawline. But what held my attention most was his pair of dark and deep-set eyes. Strangely, these separate features which were in themselves characteristically Caucasian, combined to form an indisputable oriental face. And this, I felt, set him apart from those beautiful but anonymous faces that adorned the latest fashion spreads.

He was of average height, moderate build and had a fair complexion. The blandness and homogeneity of school uniforms that so often rob young persons of their individuality seemed to fail to have an effect on this boy. Perhaps it was the way his shirt was almost fully tucked out. Maybe it was the way his pants looked - looser and more comfortable than others. Or perhaps it was because he wore brown canvas shoes rather than running shoes. Whatever it was, despite the air of conformity that hung over the institution like stale breath, he exuded a uniqueness that seemed almost bohemian.

He was sitting at a table, with his legs apart and his eyes focused intently on the pages of a book - "Of Human Bondage" by W. Somerset Maugham. On the table, there was a brown haversack covered with a muted paisley print and on top of that, there was a black file. I could see a picture stuck to the cover. After screwing up my eyes and squinting madly, I made out a pencil sketch of Nelson Mandela and James Dean locked in an embrace.

For the better part of half an hour, I sat there, just looking. He might have felt the weight of my stare, for he looked up suddenly and his gaze met my eyes. I started, and turned clumsily to pretend to be talking to someone next to me, only to find myself alone. Possibly red with embarrassment, I turned back slowly to look at him, almost apologetically.

He smiled. The bell rang. He gathered his things and left.

I was motionless, and slightly dazed. I couldn't name the feelings that were running through me then. But I know now that that was my last moment of guiltlessness.

Daddy's Drinking

The four-year-old boy made rumbling noises as he rolled his toy truck across the floor, up the leg of the coffee table, across the top and over the edge, sending it crashing onto the floor. He made the sound of an explosion and stopped, suddenly perturbed.

"Tammie," he said.

"What?" replied his pretty eight-year-old sister, who was then combing the hair of her Barbie doll.

"Tammie, why is mummy angry?" he asked.

"Because Daddy didn't come home for dinner," she said.

"Where did he go?" he queried.

"Mummy said Daddy went drinking again."

"Oh," he muttered, and sent his truck rolling along once more. Then he stopped.

"Tammie," he said. "What did Daddy drink?"

The girl looked up in irritation.

"How would I know? Stop asking so many silly questions, Chris. And come and help me change Barbie's dress."

The little boy scowled.

"But Barbie's always changing," he complained.

His sister looked at him sternly.

"Of course," she said matter-of-factly. "That's because Barbie's got lots of pretty dresses, just like mummy. And she's got plenty of money to buy some more, just like mummy."

The boy held the legs of the doll as his sister slipped a dress over it.

"And she doesn't need any silly Ken dolls," she said as she pulled up the zip. "Just like mummy."

CHAPTER II

His name was Kenneth. He was a Humanities scholar and a member of the Society of Dramatic Arts. I also found out that he was an Indonesian who was two years older than me, and I was told that he drove to school everyday.

After that first encounter, I found myself looking out for him wherever I went - the canteen, the corridors, the class-rooms, the gardens, and just about everywhere else. This pre-occupation became a constant distraction, and any day that passed without me catching a glimpse of him made me upset and irritable. With almost fanatical devotion, I skipped close to a week's lectures and tutorials, just to sit in the canteen to trace the pattern of his tea and lunch breaks.

With great reluctance, I admitted to myself that I was having an infatuation. But it was with greater self-denial that I forced myself to accept the fact that the object of my desire was a guy. Everytime I became excited by the sight of this person, every conceivable implication of the entire affair would disturb me deeply. Many a time, I tried to convince myself that my feelings ran along a platonic plane, but when my body responded as fervently as my mind, I quit the self-deception altogether.

Any other boy in my shoes then could have been disturbed by a number of things, the matter of pride being one of them. But I never felt that I was compromising my sense of pride by falling for a guy rather than a girl, probably because I had never felt a sense of superiority over the female sex. This was also probably one reason why Sylvia found me so "different". Because the shadow of this orientation had loomed in the darker side of my psyche for so many years, I was never shocked by my feelings towards Kenneth. What surprised me, however, was the intensity of this manifestation.

The underlying consideration that haunted me most of all was the raw and instinctive feeling that something was fundamentally

170

wrong. And yet, just as instinctively, I felt ready to defend what I was going through. I just didn't know how to do it. I felt that my only hope of redemption was the chance to prove to myself that what I was experiencing was something deeper than a passing fancy, and something more noble than lust.

One Saturday morning, I visited the college library, hoping to accomplish some work in Physics. The air-conditioning was on full blast, which was fine with the students, as all self-conscious youngster seemed to appreciate a showcase for their small autumn and winter-wear collections, which would otherwise remain unadmired in a tropical climate such as ours.

Browsing amongst the books, I finally located the section I was seeking, which happened to be on a low shelf. As I bent down for a closer inspection, I saw through an empty space before me, that familiar pair of brown canvas shoes. My heart skipped a beat. I knew this was a golden opportunity and my mind worked feverishly for the next move to make. Before I could devise anything, his knees bent and I found myself looking straight into his eyes.

"Hi," he said with a smile. That same smile. That same dazzling smile. And for the first time in my life, I understood how people could possibly describe their hearts as beginning to melt.

"I thought I saw you coming into the library," he say.

"My name is Christopher."

"I know," he responded. "I'm Kenneth..."

He knows, I thought wildly; how could he know? How would he know my name? How? And I never heard the words that followed. There was a pause.

"Huh, what?" I uttered.

"I said," he repeated, "I have to go. I'll catch you again some other time."

"Oh yeah, sure." What else could I say?

"It's been nice meeting you." He stretched out his hand through the shelf.

I shook it. It was firm and warm. And so he left. It's funny how you can plan, speculate and anticipate, but when something finally happens, it's as mundane as the arrival of an SBS bus.

On the following Saturday morning, which was cold and grey, I decided to do a couple of laps at the college pool. As I came out of the water, wet and shivering, I started at the sight of a solitary figure at the spectator seats. It was him. I had no idea how long he had been there and I could only guess why he was there.

He was wearing a pair of beige bermudas, a white T-shirt and an oversized windbreaker. Saturday or not, we were still within the school compound, but somehow, I had ceased to be surprised at how he could flout the rules so blatantly. He stood and walked towards me.

"Hello, Christopher," he said amiably.

"Hi, Kenneth. Please call me Chris."

"Fine. I'm Ken then. Would you like to have lunch with me?" he asked invitingly.

Standing there, half-naked, close to six feet tall and with a well-toned body, I felt as gawky as a young Pekingnese. "Sure," I managed feebly.

Lunch for Ken consisted of a single croissant and a cup of cappuccino, and he was visibly impressed by how I attacked a chicken on rye, an egg and mayonnaise on wholemeal, and two fruit tarts. So, after all these weeks, I was finally within an arm's length of the person who had put reins on my mind. He did most of the talking, and I found it so easy to be mesmerized by his eyes that I was constantly stammering hasty apologies and asking him to repeat his words.

We, or rather he, talked of many things - of school, of books, of music, and even glasnost. Such little outings to the Délifrance outlet near college became something of a regularity, but we hardly ever got together in the school canteen, for Sylvia was always around. There was a mutual understanding between us that a threesome was never meant to be, and hence I never brought up the idea of introducing him to Sylvia, and Ken, on his part, never suggested it either.

As time passed, the frivolous excitement that used to overcome me whenever he was around faded away. But unlike the way most crushes fade away into oblivion, a feeling of warmth and ease settled between us.

In the middle of our first year in junior college, Ken became heavily involved in a Shakespearean production, which I later found out to be Romeo and Juliet. I was not at all surprised when he told me that he had auditioned and acquired the lead part but nevertheless, I could not help but glow with pride when I heard the

172

news. Unfortunately, I wasn't half as prepared for the other piece of information that came along with it.

"You're what?" I exclaimed incredulously.

"I'm playing Juliet!" Sylvia replied enthusiastically. "Aren't you happy for me?"

"But what about debating?" I almost hollered.

As I have already mentioned, Sylvia always got what she wanted, and I wasn't going to make any difference. It was, as she proclaimed, a chance of a lifetime.

Ken, on the other hand, was completely devoid of any option as to who his leading lady was going to be. His coolness, however, failed to quell the uneasiness I felt when I thought of all the hours they were going to spend together just rehearsing for the play. During that period, I saw very little of both of them, and just trying to imagine what went on behind the closed doors of the rehearsal room was enough to drive me insane.

Two and a half months later, I bought myself a front row ticket for the opening night performance at the Victoria Theatre, and prepared for the worse. They were marvellous. Till this day and time, I still recall that night to be one of the most distressing experiences I have ever gone through. Before then, I had never been so torn apart by two separate, conflicting emotions.

On the one hand, I felt a pang of petty jealousy at the sight Juliet's surging passion for Romeo, for I had become so accustomed to Sylvia showering her attention on me. On the other, I was wrought with a mixture of bitterness and yearning whenever Romeo expressed his love for Juliet, for I felt so deeply for Ken. Hence, ridiculously enough, I shuttled madly longing to be in Romeo's shoes and wishing that I was on that balcony in place of Juliet.

By the time the curtains fell for the last time, I was spent and heavy-hearted. Clutching a dozen roses, I rose from my seat and trod dutifully towards the dressing rooms backstage. Sylvia greeted me with a wild shriek and a fond embrace, and it was no wonder, for the play and its players were a hit. Mustering as much enthusiasm as I could, I kissed her on the cheek and told her, truthfully, that she had been terrific.

From the corner of my eye, I sensed someone looking at me, and turned in that direction. There stood Ken, still in his garb and make-up, smiling. There was the usual radiance in that smile, but in addition to that, there was something else so subtle I could barely detect it. I could read it in his eyes as well. It was an unspoken word of reassurance and confidence, as if he had known all along how I felt during the performance.

And I felt better. Much better.

*

"I want so badly to have children of my own," Ken murmured.

It was a cool Sunday evening and we were sitting on a bench under a tree in a beachside park. We watched idly as four young children ran about, creating the type of ruckus that one would expect of them. Their parents were sitting nearby, with a mixed look of contentment and resignation on their faces.

"I know what you mean," I said as I leaned back, put my hands behind my head, and closed my eyes. "The good old 'leave-my-bit-of-humanity-behind' syndrome. I love children. But since I met you, I've been wondering if I'm going to have any." I tried to sound nonchalant about it, but deep in the hollows of my soul, I felt a tinge of disappointment. Even now, it is a feeling that I am still unable to overcome.

The minutes passed without a word between us.

Blue-green waves crowned with white foam swept across the surface of the ocean and rushed swiftly onto shore, only to be quickly devoured by the pores in the fine sand. Shields of water that crashed onto the huge grey rocks shattered into infinite sparking droplets, sending a spray of water and a smell of saltiness coursing through the air.

Nature's globe of gold, sliced dramatically by the distant horizon, coloured the sky with hues that were seen only twice a day - from dazzling gold to chrome yellow, to vermillion, and very gradually, to black, as the darkness of the night fell upon the landscape.

Slowly, but very deliberately, I moved closer to Ken and we leaned against each other. Sighing deeply, he took hold of my hand. And as we touched, a sense of tranquility evolved from within me. At that moment, something at the back of my mind clicked and it dawned upon me that this was it, what I was hoping for - something more emotional than physical; no passion, no lust, only serenity and contentment, and I was happy.

A week later, on my eighteenth birthday, Sylvia came down with flu and could not make it to school. Ken and I lunched together in the canteen and as we did so, he stopped abruptly and whipped out a brown package with a tiny card. The words were simple.

"To Chris. In all goodwill, Ken."

I tore away the wrapper and uncovered a book: "Maurice" by E.M. Forster. I read the words on the back - "A masterly and touching novel of homosexual love."

I looked at him, reached out to flick away a grain of rice from the corner of his mouth, and laughed.

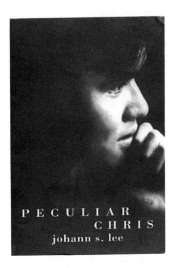

CANNON INTERNATIONAL
Block 86
Marine Parade Central #03-213
Singapore 1544
Tel: 65-344 7801
      65-440 7409
P'bk.
ISBN 981-00-3557-8

Review of
A MALAYSIAN JOURNEY
by
Syed Adam Aljafri

The publishers approached by a young Malaysian journalist, Rehman Rashid, were not keen so he financed the production with family help. Manuscripts usually are refused on editorial judgement of quality and marketability; but sometimes a "political" aspect clouds such judgement as it may well have in the instance of *A Malaysian Journey*. This lack of confidence is deplorable by any except the crudest standard, but its prevalence says a lot about courage and sticking to principle, or their absence.

The book is a patriotic voyage through the Malaya and Malaysia of the author's formative youth. However, patriotism alone is not sufficient, as is evidenced by the daily agonies of Sri Lanka, the broken bits of once Yugoslavia, the large spinoff particles of the former USSR, and other countries suffering the trauma of clashing "patriotisms". For, as reported in James Boswell's *The Life of Samuel Johnson, LL.D.* in 1791, Dr Johnson commented that "Patriotism is the last refuge of a scoundrel."

So are reluctant publishers scoundrelly "patriots" or are some writers "scoundrelly" patriots in the kind of Mexican (or Malaysian) standoff which this book has come to represent, even against the aims of the author? One best way of arriving at one's own judgement is to read the book against this background.

Rehman offers his experience, thoughts, and views on an intellectual menu of "forbidden" topics which, on full perusal, has nothing sensational or censorable. He is simply forthright to the point of charming bluntness in his journey through the Malaysia he knows and the significance he perceives about society today.

His book is a medley of events, places, and people through the early formative years of Malaysia. In the process of growing up in what he fondly imagined as a multi-cultural society, he bumped over increasingly rocky patches which eventually burst a spring or two in the suspension system of his beliefs. This led him to self-discovery, an inner voyage that was beset by storms which assaulted but also shaped his values as a Malaysian committed to higher unities than ethnicity and the apparent move towards separatisms.

This writing is presented in short episodic form, somewhat like the columns he once wrote for the *New Straits Times* and, therefore, appearing disjointed unless one is prepared to dig into possible unifying themes. These latter are more explicitly rendered in his politico-social chapters or pieces where he examines, with sharp critical eye, the "minus" consequences of several public policies intended to provide and promote "plus" outcomes, especially for the *bumiputra* element of the population.

He traces, from one standpoint, how the New Economic Policy of Tun Abdul Razak worked well initially, and how even after the premature death of Malaysia's second Prime Minister, "it was a tibute to the competence of his leadership that the economic mechanisms he installed had by then assumed such a momentum as to step lightly over his passing and continue barrelling forward with undiminished velocity".

Then, as in so many human affairs, success bred excess. "For many of the Malays whose own dreams of wealth were sparked by the burgeoning fortunes of Pernas and PNB, the NEP would seem a road paved with the proverbial good intentions...many of them had simply taken [the cheap loans to start up or expand their businesses] and bought new cars and houses, perhaps on the premise that to be successful, one must first *look* successful." This is the kind of explicit comment which, in local circles, may be orally acceptable but is NEVER put into print. The book is replete with such audacities about the commonplace.

His explicit habit extends into political discourse with the same titivating effect. On Dato' Seri Dr Mahathir, for instance, he embroiders: "As a 22-year-old member of the fledgling UMNO then, Mahathir must have wondered what his political prospects might have been, what with all these teddibly British Malays in the party's top echelons." This sort of comment is titilating to those who behave locally like first-timers in overseas "sin cities", walking past somberly while stealing envious glances at sex shops and X-rated movie posters, except the strictures are self-imposed in political and "race" matters.

So this book is laced through with quasi-forbidden (in our minds, not necessarily by law or public policy) glimpses of exciting views for the jaded mentalities who daily complain (but never in writing) about real or, more often, imagined censorship and "suppressions", simply because Rehman has chosen to write up what too many of us consider should only be spoken of furtively. Granted that even the glimpse of a bare ankle is enough to excite the viewer denied richer sights, Rehman has certainly pulled up the skirts well above the ankles.

In similar vein, he has written explicitly about his time in the murky world of local journalism where political shareholders (as distinct from actual economic shareholders) control the shots, a truth which crept up to disillusion him gradually and led to self-imposed exile of a sort.

On his second spell in Britain (the first being a MARA scholarship student), as a working journalist, he found some cheer in the fact that religious separatism affecting the mix of Malaysian students in his time had given way to junior political clubs; the remaining fly in this ointment being that these clubs reflected exactly the ethnic and race composition of their parent political bodies back home. In welcoming the fading of fundamentalism that cut Malaysians off from tolerant intermingling (an obvious ideal of his), he nevertheless decries the resort to political-ethnic separateness that had replaced it in the 1980s in the UK and other locales of Malaysian students overseas.

This book will be offensive to none but the most close-minded and petty. Certainly, it bears no seditious messages, but its excitement comes from readers who will enjoy the sensation of travelling through "forbidden territory" which, in the last analysis, is simply one man's view of his country and what has happened and is happening in and to it. It is a story well told in most parts, with refreshing vitality of phrase and turn of expression that indicate that the journalist in Rehman is still very much alive, that regardless of the changing situation, he remains optimistic and a rather (for our times) old-fashioned liberal in the genuine sense of that term.

Buy a ticket and get on Rehman's train of thought for a journey that will present familiar scenes in new ways.

© Syed Adam Aljafri, 1993.

SYED ADAM ALJAFRI is a management consultant and company director. He draws on experiences and insights gained as a

178

Malaysian diplomat, central banker, professor, industrialist, regional director of a private international organisation, for his short stories and numerous articles and book reviews. His books include *Civics for Young Citizens* (Longman) and *Ollie's Search for Golden Hope, & other stories* (Heinemann's Writing in Asia Series). His first short story, "The Matsumoto Light Horse Artillery" won Third Prize in the first Short Story Competition sponsored by the *New Straits Times* and the Shell Group of Companies in Malaysia. In the second Competition he was awarded a Second Prize (no First was given) and three of ten Consolation Prizes.

He was educated in Malaysia, and at Yale and Columbia Universities in America and the University of London in England.

Serpent's Tail,
London

Hernie Perera runs the furniture department of Benson's, the largest store in Singapore. In his spare time he writes stories. Suddenly, his comfortable life is shattered. His father is found to have terminal cancer, he loses his job, and his lover joins the 'Children of the Book', a Christian sect committed to overthrowing an oppressive government.

An old acquaintance and government official promises Hernie literary success in exchange for information on the 'Children of the Book'. He must now decide between the rewards of political corruption and his conscience.

With passion and humour *A Candle or the Sun* reveals a Singapore far different from the tourist brochures.

REHMAN RASHID
Excerpt of
A Malaysian Journey

Nizamuddin Ambia lives in a very quiet part of the country: a village nestled in the folds of low hills not far from the old palace of Negri Sembilan.

The village called Kampung Gajah has been there for a very long time; the house in which Nizam lives is one of the more recent additions to the village, and it was built the year his mother was born. Nizam's mother, Puan Zainab, is more than sixty years old now. She is a formidable lady, a widow, sharp of wit, quick of tongue, and built like a meat-safe. Puan Zainab does honour to the matrilineal Minangkabau tradition; every nuance of her carriage bears the weightily maternal stamp of the matriarch.

In poetic contrast, Nizamuddin, her eldest son, is slender, delicate, graceful, and soft-spoken almost to inaudibility. He wields his *tjanting*, the batik artist's wax pen, with the dexterity of a seamstress doing needlepoint, or a surgeon splicing nerves. Nizam is a quiet and melancholy creature, a gently troubled man with a soft, sad smile. He is thirty-five years old, and he knows not what he is doing, nor why he exists - at least, such does he profess. Very soon after graduating in "communication arts" from the Mara Institute of Technology in Shah Alam, Nizam gave up all pretence of an aptitude for commerce and the metropolitan life of the Klang Valley. Many who knew him said this was a shame, for Nizam had a rare talent for graphic design, a sureness of line that translates well into the sort of art that tourists and advertising agencies seem to enjoy the most. Nizam's work was highly "accessible", but the trouble was, Nizam himself was not - least of all to himself.

So he left the Klang Valley and went home to Kampung Gajah, Sri Menanti, Negri Sembilan, to live with his mother and dedicate himself quietly to developing his style, whatever it may turn out to be. The truth is, he finds it easier to wrestle with the conundrum of himself in the familiar surroundings of Kampung Gajah. Here, he might at least live in fitful peace with what he cannot yet fathom. Who is he? What is he supposed to be doing? Even: Why is he so fixated on all these questions?

And the hardest question of all: Are his doubts merely an intellectual conceit?

Nizam does not know.

Things seem so much surer for his siblings. His two younger brothers, Azizan, a teacher, and Eddie, a student, home now during the school holidays, both seem to pursue lives of easy certainty. Listen to them bantering with their mother in the kitchen: "The *adat perpatih* is outdated!" blusters Eddie, referring to the matrilineal tradition of this quarter of Negri Sembilan; the custom that will see this house and everything in and around it passing in time to Puan Zainab's oldest daughter, and not Nizam. His mother responds: "Men have been saying that forever." Laughter rises above the clatter of cooking utensils; it seems this is one line of argument that's been going on forever, too.

But the *adat perpatih* is an anachronism; a 500-year-old legacy of the West Sumatran settlers of this region. Enshrined now as an element of Malay custom, it persists as an embellishment of identity quaint as Minangkabau roof, and hardly more significant.

Nizam smiles his soft sad smile, but does not participate in this well-worn debate. He has other things on his mind. Things like: "What do you call someone who does not have a bedroom, but sleeps anywhere in the house?"

The point he wishes to make, in this obscurantist manner, refers to the breakdown of boundaries; the dissolution of private territory. Nizam senses that he is growing beyond the need for personal space; he is becoming a child of the universe. Like Socrates, his home is becoming defined purely by the boundaries of his skin. It is an evocative emotion - there is something holy about it, something that tends toward the ideal of the wandering ascetic, the *sadhu*. But Nizam's exploration of this peculiar, exhilarating, frightening impulse must begin here, in this shallow valley he knows so well; this aged little community tucked away in a fold of low hills in the heart of Negri Sembilan. If Nizam is to leave home, he must first *be* home.

So let me walk with him, this slight and troubled man, as evening settles on this little valley and the narrow sky above begins to drain of light and heat. In the blue cast of the evening light, these old houses seem ghostly. Here is a structure that must have been magnificent the day it was completed. How many two-storeyed wooden houses still exist? Here is one, seventy years old and black with age, its *tiang ibu* - its central pillar - an entire forest tree. What a marvel it must have been; what a marvel it remains. The descendants of the man who built it still live here, but no one dares climb to the upper storey now.

And there, on an acre of land overgrown with waist-high weeds, a single light glows in a single small house. Nizam tells me an old man lives there alone, shunning all human contact. Thus has it been for decades. All around in this quiet enclave are stories. In each glimmering of light through the trees, each fleeting shadow in the window of an ancient house, is a story. But I am on a journey that permits me little time to stop and listen; I curse the impulse that has me constantly moving on, moving on, towards a destination I know will be just another way-station once I get there...but for now let me walk with Nizam down this village lane, past these silent old houses in wide grounds out of which stretch tall durian trees laden with fruit. Any moment now, the first of the season's bounty will fall, and the heavenly aroma of this magnificent fruit will fill these dales.

The village idiot sails by on an ancient bicycle, calling out Nizam's name in a voice that sounds as though it has been filtered through sludge. He is a cheerful lad, as the mentally impaired so often are, and Nizam and he pause to exchange pleasantries in the Negri patois, a dialect of Malay almost as unfathomable as Kelantanese to the uninitiated. Zul is not the only one here so afflicted; there is a distressing effect of the in-breeding, the marriage of cousins, that so often takes place in isolated rural communities. But the village embraces and cares for its deficient, so good-natured are they, and so willing to do odd jobs for anyone.

We walk on to the end of the lane, where it joins the main road. Even this is not much of a road; it is the minor spur off the Kuala Pilah road that leads to the abandoned capital of Sri Menanti, where Raja Melewar, the first of the Sumatran princes to assert some semblance of rule in these regions, built his palace in the late 18th Century. We turn and walk back, the evening now barely distinguishable from night.

"Am I a bohemian?" asks Nizam.

"I don't think so," I reply. "A bohemian is a rebel of some sort, a defier of convention. I know you feel as if that's what you are, but I think you're much closer to your heritage than you think. It's just that, these days, for a Malay to be true to his heritage is itself almost an act of rebellion." Which is as long a speech as I've given recently. But Nizam seems quietly reassured.

We reach his house. I cast a stick into the thick undergrowth across the lane, where there used to be a ricefield. A quail, startled, takes flight in a flurry of wings. Nizam's house glows with light; his mother is in the kitchen preparing dinner. In the front porch, his latest batik painting, half done, lies stretched on its wooden cradle. On the front steps his brothers sit, smoking cigarettes. They greet us warmly, but with the reserve befitting younger siblings when addressing their elders.

Nizam will sleep tonight in the space surrounding the *tiang ibu* of his house. It is a sacred little place, and he sleeps well there. I have been given the guest room in front, which used to be occupied by an elder brother who died a few years ago. It is a sweet and comfortable room, with its floor-to-ceiling windows paned in coloured glass, opening out on a riot of hibiscus bushes and a grove of bamboo.

In the morning I am awakened by Puan Zainab in the garden below those windows, yelling bellicose imprecations at a squirrel ostensibly responsible for dislodging the first durian of the season. But it turns out to be a most delicious fruit, decidedly ripe and a promising augury for the harvest to come.

It makes a good taste to hold in the mouth as I take my leave of Nizam to continue my journey. The historian Richard Windstedt once described Negri Sembilan as "that delightful little state of lost causes and incredible beliefs, breathing from clustered hamlets and sequestered ricefields the last absurdities of the matriarchal system."

"Absurd", Sir Richard? No more and no less than any other system, you must agree. And from at least one of those hamlets clustered around its sequestered ricefields might still emerge something of lasting value...but I suppose that must depend on whether or not Nizamuddin Ambia believes his art to be a legitimate means of escape.

© Rehman Rashid, 1993.

Review of
GREEN IS THE COLOUR
by
Wong Soak Koon

Lloyd Fernando's second novel, *Green Is The Colour*, completed almost two decades after his first novel, *Scorpion Orchid* (1976) must excite the curiosity of both critic and general reader alike. After such a long hiatus what would be germinated? Clearly, the central concern of the first work, namely how people of different races, the heirs of colonial and migrant histories, face the challenges of living side by side is as important in *Green Is The Colour* as it is in *Scorpion Orchid*. But it seems to me that the second work is more sombre and the vision darker.

In *Scorpion Orchid*, Fernando uses the racial and political riots in Singapore in the early 50's to explore the demands on four youths (Sabran, Guan Kheng, Santhinathan, D'Almeida), each of a different race, as they face the challenges of a commitment to the forging of a new society which can be called home after the violence of the riots. Although a lot of hard work lies ahead, Fernando hints of the possibility of a genuine dialogue across racial lines so that commonalities rather than differences are emphasized and adaptations take precedence over puristic racial stands.

The author's vision of the flowering of a new, post colonial society (multi-lingual, multi-traditional) is crystallized in the image of the orchid of the novel's title. Like this specie of orchid, the new society is a wonderfully adaptable hybrid created by a nationalistic, post-colonial generation out of the collective past. But its survival can be threatened by hidden venom. Scorpions lurk among the roots of the orchid waiting to sting and poison.

In *Green Is The Colour*, fresh violence erupts in the racial riots in Malaysia (13th May, 1969). Again, a set of multi-racial characters is used to develop the novel's ideas. Yun Ming, the Chinese who has been "absorbed" into the system as a government official is beginning to question the dominant discourse, in particular, ideas on unity which the authorities are touting. Dahlan, once his university mate, and now a lawyer, looks with contempt on Yun

Ming's affiliation with the political powers. Dahlan himself tries to bait the conscience of the authorities by speaking out on the need for religious tolerance after the members of a Chinese religious sect and their leader Ti Shuang are arrested, not because of any crime they committed but because they appear to the authorities to be a threat to public security. Omar, the second important Malay character, fed up with what he deems the decadence of Western ways which have tarnished the race seeks a return to the spiritual protection of fundamentalist Islam. Important as these male characters are, it seems to me that Fernando gives prominence to the woman character Siti Sara. A large portion of the last segment of the novel is told in her first-person narrative or seen through her consciousness.

When the novel opens, the violence engendered by the riots has not ceased. Roadblocks necessitate detours; tension is so high that it does not take much to ignite fresh eruptions. The country itself appears to have been divided into zones even as its multi-racial populace huddle into "safe" spaces. Against such a scenario we are not surprised that some of the main characters (Siti Sara, Dahlan) undergo the horrors of rape, incarceration and torture. But over and above this physical violence, is the more insidious violence that is done to men's minds and their powers of clear and sincere expression. Language has been debased into counterfeit coinage in order to mask lies or purvey half-truths. As Dahlan sees it, "I have lived all my life by words. I have seen men make them do anything they wanted. That is the evil I have fought."

No real connection between people can be possible when there is so much muddle and so little willingness to be clear. Fernando skilfully evokes an atmosphere of fear and suspicion in which many prefer to be listeners rather than risk voicing deeply-felt truths. These self-imposed silences are volubly filled by other voices such as that of Wan Nuruddin, the Secretary General in the Department of Unity, discoursing confidently on Confucian ethics and loyalty to the government. In the post May 13th ambience an artificial togetherness has been created to prevent more painful soul-searching. Siti Sara admits that "she developed and clung to the use of plural personal pronoun" because it stirred feelings of love for her fellow citizens whether Malay, Chinese, Indian or Eurasian. In fact "she had embraced a specious feeling of togetherness with people in the abstract to cloak her unease, to disguise her semi-instinctive need to know." Like Yun Ming, she begins to see that official rhetoric merely covers the fact that racial lines are clearly drawn so as to reinforce a sense of "them" and "us." In this context the shadowy figure of another woman, Neelambigai alias Fatimah binti Abdullah whose body neither her relatives nor the Religious Department would claim haunts the reader as a sad reminder of intolerance and bigotry on all sides. Her family consider her an outsider because of her traversing of religious and racial barriers and the Religious Department will not accept her as being of the faith since there is no proof of conversion. Dahlan himself discovers that it is not so easy to simply say, "I don't care for your beliefs, I will bury her."

The individual in such a society is constantly under surveillance. Nearly all the main characters have a sense of being watched. The *leitmotif* of eyes is skilfully manipulated to reinforce an Orwellian sense that one's every move is known, noted and filed away for future reference. Panglima, Political Secretary to the Minister of Home Affairs, whose basilisk stare unsettles even as it mesmerizes, has files on everyone. Such an atmosphere breeds paranoia, even madness. The more sensitive members of the society chafe against the tension and strain of having to choose one's words before speaking. Dahlan, we learn, had already had a nervous breakdown while still an undergraduate. Siti Sara, the returnee from an American university, who now lectures in a local institution of higher learning feels as if she is under the close scrutiny of colleagues, students and even her own husband, Omar who wants her to quit her job, follow him to Tok Guru Bahaudin's community in Jerangau. That her internal turmoil threatens to spill over is conveyed in various instances. Looking at a flower in the compound of her *kampong* home to which she had returned to seek some respite she feels as if "the hibiscus exploded in her field of vision... One flower glowed so intensely bright that it seemed aflame and she gazed at it thunderstruck. She stood before a molten furnace door... It was inexpressibly wonderful to the point of being terrifying and she steered away from the disquieting splendour, fearing madness."

The novel's many scenes of violent sexual encounters, for example, between Yun Ming and Sara, and Sara and her husband show the desperate coming together of people whose inner lives are intensely disturbed. Yun Ming's violent possession of Sara is like an urgent effort to transcend loneliness and the consciousness that one has been a pawn in the political games of the powers that be. Omar takes Siti Sara with unseeing eyes in a narcissistic frenzy. A refusal to see other points of view propels him towards the confined space of Tok Guru Bahaudin's domain where one can be away from the tarnishing contact with Western ways and those not of the faith. He does not see that to do so is to deny history, both colonial and migrant. It is a retreat into an unreal world, a space that assails Siti Sara, who follows him half-heartedly to Jerangau, with its dissolution and its retrogressive, almost medieval atmosphere.

Other reviewers have found the ending of the novel optimistic. Yun Ming resigns his post, is ostensibly his own man at last and he and Siti Sara comes together to forge a new destiny. But the Kafkaesque quality of the last portion of the novel where Siti Sara is the centre of consciousness fuses the quotidian and the nightmarish and suggests that all is not well. To Siti Sara, the watchers in the forms of Tzeto, Vanar are terrifyingly present still. The only safe haven is the "little room in her head." Without dismissing the physical scars of her ravaged body, it is the wounds inflicted on her nerves that reinforce our sense of the power of the *penaungs* and *dalangs* (puppet-masters).

Are there therefore no glimpses of hope? Fernando records simple acts of kindness between people of different races in a meal shared or a fruit given at a market place. In pockets of rural seclusion, which have miraculously escaped political manipulations, families live side by side "their bonds as strong as they are unspoken." The novel is not only peopled by grotesque figures of nightmare such as Panglima, Lahab and Tzeto; others such as the simple, warm-hearted Safiah and Lebai Hanafiah, Siti Sara's father, renew our belief in the decency of common people. Although, as Orwell says, this decency is seldom brought into the corridors of power, that it is still there is reassuring. The Lebai, on his deathbed, gives his blessing to Siti Sara's conjoining with Yun Ming: "I tell my beloved child there is nothing to forgive, only love to be given." Accepting the legacy of a multi-racial history, the Lebai will not allow zealous groups "to come between me and love for all humanity." And the land too, in spite of the scars it bears of trees felled and hills levelled for sundry development projects, is still able to renew itself in fresh, green vegetation.

Green Is The Colour is clearly conceived as a novel of ideas and this is the source both of its weakness and strength. The author has to deal with a range of characters of different races without privileging any one except perhaps, Siti Sara who is given more attention. He does not stay long enough with any one character for us to know that character well. Although his characters are memorable collectively, no one individual arrests our attention. The strength of the novel is its uncompromising look at the past and its legacies for the present. It articulates with keen insight some deeply-felt but unexpressed truths about the way we see each other in this multi-racial land. When so much rhetoric is today directed toward the future, it is timely that a work invites us to pause and ask what has been and what is.

© Wong Soak Koon, 1993.

DR WONG SOAK KOON is a lecturer in Literature at the Universiti Sains Malaysia. She has published articles on Conrad, Kipling and Pramoedya Ananta Toer and is co-editing a collection of essays on feminist discourse from a Malaysian perspective.

LLOYD FERNANDO
An excerpt of
Green is the Colour

In the afternoon she dandled Safiah's youngest child as Safiah herself winnowed the *padi*. Two older children, both boys, were spinning *gasing* with their friends on a sandy patch some distance away. Tall *pinang* trees lined the little two-acre patch which was their homestead, making it seem a cool haven in the expanse of dry stubble that stretched away all round where once the green *padi* plants had thrived. Karim, Safiah's husband, had gone to Kuala Kangsar.

Sara listened to Safiah's account of the season just ended. The tractor hired from the National Padi Board broke down several times. Then the rains did not come on time. But the *penyakit merah* was the worst. "We couldn't do anything," Safiah said. "All our work was no use. So many months spent in the field, what has it brought us? Once those worms got into the grain we lost heart. The grain which we got breaks easily in the milling. Look," she stopped her desultory winnowing and taking a few grains of the *padi* between her fingers pressed hard and then showed the broken grain to Sara. "See? Half of our harvest will be like that. Lucky thing the government is going to help us, otherwise sure we cannot carry on. Already some of the families in our *kampung* don't want to plant anymore. Have you seen their *sawah*? Not dug up anymore, nothing growing, just lallang. They just rely on the fruit trees. Nothing to do but pluck the fruit. Anyway," she lowered her voice, "there's trouble here now, you know. Work in the fields also not safe." When she asked Sara how things were in the city, her wistful tone of voice made Sara feel slightly guilty about her own comfortable life.

Later she picked up a bicycle and in jeans pedalled swiftly on the narrow metalled path that ran along the river bank for half a mile before turning inland. Her hair flew, she rang her bicycle bell in exhilaration, swerving past other cyclists and a few pedestrians. She passed a little *kedai* where several young men were seated on a makeshift bench outside. Some of them were barebodied. They shouted out to her teasingly, but she looked straight ahead as she rode on.

Some yards ahead a youth signalled to her to stop. He was dressed in city clothes, dark trousers and a clean shirt with sleeves folded up above the elbows. It seemed he wanted to say something to her. She stopped, standing astride her bicycle.

"I know you," he said, somewhat brusquely. "You were at the university club in Kuala Lumpur, no?"

She said nothing, wondering at his manner.

He had a thin moustache which made his brown-complexioned face look darker. He kept looking away and staring into the distance, as if to perceive something. When he looked at her, she saw that his eyes were red, as if with anger. "I speak to you like your brother. Dress properly, don't bring shame on your father and mother."

She remounted her bicycle and rode on without a word.

The Government advisory station for farmers was a simple hut with a green and white coat of paint, standing in a small fenced-in area. A signboard gave the times when the station would be open. It was shut when Sara got there. She got off her bicycle and stood staring at the hut from the gate. Suddenly it opened and a Chinese stood in the doorway. It was Yun Ming.

"What are you doing here?" she gasped.

He was smiling. "Shouldn't you be in the university?"

"This is my *kampung*."

"I know."

They laughed. It seemed as if the tinkling of the *gamelan* was wafted again in the rural air.

She said, "I came to see my father."

"Is he not well?"

"No, it's not that. He's all right."

She took in the hut and the unswept garden in a glance. "Is this place ever open?"

"When was the last time you saw it?" He walked up to the gate and opened it to let her in. "There is some trouble."

"I haven't come this side a long time." She walked with a nonchalance she did not feel. "What sort of trouble?"

He showed her in, switching on the solitary electric bulb which hung from the ceiling without a shade. It cast a yellow light over the sparsely equipped room. On an old wooden table lay a few files, a typewriter and a table fan. He switched the fan on. A faded poster about kinds of *padi* hung on the notice board, one of its corners curling. He sat on the table and talked about an old Hindu shrine which had been discovered in an archaeological dig some years ago. Its statues had been smashed, the shrine desecrated. The persons responsible were never caught. Two days after that a gang of youths came in two cars from the town, shouting abuse, making obscene gestures at passers-by in the village. It seemed they held the village responsible for what had happened. Sure enough there were a couple of brawls, and one person was stabbed and taken to the clinic where he spent an uncomfortable night before being sent to the hospital in Taiping. Soldiers now patrolled the main roads. He said, "I came up to see what needs to be done. Last job before I go."

"Are you thinking Dahlan might come here too?" She could not keep irony entirely out of her voice. "By the way, what is happening to him?" she asked.

"Depends on him."

She did not understand why he was so dismissive, simply because he happened to be going away. Come to think of it, she did not understand Yun Ming's role at all. She said, "Do you mean if he comes up here and speaks to people saying, don't desecrate this shrine, you'll put him in?" but the look on his face made her feel as if she had said something frivolous.

"He may come here. We think he is also planning to go to Jerangau. That would be dangerous."

She said, "We will probably be going there."

"To live there?"

"Yes. My husband wants us to live in Tok Guru Bahaudin's community."

He felt repulsed and couldn't react immediately. He put his hands on the desk behind him and half sat on it. She had said the words with a certain deliberateness.

He said, with odd formality, "He's a good speaker. Bahaudin, I mean."

"Is it true what they say of him?"

"I heard him give a *ceramah* when he came to KL last year - part of my duties," he added with a smile. "You know, you can't take your eyes off him when you're listening to him. It's like you're in a trance. People become spellbound when he speaks. Have you seen them? Their eyes become glazed, they sway from side to side."

191

She said, "Many people's hopes and aspirations are centred on him."

She saw he was going to challenge her, and she walked away from him, inspecting the room, and reading the outdated circulars pinned on the notice board. "Here's one about *penyakit merah*." She went up close to the board and began reading it.

He stood beside her and glanced at it. "Yes. Advice on how to prevent it from taking hold. Not followed, you see."

Last year there were a few rice fields overgrown with weeds and lallang. This year there were going to be many more. There is a little insect that gets into the *padi* stalk, and when that happens there is little that can be done to get them out. This year people simply gave up. Many were just relying on their fruit trees. Mangosteens, bananas, rambutans, durians. One season after another. They got less, but they were certain of what they got. Why till the fields when more than half the crop could end up useless. When the fruits were in season they plucked them and sold them at the stalls just round the corner from Iskandar Bridge. When that was over it was too late to till the fields, the season was gone, they had missed the cycle, but it did not matter. They had *rezeki*.

She caught an underlying appeal in his voice unrelated to the words he was uttering. She turned to look at him and realised he had never taken his eyes off her as he spoke, and she saw in his look no reticence. The words about the problems of the station continued to tumble out of his mouth, more haltingly. Now there was discontent in the *kampung*, and two factions which differed fiercely with each other as to how their problems should be solved were beginning to have separate weddings and even separate funerals. Think of Dahlan coming into such a situation, and where were we?

She no longer was able to follow his words, the air in the room stifled her, sweeping her into disquiet. Trembling she reached out with her hand, but before he could take it she withdrew it and forced herself to look again at the curling poster. "Are you going to close this station down?" she heard herself ask.

It was some time before he spoke again. "We had an officer here. He organised courses. But the people stopped coming. After that he just collected his pay every month. We replaced him, but it was the same." He broke off. "Why are you here? Don't you have teaching to do? When are you going back? Do you have to leave the university to go to Jerangau?"

"The campus was dull," she said. "I came back after my studies, full of ideas I was going to thrash out with the students. No use. You feel you're being watched, your ideas are all carefully recorded and reported somewhere. You look over your shoulder when you say something. The students simply want to pass. The staff write rubbish in the local newspapers just so that they can say they have published something. There's a beautiful campus, shelves of books but it is a dead place. Everyone should go to Jerangau - or places like it." She was leafing through a large record book which was the office journal as she spoke. When she stopped and placed her hand on a page to make as if to read, he took it gently in his.

The sound of the fan receded, the sounds of the children's shouts outside were stilled. His hands grasped her body everywhere, hurting. He bit her lips till she cried with pain. She leaned against him as if forcibly propelled, and felt the ardour of his passion with an acquiescence which surprised her. She was moving in a subterranean channel whose current, swift and noiseless, sped her to a bank where all was still.

Sudden voices outside startled them and she wrenched herself away, panting.

She said, "Someone's coming."

He went unsteadily to the front of the office and stood listening for a while.

She whispered, "Who is it?"

"It's nothing. Just passers-by."

With shaking hands she tucked her shirt back into her jeans, and rearranged her hair. She did not look at him.

"Don't go. Please don't go."

She opened the door and walked slowly out without another word. She pushed her bicycle on the path leading up to the road, the gravel under the tread of her feet sounding unnaturally loud. From the corner of her eyes she saw again the dark, red-eyed youth who had accosted her earlier. He was sitting among companions on the wooden steps of a *kampung* house. She was aware only of his eyes fixed on her as she climbed on her bicycle. Someone sucked in his breath exaggeratedly, another gave a short laugh. She stood hard on the pedals to gather speed and rode away.

193

Her father said to her when she returned, "Where have you been? Why are you back so late? You know it's dangerous to go about alone."

Most of the television watchers had left the house. Light from the electric bulb which swung over the dining room crept uncertainly into the darkened living room yellowing the faces of those who remained. A mother, her sleeping child on her lap, sat on the wooden floor, continuing to gaze at the screen that flickered brightly with phantom shapes from another hemisphere. Two boys, sprawling on the floor jostled with each other to get a better view of the fleeting figures. The noises of the night had now become a soft, high-pitched whirr pressing upon the dimly-lit house in waves.

Panglima had come to visit.

People began to call him Panglima because, after the British reoccupation, he spoke often of the revival of religious values and of the cultural decay which the West had spread to the countries of South East Asia. He became a frequent visitor to the house of Lebai Hanafiah offering him advice on all matters, including Sara's education. If Lebai Hanafiah had any reservations, he kept them to himself. After all, Panglima was now Political Secretary to the Minister of Home Affairs but, more than that, the people of the *kampungs* surrounding Kuala Kangsar feared him for the secret knowledge he had acquired of them from the individual files compiled by the Ministry. Sara was only six at the time, and he noticed the more than common interest which Panglima showed in her.

As Sara grew to young womanhood, Panglima developed a passion for her he found more and more difficult to hide. Lebai Hanafiah instinctively knew he was going to be asked for her hand, and to avoid having to refuse him, hurriedly arranged for her to go to America "for further studies." The news of her marriage to Omar did not diminish Panglima's desire for her. He found the way she mixed easily with people of other races a convenient pretext to call on her frequently. It was sure to lead to trouble, he told her father, especially while Omar was away overseas. As an elder of the community he could not be refused, but Lebai Hanafiah was uneasy.

Sara listened to his low monotone in amazement as if hearing it for the first time. It was like the root of the tree by the river bank, snaking its way into the clear water. The words conveyed objectivity, the monotone a bitter venom. "Dahlan means well. But he is just a Western liberal. He is thinking this country is like the steps of Senate House in the University of London. He wants to be a martyr and, you know what? I guarantee he will be one if he does not look out, you see if I am wrong. He thinks he can just stand up and shout to make everybody listen to him. Then he will go into a pub, drink beer and read human rights poetry. After that he will go to bed with some white girl from a human rights group, and his conscience will be at peace, and he won't have to worry anymore about actually doing something about inequality, poverty, and race." Panglima spoke of the need to wipe out all traces of the colonial legacy and reassert the traditional heritage. "Now you take Yun Ming. That's what I like about Yun Ming." He turned to Lebai Hanafiah. "He works in my Ministry. He used to be a real - what do you call it - banana! You know - brown outside, white inside. Now I do not say that, Macaulay said that." The teeth were bared in a genial smile at his own joke. "But he realised it. That he had to change. Look at him now. He works very hard. I can trust him just like our own people. I gave him a job to do here. He should be around." He broke off, and the eyes narrowed again into their habitual suspicious stare. "Have you seen him?" Sara, whose thoughts had wafted into the night, though she kept her eyes in a fixed stare on Panglima, did not hear him. "I said, have you seen him?"

What would this ape think if she lied? What, if she told the truth? The narrowed eyes, slanted at her from an inclined head, would even see deceit where none was. Her heart thumping, she said, "You mean, Yun Ming? Yes, I saw him at the station. What is he doing here?"

Panglima took a deep breath, and looked at the television screen for a while. "Did you know he was coming up to Sayong?"

"No, I did not."

He did not pursue the point. There was time. He said, more mildly, "He is doing work here which you could do better since this is our *kampung*. But you are looking for the spiritual life. If you weren't going to Jerangau, we could use your help. We need people like you to explain things to the village folk." He paused, and his lidless eyes narrowed still more. "I could show you what to do."

Real social involvement, she thought. Providing people with the mental equipment to fight the decadence that was swamping the towns. But she recoiled at the thought of working with Panglima.

"Dahlan is a decadent," he was saying. "We must stop his influence at all costs. Look at his name, Harry Dahlan. He likes their way of thinking so much that he does not know how much he has lost. They have put their mark on him."

On you. On me. On all of us. The thought filled her with an inner desperation. She had to find a way of reasserting what was native and true. The past clung to her, a large scab that had to be shed so that normal growth would be hers again even though a scar might remain.

Bright moonlight shone down on the *kampung*. From the verandah she saw dancing streaks of silver on the waters of the river. The chug of the ferry boat carrying its last passengers came faintly across in the night. It seemed as if the wake of the boat was moving towards her in a gentle, prolonged heave. It soothed her beating heart.

© Lloyd Fernando, 1993.
Landmark Books Pte Ltd

LLOYD FERNANDO was formerly professor in the English Department, University Malaya.

Dr Fernando's works include two novels, the first being *Scorpion Orchid* published in 1976 and republished by Times Intn. in 1992 and the second *Green is the Colour* by Landmark Books, Singapore in 1993. He has also published works on literary criticism: *'New Women' in Late Victorian Fiction* (Pennsylvania State University Press, 1976) and *Cultures in Conflict* (Graham Brash, 1986). He has also edited anthologies: *Twenty-Two Malaysian Stories* (Heinemann, 1968), *Modern Malaysian Stories* (Heinemann, 1982), *New Drama One* (Oxford University Press, 1972) and *New Drama Two* (Oxford University Press, 1972).

Afterword to K.S. Maniam's
IN A FAR COUNTRY
by
C.W. Watson

It is difficult to read *In a Far Country* with any degree of confidence. By that I don't mean that it is difficult to construct some sense out of the words on the page and follow the episodic descriptions conveyed there, although there is that difficulty, too, at times. Where the real difficulty lies for me, is in getting a grip of the whole: feeling confident that I know what the novel is about, that I am properly interpreting and understanding, indeed even correctly identifying, the various levels at which the text is operating.

One easy reaction to such doubts is the familiar one of dismissing them by incorporating them within a critique; thus one argues that the doubts are part of the response which the novel's structure is designed to elicit. The structure in this perspective deliberately seeks to undermine the usual conventions of reading and create uncertainty for the reader. Consequently, I can interpret my own doubts as an indication of the success of the novel's style. Much of this argument is clearly appropriate in relation to *In a Far Country*. It should not be read as a realist novel; its ambiguity is a deliberately intended structural feature of the text, and the conventions according to which it must be interpreted are to be found not in the realism of the late nineteenth century novel, but in the modernist and post-modernist texts of the late twentieth century. Nevertheless, even though I appreciate the strength of this argument, I still feel uneasy, and I want to account for my uneasiness in terms of what I see as a promiscuous use of narrative conventions and tropes which confuses the reader at crucial moments within the text. Let me explain.

As a reader I am quite happy to go along with the task of selecting appropriate literary conventions and codes and relating them to *In a Far Country*, and certainly this is a rewarding way to approach the novel. One can, for example, reflect on the surrealist quality of the narrator's confinement to his house in the opening sections of the novel and his breaking with the daily routine of his middle-class family life style, and recall similarly constructed situations in the claustrophobic stories of Kafka or Samuel Beckett. In other episodes where the focus is less on the experience of mental and physical confinement and more on the notion of journeying, pilgrimage and discovery, other parallels spring to mind. The expeditions into the jungle, the return to the northern town and the narrator's second encounter with Zulkifli, and the recurring symbolism of Mani the goat, for example, seem cognate, in a non-specific way with some of the thirties novels of writers like Rex Warner or French novels of the fifties. Closer to Malaysia, I am reminded of the fantasy and absurdism of the Indonesian writer Iwan Simatupang whose protagonist in *Ziarah* and *Merahnya Merah* are not only observers of the unreal world of others, but total participants within it. And, finally, another literary form which invites comparison is the magical realism of Marquez, Isabel Allende and Salman Rushdie, all of whom revel in anecdotes of extraordinary characters and phantasmagoric situations, yet at the same time insert within their narrative a committed historical and political commentary.

The point of making these comparisons is not to transfer attention away from *In a Far Country*; on the contrary, it is to invite a closer reading of it, since by observing the similarities and differences in the way in which the conventions of anti-realism are manipulated, the reader is guided to a view from which she can, ideally, identify and evaluate what the enterprise of the novel is, what it is about. Let me illustrate what I mean by referring once more to the political intentions of the magical realists.

Marquez' *One Hundred Years of Solitude*, Allende's *House of the Spirits* and Rushdie's *Midnight's Children* deal respectively with Colombia, Chile and India, giving powerful and individual interpretations of the recent political history of three nations. In their case the way in which that commentary is conducted is through the retelling of historical events in gross caricature in which political personalities appear in exaggerated grotesque forms which combine the blackly humorous with the horrifically violent. The political commentary is located, then, in the juxtaposition of violence and humour, a juxtaposition which precisely because it is so alienating, forces the reader to reflect more profoundly on the political statement being made - an excellent example of Brecht's *Verfremdungseffekt*. Here in *In a Far Country* it seems that K.S. Maniam is occasionally trying something similar, but only very tentatively and unconvincingly. In several places throughout the narrative there seems to be an attempt to present specific detailed descriptions of events in the narrator's life and in the record of the lives of the significant others whom he encounters. Now at one level we can read these descriptions as indicative of the transformation of Malaysian society over the past forty years. Thus the narrator's progress from being a junior official in land development schemes in northern Malaysia to his present financial success as a property developer mirrors the economic transformation of the country from being a largely agriculture based British colony at the start of this period to the achievement of modern nation status with a fast-growing economy after forty years. Similarly, the various characters whose life-stories are recounted, or hinted at, throughout the narrative seem intended to reflect the victims and the beneficiaries of that transformation, the victims being those like Lee Shin and Andy the smoke-house man who cannot accommodate the demands of the new society and the beneficiaries, those like the narrator, Jimmy Kok and Ramasamy, who have adapted and made good. And in between there are those like Zulkifli and the narrator's wife who do not fully adapt, but manage to survive. These characters and the episodes in which they are involved, are on this reading, to be seen as case-studies. Certainly at one level such an interpretation is plausible, but unfortunately these are only the faintest gesturings towards social comment, and there is nothing substantial which might allow the reader to obtain any real sense of what has been happening to the country.

The same is true of the muted political commentary in the text. In Chapter 10 towards the end of the book, for example, there is an account of a political meeting, but this is filtered through the description of a surreal nightmare, and the narrative of the dream allows the assembling of characters and events from different periods of the narrator's life history: Mani the sacrificial goat, symbolising perhaps the common man; the friends of the narrator, Lee Shin, Zulkifli, Jimmy Kok, Ramasamy, each again perhaps - but this is not certain - representative of an ethnic voice within the nation. At the centre of the dream, however, is the "representative" and it is he who provides the focus for the satire:

'Once launched, the representative rambles on about how the administration has only the welfare of the people at heart. He cites various projects that have been completed, all in the interests of the people. The people, he is referring to, shift restlessly on their chairs and feet. It is when he beings to talk about how the multi-purpose complex represents everything that a society dreams of that we hear a raucous explosion, like a fart. The representative stops talking but the culprit isn't to be found. Security guards walk among the people, trying to identify the mischief-maker. The speaker continues with his praise of the administration's far-sightedness when we hear a bray, followed by the sound of someone urinating. The representative doesn't stop; he only hurries on and brings his address to a conclusion. Just as he takes the scissors, presented on a silver platter, and prepares to cut the ribbons the air suddenly fills with the stink of a goat's pellet-dung. But Mani is faster than the security guards and having made his comments on the occasion, bounds away. He doesn't show himself for a few days. But he must have been in the administration's black book since then.

As satire goes this is mildly amusing, but all in all it is fairly trite and there is not much substance to it. The figure of the hypocritical politician mocked by the common man has become a stock character in fiction throughout the world, not least in Malaysia. The humour here, then, does not carry us very far. There is a world of difference, between this mild general criticism and the excoriating caricatures of individuals which we find in the other novelists of magical realism.

This is one way, then, in which comparative literary criticism can help us to read selected episodes in *In a Far Country* at a more intense level. And, as I suggested earlier, trying to trace a literary genealogy or locate the novel within a genre can be a rewarding experience. It can never, however, of itself be enough. Ultimately one's evaluation of a work of fiction of this kind depends on an assessment of how far it has succeeded in the articulation of something original within the limits of the conventions it has set for itself. And it is here that the doubts and difficulties arise. I am never sure what the intention of the novel is - where in other words the originality is to be found - and, if the argument is that there is no intention, I am not convinced.

Part of the problem seems to lie in the chaos of a first person narrator, whom the epigraph at the front of the book encourages us to think of in Proustian terms. Like Marcel in *A La Recherche du Temps Perdu*, the narrator is searching, or so it would appear, to recreate the past, restoring it, almost, through literary fabrication. Thus the novel opens, like Proust, with a vividly evoked memory of a childhood, in this case the scene of the slaughter of Mani at Deepavali. This opening sequence, and I use the film term deliberately, is to my mind one of the most successful in the book. Very subtly it sets the reader up for a number of the episodes which will follow. The figure of the goat will constantly recur, both as a symbol in itself, a symbol, mind you, which seems to change its referent from ritual scapegoat to peasant rebel, and as dark image within the narrator's mind of the Dionysian spirit which undermines rigid and inflexible control. Above all, however, this introduction alerts the reader, again as in the Proustian case, to the function of memory.

It is therefore somewhat disappointing to find in the succeeding chapters that although the device or recollection, is preserved, the style of the narrative changes and we are led into the absurd and the fantastic. Despite the linking voice of the narrator, the various episodes which follow are dissociated one from another, and striking as they are as vignettes, the life and death of Lee Shin, the Spotted Lady, Sivasurian's chronicle, there is no overall coherence, either in terms of a consistent style or in terms of an overarching narrative structure. To put it another way, the reader is left to puzzle out whether this is a novel about a central character whose reflections on experience are intended as an exploration of individual subjectivity, or a farrago of portraits and stories which taken cumulatively are organised in such a way as to enable us to read modern Malaysian history from the text.

It would be wrong, however, to end on a critical note and one which perhaps says more of my own lack of perceptiveness than of flaws in the novel itself. There is some very powerful writing in the book which should not go unobserved. The description of the narrator's visit to Zulkifli's village and the horror of the transformation of Zulkifli's son, read partly as an allegory of the transformation of Malaysia over the past thirty years, partly as documentary realism, offers fine confirmation, if ever it was needed, of how compelling a novelist K.S. Maniam is. In fact this episode stands out in the narrative not only because of the graphic quality of the descriptions, but also because, with respect to two central issues, the novel here reaches its dramatic climax.

The life of the narrator up to that point, at least this is how it appears in his narrated reflections, has been the accumulation of disconnected experiences, lived through at different levels of intensity, but never providing the security from which an assured self-perception can be achieved. It is precisely this lack of assurance which has led to the withdrawal from the world, and it is the search for assurance which has prompted first the recall of the earlier experiences and then an attempt to revisit the emotion of those experiences for the purpose of greater self-understanding. It is this motive which inspires the desire to see Zulkifli again. Years earlier Zulkifli had tried to help the narrator to see the tiger, a symbol of the quality of Malay life and the Malay vision of the world, but as with other earlier attempts of the narrator to grasp at a subliminal reality beneath the surface, the journey made had ended in failure. The return to the north, then, is an attempt to take up again that earlier frustrated endeavour. In being forced to confront Zul and listen to what has overtaken Zul's family, the narrator does indeed achieve some sort of self-understanding and this is sufficient, not to allow immediate re-entry into the world, but to enable progress in that direction.

The other central issue which is raised here which provides some justification for seeing this episode as a climax is the connection made, for once very explicitly, between the nation's political history and the narrator's desire to arrive at self-discovery through an insertion of himself within that history. After Zulkifli has described the mental collapse of his son he turns to the narrator.

"He is living and not living," Zul said. "We can accept the results but we still have to look for the cause. You ran away that time. From the tiger. I've become old and wiser, when I look back I see you and others like you as the cause. We lived well, maybe too peacefully, before you all came with your ideas and energies. Ideas that can even destroy the tiger, the oldest symbol of our civilisation. You gave up everything to come to this land. We offered you what we had. But you all became greedy and wouldn't share. Saw no other world but the world of progress and money. And we had to make the sacrifices. This time I want you to experience what my son went through."

"I can try, Zul," I said.

"He saw the tiger," Zul said. "I made him see the tiger. Yet, when he went to the city, everything was destroyed."

The ideas here are familiar, the rape of the country, the destruction of tradition, the awfulness of what replaces it, but located where they are in the context of the narrative these ideas are articulated with a poignancy which compels the reader to go beyond a gesture of complacent acquiescence. Although, ultimately, I still feel unsure about the depth of thought here, and how much is really being communicated, I am moved by the style of the statement.

There is, then, much to commend *In a Far Country*. If at times it seems to suffer from a certain lack of control, the experiments it contains were nonetheless worth making and should be applauded. If there is an overall weakness of the novel, then, it lies in its being over-ambitious. Too many different styles and forms, too many literary devices, jostle together, and even though several episodes in themselves come across with a force and vigour which grip the imagination, the success of the whole is jeopardised by the very disparateness of such a kaleidoscopic narrative. Reflections on the literary uses of memory, the depiction of history as surreal, commentary on the nature of tradition and the upheavals of modernisation, are all great themes which sit uneasily together and can only be handled with great literary skill and control. That K.S. Maniam's first attempt in this direction has not been entirely successful is not altogether surprising, but with the experience of having written two very different novels behind him, he is undoubtedly moving from strength to strength, and I eagerly anticipate his next novel.

© Dr. C.W. Watson, 1993.

DR. C.W. WATSON is a Senior Lecturer at the Department of Social Anthropology, University of Kent at Canterbury.

There has hardly been a time in my life when I've stayed in a room, looking outside, doing nothing. Here I am writing - for which I see no immediate value - and watching the light come into the room and mix with the brightness inside and become indistinguishable. There are no shadows, either inside or outside the room. There have been many rooms I occupied, in houses or offices, that were filled with such even brightness. I hadn't felt uncomfortable in them; I didn't feel disturbed as I am now. I look past the roof-tops of the neighbouring houses and see a clear, blue sky streaked with white. Such plainness, I find, is suddenly unsettling. It was on such a bright morning, some time back, that I left my office premises, abruptly, and shut myself up in this room in my house. My wife and children didn't know what to make of my behaviour the first few days, then fell into a routine that emerged from the crisis.

It was another stroke of light, I think, that brought me into whatever I am trapped by now. Even language denies me plainness, straying this way and that to avoid the blankness that has come into my mind. Fortunately for my generation, we had a good dose of it in the schools during our younger days. I mean the English language. But since I left school and university, where I read economics, the English I used has had to do with adding up and avoiding subtraction. But now there is only a zero in my mind.

It was that blade of light I saw one evening which has brought me to this pass. I remember coming back to an empty house. My wife and sons had gone off to some shopping complex - there was a note with this information- and it was the servant's day off. I went into the kitchen, had a cold drink, and as I was coming into the hall, I noticed the door to my right slightly open. I wouldn't have seen it if the sunlight coming through the crack hadn't struck my face with the warm sting of the *lallang* grass.

---

lallang - Malaysian tall, wild grass.

The room is a sunken one, which an architect friend specially designed for my sons as a playroom. Located next to the kitchen and opposite the servant's room it is well within reach of the fridge, my wife's arbitration responsibilities and the servant's help. But over the years I had forgotten about its existence.

I pushed the door open and entered the room and was, for a while, blinded by the sunlight. After I had grown accustomed to the brightness, I saw nothing in the place that made it a playroom. The windows were wide open as if the occupant wanted the room aired and the curtains were made out of old *saris*. I drew them across the windows and recognized that the saris were the ones Vasanthi had brought from her home and must have worn after her puberty rites. There is a photograph of her wearing one of these saris, taken just after she came out from her menstrual isolation.

I looked around at the room and was struck by the frugality of its furnishing. At the opposite corner from that occupied by the photographs is a wide plank bed covered with a mat and a thick blanket. On top of the single pillow is a folded, white coverlet. Near the window, not far from the bed is a bronze statue of a beggar boy, hands held out and face appealing for charity. I've since returned to the room in my wife's and sons' absence and notice that nothing has changed.

I've stayed in this room as I would have in my office, at the end of the month, to track down any mis-entry in the accounts ledger or try to trace some non-entered item. But that kind of procedure hardly seems to work in my present situation. Most of the time my mind is blank and to get rid of the blankness, I've been reading, off and on, when I'm not staring out of the window, whatever books have been lying around the house. My wife, true to her sense of duty, has brought in supplies from the public library and bookshops. But nothing seems to replace the drive that I've lost, the drive that brought me to my present status of house and property owner, with a solid bank account. The fire that I had in me is simply spent.

During my most idle moments, when I'm off guard, events and people I had thought hardly worth paying attention to, come into my mind. My father's face and his last days in the estate house keep coming back to me. (Is it possible for despair to be inherited through

---

saris - Long textile worn by Indian women.

the blood?) Though in his early fifties, he looked old for his age. Perhaps he felt harassed by his wife and eight children. I don't know. All I can recall is that he would lie like a covered corpse on the long, wooden bench outside the house in the mornings. Later in the morning the corpse sat up and blinked at the bright day. Somehow it found the strength, some hours later, to go to the cooking place, make gruel from the previous day's rice and pour the mess down its throat. Then the corpse straightened itself some more and put on a shirt and shorts.

Though I scoffed at him, how strange it is now to almost look and be like him. At least he could eat a morning meal; I merely look at the food my wife puts on the table in my room and move away.

That breakfast prepared my father for the toddy drinking for the remainder of the day and most of the night. When he returned, late, my mother, sisters and brothers would be fast asleep, having scrambled and fought for whatever food and space they could get.

I couldn't understand at that time why my father never shouted back at my mother when she scolded him. One of the highlights of estate life was to see and hear husbands and wives go for each other almost every day. Other men beat their wives and abused their children under the violence toddy brought on in them. But my father was worse than the stiff corpse he had been in the morning and early afternoon.

The kerosene hand-lamps danced all over the long row of houses when the men returned. The women's faces, under the dim lights, took on heightened anger and indignation. In my house, only I came out, my mother being too exhausted to care. Seated on the steps beside the lamp hung on a nail, I watched my father. Perhaps he had grown used to my presence or he was indifferent for he didn't notice me.

The stiffness that had held up his body during the day, disappeared. He was a mass of pulp; his head lolled from side to side. His stomach was caved in; his shoulders hung down as if at the end of invisible strings. In short, he was collapsed like a puppet put away in a box when the show is over.

As far as I can recall there had been only one great adventure in his life - his escape from India to Malaysia. There were times when he muttered and mumbled during his toddy-soaked carelessness, and it was through these moments of indiscretion that his story came through to me. Thinking back, I realize that that was how he tried to pull himself out of his limp helplessness.

The faint, flickering light and the night silence created shadows and echoes that could have been of another man and another place. The place was another country, India; the time, another era that comes through to me in a strange way. Can memories be inherited? Can repetition make actual the past?

When my father returned home, his uncertain tread brought me out as if to a rescue. Also the duty of handing him his blanket every night had fallen upon me. He received the furry thing as if it was an animal, with unconcealed disgust. He sat wrapped up in it for a while until even I began to feel the cold bite into my flesh.

Then he spluttered and growled and chuckled.

"What animal brought me out here?" he said, falling into a steady stream of words. "You prick me everywhere as if you want to pickle me alive. Remember those nights I came home straight, steady and serious? You didn't sleep turning your back on me. Now you don't even know I'm alive."

At first I thought he was addressing my mother but as he talked on I began to feel he was flinging his words, frustration and anger at something invisible.

"You kept me from sleeping the whole night. Through the open window I saw the stars up in the sky. Did they shine on a better land? Was there drought in those other countries?

"My great-grandfather told me many stories. About those stars. How they had guided our travellers, the bold ones in the family, over lands never trodden by feet before. Ah, those men carrying their boats overland, passing through sandalwood-scented forests! How many were there to carry the boats? How big and heavy were the boats?

"The ship we came in was crowded and foul. The hulls were rusted. When I drank water from the taps there was only a taste of rust. And the human dung - all over the place. The men not even closing the door. The door too rusted to be closed. The women with just the saris over their thighs, to hide their shame. Sometimes no water even to wash, to flush away the human filth."

The months and years of such talk overlap and has become its own reality. Such occasions made me forget who I was and to whom I was listening. The lone voice in the half-darkness removed my self-consciousness - I was about thirteen when these confessions began - and allowed me to escape from brow-knitting thought. There was a certain yearning in me for visions and mysteries that could destroy, even for a short while, the bareness and harshness of my surroundings.

My father carried me away with him when he talked of those early voyagers who either carried their boats across vast tracks of jungle to launch themselves once more into a fresh sea or build another one to reach the land of their dreams. What country could match the complexity of their dreams? How could frail boats transport them into their dreams? My father drew from his memories the discovery of a fabulous kingdom by his forefathers.

"They were not right in the head, those travellers. Why didn't they continue to stay in the land where they built their temples? Go and see them. As good as the ones in India. A little India just here. Were received with respect and honour. Given the chance to lead and to rule. What did they do? Lost their dreams. Went again on their unquenchable travels.

"Those temples. Nothing like them nowadays. Clean and upright. No need for rich men to donate bells with their names inscribed. Even when dug up from deep inside the ground, they were not cracked. Could make a sound that holds together the whole world."

Where was this kingdom and the bells that though buried for centuries retained their pure music? My father was an avid reader of Tamil newspapers, that was, until drink overtook him. Had he read about some archaeological discovery? There had been passing mention of some diggings, somewhere in the north, in the English papers. But he gave me such details as to make me wonder if the source was not himself. If he hadn't invented that glorious, utopian reign of his ancestors, why was such a find suppressed? And who kept it from public notice?

He went on: "People coming together like brothers from the same family. Not strangers from different countries. Look where we are now. Shadows in the darkness, not even hearing the other person breathe. Not even caring.

"Those stars were wrong to bring us here. But how can we stop ourselves from following their pull? Everything is joined together. One land's grass dies, another land's jungle is cool and full of fruits. Like blind bats we come to the fruit trees. Then we're caught in the net."

He wrapped the blanket more closely round his shoulders and sat there rocking himself. He turned his face once or twice in my direction and seeing me there on the steps, seemed to be reassured.

"Wife and children. Just cycle after cycle. Can't break the turning of the wheel. I tried. Yes, coming in those peoples' dung-filled ship, I looked out at the water rolling past us. How vast and clear it looked! Going somewhere deep down. Had its own life. Our lives just small handfuls of dirt. Dropped into the ocean, they just disappeared."

There was one terrible night when he didn't even talk to himself. He wasn't bunched up and formless. Had he swallowed a different kind of drink? He had risen out of his helplessness like a ferocious giant. He stormed there on the cement verandah, his arms raised like huge axes ready to chop down anything that came in his way.

"So what do you want me to do?" he railed. "Build a diamond palace for you? Cut down the hills and plant the flat land with honey-dripping bushes? I took you away from that dry, gossip-diseased family and land. Yes, I thought I would find heaven. But people can be wrong. A man can be wrong.

"The price has to be paid. I'm paying it with blood. With all this suffering. Ah, you're laughing. Saying, 'A fool for following the stars!' Fools sometimes walk into hope-giving things. Fools sometimes fall into insect-gnawing ravines. Do you understand?

"I've tried to understand but my mind is all mixed up. The knots are too many to untie. You're not helping, only laughing at me. Getting angry, spitting on me, making me suffer some more. Why must there be suffering? We suffered there in India. Now there is only suffering. No escape like the last time."

He withdrew deeper into that blanket, slid down and went to sleep on the bench. I sat on, watching, waiting. There was only the strangled breathing that came from the huddled figure under the blanket. The oil lamps had already been taken into the houses and what remained was a starless night. That brought on in me a helplessness almost like that of my father's. A world was blotted out. There remained in the darkness only a voiceless, faceless being.

Fear embraced me like a big-pawed, furry animal. Was that only a young boy's imagination playing tricks on him? I sat there on the steps for a long time, unable to move. My body became slowly covered with sweat. I breathed against the fear, trying hard to regain some confidence, some sense of security. The figure under the blanket offered me no help, only lay still as if its suffering had turned it into stone.

In the distance, through the fearful darkness, I saw the slaughter house. A light came through, somehow, from beyond, like memory recreating a forgotten incident or encounter. The slaughter shed, open on all its sides, stood out there clearly. No goats were tethered there but they would appear when Deepavali was about a few months away.

When I came into adolescence, Deepavali was, for me, held within a circle of mystery. My father's drinking seemed trivial; my mother's suffering was hardly worth the attention. People seemed to be taken out of themselves. The estate lines were transformed. The songs that came from the valve-set radios reached into a more complex and deeper harmony. Somehow the dingy, green plank houses did not rest just on earth-bound stilts; they cushioned themselves on an invisible axis of enchantment. They were unusually clean and neat. The children did not have to be told anything; their faces were washed sober by an air of responsibility.

All this happened after the goats appeared. The older boys roamed the plantation late into the evening with the goats. They returned home with the herd, not scratched or bruised from a fight with each other. Not one of them was bitten by snakes or had to be rescued from wandering away too far. An uncanny kind of order took charge of the lives on the estate.

My own preoccupations and forming personality were held within a stillness and calm that went against the self-centered turbulence I had seen in boys of my age. While they were boisterous, their energies didn't take them into destruction. They didn't swing a cat by its tail. They didn't stab sharp sticks into the anus of a dog. They didn't throw stones, hidden behind hibiscus bushes, at a passing car. They didn't twist and snap the stems of flower plants in the office grounds. They were all curiously self-restrained and loyal to some ordering force outside themselves.

The goats they herded were tied to iron stakes beside the slaughter shed. When it rained, the boys scurried like a wave of ants to these stakes, untied the goats and housed them inside the shed. Their parents watched them, filled with pride and a sense of awe. They too, appeared to be ruled by an awareness beyond that of the ordinary selves.

The goats munched ceaselessly on whatever was pushed into their mouths. They were given grass, banana skins, drum-stick tree flowers and, on occasions, rye cakes. When *pujas* were held on Fridays, the women hurried out to the goats with whole bunches of bananas and rice boiled in brown sugar. It therefore came as a surprise to me to see their behaviour change a week or two before Deepavali.

Nights grew darker than in the previous months. The stars, shining above an awed estate community, now steadied their light as if for a demoniac scrutiny of the world. These were not the stars my father spoke about. They didn't shine an encouraging and benevolent light upon the inhabitants of the earth. They were withdrawn, unsympathetic and mysterious. The estate population reached a frenzied climax on the eve of Deepavali. The nights before the eve seemed to be plunged into deeper darkness and the households lighted hurricane lamps as a kind of defence against the unknown. Even then there were scary patches of shadow between the houses. From where I sat, on the steps, I saw the houses appear precariously out of nothingness and I felt when morning came they would have vanished. But there was certainty in the actions, speech and gestures of the tappers, weeders and gardeners. The clerks, typists and accountants, though removed from the estate lines by a short distance - they lived in small, wooden bungalows - adopted the remote air of the cautious and uninvolved. Perhaps, having watched the annual ritual for years, they preferred the detachment their British masters had impressed upon them.

I don't know.

The morning had an unusual calm about it - the calm the condemned feel before their execution. The men, women and children were silent and restrained like the tethered goats beside the shed. As the morning progressed there came to me the thought that we were slowly being drained of our blood. The light was parchment thin, like the bloodless skin of a man who has lived too long in an icy cavern.

I walked about the estate, lingering under the cool shade of the trees. There was a restlessness inside that forced me into some kind of action. The walking didn't help for it seemed to carry me towards

---

pujas - Special prayer session.

the slaughter shed. And I didn't want to be there at all. Yet I knew the mystery that I longed to confront waited for me beside the cement floor with its little drains and tall pipes. The water would gush and wash away the year's dust and dirt before the awful ritual of slaughter began.

My father, as did most of the men, went out early and returned by mid-afternoon, primed with toddy. In their absence the women and children squatted down to an early lunch. There was an expression on my mother's and sisters' and brothers' faces I couldn't quite place. It was a kind of despair or some secret joy or perhaps it was just desperation. Why should my brothers, so much younger than me, feel cornered and fearful? The men's absence, even if only for a few hours, carried the sense of a final betrayal.

The men returned. The afternoon sky was already tinged with a rusty glow. The children ran out to grab from their hands the little bundles of *vadais* and *murukus* that would prevent them from paying too much attention to the killing of the goats. Already long knives and shorter blades were being sharpened on whetstones. Women ground, gratingly, the chillies, coriander, cummin and poppy seeds in anticipation of the cooking to be done for Deepavali. The day stretched before them like a long vigil.

All over the estate men moved with the weight of habit and determination. The children hung about in knots of curiosity and eager expectation. As they watched the younger men bring down coils of seasoned and well-used rope from hidden stores beneath the rafters, they felt they were entering a ritual that would take them a step further towards adulthood.

Other men cut down banana leaves, the juice from the stems spiking the air, and piled them up without cracking the spine or shredding the edges. These the boys helped to carry to the shed hearing behind them the command: "Don't tear any of the leaves! I'll cut off your tail before it can grow!" The girls who stood watching the boys at their tasks, giggled. They had seen the "tails" when they went to the communal bathroom and caught, unawares, the boys bathing naked. They would see the "tails" again this time that of the bull-goats, when the broad shouldered men slaughtered the animals.

---

vadais - Indian doughnut.
murukus - Indian spicy tidbits.

In the late afternoon, time seemed suspended. The goats bleated and their cries dispersed quickly in the emptiness under the now red sky.

Women's voices, issuing orders to the older girls, reached my ears as faint distortions. Between me and these waves of activities came a clamouring silence. Now and then insects ticked loudly as if they would split their tiny throats in some mad sacrifice. Then the silence overpowered them and they were lost to my consciousness.

Somehow at this point, I find myself stationed at an old well in front of the shed. The covered up well provided a slab-like seat and I sat on it, quiet and remote, watching what went on. The men who would slaughter the goats were old hands at the job but had beside them younger men who were apprentices. These slaughter-trainees merged themselves with the more experienced men as if they were their shadows. Inside the shed waited the skinners and dismemberers. They shuffled, whistled, sang old Tamil songs and drank toddy from dirty flagons while waiting for the carcasses to be brought to them. The two teams taunted, jibed, provoked and abused each other.

There were about eight goats tied to separate stakes at a site a few yards from the shed. The slaughterers had thought it unwise to let the goats smell their approaching deaths. This precaution became necessary after an incident a few years back. Among that batch of five or six, there had been a dappled bull-goat. During the months that it was bred for the slaughter it acquired a personality and a name, Mani. The estate women had fondly tied a brass bell to its neck and, therefore, its name. Mani was not tied up for the night like the other goats; nor was it led on a rope for its grazing. Mani was too gentle to rebel, too courteous to steal food from the pots and pans.

Mani's lustrous, spotted, black-and-white body hung like a charm in the doorways of the estate house kitchens. Sometimes Mani gave in to the whimsical tenderness of a woman and allowed himself to be stroked. He let some of the young girls brush his coat until he shone like their unviolated virginity. But he was there all the time, the faint yet unriddable scent of a hardly understood nostalgia. His bell tinkled, awakening memories that had nothing to do with the struggle for a living in an estate far from a motherland.

Where did he come from? They bought him in a neighbouring estate but he came whole and fresh from the centre of a mystery.

213

To this day he puzzles me. He lived briefly among us and then he was slaughtered. He was an animal but he saw life differently. How was his behaviour the days before his dying to be understood? Was there another kind of deep-seated awareness?

Some three days before Deepavali, Mani disappeared. The women and the young girls became distracted. A few of them joined the boys in looking for Mani. They clucked and called out seductively, "Mani! Mani! Mani!" The boys had banana peels and one young girl even took the trouble to make brown, sugared rice, Mani's favourite. But Mani was not to be found. The people were forced to call off the search.

Mani returned by himself the next morning. There he was beside the shed, on his haunches, an unfathomable expression in his eyes. He didn't so much look at you as beyond you. Into those smoky eyes there came to be crowded all the space that lay beyond man, far from his reach. This vastness terrified me, made me shiver and withdraw into myself. There was, I thought, a subtle insult in that look. Man, he was saying, go ahead. Lock yourself up in the narrow prisons of your making. Me, I'm going out there, into the incomprehensible mystery you can't grasp.

So I shied away but still watched him from a corner of my consciousness. He got to his legs and strutted about, glorying in some discovery only he could have made. His shaggy body - he had not been brushed since his return - tensed against the light that filtered through the jungle, rubber trees and more domestic plants, down to the roof of the shed. His eyes glinted with the fire of a smouldering anger.

Most remarkable of all, at that stage in his life, was the ease with which he lived in complete isolation. He didn't come near the kitchens any more; their doorways were filled neither with memory nor with nostalgia for him. This behaviour not only intrigued the women, both young and old, but also drew from them a respect that verged on reverence. Though Mani indicated he valued his solitude, they never left him alone.

He was approached, besieged and clamoured around at all hours of the day, particularly in the mornings and evenings. They didn't seek to tie a bell at his neck though he had lost the previous one. Instead, they garlanded him with a variety of flowers. Mani neither looked at them nor acknowledged the flowers around his neck. His

214

indifference bore the awesomeness and ferocity of the goddess, Kaliamma.

The women thronged like supplicants around him. Did they want another god in him? One old woman even went so far as to anoint his forehead with sandalwood paste, *kumkum* and holy ash but Mani kicked so violently at her that she had to abandon the attempt. But the other women would not give up so easily. They tried to get through to whatever he represented for them in subtler and more persistent ways.

They talked to him.

"Mani, why're you behaving like this?"

"Yes, tell *amma*. Everybody here wants you to feel happy. Remember the *kanji* water you used to drink? With just a pinch of salt and onion slices? Not too watery or too thick. You drank it like honey. Come to amma's house, Mani. Wear your bells again. The sound makes me glad I'm living."

"Don't listen to her too much, Mani. Listen to me. My words are sweeter. And my palms even more sweet. In some peoples' palms whatever they hold goes sour. In my palm they become crystal sugar. You always came quietly to my house. Like a saint. Look at you now. You've become too proud. Be gentle and simple again, Mani."

This woman went towards Mani with rice boiled in milk and honey, but he only turned his head away.

"That's right. You're too good for our food. Show us what you really want. Something special that only gods and goddesses can prepare for you. Take us and show us. Might be good for us too. Cure our blindness, take the evil away from our tongues. Make us see what you see."

This was the philosopher-woman. Whenever anyone had problems, he or she ran to this calm, knowledgeable woman. The philosopher would chew her *sireh* and betel nut shavings, spiced with lime and dried *kerambu*. She had a melodious voice and just listening to her drove your problems from your minds and hearts.

---

kumkum - Red powder worn as a dot on women's forehead.
amma - Mother.
kanji - Rice gruel.
sireh - Leaf eaten with betel nut shavings.
kerambu - Indian spice.

Mani, after listening, made a noise in his throat that resembled a man's hawking just before he spat.

They turned aggressive towards him and finally left him to his own devices. Mani used this freedom to wander all over the estate, it seemed to savour and relish whatever was not human. He ran with the dogs and hid with the cats. Once he got a black cobra to open out its hood and, to the tapping of his hoofs, sway in dance. As the days drew nearer to Deepavali, he gave up all these treats and rested, without eating, beside the shed. His eyes were dull and smoky with a despair man could not even know.

That Deepavali eve the slaughterers were in an unusually savage mood. Was it because Mani had been given too much attention? They didn't give him a glance though he lay docilely waiting for his execution. They only had to reach out and they would have got him. No, they had to reserve him for the last.

The killing began in the late afternoon. Two men held the legs while the slaughterer turned the head until the throat bulged like a tube. The long knife went to work, moving up and down until the bleating at the first slitting turned into a rasping whistle and finally into just wind struggling to be released. The blood gushed into the yellow, enamel basin an assistant held under the neck. Then the lifeless body was thrust aside and the next goat brought to the knife.

All this while Mani had been quiet and complacent, a mass of rough and shaggy indifference. Though flies had begun to buzz over the offal now piling up on the shed floor and settled distractingly on his ears and snout, Mani didn't shake himself free from them. He turned stony eyes on the meat workers and looked away.

There was too much nakedness, fat flesh, mutton and blood everywhere. Skins had been cleanly removed from the goats' bodies as one would take off deep fur coats in readiness for spring. There was just too much neatness and reduction. A goat didn't seem worth its killing: a pile of chopped up meat on a banana leaf and a bowl of blood.

As the goat before Mani's turn shivered and lay still, an unearthly sound made the men abandon their activities and listen. No man or animal could have drawn such a deep moan from a throat. Is it an exaggeration to say, in retrospect, that the rasping boom came from some horn in the earth's centre? We were startlingly put off our tracks. Confused and surprised, we stood there in the post-afternoon light like half-formed creatures, the life-force yet to be triggered off in our bodies.

There was gritty granite dust in the air - a sudden obscuring of everything we had known. In that still, unexpected confusion we saw Mani bare his teeth in a devilish grin. Then he stood up and gazed at us through eyes that held in its fires a millenium of innocent anger. Then Mani turned and bounded towards that immeasurable green, the jungle.

Something broke and the men released from their trance, gave chase. Knives, thin blades and scrappers fell behind them like so many useless instruments of pillage. Someone grabbed a coil of muscular rope as he joined the mass that scuttled towards the disappearing animal. Shouts, cries and curses, only half-human, pursued Mani faster than could lean, young legs.

A sudden silence descended upon those remaining behind. We didn't look at each other, mesmerized as we were by the lightning disappearance of Mani. Flies, now a thickening blue blanket, clamoured voraciously at the mass of uncleaned offal. The buzzing monster seemed to consume itself more than it did the hidden intestines, stomachs and livers. The severed goats' heads looked down from a cement shelf, their expressions sculptured by death. One head, the eyes open, looked mockingly at the entranced people. Another, the eyes closed too tightly, stretched its lips into an impossible line of scorn. A third had both eyes slightly open and jaws that seemed to have been wrenched apart by surprise.

The sky had dipped into a greyer shade when the men returned with the struggling Mani, his legs trussed up with rope.

"You can't run away from us,

"We'll deal the final blow," the younger men sang as they marched with Mani to the slaughter block.

Mani stopped struggling when he saw the shed, the flies and the goats' heads. He didn't go limp; there was only a strained quietness in his body. His head was held erect, an amused indifference in his eyes. As they placed his neck on the wooden block, he made a guttural sound that resembled a human voice. The men left him tied up at the legs as they held him down for the knife.

The burly slaughterer, a peculiar viciousness filling his movements, sharpened the long knife again. His thrust against Mani's bulging neck was more than professional: his knife drew a trickle of blood even before it moved. Mani took the sawing blade without flinching and those of us whose nerves had been heightened by Mani's escape and capture, heard the knife cut into the animal's bones behind the throat.

"So you'll run away from us, will you? Try now!" the slaughterer said and pushing away the men pinning down Mani's legs, he loosened and flung away the ropes. Then, with one blow, he severed the head from the body and held it up for the people's inspection.

Mani's eyes had not closed and I thought they looked in the direction of his body. Could there be communication between the dead mind and the dead body? We almost jumped out of our skins when Mani's body stood up and tottered, shakily, towards the slaughterer. The children screamed and ran to their mothers. The burly man, still holding the head, took a few steps backwards.

"Close his eyes! Close his eyes!" the older men and women shouted but the slaughterer was too dazed to obey even such a simple command.

Then Mani's body turned and trailing blood like splotches of vengeance, hobbled towards the jungle fringe. Midway it steadied itself and now that it was just a body, all the muscles strained and stood out so that we got the impression that Mani, in death, grew in stature. The body circled - the children screamed again - and came towards us. The raw flesh at the neck looked like an eye in the severed throat and Mani cried blood as he took off into a last, spasmodic gallop around us.

"Close the eyes! Close the eyes!"

Some elderly man seized the head and massaged the eye-lids shut. Almost immediately Mani's body whirled, leapt and fell to the ground beside the slaughtering block. The man who was still holding the basin got out of the way, spilling globs of Mani's blood on his shorts and knees.

That was many, many years ago. The slaughter still continued every Deepavali eve but I didn't go near the shed. On that particular night when I watched my father's drunken form, I bristled with a vague restlessness. There come to my mind other incidents and episodes which had nothing to do with goats or their slaughter.

I am reminded of another shed, this time the smoke-house of the estate. And another man, Muniandy. Andy, for short, also for the dirty brown shorts he wore. He wore nothing else. His bare body sprouted greying hair on the chest and in the small of his back. There hung about him a perpetual burnt rubber smell and he was darker than the other workers because of being 'smoked' in his work place.

When I began to notice him, he was already in his early fifties. He was remarkable for the way he made himself inconspicuous. If he spent a long time in the smoke-house, you could hardly separate him from the smoked rubber sheets. I suspected that he often lay on the piled sheets not only for the springiness of a mattress but also for the criss-crossed lines he got on his back. Walking behind him, you imagined a smoked rubber sheet was going to some rendezvous in the dark.

Though he occupied a house not far from my own in the same row, I never knew when he came home or if he did at all. Something must be said about the way my mind worked at that time. It couldn't shut itself off to subjects and areas; it could only focus itself on something of its own choice. This shut-and-open habit carried my response to life, spasmodically. This went on until I took over conscious control when I was older.

Perhaps my mind fixed itself on Andy for no reason at all but when it did he became the most absorbing subject. So I became a follower of his movements, a sort of secret or private eye and began to work out what he was doing at all hours of the day. But the man could be elusive. Even when I kept the strictest watch, he escaped the net of my vigilance and would be in the house when I thought he was at the smoke-house.

From discreet inquiries, I came to know a little of his past. Like my father, he had come to Malaya with only a wife. For some mysterious reason the wife - a traditional Hindu woman if there was one - withdrew completely into herself and died only a few years after her arrival in the country. For a time it looked as if Andy would follow in her footsteps but recovered sufficiently to volunteer to take charge of the smoke-house. From then on this dark shed next to the estate factory became his entire world.

What went through his head? So many ideals and desires clamoured in mine, I wondered how he could live through an enforced suspension of all ambition. The smoke-house rose like a squat stake to which he allowed himself to be tethered. Had his mind become clouded by all that smoke inside the shed?

There were occasions when I went to the estate factory and helped my mother to flatten the thick, coagulated latex into lined, thin sheets. To escape the stink the chemicals and the rubber raised in the factory, I walked up to the smoke-house and stood about for a while looking at the rubber saplings that would, in a few years, produce latex. Usually Andy would be inside the shed but there were times when I caught him seated on a rough, wooden bench outside. We never talked but some communication was made when our wandering eyes crossed paths and we looked into each other briefly.

At such moments I became aware that he wasn't all that empty inside. Andy as a person was lost to my sight. He was replaced by a vague, dark shape - sometimes a lion, at other times a dragon or a muted sea or all three together - which I had no power to understand. I turned away quickly, dissatisfied with myself for at my post-adolescent stage I was being looked up to as a sage by the estate.

There were other times when he looked beyond me and into a vastness that made me feel diminished. Then I was no more than a speck of dust in that infinite conception that was his world. Was I making up thoughts for myself, having read H.G. Wells and Jules Verne and their preoccupations with space? There appeared before me, when I gazed at his sightless eyes, a billowing yellow fog behind which teemed incomprehensible shapes and bright gleams of an unknowable universe.

Did he exist only for these and for the sprawling universes *The Ramayana* and *The Mahabharata* created? (At that time I didn't pay much attention to the estate story-teller who narrated portions of these epics; they have come to figure more importantly in my thoughts only now.) I saw Andy then, a passenger in one of those time or futuristic machines, returning to his planet where eyes were not necessary and seeing was done with the whole being from some centre within oneself.

The Ramayana - Indian classic.
The Mahabharata - Indian classic.

His fleeting, ghost-like existence certainly pointed to this invisible centre. I sometimes wondered if he was in occult, secret communication with his dead wife. (Superstition was so rife on the estate that such a view wouldn't have been unorthodox.) He entered his house, the door opened swiftly by eager, waiting hands. The door then closed on a silent, intimate relationship for the duration of Andy's stay within. He seemed to need no one's company or reassurance. The cooking and the eating were conducted silently, the spirit of his wife all the time beside him. We never heard him grumble, mutter or talk to himself - signs that would have shown he needed and understood the language of our world.

And then moving, waif-like, he was at the smoke-house. He was to be found there at all hours of the day except for the one time he went into town. That happened on pay day, when he wore a white *vesti* and shirt to receive his salary and then go off to buy the month's provisions. When he returned from town, he smelled faintly of toddy. On his shoulders he carried his hemp bag containing his rations for the month. His vesti was a little crumpled at the knees as if caused by his kneeling at the temple beside the road leading to the town.

Mostly, he dissolved into the smoke and shadows of the smoke-house. Soon I began to associate that shed with his presence. If it was a bright afternoon, he was the sunlight that lay spangled on the rubber-tree logs and the grass. He was the dark grey shades on the smoke-house walls on cloudy, rainy days. On festival days such as Deepavali, he was the colourless solitude that fell on the silent smoke-house.

Andy, the smoke-house man and the smoke-house became inseparable. One gave the other life and the other robbed one of life. Wood turned into flesh; flesh turned into wood. And the two went up in smoke. Andy led an invisible, separate existence in the smoke-house. His life was consumed by the coconut-husk and rubber-tree log fire that produced the smoke. The years became ashes and the man rose out of the ashes as the bony remains of an incomplete cremation.

A younger man was needed for the job and retirement was thrust upon Andy. He had to vacate his house - not that he seemed to

---

vesti - Cloth worn from waist downwards by Indian men.

221

have lived in it - and the bonus and his savings were so meagre that he couldn't rent a place in town. He stayed for a while with his neighbour but the wife had such a virulent tongue that Andy was forced to take to the streets of the town.

There we saw him wearing his white vesti - later this garment turned into an unapproachable and dirty black - and lying on the cement walks fronting the shops. Andy soon stank so much that the Chinese shopkeepers had to kick him so as to be rid of him. I witnessed one such kicking and saw Andy receiving the blows in his mute, unprotesting way. He shuffled away to another refuge. The last I heard of him was of his body being found beside the large furnace where the town's rubbish was burned.

What I registered at that time was the indignity of Andy's and my father's deaths. Though I never noticed my father and Andy talking with each other or going out anywhere together, Andy's departure from the estate further deteriorated my father's condition. He fell more frequently into his depressed moods. He talked less and whatever he said hardly made sense. Andy's death worsened his depressions; they became prolonged. One morning he coughed up blood and the verandah was tarnished by those thin spatters of fatigue. Within hours he was dead. During the final spasms, he kept his eyes closed on a world in which he had found no home.

Andy's and my father's deaths strengthened my resolution to leave the estate but escape came only years later. There was school to be finished and a profession found. These were the years of loneliness which schoolwork wasn't enough to banish. I became a scavenger and a parasite: I fed my mind with visions culled from my reading. I read voraciously, defying the noise and the poverty of my surroundings. Sometimes my mother sat in the doorway, watching me, and there was that look in her eyes that said I too would be lost to her.

© K.S. Maniam, 1993.

THE GOSPEL ACCORDING TO GOPAL

Gopal Baratham's
Sayang and *A Candle or the Sun*
by
Salleh Ben Joned

Something seems to be really happening in Singapore. Premier Goh's announcement early in the year that Singaporeans had finally discovered fun and were looking forward to the emergence of a "culturally vibrant society" seems to be unbelievably true.

The first person to add her own "bubbles to the Singaporean champagne" (metaphor courtesy of Premier Goh) was venture-capital-consultant-poetess Anna Wong with her Lady Godiva-blessed book-launching sensation (see *As I Please*, July 3).

Now we have a neurosurgeon-novelist with two simultaneously published first novels surprisingly frank (for Singaporeans at least) in their treatment of sex, religion and politics.

Gopal Baratham, who is in his mid-50s, is a very zappy writer, and the bubbles he has added to the Singaporean champagne will no doubt dazzle readers who have only recently been released from the clutches of puritanism. I wouldn't be surprised if *Sayang* at least becomes a bestseller in the republic; it has all the right ingredients - sex, drugs and violence - and doesn't make too much demand on the reader.

If *Portnoy's Complaint* is a minor epic of masturbation, *Sayang* is a would-be epic strictly not meant for minors; it literally begins with sodomy and ends with 'dry sex', a night-long intercourse sans movement and sans orgasm. And all this sex business is intertwined with religion in a way that the average Christian will no doubt find blasphemous.

Why 'blasphemous'? Because the major characters in this 'soft porn' sentimental thriller are improbable reincarnations of the central figures in the drama of Jesus Christ, and their story is a profane re-enactment of that drama in the context of modern-day suburban Singapore.

The names of these characters and the echoing of familiar motifs of the Christian drama loudly proclaim the parallelism. And if the reader is too dense to notice it, the author makes sure he does by spelling it out for him. (There is one thing you can't fault Baratham for: he is very helpful when it comes to spelling out the meaning of his writings to you; this is true of both novels under review.)

The novel's hero, retired school teacher Joseph Samy, has been married for a long time to a woman 20 years his junior named Marie; they have a son in his 20s called Kris. The name is really from the Malay word for that infamous dagger; it's chosen with the idea that it'd be mistaken as short for *kristian*.

So, we get Joseph, Marie, Kris. And virgin birth too? Oh, yes. Marie or Ri is one of those women who "enjoy it up the back way"; she got mysteriously pregnant by Joe without his ever penetrating her the normal way. And she insisted on remaining a virgin until Kris was born, thus making him literally rip his way into the world.

Kris turns out to be a son without a mission that leads to him being literally crucified by the drug goons whose operations he had tried to expose. There is also a Peter, nicknamed Rock (Really? You've got to be joking!); this Peter the Rock actually does in this novel what that other Peter the Rock did in the Bible. And the Devil? Who else but the leader of the drug syndicate, a hazy half-character named Logam. And the Holy Ghost? Someone called Gopal - I think. Christ!

There is a lot of f---ing in this book, but as Holy Ghost Gopal would no doubt say, they are necessary accompaniments to the real business of the book. Or, in the words of one of his characters who actually f---ed her way out of a guilty conscience, "I'm not f---ing well just talking about f---ing!"

About what else then? "*Sayang*" (love), of course. That's the gospel of the book; that's what all the sodomy, the fellatio, the crucifixion, the dry sex are all about. All of them have to happen before Joe Samy can penetrate the mysteries of "*sayang*".

Why the Malay word? Because the English "love" is hopelessly inadequate to be the vessel of the Gopal Gospel. And what is "*sayang*" according to this gospel? Hear this: "*sayang*" is a "a love bound to sadness, a tenderness trembling on the edge of tears", something that is "only possible between creatures born to perish", whose value is inseparable from transience itself. What a revelation!

Stuck all night long inside Ri who is dying of AIDS, (yes, Sayang is very up-to-date), Joe the compulsive fornicator and sentimentalist affirms that once you have discovered true love called "*sayang*", the need for orgasm is transcended. From sodomy to "*sayang*" via crucifixion and AIDS is one tortuous journey for Joe Samy. In the words of a de-frocked priest he befriends in Thailand: "The ways of God, Joseph, are not just mysterious; they are ... downright obscene."

Reading *Sayang* was quite a frustrating exercise for me; it was like having one coitus interruptus after another. Gopal Baratham, I think, has a talent for comic writing; there are enough hints of it in this novel. But every time the comic impulse raises its funny head, he knocks it. *Sayang* lah, Encik Baratham! (What a pity, Mr Baratham!)

Joe Samy, who is the narrator of his own story, is probably also the author's mouthpiece. With all his imperfections and charming naivety, he at times sounds like a sort of aged but still potent Catholic Portnoy from Singapore, especially in the beginning.

The tone of the opening chapter, the way Joe talks about his wife's preference for "the back way", and all that virgin birth business, leads one to expect an irreverent romp through the sacred territory of Catholic mythology. Instead, we get sentimental droolings about "*sayang*" in between stretches of self-indulgent sex scenes, improbable talk of crufixion and even more improbable rumours of resurrection.

As to the supposedly satanic figure, Logam, he simply fizzles out into nothingness - which is his proper territory.

Sayang is thus a potentially comic novel that gets smothered by sentimentality, misplaced blasphemy, compulsive solemnity and pages of sheer pretentiousness. If only its author had trusted the creative instinct which I suspect he has, it's just possible that we might have got a Rabelaisian romp of a book.

A Candle or the Sun is a novel that is truer to the author's instinct than *Sayang*, but, unhappily, far from perfect.

It is marred by Baratham's incorrigible compulsion to explain almost everything, even to the point of repeating himself. There is also the appearance of patchwork in the structuring of its material, most clearly evident in the use of previously published short stories now supposedly written by its writer-hero.

The subject is the sensitive matter of religion and politics in an island paradise where conscience and freedom are drowned by affluence. The themes are the interconnected ones of political commitment and indifference, of resistance and submission, of compartmentalising one's life into the morally compromising and the morally innocent.

The fact that a political novel of this nature, so closely reflective of recent political events in the republic, was actually written, published and allowed to circulate speaks well of the literary situation in Singapore.

The novel, according to a report, was actually completed in 1985, but no Singapore publisher dared to touch it. It was eventually brought out in London by a relatively unknown publisher.

The date of the novel's completion is worth noting, because its political plot about a group of church workers conspiring to incite resistance against the state uncannily prefigured a more or less similar plot that actually happened two years later (the so-called Marxist incident of 1987); that is if the author had not revised it after the incident.

The interweaving of private and public dilemmas in the story of its writer hero, Hernando Perera, is quite ably done. And in the portrait of Samson Alagaratnam, "a highly-placed official in the Ministry of Culture" who speaks in the manic idiom and accent of a disc jockey, Gopal Baratham shows his skill as a satirist.

It is Samson, Hernando's childhood friend, who presents the desperate hero with the temptation of security through betrayal - betrayal of both friendship and his vocation as writer. But Hernando lives to discover that one cannot serve both God and Mammon, and that to think life can be morally compartmentalised is a delusion.

In a number of ways, *A Candle or the Sun* is a more satisfying work than *Sayang*. Both, however, suggest that Baratham's real talent probably lies in comedy and satire. Let's hope he agrees with this diagnosis and confirms it in his next novel.

© Salleh Ben Joned, 1993.
With the kind permission of the *New Straits Times*.

GOPAL BARATHAM
Karma
A Short Story

Rattlesnakes are full of surprises. At their rear end they have a noisy apparatus which distracts enemies and causes them to strike at their tails instead of their heads, where their brains...and their fangs are. As with other snakes they have no noses and smell with their tongues, so when you see a snake gliding across the grass, his tongue darting ahead of him, he is not trying to frighten you: he is merely taking the air. The most surprising thing about these creatures, however, is their capacity for love. When they mate the male inserts his bifid penis, which resembles two light-bulbs stuck together, into the female and they stay wrapped around each other for nine whole days. During this period, they seek neither food nor water, nor do they appear to excrete, for they have a common orifice, called the cloaca, which houses both their genitals and their organs of excretion. Using the orifice for one function precludes their using it for the other. Such commitment to love is difficult to find anywhere. When mating is done the penis is withdrawn into the cloaca and it becomes impossible to distinguish male from female. This story, however, is not about reptiles. It's about humans.

It is a story of Ganesh and Gita. Ganesh resembled the elephant god of his name. He was a stocky fellow, with a low hair-line and an enormous nose that led his face. Gita, on the other hand, was a song, beautiful and slender as a note played on a single-reed instrument. They were the most improbable of couples.

At the time when Ganesh and Gita lived, men believed in God and God believed in Man. That is to say, God deceived Man at every turn, played cruel tricks on him but, nevertheless, called on Man to serve His unknowable purpose. Like the people around them, Ganesh and Gita were Hindus: devout Hindus. They believed in the cycle of birth, death and re-birth, the spiral of *karma*, which if you lived your life correctly carried you upwards towards everlasting enlightenment but if you didn't dragged you down to the level of beasts.

As soon as they set eyes on each other and, much to their dismay, Ganesh and Gita fell in love. Theirs wasn't the eye-evading, flower-throwing love that culminated in day-dreams and poetry. It was a love that demanded sweat and smells, sticky secretions and the exchange of unmentionable body fluids. Even with God around this would have been alright. Except for one thing. They were married. But not to each other.

As a young lad, Ganesh had married the bride appointed by his parents. And he couldn't complain about the girl chosen for him. Vasantha was as light and sprightly as spring rain. Gita had done likewise and her man, Prem, was a model of propriety and husbandly love. So they had no reason, no excuse, no case that even a Californian court would countenance to find each other. But find each other they did.

And, when they did, they couldn't believe what they had found.

It seemed absurd that flesh could sing so sweetly that time stopped; incredible that the circumscribed pleasures of Eros could make them cling to each other for days, nights and days again. Dripping, dancing and in positions that would have made *houris* sweat they spent time, if one could call what felt like eternity time, in a pleasure that flowed between them like the swing of the sea.

But they were good Hindus. Religious folk. And like all religious folk they questioned what God intended by causing them to come together. Joyfulness could never be its own reward.

"God is telling us that a child wants to be born," said Ganesh in his simple way. "He is telling us that out of the unformed elements of the universe a life is crying out for an existence. We are the vehicles of that purpose."

"Then why not a child from you and Vasantha or one from me and Prem?" Gita questioned. "That would be proper and it would not offend the code of *dharma?*"

They questioned even as they clung to each, questioned even when breathless with pleasure. But questions unanswered are more damaging than those attended to. They erode joy, interrupt ecstasy.

Once, even before the ebb of their pleasure was complete, Ganesh, suggested, in the touching but somewhat stupid way that elephants have, "It could be that the astrologers were wrong when they matched horoscopes. It could be that we were designed for each other and would be husband and wife but for a man's misreading of the stars."

228

Gita was not satisfied with this. She was a song and songs, as we all know, work in a roundabout way. So, even as she rejoiced in her love for Ganesh, she searched for its true meaning, worried about its significance.

Then, as though God had intended it, she found in a magazine an article on rattlesnakes.

"It is clear," she said, as she lowered herself on to her lover, "that in our past existence, we were rattlesnakes. Some memory of this remains. That is why we are as we are." She continued when Ganesh was securely inside her. "You and I have been good Hindus. We have, except for this one transgression, obeyed all the dictates of *dharma*. All God can do to punish us for our present failing is to return us to our former state. When we are born again, we will be born as rattlesnakes. And is that not what we really want?"

"How can we be sure that when we die God will return us as rattlesnakes?" asked Ganesh. Worry made his tiny eyes wide.

"We can't be sure but we have to trust in God." Gita felt her lover begin to shrivel inside her. She put her hand over his mouth, moved a little and made him firm again before she let him speak.

"And to return as rattlesnakes...?" Fear at what Gita was about to suggest made it impossible for him to complete his question.

"We must die now and go back to our former lives."

"Kill ourselves, you mean?" asked Ganesh, now clearly terrified.

"Yes."

Songs persuade and it didn't take Gita long to convince her lover that the course she planned was the right one.

The rains came and the river rose. Rose till its muddy waters invaded the huts of the poor living on its banks. Gita, dressed in a plain white sari, and Ganesh, in a yellow silk dhoti, hurled themselves into the swollen river. At their birth, the astrologer had warned that water would be dangerous to them and they should never go near it. Because of this neither had learned to swim. The astrologer was, of course, right. Water is, indeed, dangerous to non-swimmers. Ganesh and Gita drowned.

* * *

The desert in Arizona is hot and arid. The air is so dry that human skin flakes and becomes like scales. Gita was glad that she was a snake. Her belly was heavy with eggs and she was aching for a male who could make them come to life. Nevertheless, she waited till the cool of dusk before she emerged from under the rock where she had found shade.

She knew she had to be careful. She yearned for a male. But not any male. She yearned for Ganesh. He was around, somewhere, and she would find him. Of that she was sure. But she had to be careful to avoid the attention of other males in heat. Whatever the eggs told her body to do, it would be pointless spending nine days entwined with a stranger. So she avoided the flat easy paths that randy young rattlesnakes took and stuck to the rocky high-ground, even though the stones grated against her full belly and threatened to tear up her soft underscales.

Dawn was beginning to break and Gita had almost given up hope, when she found him. He was lying against a rock. She shot out her tongue to get the male smell that would make her orifice damp and the eggs in her belly churn. Nothing happened. But she knew it was Ganesh. Her Ganesh. So she slithered across and began wrapping herself across his body.

Ganesh seemed disturbed by her action. Almost ashamed. But Gita was not put off by this. He had always been a little shy. She pressed her damp orifice against his and began the gentle gyration that would cause his penis to protrude. She couldn't wait for the bulb of gristle to spring out and lock into her opening. Nothing emerged. She flicked out her tongue to smell him again. There was no sharp male smell about him. Instead the odour that she got was exactly the same as that which came from her own body. As *karma* promised, they had been reborn as rattlesnakes. But as female rattlesnakes.

As always, God has the last laugh.

© Gopal Baratham, 1994

Gopal Baratham is a neurosurgeon and has published four books in Singapore and one in the United Kingdom.

GOPAL BARATHAM
An excerpt of
A Candle Or The Sun

one

I am at work before anyone else not because I am conscientious or particularly like my job but simply because it is the best way I have of keeping Chuang from ruining my day. Chuang is the general manager of Benson's, the oldest department store in Singapore. I run the furniture department. When I first started with Benson's five years ago, I used to arrive around nine like everyone else. Invariably Chuang was already in the department rearranging the sets we had on display.

I would come in to find him chanting, "Latest statistics has proof that changes is what peoples most want to have." Then, nodding sagely, he would add. "Variety is one of the spices of life, ah?"

When I remained silent, he would ask, "You getting my points, Hernando?"

If there is one things in the world that really upsets me, it is being called Hernando. I can still remember the horror of discovering, aged five, that I was not just Hernie as I had supposed but Hernando Perera. "Why? why? why?" I wailed, punching my mother's body and kicking at her shins. When she did explain, several years later, I was the worse for the knowledge. My parents, Fred and Clara, had fallen in love while dancing to a tango called "Hernando's Hideaway" and held the tune responsible for all that transpired. Knowing this, I was unable to rid myself of the belief that I had been conceived to the rhythms of a tango and every time someone called me Hernando I was reminded of this.

I had for years agreed with all Chuang's suggestions (hoping the sooner to be rid of him) until I discovered how simple it was to avoid his early morning attentions altogether. I simply arrived an hour before he did, sent for the workmen and began rearranging the furniture displays myself. By the time Chuang came in, the job was almost finished and it required a much braver man than our general manager to order the workmen to redo a job they had just completed.

I take no special pride in running Benson's furniture department and would not have minded Chuang's intrusions except that it took him several hours to decide on the rearrangement he wanted, hours during which I was expected to hang around offering suggestions and murmuring approval. Not only did this waste my day but when he finally left I usually found myself no longer in the mood to do what I really liked doing, which was to sit at my desk and dream, occasionally jotting down an idea, an incident or a sequence of words I might find use for in one of my stories.

I don't write many stories, though there are always several buzzing and bumping around in my head, rather like flies behind a window-pane. I usually write when the buzzing gets intolerable or when a plot refuses to unravel itself till I pin it to paper. Once a story has actually been written, I tend to lose interest in it. It becomes an object which I may like or dislike but which has an existence of its own. I suspect that women feel this way about their grown-up children. I could find out by asking my mother, I suppose, except that she probably regards me as a tango come to grief. Had I known how much my stories would come to direct the course of my life I would have regarded them more seriously. On that morning, secure in the cool basement of the furniture department, I could only see them as little indulgences which I used to fill an existence in which not too much happened.

I sent for the workmen as soon as I got in. It was early December and I had arranged, using our latest dining-room suite as the centre piece, a Christmas dinner tableau. I had situated this in the darkest corner of the furniture department so as to heighten the effect of cosiness produced by the artificial fire. Opposite the fire a false window looked on to a painted snow-covered landscape. To increase the effect of winteriness I had lowered the room temperature several degrees and placed rotating fans at strategic spots to provide chilly drafts. Thus I succeeded in justifying the thick carpets and heavy curtains with which I had decorated the room. Early in my working life I had discovered that salesmanship consisted not of providing people with what they needed, but with what was essential to their dreams. I was confident that our dining-room suite, complete with carpets, curtains and an artificial fireplace, would shortly be snapped up by people occupying oven-hot semis in the newer and, as yet, treeless housing estates on the island. The possibility of winter is essential to the happiness of people living in the tropics.

Chuang bounced into the room just as the men were finishing. "Very excellent," he said, clapping his hands. "I think, Hernando..."

I gave him a look of such venom that he stopped talking and stepped backwards. It took him a moment to readjust his expression before he again bounced forward clapping his hands.

"Very excellent, Perera," he began. "Chinese say pupil's supremacy is master's reward." He smiled to himself and bowed slightly to acknowledge my gratitude. "The times I spend for you in your junior days, not wasted now, ah. So tiresome I became that sometimes I could not stand, but not wasted, see."

He pranced around the room, nodding approval, rubbing his hands together, a full fixed smile on his face.

"Nothing to do to improve," he said, adjusting the artificial fireplace slightly and drawing the curtains a fraction before he left.

With Chuang gone, I began to settle down. I placed on my desk several design magazines opened at random, a file containing invoices and a pocket calculator. On a pad beside me I jotted down words, phrases and a complicated system of arrows •and hieroglyphics by which I plotted the course of my stories. I was now ready to enjoy my dreams, some of which I might write down. Only very occasionally did Ahmad, our senior salesman, disturb me with a request to authorize payment by cheque or to deal with a difficult customer or a VIP.

I resented these intrusions, the more perhaps because I had been working for some time on a character in whose life there were none. I was trying to fashion a man so totally liberated that he had nothing to do with events outside his imagination. Without friends, job, family, needs, his mind was freed to roam where it pleased. My man would hear sounds but have no need to speak. The images that filtered through his eyes he would distil into their essences and with these he would build his visions. Gradually he would shed all the body's demands - hunger, thirst, lust - until he was pure awareness, enjoying consciousness for itself. I leaned back in my chair and closed my eyes. It would be lovely but was it possible? I began wondering. A Hindu mystic, ascetic, the world of forsworn, taking to the Himalayas, would hardly have enough around him to make pure consciousness worthwhile. Or would he? Would the past he had forsaken help or hinder?

"Mr Perera," said Ahmad, touching my shoulder, "telephone."

"Ahmad," I said, opening my eyes very slowly then looking sternly up at him, "you are the senior salesman here and quite qualified to deal with all telephonic enquiries."

"But she asks for you by name, sir. Very urgent she says."

"Who says, Ahmad?"

"The lady, *tuan*." Then, getting the point of my question, he added, "She says her name is Su-May, Mr Perera."

"All right, Ahmad," I said. "You get about your work. I'll take the call on my extension."

I was surprised. Su-May rarely phoned. At the outset of our affair a year ago I had been at pains to explain that the last thing I was looking for was a torrid, nerve-racked romance replete with anxious phone calls and unnecessary trysts. She had laughed and agreed. She said she was nineteen and had got over that kind of things years ago. Our initial meetings had indeed been marvellously light-hearted and inconsequential but somehow, and quite contrary to our intentions, tenderness and passion crept into bed beside us and sweetened our coupling.

I swallowed several times before picking up the receiver.

"Perera speaking," I said in a deliberately well-modulated voice.

"Hern," she said breathlessly, "can I see you this evening?"

She sounded so vulnerably close that it was with some difficulty that I managed to inject a note of irritation into my voice. "God, no, Su-May. My parents are coming over for dinner tonight and you know how upset Sylvie will be if I'm not home early."

"Oh," she said, her voice shrinking. "I'm sorry." Su-May was very sensitive about any suggestion that our affair upset things between me and my wife, Sylvie.

"And you know how I hate you calling me at the office." I could just make out the small but sharp intake of breath and, without my quite wishing it, let my voice soften. "Won't tomorrow do, darling?"

"I suppose...but I was hoping..."

"Can't we talk on the phone then, Su-May?"

"It's not easy to explain things...on the phone."

"Just give me a rough idea what it's about."

234

"So difficult like this, Hern," she said. "No problem when you are with me and I can touch you. Then you understand but like this it's no good. You know, Hern..."

Suddenly I was afraid, and to quell my fear I joked: "I know what this is all about, Su-May," I said, "it's another man, isn't it?" I forced myself to laugh out loud. "You found yourself a nice young man. You want to chuck up old me and marry Mr Right? OK, you have my blessing but you must invite me to the wedding." The silence at the other end of the phone was so complete that I thought we had been cut off. "Su-May, are you still there?"

"Yes, Hern." And after a slight pause, "Yes, my love. Can you meet me tomorrow then, around six?"

"OK, where?"

"Up in Tampines. You know...where you used to pick me up when we first started."

"Why there?" I asked, my voice rising. "For heaven's sake, Su-May, don't say you've taken up with that mumbo-jumbo bunch again?"

When we first met, Su-May had been deeply involved with an unorthodox Christian group styling themselves the Children of the Book. I had assumed, obviously wrongly, that our adulterous affair would make it impossible for her to continue with them.

"Hern," she said, her voice very steady. "I never left the Children, you know. Stopped talking about them, that's all." In a voice now almost gay with relief, she said, "See you around six tomorrow." And hung up.

Su-May's call upset me more than I was prepared to admit. At the start of our affair I had seen her often enough in the company of her religious friends, young people in their teens or twenties who bubbled with a vivacity I could not remember. I resented this as much as I did their slim, clean bodies smelling like babies fresh from a bath. They laughed often and without cause, frequently tickling a member of the group slow to join the chorus of giggles. The leader was a lad named Peter Yu whom they jokingly referred to as "The Reverend". Apart from his being a little more intense than his fellows, there was nothing that distinguished him from the other Children, and I had not discovered in what way he was looked upon as a leader. When Su-May was with the group there was an enormous gulf between us. I was excluded from the secret that was the basis of their mirth, and untouched by the wonder they found in each other and the world. I attributed this to the difference in our ages. Today, I told myself, ten years is a long time, the equivalent of a generation, a time-gap that can never quite be bridged. But my explanation never quite satisfied me. Moreover, there was another aspect of the whole business that bothered me. Born a Catholic, I had become a resolute atheist and yet could not, whenever I saw Su-May with her religious friends, help thinking of the lilies of the field who were more glorious than Solomon.

After Su-May's phone call it was impossible to think of my story. The character I dreamed of had, freed from the directives of his body, possessed a sort of biological weightlessness that enabled him to do with his sensation as his imagination dictated. How could I write about such a person when I myself was burdened with jealousy and trapped in doubt? Everything around me brings me back to my situation. A group of schoolgirls gathers round Ahmad, who is slightly deaf. He obviously does not understand what they want. They burst into giggles. I think of the Children. They, too, laugh a lot when I'm around. Perhaps at me. But why? Have I some mannerism, some deformity, some obnoxious secretion of which I am unaware? I pick up a Christmas card with a picture of Jesus on it. It is a young Jesus, a sexual Jesus but a Jesus possessing a formidable gentleness. He reminds me very much of Peter Yu. Suddenly I know what the Children find so funny about me. Peter and Su-May are lovers. Have been for years. But Su-May's affair with me was no infidelity to Peter. Oh, no! She had, in fact, begun it at his instigation, as an act of charity towards an older man terrified of the passing of the years. I had completely missed the point of the exercise. No wonder the Children laughed...

By afternoon I had quietened sufficiently to begin thinking of the story again. Perhaps my own bondage told me that my man had to be totally aloof if he was to allow his imagination to respond freely to the promptings of his senses. But how could such a situation come about? Taste, touch, sight, smell competed with one another to dominate consciousness. Linked to these were the body's responses, which were bound to interrupt the process of fantasy. Awareness without strings was only possible in science-fiction, in disembodied brains floating in glass jars. But that was not the kind

236

of story I was trying to write. Somewhere in the back of my mind was a situation I had read or heard about which would solve my problem. What it was I could not for the life of me remember. That evening as I made my way circuitously back home, ambling along side roads flanked by the old houses which I love, I cursed Su-May, Peter Yu, the Children of the Book and everything that had interfered with my exploring a theme that was beginning to interest me.

As I entered my flat, the smell of cooking hit me. My mother was making a prawn sambal. The prawns fried in onions, tamarind and red chillies acquired a burning, all-pervading flavour that simultaneously attacked nose and eyes. The pungency of the confection, however, was only an alibi for my tears. The smell of prawn sambal cooking took me far back into my childhood, to the days when I used to hang about my mother's skirts while she cooked. Now as I stood outside my own kitchen, sniffing the prawns beginning to brown, I wondered why smells often took me to the edge of tears and why they led so often to the days I had spent alone with my mother, days even before Sylvie had begun to be a part of our family.

Abandoned in infancy by her Chinese mother, Sylvie had been left to the mercies of her Indian father, who comforted himself for his wife's desertion with whisky and a succession of mistresses Sylvie referred to as aunts. A year younger than me and living two doors from us, she quite naturally became the daughter my mother wanted but never had. Very early on, the two women decided that Sylvie and I should marry, and I was given neither choice in the matter nor a chance to protest. In adolescence the rowdy games of childhood gave way to erotic ones and, when we finally fell into bed together, it was more an acknowledgement of our changed needs than a consummation of fierce passion. Now in our thirties, we acted like a couple who had a lifelong marriage behind them and, in a manner of speaking, we had. Not that I have any cause to complain. Sylvie, a lovely hybrid, with a laugh that bubbled from deep inside her, was the most companionable of bedfellows and knew me well enough to treat everything about me with matter-of-factness that only genuine intimacy permits. And, what was more, she talked in mismatched clichés which gave her conversation a jokiness and ambiguity I found intriguing.

As soon as I entered the kitchen, she stopped chattering with my mother and kissed me, putting her right hand against my chest as she always did. (A hundred years ago I had asked her if she did that to stop me getting too close. "It's the currents," she had said. "I make another contact so they can go round and round between us and never have to stop for breath.")

I embraced my mother and asked, "Pa not here yet?" I missed the smell of cigarette smoke that always accompanied my father and was usually strong enough to overcome even cooking smells.

"Ssh!" said Sylvie, touching my lips.

"He's resting," whispered my mother. "Pa's not been too well lately."

"Flu?"

She shook her head, her face suddenly bleak. "Only the good Lord knows what it is, Hern."

"Tell him, Ma," said Sylvie.

"You know the smoker's cough Pa's had for years?" said my mother, her manner as subdued as her voice. "Well, it's been getting worse and recently he's been coughing up..." her voice became hardly audible and she paused for a moment before she said, "blood."

"Good God!" I said, forgetting to keep my voice down. "What does the doctor say? What about having X-rays and things done?"

"The doctor says it could be quite serious." Her voice was low and accusing. "He says there are suspicious markings on the X-rays." She nodded slowly several times.

"For heaven's sake, Ma, what does all this mean?"

"More tests and things," she said flatly.

"You know what doctors are, Hern," said Sylvie softly. "They punch a hole in your boat and watch you sinking as your confidence runs out."

"With no straw to clutch on to," I said, laughingly, elaborating on her already incomprehensible metaphor.

"Clever boy," said Sylvie, patting my arm.

"He goes into hospital next week," said my mother, dragging us away from our complex word game. "For more tests."

"Where's he now?" I asked.

"Resting," said my mother.

"In my work room?" I asked, my voice rising.

"No, dear," said Sylvie soothingly. "In our bedroom." She touched my cheek. "You get on with your typing if you must, but shut the door so you don't wake Pa."

Sylvie always referred to my writing as my typing. In part this was disparaging, an expression of her resentment at being excluded from an act in which I so often engaged. Mainly, however, it was proof of her matter-of-factness. Whether or not I was a writer was arguable. A few of my stories had attracted comment but I was, in no sense, established or well known. By talking of typing rather than writing, she was describing an action, not a purpose and was, in her own way, protecting me from my expectations. Comforted by these thoughts, I embraced Sylvie and my mother together.

"I'll be very quiet," I said. "Call me, but only when dinner's on the table."

She did - twice. I was by then so involved in the story that she had to knock on my door and shout, "The food's icing over," before I could tear myself away.

My father, usually garrulous the way retired schoolteachers often are, was silent, chewing his food with a thoroughness that betrayed his lack of enjoyment of it.

"Feeling better for your rest, Dad?" I tried.

"A trifle," he said. "Just a trifle."

"Do you have pain with the cough?"

"Nothing agonizing," he said, smiling to convince me. "Just creaky aches and pains and a feeling of intense tiredness." He smiled again. "So much like sadness."

"They'll have you right as rain soon enough, my sweet-heart," said my mother, uttering one of her gutsy little laughs.

"Quite right you are, doll," he said. "As always," he added gruffly. He had on his face a look meant to indicate that, whatever his fate, she could be sure he would see it through with courage.

My parents Fred and Clara Perera had met, fallen in love, lived and would die in the spell of the films and music of the 1950s. Even as they talked, I could see my mother rehearse the moment when she finds out that father's disease is incurable. "How long has he, Doc?" she would ask. The doctor, grey-haired, his face lined with the suffering-he-has-had-to-share but nevertheless retaining its kindliness, would say with a wisdom that transcends mere personal experience, "It is not the number of days we have left but the use we make of them that matters." She knew she would be smiling and brave to the end so that Father would never know that she knew. And my Father would, right up to the bitter end, remain his gruff, kindly self, sneaking grimaces of pain but only when he thought Mother wasn't looking, sparing her the agony of knowing. Yet deep down each one knew the other knew and their pretence was but another aspect of their love. Then suddenly would come the news: there had been a terrible mistake, a mix-up of X-rays. The nightmare is over and staring into each other's eyes they find the happiness-ever-after as the camera zooms out, leaving two figures alone but blissful in a landscape of unending green.

"Right as rain they'll have you," said my mother, reaching out for Father's hand. "Just you wait and see."

My parents left after dinner and I returned to my writing. I was more than halfway through and the story was by now telling itself, incidents racing ahead of the words I had for them. At each pause in my typing, Sylvie called to ask if I had finished. I answered with a fresh clatter of activity on the machine. Her intrusions, though mildly disturbing, moved me to write faster. After a while she stopped calling out.

The aroma of my mother's cooking had started me off on the tale of a man who had lost all his senses except his sense of smell. The sensations that came to him through his nose made no demands on him. Instead, each carried with it a fragment of his past which, undistracted, he relived in its original intensity. The man I wrote about was very old and I called my story "Roses in December". By the time I finished, the traffic and other city noises had died away. It was early for the birdsong that, swelling as it did from the concrete heart of Singapore, awoke me every morning but the breeze that preceded daybreak was beginning. This came from the sea as a steady cool breath on which were superimposed shorter, sharper bursts. A little like applause, I thought, clipping together the typewritten pages.

ALEX LING
Excerpt of
Golden Dreams of Borneo

They left the Rajah behind in his chambers to write his famous 'Rajah Diary', his legacy to future historians.

Rajah Charles's approach to writing mirrored that of his contemporary Lord Acton, taking a heavily factual approach. However, historians are an argumentative breed and not all the events he recorded would be considered 'historical'; there would always be a debate as to the facts he selected, as well as between the subjective and objective schools of thought.

Rajah Brooke did not care for the scientific interpretations and meanings of history, and even less for academic and high flown philosophies of history. History for him was not a continuous 'process of interaction between the historian and his facts...including dialogue between the present and the past', but selective 'factual' events considered to be 'objective', important and historical.

Stephen had a more developed concept of history; the real meaning of history could be discovered in history itself - in the objective record of past events. One's interpretation of and views on history would depend on one's basic idea of the nature and destiny of man, and one's conception of man's relation to God, and of the causes and effects at work in the mortal world as a whole.

But Stephen admired *Ten Years in Sarawak* for the industry and perseverance it demonstrated. He similarly admired the Rajah's efforts to study French and recite French poetry, even though he had a horrible and peculiar accent, despite numerous lessons from his French tutor, Monsieur Poncelet. Certainly, linguistics and history were not his forces.

Half an hour after Stephen's departure a dull thump at the solid dark-red meranti door was followed by louder knocks.

'Come in, sit down,' bade the Rajah, looking towards the Sea Dayak warrior, Penghulu Munan and then Mr Bampfylde, one of his most senior officers, who had just returned from Simanggang in the Second Division a few days ago. 'Yes, now what's the problem?'

'Your Highness, it's about your letter giving permission to

Penghulu Munan to bring his mother and some of his relatives from Krian [Kalaka] to settle down in the Rajang Basin,' briefly explained Bampfylde, always feeling as nervous as a mousedeer in front of Rajah Charles, the Lion of Sarawak.

'Yes, what about it?'

'It's not clear, Your Highness!'

'Who the devil says so?' The Rajah stood up behind the desk, pushing away his diary, his brow furrowed.

'Demetrius Bailey! Our Resident in the Second Division wanted certain clarifications.'

'Clarifications! Bailey always does! The permission granted is as clear as the water from Matang Mountain. What else does he want?' Demetrius' stubborn attitude was incomprehensible. Despite the numerous faults and blunders of Demetrius, the Rajah knew well that he was the only graduate in his service, being an ex-Jesus, Cambridge, man. Charles Hose, the Resident in Baram, and Vyner, the Rajah's son, had failed to complete their studies at Cambridge.

'Firstly, the definition of relatives?'

'Relatives! Good God! Do I really have to incorporate a preamble on interpretations? Bailey is always so superpedantic! Just tell him anyone related to Penghulu Munan under their Adat law; for all I care, everyone he chooses in the nearby region or related in any way.'

'Then, how many families, Your Highness? Penghulu Munan is thinking of about four hundred families. Bailey thought that would induce a wholesale migration to the Rajang Basin. In that event, it will be bad and against our normal policy on the control of migration.'

'No, no, Penghulu Munan...now, you tell me really, how many families you really intend to move?' the irritated Rajah asked him in the Sea Dayak language.

'About forty families, Tuan Rajah. Cheyne Ah Fook, the court writer, deliberately said four hundred families to Tuan Resident Bailey, to mislead him and make life difficult for me.'

The Rajah knew Cheyne was always protective and in collusion with Bailey who, out of sheer frustration, once imposed a fine of $20 in court on Seng Kim, a shopkeeper from Simanggang bazaar, who catered to the Fort Alice mess, for the unforgiveable and heinous offence of running out of soda water!

The Rajah gave his final approval. 'Well in that case, move thirty families! That's more than enough. Isn't that right, Penghulu Munan?'

'Terima kasih, Tuan Rajah, that's enough.'

'Now, Penghulu Munan, tell me about our rebellious ringleader in Batang Lupar, Bantin. What is he up to now?' The Rajah's moist eyes suddenly glistened with keen interest.

'What else! That arrogant and hard-headed enemy is carrying out sporadic surprise attacks against and plundering the friendly Dayaks along the upper river.'

'I see...yes, it's all Bailey's fault.' The Rajah grew angry. 'Bailey has antagonised Bantin by imposing a severe import tax on the brassware he imported from Dutch Borneo. He forced Bantin and his people to stay along the main river. Well, if peaceful negotiation is of no use, I think we should prepare an expedition and punish Bantin more severely.'

This volte-face stunned Bampfylde into a gasp of horrified surprise: 'Your Highness, I thought you said a few years ago, actually in front of Penghulu Munan that "the days of warlike expeditions were past...it is no longer required that they should be great warriors".'

'Well, we must review the situation,' explained the Rajah, 'New circumstances often force us to be more circumspect...if Bantin has indeed changed his mind after smoking the peace pipe with us, why shouldn't we retaliate against his raids? We have sent Penghulu Munan to talk to him on several occasions but to no avail. Anyway, Mr Bampfylde, you may leave now, as I want a quiet chat with Munan.'

Bampfylde left them undisturbed, wondering why the Rajah wanted to be so secretive and so pro-native, and worse, so pro-Sea Dayak!

'Penghulu Munan, don't worry. You will launch an expedition from the Rajang side and bring your fighters towards Batang Lupar to attack Bantin from that side of the river as shown on this map, and Bailey will attack upwards from the lower Batang Lupar. This pincer attack will give Bantin the shock of his life! He won't know what hit him! This is top secret, don't let anyone know. Not even Bailey nor Deshon, our Resident in the Third Division. Don't let your wife nor your mother know. Nobody. Is that clear?'

'Yes, Tuan Rajah!'

'Our Resident Bailey, in Simanggang, is presently not in good health, and I will send him to Europe on furlough after the successful expedition. I'll let you know the exact date of the expedition. Be patient when you deal with Bailey.'

'Yes...'

This would be the first time that Rajah Charles had permitted a non-European officer to lead an expedition against the rebellious Dayaks.

The Rajah knew the Dayaks' minds, feelings, and inspirations, much better than those of his own countrymen. A hundred times better. Only Rajah Charles could achieve this quality of intimacy between a ruler and his trusted Sea Dayak subjects; all this while, he was aware that there had been no love lost between Penghulu Munan and Bailey ever since Bailey appointed Ampang over Munan's brother, Antau, as the Penghulu. Then a bitter dispute arose between them on the interpretation of Adat law imposing restrictions on the old jungle whereby it was not allowed to be felled for farming but only for cutting timber for house building. Penghulu Munan and Bailey, both arrogant, had nearly come to blows on a boat near Fort Alice.

Despite this contretemps, the Rajah admired the warrior-like quality in Penghulu Munan, one of nature's gentlemen, who was daring, hardworking, and always walked with that air of confidence. The appearance of being gentlemen was the quality that Rajah Charles always looked for when recruiting natives and expatriates for his service. As far as he was concerned, Irishmen were not gentlemen, for some unknown reason; New Zealanders and Australians were inclined, more often than not, to be wild; and Americans were the crudest, most big-headed and ruthless of all speculators, with the exception of American Methodist missionaries.

The old Rajah knew that only Penghulu Munan was more than a match for Bantin. 'Only Dayaks can attack Dayaks to make them feel it is in any way a punishment' had always been the Rajah's philosophy. The Rajah remembered the Chinese idea of 'using poison to neutralise poison' in raising Sea Dayak levies.

'I'll lead an expedition against Bantin, if necessary,' said the Rajah.

'No need, Tuan Rajah, I'll fight for you until Bantin is captured or killed.'

ALEX LING was born in Bukit Lan, Sibu, which lies on the Rejang River, in 1946. He has graduate and postgraduate degrees in law from Cambridge University, England. He later became involved in the timber business in Indonesia and Malaysia. At the time of writing, he is the Managing Director of the Bukit Young Goldmine Sdn Bhd and Chairman of the Hock Hua Bank (Sabah) Bhd.

He has a special interest in the history of gold, its discovery and influence on history. In writing this historical novel, he had access to original material, unpublished official records and interviewed some of those involved and their descendants.

Published by:
POLYNESIA TIMBER SERVICES
PTE. LTD.
79 ROBINSON ROAD
25-05 CPF BUILDING
SINGAPORE 0106
H'bk. MYD $60
ISBN 981-00-4805- X

JOHN MADELL
Cover Story on Claire Tham's
Saving The Rainforest

Claire Tham's *Saving the Rainforest* is the second collection of her stories to be published. Like the other books under review, it is somewhat unfortunate in its physical presentation. The blurb on the back, stressing Tham's concern with characters who push against boundaries, is given crude reinforcement by a front cover photo of a bird cage and a padlock - both open. She deserves better; the quality of her writing can speak for itself.

The narrator of the title story is a single woman of 39 who has made for herself a "cool detached exterior" with which to confront the world. She envies the exciting life, as she sees it, of her ex-hippy friend Ethel, who runs a health food shop and has a 19 year old son named Rainforest Peace (Ethel spent time in California), known as Rain. Perhaps predictably he is an eco-freak who wears a silver chain with the words 'Save the Rainforest' in filigree. Perhaps also predictably the narrator finds herself drifting into a relationship with him. He plays jazz saxophone, inspired by a photo which sounds like Herman Leonard's picture of Dexter Gordon, and which the boy sees as a symbol of freedom. The narrator comments:

"It was an odd ambition for a child to have, here, anyway, and indeed his whole life, apart from the shaky desire to play tenor saxophone, seemed ambitionless, shot through with a studied aimlessness that I didn't understand."

Here are brought into focus the contrasts, in age ("child"), outlook and attitude; we assume that "here" is Singapore, where as the narrator goes on to tell the boy:

"There's no scope for a Bohemian life."

Tham's talent is to convey, through sharply imagined moments and convincing dialogue, the surprise and confusion within her self-aware narrator as she confronts her feelings for someone so much younger and apparently so much more assured. His self possession deserts him, however, when she meets the rest of his band and he introduces her as his aunt. Rain's ex-hippy mother has disapproved of the relationship and is relieved when, after the mishandled introduction, it ends. She asks the narrator what she will be doing next.

"Surviving, mostly, I said."

One might have hoped for a more positive ending, but at least this convinces by its understated realism.

The scope of Tham's imagination is evident in her ability to put herself inside the experience of a range of narrative voices. Several are men - a middle-aged banker who believes in "the sanctity of the ordinariness of everyday life" and who learns from an employee that his teenage son has picked him up in a bar; a Chinese restaurant owner, also middle-aged and living in England; deserted by his promiscuous English wife, he acquires a Chinese child-bride through an agency:

"She has such neat features, she stays at home, she looks after her sons. What more could a man want? Twice a day, I try to remind myself - it is all I ask for."

The same sense of regret for the loss of something more exciting, more risky if less comfortable, occurs at the end of *The Forerunner*. A teenage boy, solid and conformist, envies his older brother who could "glide through barriers and emerge the other side", but who ends up drugged and dead in an accident. The boy thinks of the dead brother's girl friend, whom he blames for the death:

"I don't hate her any more. I wish I did. At least you know you're alive when you hate someone."

Tham's characters are drawn mainly from a middle-class milieu, and there's a sharp awareness of the tensions between the pull of tradition, the implicit conformity in such a background on the one hand, and the "burning inchoate desire to escape" on the other. The final story concerns Mrs Tan, who falls for the young American leader of the 'Renewal Charismatic Free Church'; she contrasts him with her husband who was "safe, steady, constant and never caused the slightest anguish. Truth to tell, he was rather dull."

Tham's central characters share an awareness of the limitations of their environment, the boundaries of ordinariness, and at the same time are fascinated by the excitement, even at the risk of anguish, beyond those boundaries. Whatever their age or sex, Tham creates them with equal skill and confidence. She does not mention Singapore explicitly. You are left to assume that this is the setting, the site of the conformity and the rebellions against it. She recognises both the imperatives to rebellion and its dangers, and avoids easy judgements. Like her own characters, she takes risks, in dealing with such a range of narrative voices, for example. In contrast with the other writers discussed here, the endings of her stories never seem contrived or tricky; they arise in a natural, often understated way from the body of the story.

Claire Tham has chosen to begin in what many regard as the hardest fictional format - the short story. It would be interesting to see how her skills translated into the more expansive space of the novel. Her present work makes clear that the tensions produced by the diversity within Singaporean society offer a rich field for writers with the imagination to recognise them.

© John Maddell, 1993.

John Madell is a senior lecturer in English at South Bank University, London.

Published by:
LANDMARK BOOKS PTE. LTD.
5001 BEACH ROAD
#02-73/74
SINGAPORE 0719
P,bk.
ISBN 981-3002-41-7

SIMON TAY
Drive
(Excerpt from *STAND ALONE*)

"At least I'm consistent," he said and everyone moaned. It was only ten minutes and he was always late: didn't constancy change his defect to character, amongst friends at least? This had been his argument.

"Forty-five minutes late, if you want to count the fact that you were supposed to join us for drinks."

"Well, don't count that, Lizzie. I called to tell you I couldn't make it, didn't I. And I'm here in time for dinner, right?"

His friends moaned again.

"And I couldn't help it."

"Yes."

"Really. The boss went on even longer than usual. I couldn't just tell him I had to go because you were all waiting. Give me a chance."

He looked at them. Lizzie, Choon Ming and Kathy, Ken and Mei Lin - dressed in their office clothes, each with a bowl of steaming hot Hokkien prawn mee. Choon Ming, like him, still with a tie, Ken with his sleeves rolled up, almost finished with his first bowl. He grinned broadly.

"You guys do know what work's like, right? Come on."

Behind the grin, he remembered how important the meeting had been. He had finally got his boss to listen, to really listen to the ideas he had worked so hard on. His ideas would work and when they did, he was now assured the boss would know the success was due to him. That credit, he had realised, was as important as the work itself. Now he could relax.

"Okay, okay. Enough. Shut up and sit down. You want big prawns or not?"

"Ya, with mee beehoon mix."

He sat next to Lizzie. She had waited for him in her office as they first agreed, even though her work was more or less finished. He imagined she had tinkered with some details of a presentation due next week and then rearranged the small plants she kept on the window sill of the small blue office he had visited once. Immediately after his meeting, he had called her to tell her not to wait, but he was already late by then. He smiled at her.

"I forgot your instructions, Liz, and couldn't remember which floor to park on."

He regretted saying that. She looked at him over her bowl of beehoon, biting off the white strands sharply. Her look reminded him that if he had met her and gone together like they had planned, that would not have happened.

"What's new." She sniffed at the chilli powder in the soup.

"Then I saw your new Honda, Ken. So clean I knew it was yours. So I parked near it. I'm glad Mei Lin persuaded you to finally remove the plastic seat covering."

They all laughed, including Lizzie, and he felt as if she was on the way to forgetting that he'd been late.

"Okay, your food's here," Ken said, "stop the bad jokes and eat."

He picked up his chopsticks and dish of chilli powder, but then stopped.

"Hey, it's giant prawns. I ordered big only."

"What's the difference?"

"Three dollars, Lizzie. And besides I don't want to eat more than I asked for. Miss. Hello. Ar-lo, Ah-moy, Ah-moy. Shiau Chieh."

"Sssh...Don't make trouble."

"Trouble? The old lady won't mind. It's just some mistake."

"Just eat it, okay? The people at the next table are staring."

"So what if they stare, Liz? Shiau Chi-eh."

"They may make trouble. They're the kind who carry bearing scrapers and won't think twice about using them."

"Over a bowl of prawn mee, which they don't even sell? Don't be crazy, Liz. This is Singapore you know. Not some gangster town."

"No, she's right."

"Et tu, Mei Lin?"

"There was an article in the papers last week. About a staring incident. Two groups eating fish-head curry. One complained about the size they ordered too loudly for the other and they fought. One man killed with a knife."

"OK, Mei Lin, Liz, you win. I'll eat this bowl. But tell me, this case in the papers, the other patrons decided to *tah-pau*, right?"

*

It was quite late when they left and the car park was empty and dark. Lizzie and Mei Lin were getting a lift from him and walked slightly ahead. He said goodbye to the others, making vague plans for tea at Choon Ming's new apartment. There was a light blue BeeM and Lizzie started towards it. He followed but, when he was nearer, saw it was not his car. His car was on the other side.

"It's not mine, Lizzie," his voice echoed loudly in the carpark.

"It's exactly the same colour."

"It's got spoilers all over, OK. The one on the boot's the size of an aeroplane wing. What a thing to do to a BeeM. Maybe it belongs to our friends back at the next table."

Mei Lin laughed and Liz shooshed him. As they walked back towards him to continue searching for his car, he read Lizzie's look: "You should have listened to me and parked where I told you to."

Taking them home meant going all the way to Serangoon Gardens, completely past his house at Bukit Timah. But it was the least he thought he should do after he had kept Lizzie waiting. At 12.15 he was doing almost 110 on the CTE, heading back to town. He was used to it. Since they had met in his second year of Uni and started going out, he had done so, after the teas in the canteen, the movies, the dinners, the parties with the rest of the group.

Then, he remembered, there had not even been a highway. It was all the way down Toa Payoh Road and then turn left into winding Lorong Chuan. And his car, the Mazda. Old, yellow and so slow the trip there and back home must have taken an hour, if it didn't overheat. Or, at least, that was what he would say, so if it was early morning he could switch off the engine and sit with Lizzie in the car in front of the house, just talking. Mostly talking. A hundred and ten was the most the old Mazda ever did and that had taken a long stretch of straight, downhill road. At the same speed the BeeM had plenty in reserve and thinking of this, he accelerated to relish that difference: 120 and he felt comfortable, safe. He turned up the Mozart. This was the way to drive, he thought.

He first spotted the car at the first flyover, the one that goes over Toa Payoh Road. In the far right lane, highbeams on, glaring into his rear view mirror and cabin. Gaining fast. It must be doing 160 he thought. Madman. He put his indicator on and started moving over into the middle lane to let the car overtake. As he did the car also moved into the middle lane. He pulled the BeeM abruptly back to the right. A tyre screeched. The car horned, flashed its lights and, as it pulled alongside, the driver stuck his fist out of the window, into the rushing wind: a thumb wrapped under the closed index finger, pointing at him.

A black RX-7. The driver in his early thirties. A bastard. An incompetent bastard. Travelling so fast and trying to overtake on the left. Then daring to show him that sign. The BeeM dropped a gear and accelerated steadily. A hundred and thirty and then, changing up again, a hundred and forty, catching the RX-7. He could see that it had red trim all round, a large spoiler at the back and body coloured bumpers. He saw the number and remembered it so he would report it to the police. That would teach the bastard. Then the RX-7 pulled right into his path.

He braked from instinct alone. Tyres screeched and the BeeM twitched as he wrestled with the steering wheel. The RX-7 pulled away. He swore aloud and accelerated. The BeeM raised its front slightly as the speed climbed again. They raced down to the end of the CTE, to the junction near Farrer Park, and the RX-7 slowed in the turn. The BeeM cornered hard and caught up. He horned loudly. Then he saw the junction lights ahead turn red.

The BeeM's tyres dug in desperately. The car swerved slightly to one side and he could feel himself being pulled hard out of his seat and against the safety-belt. It stopped, just before the lights. The RX-7 went through and ran the lights at the next junction as well. It raced away, horning its victory in the late and quiet of the night.

II

He sat at his desk. His eyes throbbed lightly as if he was about to get the flu. It had been like that the whole morning: tired and achey. He got in slightly late and when he did, simply couldn't get going. He hadn't worked at night either. He had changed and simply lain in bed, trying not to think of what had happened, but not finding sleep until maybe 4.00. Now he was behind with the report promised to his client. He tried to work but after an hour, when it was obvious he would not make the deadline, he simply tidied up the main part he had finished the week before and sent if off, after calling the manager he was dealing with to promise the rest in two days. He had to tell someone what had happened.

Ken listened with interest. A similar sort of thing had happened to him before, he said with sympathy. His had been the driver of a grey Volvo. Mercs and Volvos, Ken expounded, these two makes of car were driven by smug middle-aged men who drove as if paying more road tax entitled them to more road. The Volvo had taken offence at something Ken had done. Maybe overtaking him in a corner or horning at him to get out of the way. Whatever.

At a traffic light, the driver got out and went over to Ken. He stood there and rapped on Ken's window: about 40, gold Rolex watch, jade ring and paunch. Ken just stared straight ahead. He was angry, but there was no point getting into something like that. The man walked around Ken's car looking for an open door but Ken locked them all automatically. He knocked hard on the back windshield, at Ken's STANFORD U sticker and started shouting.

"What did he shout?"

"Oh, I can't remember. Something like - 'You university people think you're smart, right?' And, of course, various obscenities in dialect."

"And then?"

"The lights changed and I drove off. No point getting involved with that kind of person."

"What kind of person?"

"You know."

"The type Lizzie thinks carries a knife or bearing scraper."

"Ya. Or a crowbar under the driver's seat."

He didn't say anything more. Maybe Ken was right, but at that point when he was chasing the RX-7, it never occurred to him to just let the driver get away. He would probably have been the one to walk over to the RX-7 at the nearest light and knock on the window and shout. And he would have, if the other driver hadn't gone right through the light. Just thinking about it made him angry again. He couldn't help it. What Ken had done seemed like an act of cowardice.

When Lizzie called, he mentioned the incident and she was appalled. Both at what the RX-7 did and what he had done in retaliation. Chasing each other...like some idiot detective movie...how much danger if they had collided or if he had lost

253

control. It really wasn't a question, but he answered anyway: he knew what he was doing; he was an experienced driver; he would never have lost control. That wasn't the point, he knew very well what her point was. He said he did not and there was silence. Lizzie said she had to go and hung up. He put down the phone, picturing the usual slight frown and pursed lip of disapproval on her face. She didn't understand. And wasn't willing to try, even after all these years. That was the whole problem with Lizzie.

What could he do? He thought of making a police report, but that would expose his own actions. Or the RX-7 might make a complaint as well. He wasn't ashamed of what he'd done but the police, he realised, might not see things the same way. No report. He thought for quite a few minutes at this problem, from different angles like he did with his work. Nothing, he concluded, could be done now. It should all have been handled on the spot, at the moment itself: go through the red light, chase the RX-7, settle the matter. Now it was too late. He picked up a file and suppressed a sniff. He was feeling really flu-ish now.

III

"I'm so angry, I could kill someone."

"Slow down, calm down. Don't slam the cup like that."

"I can't calm down, Lizzie."

He stared into his cup. The coffee was steaming hot. He looked around the table. Lizzie held her cup and saucer on her lap. Choon Ming's and Kathy's were on the Italian marble coffee table. Kopi tiam cups, the real things with thick rims and green flower patterns on white. Old cups in Choon Ming's new apartment. A nice touch, he thought, and suddenly felt sorry for being late again and arriving with his anger, like a vivid purple so out of place in the pastel living room where they sat around with their cooling cups.

"Sorry about the cup, Ming."

"No problem. They're tough. That's one of the reasons we got them."

"Where did you get them?" Lizzie asked, "They're almost impossible to find."

"From the Kopi Tiam at Peranakan Place."

"I didn't know they sold cups."

Ming cleared his throat and it was Kathy who answered.

"They don't. Ming sort of appropriated them. You pay for a cup of coffee and take it out to the mall to drink. Finish the drink and put the cup and saucer in your bag. Repeat six times for a full set."

"You can't find any place that sells them," Ming finished.

He saw Lizzie's frown and broke the silence, "Bravo, I should have thought of that. No wonder they just use normal cups now."

Ming beamed and he laughed. Lizzie said nothing.

"Now what did you want to kill someone about?"

"Look Ming, I'm sorry for bursting in like that..."

"Forget it. We're used to you. What happened?"

"Someone scratched my car."

"No."

"Goodness!"

"Who would do something like that? What happened?"

The chorus of shock soothed him and he began the story:

- Holland Village: just putting his shopping bags into the car boot when he spotted it - a long deep gash above the rear lights, just under the lid, running all the way from the left-hand side to the right. Disbelievingly he looked at it and rubbed the scratch with his fingers, as if massaging it. The gash were deep and broad, gouged in with a lot of strength. Maybe two or three coats of paint. It wouldn't look better even after polishing, he knew. He shook his head, put away the bags, bent down and looked at it more closely. He still couldn't believe it. It was common enough but it had never happened to him; he scrupulously avoided the type of places in which common wisdom said that sort of thing might happen. Now it had happened in Holland Village, in broad daylight. That damn RX-7 driver.

"Wait a minute, how do you know it was the RX-7 driver?"

Because, Lizzie, he saw the RX-7 in the carpark at Cold Storage.

"I thought you said it happened at Holland Village?"

No, no he noticed it there. Earlier he had seen the RX-7 at Cold Storage. He was just about to leave when he saw the car there. It was quite dark in the basement carpark, but it was the right one: red trim, spoiler, skirting all around. He thought of waiting for the driver to come back but he had no idea how long that might be. Besides, for all he knew, somebody else might be driving the car - the driver's brother or friend. So he just went off. But he now realised the RX-7 driver must have been there, seen his car and scratched it. At Cold Storage. It was just that he did not notice it then - because of the lighting - and saw it only at Holland Village.

"Shit, you should have scratched his car."

Would have, Ming, if he had known what the RX-7 driver had done. In fact, he thought of it: there was no one around, he had his keys in his pocket and felt their sharp ridges on the tip of a finger. Either the tyres or the paintwork. He had walked right up to the car and stood there for a while, his hands in his pockets. But he might be caught. He went back to his car. He thought of writing a strong letter but what's the point - this kind of person might not even be able to read. He laughed.

"But it could have been someone else. Just a common vandal. You might be jumping to conclusions. The papers once reported that a car vandal they'd caught scratching a Porsche explained he had done it as a way of showing his admiration."

Sure that was possible, Lizzie. Possible. But what was the likelihood of that compared to what he'd concluded: that it was the RX-7? Which was more probable?

"Well, did anything else happen? Anyone else who might have done it?"

The blue Toyota. At first, he had not been able to find a space in the Holland Village carpark. He had circled and, as he edged past the narrow corner at the end of the carpark, seen a car pulling out; waited, his indicator on, tearing out tabs on the coupon; looked into the rear view to make sure the car could get around his safely; then, spotted the blue Toyota. It was waiting for the same spot and started edging forward immediately the other car pulled out. That wouldn't do; he had been first. He tapped his horn and started to back up. In his rear view mirror he saw the driver of the Toyota. A small man in his forties, wearing glasses. He stopped right in front of the Toyota and horned loud and long. He released the safety belt and started to get out of his car. The Toyota stopped and started backing out of the lot. That was better, he thought. He waited until it drove away. The driver looked mildly at him and raised a hand, palm up: it was just a mistake. He probably hadn't seen the BeeM waiting. That Toyota driver wouldn't have scratched his car.

"Nothing Lizzie. Nothing else happened. Look, you either believe it was a common vandal who decided on this particular day, in

256

broad daylight, to scratch a BeeM, or it was the RX-7 driver and I'm going to fix him somehow, okay?"

"Are you going to report him?"

"There's no proof, Ming. I know it was him but I can't even prove it to Lizzie, let alone the police. I'm just going to have it repaired, I guess."

"Boy, that's sick. I'm really sorry to hear this."

"Ya, Ming. Thanks," he finished, and felt better for the sympathy. He drank a bit of his coffee and reached for one of the huge, creamy cakes.

"Tea and sympathy. Or rather, coffee," he said and laughed.

IV

He pulled the BeeM into the street in front of Lizzie's house and switched off the engine. It was still early, only 10.00. Coffee and cakes had been followed by ice cream and then sandwiches and fruit - a plate of cut kiwi, strawberries and seedless grapes. Then Ming opened the sweet wine he had brought as a gift and it went well with the desserts, leaving them warm, stuffed and cheerful.

"Talk a bit?"

"Come in for a drink. Perhaps some tea."

The BeeM's doors locked at the turn of his key, with a pneumatic thump which was loud in the silence. She worked the lock of her gate in the frail moonlight. "Rust," she muttered.

"Here Lizzie." He took over, twisted the key again and the gate squeaked open, "I still remember how to do it."

"Yes, I guess you do."

He wanted to talk to her about the incidents with the car. Not about the scratch, which could be repaired, but about what she thought of his actions. Did she really think he was wrong, given the circumstances? Or was it that she was worried for him?

"I just don't want you to play macho with these kind of people. They have different values. They're from a different world."

She did care for him: okay, he would be careful. But Singapore wasn't big enough for different worlds, he laughed.

Then they talked about other things: their university days together, the morning walks they used to take in the Botanic Gardens, his ambition to afford a beautiful old house, like one of those near the Botanics, about his work as a means to afford his ambitions, but which ironically left him not enough time for those morning walks, and about a possible trip to Italy next year, together. Then it was almost 1.00 and he said he had overstayed, kissed her with an old passion and let himself out. She listened behind the drawn curtains in her bedroom until his car turned the corner and was out of hearing.

*

He sensed the car before the headlights blazed in his mirror and it pulled up to overtake him on the right. It was going fast and he saw it for only a few seconds, but there was no mistaking it. It was the RX-7. The BeeM accelerated from 80 to almost 125. Fifty metres behind and gaining. Black body, red trim, skirting and spoiler: it was the car alright. Then he didn't have time to think of anything else.

The RX-7 pulled sharply into his lane and he had to brake and swerve. The BeeM pitched and slowed beneath him and the RX-7 rushed away. The bastard was up to the same tricks. He swore and accelerated. As they crested the Balestier Road flyover, he managed to get the BeeM alongside and then slightly ahead. The road sign warning that the expressway was ending flashed by. He pulled over to the right, into the RX-7's path. It braked with a screech. He monopolised both the narrowing lanes. In his rear view he could see the driver clearly: a man in his thirties, with permed hair. It looked like the same man. It had to be. He smiled, lifted his hand above his head with the middle finger out, and braked hard. The RX-7 screeched. He pulled away and heard the RX-7's engine whining, trying to catch up. He held it off as they entered Keng Lee Road and they both ran two amber lights.

Towards Newton there were cars, mainly empty taxis loitering in the right hand lane or crawling on the left, looking for late night passengers. He began to weave in between the cars, from the middle to the left and back again, slowing slightly. The RX-7 did the same and by the time they'd reached the Circus, had caught up. The traffic was too much. He thought of going home or straight to the police station but couldn't make up his mind before the Balmoral Road junction. The light was already red and even from a distance he could see that there were cars going through, across his path. There would be no jumping this red light.

He eased off about 30 metres before the junction, in the far right lane, near the canal. As he slowed he looked across and saw the RX-7 in the left lane, also slowing. It had been a good run and he felt the better for it. It had got it out of his system. He stopped at the junction with the RX-7 two empty lanes away. Its window came down electrically and he saw the driver quite clearly. A plain face, dark from the sun, no glasses, permed hair. On the right wrist, resting on the steering wheel, a thick gold chain. Maybe Lizzie was right: he was from a different world, a different "orbit".

He smiled and turned the Mozart up. Then the hand with the gold chain came out of the window, formed a fist with its thumb between the index, and middle fingers, pointing straight at him.

The nerve of the bastard.

"Know how to scratch cars only, right? You stupid bastard."

The driver looked across at him and again showed him the sign. The hand went back inside and the window went up. He had made his point and turned away, watching just the lights. He didn't hear anything until the RX-7 driver was out of his car. Then hearing the door close and the footsteps, he turned around. He was one lane away and walking towards the BeeM.

"You don't anyhow say," the RX-7 driver shouted gruffly through the night air, "I never touch your car. Your kind think you're so smart. Call me bastard for what?"

He was lying. The bastard had vandalised his car and should just admit it. He instinctively got out of the car. It was only when he closed the door behind him that he saw the short, thick crowbar in the RX-7 driver's right hand, clinking against the gold chain.

© Simon Tay, 1991
With the kind permission of Landmark Books Singapore.

Simon Tay was born in 1961, read law at the Nat. Univ. of Singapore. In 1986 he was Singapore's best young poet and has published three books *Prism*, *5* and *Stand Alone,* which is his first book of fiction published by Landmark Books, Singapore.

Review of
GIFT FROM THE GODS
by
Paul B. J. Toy

The justified world wide success of Jung Chang's searing memoir, *Wild Swans* has focused attention on women writers and women's experience in the Far East. Suchen Christine Lim's novel, *Gift From The Gods,* offers another perspective from the viewpoint of the Singaporean Chinese. Like *Wild Swans,* the book follows the events of three women's lives - a grandmother, her daughter and granddaughter - but it does not weave them into the history of the nation. The focus is on the domestic rather than the political. Outside events rarely impinge on the characters' lives. This reflects the isolation and restriction of the women's existence. The strength of the novel lies in the depiction of those areas in which women have influence and input - the family structure and religious life.

The sense of the low status and restricted opportunities suffered by women is powerfully brought out. A daughter is everywhere seen as worthless:

> "How sad it is to be a woman
> Nothing is held so cheap
> Boys stand strong and firm
> Like gods fallen out of heaven
> No one is glad when a girl is born."

The first half of the novel is dominated by this curse of birth. A mother is beaten to death for producing a sixth daughter. Tales are told of girls being thrown into the river, or pressed to death in mud by their angry fathers. The protagonist Yoke-Lin is expelled from her husband's home for not producing a son. The only route of escape is to achieve security as the wife of a rich man, and to do that Yoke-Lin must work as a "dance-hostess". Her sex becomes the only card she can play in the game.

In many ways, she only exchanges one position of inferiority for another. Now, as a dance-hostess, she is disdained by both men and women. Whether the man she must catch is old, young, handsome or ugly is immaterial. He must be rich and stay rich.

"Love never fills anybody's stomach."

Her constant fears are of growing old and of younger rivals. Even as a wife, one is subordinate not only to the husband, but also to elder female relations and to senior wives. And to exchange the insecurity of a concubine for the position of a wife, she must produce a son.

Alongside the main story of Yoke-Lin, we see glimpses of her daughter's life. At her mother's insistence, she has been educated and so has achieved independence from the treadmill. She becomes a university graduate and an assistant museum curator. However education does not mean the Chinese classics, but learning at an English school - in the language of the country's colonizer and the international imperialist. She becomes free but isolated - cut off from the support systems of family and religion as well as the chains of prejudice and oppression.

The novel is well structured from a formal point. It begins with a birth and ends with a funeral. The first person entries in the journal of Yenti, the daughter, contrasts well with the narrative sections of Yoke-Lin's life. However, the handling of some events is less assured. Certain incidents, such as the appearance of an underworld "Mr. Big" are suddenly introduced and just as suddenly withdrawn, without explanation or development. Suchen Christine Lim succeeds best with sharp focused vignettes. The interlude telling of the capture and death of a rate is excellent. It is in the handling of dialogue that her control of her material slackens. Far too much of it is repetitive and lacking in individual characterization. The most unfortunate failing appears in the ritual that Yoke-Lin undertakes in Ping Shan to obtain the gift of the gods - a son. This needs to be the climax of the book, and the experience is conveyed in an ecstatic stream of spiritual and erotic prose-poetry. Sadly this never rises above the mundane, and the language is unable to match the vision.

Gift Of The Gods does not fulfil the expectations and wishes of the reader, but those expectations are raised by the promise of the book's theme and by the early chapters. Unlike *Wild Swans*, the characters do not impress as symbols of a nation as well as individuals. The novel is a single instrument rather than an orchestra, but it may serve as a *cantus firmus* for further work from this author. I hope so.

© Paul B.J. Toy, 1993.

Paul B.J. Toy is a playwright and an actor researching medieval drama.

SHIRLEY GEOK-LIN LIM

MONSOON HISTORY
Selected Poems
With
An Introduction
by
Professor Laurel Braswell-Means
McMaster University

'While maintaining touch with her native Malacca, Shirley Lim manages to encompass a whole world beyond Malaysian shores ... There is throughout ... that certainty: no other word, no form would do to express this thought, that feeling. (She) edges ahead of her rivals by the sheer confidence of her verse'. **Martyn Goff,** Chief Executive, Book Trust

'Palpable, distinguished by a consistent perpicuity and elegance of form, imagery and diction, the poetry of Shirley Lim deserves pride of place in the literature of Malaysia and Singapore'. CRNLE

'The poet is in exile, but a counter-exile that permits an embracing of all contradictions' *World Literature Today.*

SU-CHEN CHRISTINE LIM
An Excerpt of
Gift From The Gods

Birth

How sad it is to be a woman;
Nothing is held so cheap.
Boys stand strong and firm,
Like gods fallen out of heaven.
No one is glad when a girl is born.

Hakka Cradle Song

Yenti's Journal

My father ran away to join the Communists in the Malaysian jungles the night I was born. I don't know him. The two or three times when I tried to find out more about him, Mother pursed her lips and remained silent. That was her way of telling me that that past in her life was dead. It had been willed out of existence.

1

The tropical thunderstorm had stopped as suddenly as it had begun, petering out into a light grey drizzle that fell continuously all afternoon. The dark trunk road, that ran from Taiping to Ipoh, cut through the plantations of straight rows of rubber trees, dripping with the wet. On the right of the village lay the railway, and on the left, the rubber plantations stretched as far as the eye could see, stopping abruptly at the edge of the tin mines and the slopes of the secondary jungle. Beyond this rose the mountains of the Main Range, jutting thousands of feet into the grey wet skies.

The farm lay at the edge of a plantation. Everything in the wooden farmhouse smelt damp because of the rain. Seventeen-year-old Pang Yoke-lin lay among the crumpled sheets of the four-poster bed, moaning softly.

A thin frail-looking girl, her face was bathed in sweat. The child inside her was due, and yet it was reluctant to emerge. She could feel it struggling and straining inside her, no longer a part of her, but something foreign with a will of its own. Her muscles were becoming tighter, and more and more taut with each new cycle of pain. The veins in her legs were swelling with the strain and she bit her lips as yet another wave of pain ripped through her pelvic region.

"Stop crying and push. Push!" First Aunt hissed in her ear.

Yoke-lin was breathing hard. She wanted to push the life out of her womb - get rid of it and hurl it into the laps of the Chows! She pushed and pushed at the urging of First Aunt till all that was loving, tender and affectionate was forced out of her heart.

Night came. From her bed in that tiny bedroom of the farmhouse, Yoke-lin saw the hard profile of her mother-in-law. The coarse hands of the farm woman were lighting a pair of red candles on the altar of her Hakka ancestors. Softly intoning their names, she called their spirits home to witness the birth of the family's first grandchild.

The father-in-law, Old Chow, his weather-beaten face creased with worry, silently took down the kerosene lamp he reserved for festive occasions. He was concerned over the unusually long labour. Why was his grandson so reluctant to be born? Unconcerned about the mother, he feared that the long hours of strain might harm the baby.

He lit the lamp and pumped it till the room was bright as daylight. It was a good omen, and a good thing too that he had bought the lamp. The village was newly established by the British forces, and it had no electricity yet. "Government people, phui!" he spat, dismissing the officials' promise of a better life in these well-guarded New Villages established under the Emergency. What had that got to do with him? He was a farmer. All he wanted was to be left in peace to grow his crops and rear his fowl.

He strode into his daughter-in-law's bedroom and hung the lamp from a beam of the ceiling. Then he closed the room's only window, shutting out the black night. Like all peasants, he was superstitious - no one could tell what evil spirits might lurk out there, ready to harm the new-born.

The room was warm and bright. First Aunt bustled in, pushed Yoke-lin to one side of the bed and began lining it with cheap absorbent paper.

"The baby is due. I'll fetch the hot water."

Unable to bear her pain any longer, Yoke-lin let out a groan, then another and another, louder and louder. The pain in her loins was excruciating.

"Open your legs. Wider, ah! Wider!" her mother-in-law leant over her. "Hold your breath. Don't scream!"

"Remember, the medium said don't let out too much air!" First Aunt cautioned her.

Yoke-lin gritted her teeth and tried not to make a sound, grasping her bed's headboard till her knuckles went white.

"I can see his head! Push, push!" First Aunt cried.

"Harder! Harder!" urged the mother-in-law. "He's coming!"

Yoke-lin obeyed with anger, frustration and despair.

"Aiya, where's Ah Chong? Has anyone looked for him? A father to be and he's not home yet!" the mother-in-law complained.

"You go, sister-in-law, you go. I'll look after her," said First Aunt.

Yoke-lin shut her eyes. She strained with all her strength like one pushing out her last breath, her soul and all the sinews of her heart, pushing out that part of her body which had been defiled. Soiled and defiled! Her eyes choked with angry tears. Cry after cry of rage escaped from her. She pushed until she thought her bones would crack. What did that man care? Night after night, he had shoved her on to the bed, planted his seed and left. He did what his father ordered him to do and that was that!

In their old age, fearing the end of their line, Old Chow and his wife had wanted a grandchild quickly. But their only child, Ah Chong, was more interested in "playing politics" than in marriage, the villagers said. Old Chow, a violent man, had had to box his ears on the wedding night.

"Go in and do it!" Old Chow had roared. "I paid two hundred for her, you know or not! I want a return. You hear me?"

The whole village heard him. For days afterwards, the villagers talked of nothing else but Ah Chong and his bride. "Have you done it?" the farmers guffawed.

The baby was coming. Yoke-lin could feel something tearing through her.

"Push, push!" Her mother-in-law held her legs.

"Push!Push! With all your strength! Push!" First Aunt held her thrashing arms.

She was being torn apart. A long animal howl escaped from her as she shut her eyes and let the darkness slowly flood over her.

When she opened her eyes again, the room was bright and warm, the air damp with the smell of blood, and the papers under her were sodden wet. Pale and worn out, she could feel the sweat of labour flowing unchecked, soaking her sarong and the sheets beneath her. She lay back, exhausted.

"Aiya, no good, no good, a girl!" First Aunt was bending over her, looking distressed. The two of them stared at the pink bundle in her arms.

The father-in-law strode into the room. Without a word, he unhooked the kerosene lamp and extinguished it, plunging all of them into darkness.

Hours later, old Mrs Chow snuffed out the red candles, leaving only the oil lamp burning. The room was filled with shadows while outside, scattered dots of light showed the houses of the villagers. A warm breeze brought the foul smell of pigs' swill and manure. The heavy peasant woman let out a sigh and sat down on the earthen step of the doorway.

"It's fate. What else but fate," she muttered, trying to explain the incomprehensible to herself. "I did everything; saved the money for the bride, took her to the temple, made the son marry her and prayed to the ancestors day and night."

"The girl's young. More grandchildren to come, maybe a son next year," First Aunt consoled her.

"Aiya, that's my prayer. My old mother had sons. No pain, no difficulty. They dropped out of her like piglets, ah. Six boys, eight girls, one each year. All lived. Fifth Brother was born in the rice field. Ma bit off his cord with her own teeth! Born in the open, and yet he lived. But mine, they die! We Chows are cursed!"

"Choy! Choy!" First Aunt exclaimed. "Ah Chong will give you many grandsons yet. Where's Old Chow?"

"Gone to look for Ah Chong."

"The guards are so strict, they won't open the gates so late."

"I could see from his face," Mrs Chow continued, "Ah Chong's father was bitter. I thought he was going to slap Yoke-lin!"

"A girl! In my village in China they threw girls into the river," said First Aunt.

"In our village, Ma said that the fathers pressed their girl babies into the mud!"

And in her bedroom, Yoke-lin was sobbing quietly. She was a failure. During her twelve months in this Hakka household, the man who gave her this child had come and gone without a word. Sometimes, he was gone for days, and his mother would scold and blame her, saying she was a useless piece of wood, unable to hold on to the man she had married. What could she do? They never spoke. He came to her only when he was drunk. The few times that he had shown any interest in her, she was already big and clumsy with child, and he merely gave her some extra food to eat. Most of the time, they were strangers, doing what they had to.

But their child now lay sleeping by her side, the pink little face puckering up in tiny wrinkles. She had thought that this marriage would free her from being trapped in a fate like her mother's. Her mother - poor, illiterate, ignorant and stupid had lived with one man after another, dragging her brood of girls from small town to small town: Kulim, Bukit Mertajam, Batu Gajah, Telok Anson, an endless drabness in dim wooden huts upon which the rains pelted mercilessly and water dripped into rusty tins. Always on the move, always poor and in debt, never knowing when someone would buy them a meal, she grew up believing that a proper marriage was security.

Outside her bedroom the two older women were still whispering, their voices low and anxious as they waited for their menfolk to return. With the Emergency curfew it was not safe to walk about at night.

First Aunt came into the room. "Sleep," she ordered Yoke-lin. "After labour must rest. Boy or girl, you rest."

Yoke-lin's eyes filled with tears at this bit of kindness. Her own mother had not been so lucky. The trishaw rider with whom she had lived for many years had killed her when she gave birth to her sixth daughter. His face red with drink, he had raged like a mad bull because the baby was not the son he expected. He pulled her mother by the hair and dragged the still bleeding woman from her bed, slapping and punching her. Something was wrong with her body that could not produce a son. Again and again, he banged her head against the wall. His ancestors' graves were cold and it was her fault. Finally, her mother had collapsed. The children huddled under the table, wailing. That night, the sounds of pain from that tormented, writhing body on the floor had bewildered them. By morning their mother had bled to death. Yoke-lin, at the age of eight, became an orphan.

The baby on the bed let out a lusty wail. Yoke-lin awoke with a start and gathered her baby daughter into her arms. The farmhouse seemed full of angry people speaking in loud staccato Hakka.

"The fool! He's already dead!" Old Chow's voice rose above the din. "Let the horse-face guards shoot him! I have no son!"

"Choy! Choy! How can? Your one and only son!" the women gasped.

"What d'you want me do, ha? If not the soldiers now, it'll be the communists later! You think once inside, they'll let him come back to us?" Old Chow asked, exasperated by the events.

"Heaven, hear me, a poor mother! What wrong did I do that you punish me like this? I kowtow from temple to temple, and still I suffer like this?"

Old Mrs Chow knocked her head on the altar so violently that the ancestral tablets rattled.

"Sister-in-law, Ah Chong's mother, don't cry so. Not your fault. No one said you did wrong." First Aunt's voice rose and fell as more and more relations crowded into the farmhouse to have their say. Because all were from the same clan, the same village, or related by marriage, each felt he had a right to comment and advise the Chows on what to do. This was a family matter. A crisis had occurred, and the family must come together, to talk things over, to confer and decide on the best course of action to take. Such things, however, often lead to the teeth biting the tongue, as the old Chinese used to say, for no matter how close the family, members are bound to argue and quarrel at such times.

"If a son does wrong, a mother, what can she do? I don't have to be a god. I have eyes to see. I know Ah Chong's father blames me in his heart!" Mrs Chow raised her voice to clear herself from blame. "Why me? My fault that we've only one son ah? My womb bore him three sons! Remember, you aunts and uncles, three sons I bore him!"

"Sister-in-law, sister-in-law, peace, peace," an old uncle said. "We remember."

"Uncle, let me say this," she continued. "Why he blames me? Why not blame the war? Why not blame the Japanese soldiers? They killed his two sons! And why not fate? I blame my fate. Ill-fate! Did Ah Chong listen to me? Ah Chong, I said, don't play with fire. This politics is fire! It burns! You all heard me. I cry, I scold, but who listens to his mother in times like these?"

"Oi! What for cry?" Old Chow's younger brother asked. "The bird has flown! Heads will roll! You can all be sure of it. Ha! Cry now, what for?"

Anger and fear, mixed with scorn for his wailing sister-in-law, were unmistakable in his loud voice. Like many relatives gathered there, he had grown-up sons, young farmers who could be unjustly implicated by Ah Chong's treachery and suffer at the hands of the authorities. Under the Emergency laws, anyone found helping the communists would be jailed or deported. It was bad enough that Chinese farmers like them had to live in villages fenced in by barbed wire, without one of their own kind bringing trouble upon their heads.

"Brother-in-law, Ah Chong brings trouble, I know," Mrs Chow cried. "I, his mother, bear the blame, the shame. Blame me, blame me!" She beat her chest. "I'd die first before your sons are harmed! My son, it's my son who has run into the jungle!"

"Shut your mouth, Ah Chong's mother! You spoiled the boy!" Old Chow's calloused hand banged on the table. His dark sun-burnt face was taut with the effort to control himself. Across his forehead the harsh lines deepened into the frown of a man frustrated by life's misfortunes.

"Dry your tears, Ah Chong's mother! No more tears, ah!" he shouted. "I shall tell the government people, no son, I have no son! Do what they like with his body! Shoot him! Kill him! I and my brothers...aah, they have sons! All Chows! They can have my farm!"

269

At this, Mrs Chow broke out into a loud wail like a pig being slaughtered, weeping and snivelling in turns till her voice was hoarse with grief. This was the farm for which she had toiled all her life. How could her husband do this to her? How could her son leave her to such grasping relations? They, the Hakka farmers, had always clung to the land. But how could she if she had no son to inherit the land? For what purpose had been her life then? For what? The gods had promised her a grandson. Why hadn't her son waited? What had pulled him away from duty and home?

Mrs Chow's leathery face looked bewildered. No one could give her an answer. At this time, many peasant women were losing their sons to the war in the jungle. They too could not understand their young sons. The family had always been the centre of their world; how could they comprehend even one-tenth of the magnetic pull of the Chinese Communist slogans: Nation Before Self! No Nation, No Home! All that old Mrs Chow understood was that once her son had joined the communists, he was as good as dead. He would never be allowed to return to his family.

In her room, Yoke-lin was listening as the tears streamed down her face. Once again, it seemed, she had been abandoned. Her baby daughter, hungry and fretful, let out a thin wail.

"Stop the piglet's cry!" her father-in-law yelled. "No crying under my roof! I am not dead yet! Stop the tears! Change the luck! Get that broomstick spirit out of my house! Nothing but bad luck since she came! Out! Mother and daughter out! You hear me in there! Out!"

© Su-chen Christine Lim, 1991
With the kind permission of Graham Brash, Singapore

Su-chen Christine Lim, a Singaporean has published several books including *Gift from the Gods, Rice Bowl, The Amah,* and two volumes of short stories.

LOVE LIBERATES, LOVE REJUVENATES

Basanti Karmakar, *Love in the Throes of Tradition,*

by

M.A. Quayum

"The doctrine of love is not old, nor is it new," Emerson writes justifiably in his essay "Love" (*Works of Ralph Waldo Emerson*, London: George Routledge, p.41). Writers of all ages and cultures, and of all statures, have been influenced by love in different degrees. It is customary for most writers to treat love as a primary force of life, a divine rage, a noble sentiment, a sublime gift, that protects man from the manacles and monotony of tradition and shackles of society. Love, they believe, is an energy that saves man from the bogs and quagmires of life and induces a sense of hope, conviction, and meaning in him. "We are all born for love. It is the principle of existence, and its only end," Benjamin Disraeli writes in *Sibyl* (qtd. in "Popular Quotations", *The Webster Encyclopedic Dictionary of the English Language*, New York: Avernel, 1980, p.109). "Our life without love is like coke and ashes," Thoreau comments in "Friendship" (Henry Seidel Canby, ed., *The Works of Thoreau*, Boston: Houghton Mifflin, p.767).

Basanti Karmakar's first novel, *Love in the Throes of Tradition*, adds a new chapter to this theme of love. Its title is self-explanatory. She treats love as a liberator and rejuvenator, or as a Messiah of the socially and sexually oppressed people of modern India. Love is the theme of her novel, love that defies the demoded values of a decadent culture and brings freedom and peace in the life of her otherwise morally and spiritually thwarted characters.

The novel contains several stories of passionate love, spanning several generations of two Bengali-Indian families. Basanti Karmakar is herself a Singaporean of Bengali-Indian descent. Therefore, it is appropriate for her to return to her roots and relate stories of Indian love in her first novel.

Basanti Karmakar begins her novel by narrating the somewhat unusual but affecting story of Mohon and Suki. Then she gradually moves into the stories of Manjira and Subir, Manjira and Biresh, Rita and Nikhil, and finally the story of Kamal and Suparno. In between these stories of passionate love, she, introduces stories of parental/filial love adding significantly to the depth and strength of her novel. By weaving so many tales of love in her novel, she demonstrates her deep commitment to the doctrine of love, although ironically it makes her plot a trifle knotty and labyrinthian.

The story of Mohon and Suki occupies the first half of the novel, which is also the more poignant half, the more gripping half. Mohon, a father of two in his fifties, and Suki, a widower in her twenties, are both prisoners of tradition and prisoners of sex. They are both terribly oppressed; he by a frigid wife, and she by a fearful mother-in-law. Both are victims of a bad marriage from which neither can disengage for fear of tradition. Therefore, although they feel despondent and defeated, they reluctantly accept their fate. But then love appears on their horizons and sets them free. Meek Mohon is transformed into a gallant man by love and so he courageously elopes with Suki in the face of all odds and marries her secretly. This marriage brings happiness into their life.

Life with Suki opened up another world for Mohon which he had never dreamed possible. At fifty-two, a mere girl of twenty-two gave him an ecstatic joy and peace he had hardly bargained for. Doubtless, marriage gave Suki the security, future, home and respectability she needed, apart from happiness and love - a love so intense and profound that it consumed every moment of their lives, and they lived to the fullest. (p.40)

But this intense happiness that they discover in their love and matrimony disappears suddenly with the untimely death of Mohon, and Suki is left again in a desperate state with her two minor children. This time it is Anjan, Mohon's son by his first marriage, who comes to the rescue of Suki. Induced by his filial love for Mohon, Anjan hazards the hostility of his mother and sister, who are immersed in the values of Hindu orthodoxy, as he accepts Suki as his step-mother. This heroic act of Anjan, which is made possible only by his unflinching love for his dead father, saves Suki from an overwhelming moral and social crisis and reinstates her in society.

However, with this heroic act of Anjan, the episode of Suki comes to an end, and the novel takes a new direction. From here on, it is Anjan and his family who move to the foreground, and Suki, the central figure of the first half, is reduced to a minor character. This failure to accommodate Suki as a major character in the second half of the novel is a definite structural weakness in the work of Basanti Karmakar. It creates a rupture in her plot, dividing the novel into two almost disconnected halves, which Anjan cannot bridge sufficiently.

Another structural weakness is that she incorporates too many scrappy stories in the second half of the novel without doing sufficient justice to any of them. For example, the triangular relationship of Subir, Manjira, and Biresh, which is so intriguing and absorbing, does not get enough attention from the writer. She does not explore the psychological complexities and moral difficulties created by the incestuous relationship of Manjira and Biresh. On the contrary, their story is related in a disinterested narrative voice - vaguely, hastily, and inadequately. In fact, Manjira and Biresh are never seen to think much about their relationship; they are never seen to suffer intensely for each other, or express sufficient longing for one another, especially after their rash sexual act in a holiday resort. In sum, they are too passive and barely passionate in love. They are also curiously free from the guilt feeling that is generally present in a mother-son amorous relationship (Manjira is Biresh's step-mother, and their relationship develops behind the back of Subir, Biresh's father). These weaknesses of the novel obviously make it less effective to the reader.

But despite its weaknesses, the novel has its strengths. Basanti Karmakar's depiction of love in Indian society and her portrait of Indian society as a whole are realistic. She has given a graphic picture of the sexual and social repression in modern India, especially in the Hindu culture. Interestingly, she does not include a single Moslem character in her novel. This is perhaps because being a second generation Singaporean writer of Hindu background, she is not sufficiently familiar with the Indian Moslem culture. Her main quarrel in the novel is with the age-old values of orthodox Hindu consciousness and culture that breed bigotry, inequality, and strife in society. For example, she rejects the caste system, dowry convention, and the inhibitions related to Hindu widowhood. She also rejects the system of conventional marriage in favour of marriage of mutual love. She believes that conventional marriage is an impediment to the emotional growth of the individual. It takes away the individual's freedom and makes him/her subservient to the collective will of society or its prevailing tradition. Basanti Karmakar is a liberal humanist who believes in the autonomy and self-reliance of the individual. Being a woman herself, she is, of course, especially interested in the liberation of women. She believes that women are the more exploited sex, that they are more exposed to the rigid and repressive values of modern Indian society and culture.

Over and over again, Basanti Karkamar shows that India is a jailhouse for women. The repression of women in India is intense. They have little freedom to express their emotion, opinion, or feeling. In sex they are treated as being inferior to men; in marriage they are forced to accept their fate. This is true for all the leading women characters in the novel - Suki, Manjira, Rita, and Suparno. They are all victims of tradition and sexual discrimination from which they are all eventually redeemed by love. This is the central message of Basanti Karmakar, that love can remove all intolerance and inequality, bias and bigotry, and bring about a life of balance and harmony. She sees love as a liberator and rejuvenator of those who are caught up in tradition and the decadent values of society. Love is the only way to restore the lost humanity of mankind, she believes.

As a first novel, *Love in the Throes of Tradition* is a brilliant work. It is written in a simple and lucid language, but its theme is profound. Basanti Karmakar writes: "I am a retired school teacher and have taught for twenty-two years in English medium schools in Singapore." I think her wisdom and experience are well reflected in her novel. Certainly, reading *Love in the Throes of Tradition* was a rewarding experience.

© M.A. Quayum, 1992.
With the kind permission of C.R.N.L.E. Reviews Journal

M.A. Quayum is an academician from Bangladesh currently teaching at the Nanyang Technological University of Singapore.

Introduction to
LOVE IN THE THROES OF TRADITION
by
Robert Yeo

Basanti Karmakar has told a very affecting story spanning several generations.

The work is fiction, of course, but there is no mistaking the fact that its details (characters, setting, customs, etc...) derive from her early years in Calcutta. This is therefore a loving act of recall from a Singaporean of Bengali descent who has been able, in her retirement, to weave tales told to her or incidents in her life into this rich tapestry.

For some people, a lifetime of commitment to what society considers the necessities - school, work, marriage, parenting - have all but suppressed the urge to create. It is to Basanti Karmakar's credit that, in her retirement, she has been able to rise above the smothering weight of necessities to produce this wonderfully long creative release.

There is no doubt that she has returned to her roots but instead of autobiography there is fiction. Her memorising is affectionate which explains why these are love stories in the Indian phase of her life.

I hope that the author will enjoy the success this book deserves and go on to write another which will chronicle the Singaporean phase and bring the past she has evoked so vividly to the present.

© Robert Yeo, 1992.

ROBERT YEO has published three books of poems, one novel and numerous anthologies of short stories, plays and poems for both the general and school readers. In addition, he has written four plays, all of which have been performed in Singapore, Hong Kong and New York.

He is now Senior Lecturer in the Nanyang Technological University, National Institute of Education, Singapore.

BASANTI KARMAKAR
Excerpt of
Love in the Throes of Tradition

Chapter 5
Suki and Anjan

Who was it who had said that no one is indispensable? That must have been some confounded wretch with his contrived wealth or some extraordinary being able to live entirely on his wit.

Suki was neither. She was an ordinary, average human mortal who could but depend on others for her and her children's survival. Her dependence on her husband had been moved down too soon. With Ram's death not only was her intended career completely demolished, but it extinguished her flickering hope of inheritance. Finally the devastating storm razed to the ground her aspiration to use her two hands to earn a living for her and her children's survival. She was now in the throes of a terrible trauma. With her children, she became a convoy, lost and stranded in an immense desert, faced with a hopeless mirage.

When Madhuri came again Suki ventured to ask her if she would rent her father's place to her.

"But how will you pay the rent?" was Madhuri's most natural question.

"I had learnt the art of making earthenwares and ceramics from your father. I had intended to start my own business here and your father fully approved of it. If you rent the place to me I could start my own business and pay you the rent."

"You can't. The potter's wheels and the kiln are all completely broken by the storm."

"I've a little money saved up, I could invest in new ones."

"But my husband and I have other plans. I've actually come here today to talk to you about this house and settle everything for the future."

Suki braced herself for the worst.

"I don't know if my father ever told you that I inherited this property immediately on his death. It was given to me as my dowry with the condition between my husband and my father that my father would stay here as long as he lived and immediately at his death it would become my property. Now my husband and I are its owners. We don't intend to rent it out because it won't be profitable. We want to sell it and invest the money in our timber business, we need the cash badly."

"I see. No, your father never told me. I'll look for accommodation elsewhere," answered Suki in a state of bewilderment.

"You don't have to leave immediately. Perhaps by three months you'll be able to find some accommodation, I believe."

"I'm touched by your generosity," was all Suki could say.

Where would she go with her two children, she had no idea. Her predicament was killing her. She lost her appetite. She lost sleep. She was desperate. Her future became a losing battle.

There was only one opening for her and that was Charity. But where from? She knew Charity was not accompanied without Contempt. Well. Charity with Contempt then, her children had to live.

She had made up her mind. Durga and she were once wives of the same man and now widows of the same man and that was the common denominator between the two women. Both had children by the same man and that was also common between them. Surely Durga could not be heartless against her husband's children, even though by another woman. Suki herself had never been jealous of Durga or her children; so why should Durga be? But the naive and inexperienced Suki was unfamiliar with the ways of the world and did not quite know that to a woman only her own begotten children matter and that mother-love is selfish.

She also remembered Uncle had told her that Anjan was as generous as his father. "Why hadn't Mohan told his son about me? As a man Anjan would certainly have considered me and the children," she thought bitterly. She decided to approach his family as she had no choice. All she wanted was the children's inheritance, their birthright.

"Lal, will you do me a favour?" asked Suki after days of much consideration.

"Yes, Ma-ji, what is it?"

"Will you accompany me to Durgapur town tomorrow afternoon after your work is done? It's Sunday and we'll go by horse-carriage."

"Of course, Ma-ji. What time do you want to go?"

"Any time after lunch."

"I'll be here by three. Would you mind if I bring my wife along? She'd like to see her brother and his family, they live in the town."

"Of course not, bring her along."

They arrived at the town about four in the afternoon. Lal took them first to his brother-in-law's house, occupied by a very homely couple living with a brood of children and a herd of cows. His brother-in-law was engaged in milk delivery.

Bare of all ornaments, Suki had put on a plain white saree with a thin blue border and had tied her hair into a tight knot behind her head and closely covered her head with her saree. Anyone could see that she was a widow of very austere circumstances.

"Ma-ji, tell me where you want to go and I'll take you there. My wife will wait here," Lal offered.

"No, Lal, I know this place very well. I'll return after I've visited some people, it won't be long."

It was almost six years ago that she had lived here. Nothing had changed visibly since she had first arrived as a young bride. As she walked she came across her former home, the home that had left indelible scars on her emotions. She could not hold back the pain that surged to her mind. Like a thunder-clap she was reminded of her mother-in-law. Poor Suki, she shuddered, what torture she had gone through in that house of doom.

Suki turned the bend and after a short walk stood before Mohan's hardware Store, now securely locked. Here she had met the man who had loved her till his death and had called her as he breathed his last. She tore away from his Store and proceeded towards his house with much misgiving tugging at her heart. Only her desperate plight had brought her to face the family. She guessed her attempt would be futile but she would try. She could not let her children be thrown out after three months' charity. And why should they be deprived if their father was a man of means?

At last she stood before the house. She had never seen it before. Only a very wealthy family could live in such a sprawling homestead; its immensity overwhelmed her. But its former owner never found much happiness within its walls and she hoped the present owners were happy.

The door was shut and that gave her some time to stand there and think. She was holding Hari to her breast while Ajoy was holding on to her saree. As she was reaching out to knock at the door her heart sank within her. Her courage began to rise and fall like the tide. Should she turn back after coming all the way and leave her mission unfulfilled? There is more to mother-love, it is a woman's inborn instinct that fears no humiliation, shame or even death. She mustered her courage and her emotions together.

Radha had taken her father's death rather seriously. His youngest, since childhood she had attended to her father in a very affectionate way. In the evenings when he returned from work she would bring him his sandals and place them before his feet and take away his shoes. Next she would wipe his sweaty face with a damp towel and serve him his evening tea, and during the scorching summer she fanned him as he ate his meals. With the years her affection is dimmed. From early teens she became engrossed in her own self. One of the brightest pupils in her class, and her father was proud of her. Gradually her attention to him ceased as she grew older. Still he was the most infallible man to her.

After their afternoon siesta, on that fateful Sunday afternoon, as usual they were gathered together in their spacious sitting room, sipping their evening tea and fondly remembering their dear departed father and talking of the good old times they had had together with him. Now that he was no more in their midst they missed him more than ever. Unexpressed, they even felt a certain guilt in their hearts for their little indifferences and slights towards him while he lived.

Only Anjan realized how his father had detached himself very much from his family during the latter part of his life, though he was never to know the great happiness and more welcome heaven his father had found with Suki and his new son, a heaven over-flowing with love, tenderness and the fulfilment of being wanted where his absence was missed with dismay and his presence looked forward to with joy.

"I feel so sorry and guilty that father actually died in harness, so to speak," said Anjan sadly.

"What do you mean?" asked Radha who believed that she alone missed him most.

"Well, father should have retired and taken a good rest," continued Anjan, "then he could have lived a few more years. He wasn't that old, he hadn't passed even his sixtieth year. We never even celebrated his birthdays ever. I sometimes wonder if he found his home that attractive and welcome."

"You didn't even want to run his Store," added his mother sharply, "and not even now, and it's going to the dogs."

"I'm not thinking about the Store. I'm thinking about father. No, I didn't want to and I don't want to run the Store, I told you that before and please don't repeat that again. I feel guilty I couldn't keep my promise to father that when I'm earning well I'd support the family and he could go on a tour or rest at home; that day never came for him for me."

"Your father was simply married to the Store and spent all his time sitting there. It was better than doing nothing and hanging about the house. As for finding his home unattractive and unwelcome, just what do you mean by that?" demanded his mother. "And whom are you hinting at?"

"I'm not hinting at anyone. Father used to come home, then he played with my daughter for a while, and then he kept to his room."

"What did you expect us to do?" his mother and sister were keen to know.

"No one expressed any warmth or welcome when he returned home after a long and tiring day."

"I'm no more a little girl to tend to him all the time, I've my own life to lead," declared Radha.

"You're being extremely blind and unreasonable. Who used to cook and serve him his meals every day?" asked his mother.

"So is our dog served with meals every day because he's a good watchdog," observed Anjan dryly, exasperated by their selfishness.

"There's a knock on the door, I'll open it," said Radha who was sitting near the door.

An attractive slim, young woman, dressed like a widow, with two children stood in front of the house. One was a baby in her arms, hardly six months old, and the other a boy, a little over two years old.

"Yes? Who are you?" asked Radha.

"I believe this is Mr. Mohan Das' house?" asked the visitor.

"Yes, he was my father, he died some time ago," said Anjan.

"I know, he died six months and eighteen days ago today. And you must be his son and this is your sister, I believe."

"You knew him then?"

"You knew him then?" asked Anjan, quite taken aback.

"Who are you and what do you want?" asked Durga.

"I'm Suki...I...I don't know how to tell you," Suki stammered and bit her lips in embarrassment and agitation, at a loss for words. She was all alone and felt helpless with her two babies while the whole family now assembled at the door, and looked down on her like an army. Make it now or never, she told herself; hell, fire or thunder, I have to say what I have come to say.

"These two children are your husband's children," Suki said softly and clearly for everyone to hear.

"WHAT DID YOU SAY?" exclaimed Durga. It was not a question that required an answer. It was a thunder-clap. It was a rude shock. It was a sudden realization difficult to grasp. It was an outburst of incredulous surprise by an injured-self pitying wife. She suddenly feel from her high perch of smug satisfaction over the husband whom she had intimidated all her life and had taken for granted.

Stunned, the family stood there as if a witch's spell had been cast over them. Without any warning they were hurtled down an avalanche of confusion, conflict, disbelief and shame. They stared at each other with blank but questioning looks, hardly able to believe what they had just heard. But they did not dare ask the counter question, "Really?"

An aeon passed by. The silence frightened Suki. She herself had been so engrossed with her own trepidation at meeting the family and revealing her own identity to them that she had not envisaged the trauma and the profound shock that she would generate in them. Little did she guess what she herself would now face.

She never realized the emotional onslaught she was causing them. They were all dreaming the same ugly dream together. How could their benign and respected father, the dedicated patriarch of the family, have kept a woman secretly for sex, the ultimate in infidelity! What a fall! Their minds twitched in shame for him. All his goodness and sacrifices melted into water and flowed away into the gutter forever.

Durga woke up from her ugly dream. Little had she ever thought than the conditions she had imposed on her husband's sex life and which he had accepted passively, having no other choice, had humiliated him beyond her imagination. Once upon a time she had a voluptuous body with full pouting breasts. But as she forcefully turned frigid and imposed abstinence on herself she became flat chested with hanging breasts, and her body had withered like a piece of driftwood on the sand and lost its lustre. Now when she looked at Suki's shapely, statuesque and curvaceous figure standing before her she became so insanely jealous that she could not contain her rage over her husband. He had cheated her and betrayed her. The frustration that she had once caused her husband was now visited upon her and it overpowered her. She shook herself from her shock and now turned to attack her opponent standing helpless before her.

"How dare you come to this respectable house to debase my beloved husband? I know him too well," she screamed.

"He was my husband too, I would not debase him for all the world," answered Suki softly.

"My father was your husband! What a big lie! You shameless woman! He wouldn't step on your shadow," sneered the self-righteous Radha.

"Whoever you are, we don't believe a word you say. Somebody's kept woman that you are and now you come here to blackmail us with your filthy lies. Who knows who fathered these illegitimate brats," went on Durga, screaming like a banshee. "Anjan, shut the door on this dirty whore's face."

She had shocked her own family. Anjan could not believe that his mother and sister were capable of so much fury and filth that poured from their mouths likes serpents' venom.

"Mother!" he upbraided her sharply. "Behave yourself! How can you speak like that! Have you lost your sense of decency?"

Suki was stunned, she had told them the truth.

Anjan's outburst did little to quell his mother. Instead, she became more outraged and went on jabbering like a cantankerous woman suddenly gone berserk.

"How dare you humiliate me before this whore?" she screamed.

"No, mother. I won't stand such undignified and shameless words from you. If what we've just heard is true, then these children are my half brothers and she..."

"I'm ashamed of you, son. What proof has she that your father had married her and that the children..."

Suddenly it turned into a quarrel between the mother and sister against the brother. It become a free-for-all within the family as abusive and selected words for the occasion were hurled at each other with gusto.

Poor Suki became an unwilling witness to their increasing high tempers. Shamed and humiliated beyond her imagination, and treated like a common whore and branded as such by the two self-righteous women, she could not help the tears springing to her eyes.

"Ma! Ma, look! inside the room, there's my Papa!" suddenly screamed the little Ajoy, clapping and jumping with childish glee and tugging at his mother and pointing at his father's picture, enlarged and garlanded with fresh marigolds, hanging on the inner wall of their sitting room.

He had turned the tables. A sudden hush. All eyes turned to the life-size photograph inside the room where Ajoy had been peering with childish curiosity, absolutely unperturbed over the adults' squabble. At that moment an earthquake could not have surprised them more than that child's innocent outburst of his love for his father.

"Ma, I want my Papa, my Papa. I want to hold him and kiss him, he will carry me. When will Papa come home? Tell me, Ma. Ajoy wants Papa." And suddenly he began to cry, tears running down his cherubic face, overcome with longing for his father. His mother had told him many times about his father's death but he had neither understood nor accepted his father's death.

Anjan bent down, smiled at the little boy and carried him in his arms and took him inside the room to see, feel, touch and kiss his father's picture. He came to his mother laughing through his tears with, "Ma, I kissed my Papa. Will Papa come home with us?"

His love knew no bounds. It melted their hearts. There was a sudden surge of compassion for him as proved his love for his father above all. So sublime, so innocent, so ethereal, it left them like a vacuity on earth; they felt empty.

Durga could not contain herself; putting the end of her saree to her eyes she hastened inside the house and burst into tears so did Anjan's wife. But Radha was unmoved; disdainful, she never shed tears for anyone, she went and locked herself in her bedroom.

Suki's humiliation was complete. Never in life had she been so shamed; taken as a lustful whore, a woman of easy virtue, as if she had been mercilessly lashed with raw hide on her bare back. What a debasement! Burning tears streamed down her face, she bent her head in utter dejection, collected her children and turned to go. Her mission had failed.

"Please don't go away, come in and sit down," Anjan begged.

How dare he ask her to come in and sit down after such a shabby treatment! She turned her face away. Beaten and defeated, she could not speak.

"Please accept my sincere apologies for my mother's and sister's rude behaviour," implored Anjan, standing submissively before her with his palms joined. "Just spare me a few minutes, I must have a word with you; I was waiting for you."

"Waiting for me!" Suki could not believe her ears.

"Yes, I was. I'm glad you came at last."

As his eyes met hers she knew he was alone with her.

"Your son has dispelled everyone's doubts. He has identified himself with my family and has established his lineage. Won't you come in and sit down and talk?"

"No. I must go now, it's getting dark."

"I'll accompany you then, I can't let you go alone."

"You are very kind. I don't understand how you were waiting for me."

"I'll tell you one day because we shall meet again."

Anjan carried Ajoy in his arms and escorted Suki to Lal's brother-in-law's house.

"Oré baba! That's Ram Chandra's house," exclaimed Anjan when she told him where she lived. "He is related to me on my father's side."

"He was like a father to me, I called him Uncle. He died about a month ago."

"Oh no! He was such a good man. He came here a few days after my father's death."

"Yes, I sent him here, I was desperate, I had no news of my husband."

"I can understand your feelings. Please forgive my family and accept my apologies again."

"You have your father's generous heart. Uncle was right."

Suki went back in a happier frame of mind and with a glimmer of hope for the future.

284

As they walked past Mohan's hardware Store and Anjan pointing it out to her said, "This was my father's Store."

"I know, I met your father here."

"Really! And I never knew. My father kept his secret well."

Suki smile shyly.

Published by:
YANG PUBLISHERS & CRESCENT DESIGN ASSOCIATES
44 Jalan Sembilang, Singapore 2057
P'bk.
ISBN 981-00-4753-3

BASANTI KARMAKAR
Love's Fearful Passage

Introduction

Love's Fearful Passage is a novel which spans three generations in the life of a Bengali family. The only historical incident of any significance referred to in the novel is the beginning of the Pacific War. The capture of Singapore by the Japanese is mentioned because it prevented the principal protagonist, Tuphan Kumar Lahiri, who had left a thriving law practice in Singapore, from returning to Singapore from a sojourn in India. This incident places the story in its time-frame in history. Apart from the prologue and epilogue, which are set in Singapore, and a brief episode in London, the story takes place in rural Bengal.

Though not a historical novel in the accepted sense, it describes revolutionary changes in the social attitudes of a once conservative Bengali family which took place in the middle decades of the twentieth century. It began with people with traditional Indian attitudes, who followed rigidly age-old Hindu observances in family and social life, and ends with young people whose social attitudes have been changed by Western education and ways of living. There can hardly be a greater contrast than that between the marriage practices of Sagar Choudry in the beginning of the novel and those of Munmun and Bejoy at the end. In between, the reader can see how the ancient observances begin to crack under the hammer blows of persons such as Kumar Lahiri.

Passionate love is depicted with no holds barred. This is especially so with Kumar's love for Asha, a love so intense that its frustration leads to intemperate language and actions on the part of Kumar. The novel also depicts hatred and its consequences in stark terms. These two opposing emotions, love and hate, together with lust, bring forth a harvest of deaths. One demise follows another, culminating in the multiple deaths in quick succession of Amar Lahiri, Kumar and the doctor, rivalling in the profusion of deaths some of the most lethal of ancient Greek tragedies and those of the English Elizabethan dramatists.

The novel depicts the lives of Bengalis from the period before the Second World War to almost recent times: the lives of the poor, simple folk as well as those of wealthy people in high castle. As satire, it is highly critical of certain destructive Indian customs, the caste system, the dowry conventions, police and official corruption and police brutality, and principally of Sati-Daha, or the enforced immolation of widows. The last was outlawed by the British authorities about 1840, yet persisted sporadically up to recent times. On the other hand, it also portrays tender filial and marital love, and the kindness and unselfishness which some simple and poor people are capable of.

There is considerable character evolvement or development, but the only characters which are finely drawn are Asha, Kumar, Kusum and, to some extent, Amar Lahiri.

Stylistically, the unorthodox use of words and expressions are part of the author's style and linguistic background, and much of the dialogue appears to be the distinctive speech of the Indian (Bengali) characters. It is straightforward and highly subjective as the author expresses without reservation the thoughts, feelings and motives of the characters. There is some use of interior monologue.

The author makes use of startling coincidences, notably the meeting of Bejoy and Munmun in London, and their subsequent marriage, after which they discover that their step-mother and mother respectively are one and the same person. In the case of the rescue from death by enforced immolation of Asha by the very timely, fortuitous arrival of an immense storm followed by a flash flood, of which not the slightest intimation is given previously, the author's use of the "deus ex machina" technique strains the reader's credulity to some extent, and imparts a fairy tale atmosphere to an otherwise stark realistic story.

The novel's portrayal of human passions and emotions is powerful. The interweaving of strands in the lives of three families is skilfully done. Final outcomes in the lives of the protagonists are shown to be the product not only of their character, but also of relentless fate, with nemesis being the more powerful of the two factors, as in the deaths of Kusum, Amar, Lahiri and Kumar.

The novel is not for the squeamish, but the final outcome is happy, which will satisfy those who do not relish tragedy in the Aeschylean pattern.

Desmond P. Pereira

287

Prologue
A New Family

Sisir Nayak personally went and met Munmun, her husband Bejoy, and her mother Asha, when their boat arrived in Singapore from Calcutta. An insufferable man with a disdainful disposition, Sisir Nayak had never performed a benign act for any one and preferred to leave people to their own fate and affairs.

But Munmun had been very special to him, almost a daughter. While she studied law in England she had kept in constant touch with her warm letters to Sisir Nayak, her late Uncle Tuphan Kumar Lahiri's law firm partner, in whose firm she expected to practise one day. Sisir Nayak, once not a very well-to-do lawyer, was set up in business by Tuphan. Ultimately when the two men became very good friends Tuphan made him a partner in his law firm.

"How do you do Mrs. Chander. You must be Munmun's mother-in-law," greeted Sisir Nayak.

"She's both, my mother and my mother-in-law," added Munmun proudly.

"Both!" exclaimed the lawyer who believed he could never be shocked or surprised at anything.

"I'll explain to you one day," assured Munmun flashing a warm smile.

He accompanied them to Tuphan's little bungalow by the sea, now inherited jointly by Munmun and her brother Gopal, a bungalow by the sea beach before the massive reclamation of the sea-shore land to expand Singapore, the evergreen island in the sun, to make way for Singapore's growing population.

As his car drove up to the unpretentious porch it was evident that the house and surrounding garden, neglected and overgrown with weeds, had just been cleared and made ready for the new occupants. But what plunged Asha into an ecstasy of mixed joy and sorrow was the name of the modest bungalow ASHA ARBOUR, painstakingly etched in black on a diagonally sliced-off piece of log with its bark still intact all round it, and fixed on the door of the facade as an ornament and memorial to an episode gone by.

It was a preserved piece of art conceived in the innermost depth of the anguished lover's heart, for the woman whom he had expected to make the mistress of his home one day, and now the very sight

288

of it reached and touched Asha's heart just as Tuphan had intended it to be. He was gone but ASHA ARBOUR opened up streams of memories both happy and painful, of hopes and desires never fulfilled, of dreams that were dreamed but never realized, of thirsts and longings never quenched. ASHA ARBOUR opened up avenues through which Asha now passed in undulating waves of emotions which she had never expected would surface again, emotion that brushed over her and became embossed in her heart for her only love. And now Asha in her melting mood realized with some self-commiseration that her daughter and son, Munmun and Gopal, would inherit ASHA ARBOUR as if from a father.

That evening Burton Tan, the son of Tan Kim Chye, visited the newly-arrived family. When his son started going to school Tan Kim Chye decided to add an English name to his son's Chinese name. A great admirer of Richard Burton, he decided to call his son Richard, but to his dismay he discovered that Richard was common English name among quite a number of local Chinese, Eurasian and even Indian boys, and he did not like a commonplace name for his son. So he gave his son the name Burton, and soon Burton Tan was perfectly happy to be called Button or Baton.

"When my father heard about your arrival he sent me here immediately to welcome you," began Burton Tan. "Father would have come himself to meet you but he's been advised by his doctor to take complete rest at home due to some heart attack he suffered recently."

"I heard about your father, Mr. Tan Kim Chye, from my Uncle Tuphan, Mr. Tan," began Munmun.

"Of course. Your Uncle was my father's solicitor, and please call me Button. My father sends you his regards. He also says could you and your family have dinner with us tomorrow evening? Your law partner, Mr. Sisir Nayak, has agreed to come."

"With pleasure. My husband and I shall be at your house tomorrow. But I don't think my mother will be able to go; she's very tired after the long journey."

Tan Kim Chye was an importer of Chinese herbs and medicines, and no one knew exactly what he imported and sold until a law enforcer happened to stumble on his import that was supposed to be a drug, for which he could be sent to the gallows or imprisoned for life. Tuphan Kumar Lahiri was his lawyer and managed to save him. In gratitude he begged his lawyer to accept a humble gift, and that turned out to be the little bungalow by the sea, a short distance from Tan Kim Chye's garishly imposing house.

Tan Kim Chye greeted Munmun and her husband. "I'm highly honoured to meet my late lawyer's niece, who, I've been told, is a lawyer. It's very likely I and my son will need your professional services also."

Munmun, Bejoy and Sisir Nayak enjoyed a sumptuous dinner with Tan Kim Chye and his family. Suddenly Munmun's gaze became riveted by a little post-card size picture on the ancient Chinese black wood altar-table. She walked across the room and stood entranced at Tuphan's framed-up photo that had once appeared in the local newspapers when he won the case. Tuphan's photo stood side by side with the photos of his family's ancestors to grace the antique altar. Tan Kim Chye's eyes followed her as she stood before the picture. She had only a memory of her Uncle and she had never seen him in his full solicitor's suit as he had appeared in the High Court to defend his client.

"I never asked him for his photograph, so I cut this out from the newspapers. He was a man who detested show and pomposity. I always wondered why that handsome uncle of yours never got himself a wife as girls would have swooned at his feet."

"After the War when I heard about his death from Mr. Sisir Nayak I was completely devastated. What happened, Miss Munmun? Will you tell me how he died?" asked Tan Kim Chye sadly.

Munmun nodded her head and said, "I'll tell you whatever I can remember about my Uncle Tuphan, as I had known him for a very short time only. But I heard all about him from my mother, Mrs. Asha Lahiri."

After Tan Kim Chye's family had retired to bed, Munmun began her story for Tan Kim Chye and Sisir Nayak who had been her and her brother's trustee.

Chapter 1
ASHA

No one ever knew when Asha learnt to swim, a feat that gave her her second life. During her growing years her swimming tutors

290

had ranged from her father to her two elder brothers and their friends. The pond behind the family's backyard became the neighbourhood children's watery playground in which Asha gained the skill and tenacity of an Olympic swimmer.

Asha's growth was strictly watched by her orthodox Bengali parents, as if girls were born to spring undesirable surprises detrimental to their virtue. Like her brothers, who had been early taught to look upon every female as a mother or sister, she addressed every male as uncle or brother, until at age eleven she met Kumar, her second brother's classmate and friend. Try though she did, she could not bring herself to call him brother. Kumar was different. The very sight of him changed the erstwhile girl into a woman and planted the seed of desire in her breast, a fantastic awakening for the little girl who could hardly cope with her sudden encounter. A feeling of devastation shattered her child's mind, and in its place prevailed a tender sensibility of enchantment. She was overwhelmed. Yesterday's child had turned into a bashful nymph.

The youngest, she grew up with her brothers and was accepted as a playfellow by them and their friends. Though often ignored, she came to accept her inferior position and addressed her brothers' friends as Ramesh-Da, Nikhil-Da or Ajit-Da, adding the brother-suffix "Da" to whatever their first names happened to be. But she could never call Kumar "Kumar-Da".

A tomboy since childhood, she loved to dress in her brothers' shabby old shorts and shirts, matched up to the boys and played boys' games: marbles, kite-flying, tree-climbing to pinch and pocket neighbours' mangoes, and not the least, swimming, her favourite sport. The boys hardly took notice of the tomboy and she was quite happy to hang around unobtrusively in their periphery.

But when her eyes fell on Kumar he changed everything for her overnight, though he had hardly noticed her existence. He became the dream-boy to the child-woman. Hitherto she had looked into the mirror only when combing her hair after a bath, but now for the first time she sneaked up to her mother's wall-mirror to see her glowing face. Would Kumar like it? It did not matter. She smiled to herself. He was her discovery, a rare pearl from the depths of the ocean, so perfect, so absolute, and yet it did not shine vulgarly, screaming for attention. She glorified and basked in the warm, subdued and suave lustre of the pearl, hardly able to take her eyes off from his godlike face and figure. Never mind that he had not noticed her; she had already placed him in the innermost sanctity of her heart that was still in bud. Each time she set eyes on him she was hurtled down an avalanche of feelings that deluged her in blissful oblivion where she wanted to remain forever. To call him "Da" or brother? Oh no! He never fitted to that appendage in her life! He always remained Kumar to her.

Kumar, always the top student in his class and naturally afflicted with over confidence in himself, also excelled in sports and there was no boy who could beat him in any outdoor activity, especially in swimming, until one fine day he found himself beaten by Asha. Both were shocked beyond belief. She never intended to and only did what she had been doing always without anyone ever batting an eye-lid. And that brought her to his notice. Having grown up in a family with boys he had developed an utter disdain for girls! Defeated by a girl! How could that be possible?

It was a warm Indian summer afternoon and in the humid heat it was an ideal time to dip, swim and loll about in the cool water of the back-yard pond over which the surrounding trees cast long shadows of their overhanging branches that swayed gracefully in the wind and kept the water cool and fresh. The boisterous group of boys on their school holiday had gathered at one end of the pond to race to the other end, a pretty good distance away. With a shrill "Go" all heads bobbed up and down while their bodies and limb swished-swashed to the finishing line. And who should emerge at the other end before anyone else, but Asha - calm, cool and unobtrusive with her little pigtailed hair dripping upon her back like a mole's wet tail. No one noticed her, and she would have remained unnoticed as usual had it not been for Kumar.

"Nirod, who's that girl who beat us all? She seems to be the first!" asked the much chagrined and disturbed Kumar, blinking and doubting what had happened.

"That's Asha, my sister. She's not counted in the race. Makes no difference she's first or last," continued Nirod in perfect brotherly demeanour. "My sister's a cat-fish, swims like one. My father says she'll never drown. Just leave her alone."

But Kumar certainly did not leave her alone. For the first time in his life he focussed his attention on a girl. She bugged his thoughts, never leaving him alone. How could it be possible! Beaten by a girl! And younger than he! The more he thought of her the more she grew on him.

BASANTI KARMAKAR writes: "I am a retired school teacher and have taught for twenty-two years in English-medium schools in Singapore." She adds: "Living all my life in Singapore except for a few holiday stints in my parents' home in Bengal, I have been exposed to a conglomeration of multi-cultures, cursorily brought over to this evergreen island by adventurous immigrants who came not exactly to nurture their cultures but to seek their fortunes. I was naturally fascinated when my late father, who arrived here in the early part of this century, used to relate his society's customs and traditions... The story is my own but many of the incidents are taken from true life. I am therefore grateful to those people who opened their bruised hearts to me and to whom I could offer only some words of comfort. I would also like to thank Robert Yeo who took an interest in my story and introduced me to my publisher, Professor P. Lal."

Her first novel *Love in the Throes of Tradition* was published in 1990; that work was described by a reviewer, M.A. Quayum, in the *CRNLE Reviews Journal*, as "a brilliant work." Another reviewer, Ranu Dally, in *The Graduate*, journal of the National University of Singapore Society, wrote, "Karmakar's feminist voice is clear and strong and in her criticism she is both iconoclast and moralist."

Love's Fearful Passage, is her second novel. In many ways, it is similar to the first: a family saga covering several generations, set in Indian Bengal and focuses on the conflict between constricting tradition and liberating modernity.

ARTHUR YAP

cianjur *

the woman & buffalo at a distance were so still.
rice seedlings would have grown from her fingers
if she had not hurried on. an extravagant sunset.
lush flowers, the decaying smell of the wooden house;
rotting balcony, moss-legged cane furniture.
the serial chirping of insects. a naked bulb,
later lit; the pool of ants' wings a prayer mat,
this day's announcement of approaching darkness
thick & crepy as a physicality.

the inside of the house was its outside in reverse.
clumsier rotting furniture. nothing worked, try taps,
the telephone in a smoulder of dust.
an empty, empty hoariness; & its own despair.

all around the house, tall trees, vine-clung,
wild jasmine located by scent, chequer-board
padi fields. slope upon slope,
undulating till the last touched a level
& took away with its splendour one's breath'
a sere coconut leaf javelined the ground.
runner plants fingered their way &,
touching the house variously, never let go.

the distant orange sun taught different greens
for different identities. acid-green seedlings,
sunsteeped tree greens, brown greens, orange greens,
the violent green of a streaking kingfisher.
green noises from wet fields;
the eeriness floating off the hills, green ghosts.

& green were we when we got here
miles from anywhere, this dilapidation
described to us as a chalet-style hotel;
this ruin being hugged by all this grandeur
& gradually being strangled for not being a part.
matually encroaching, it could not vanquish.
it could be vanquished.
it could be very vanquished
before our eyes.

* In Indonesia

nightjar

here, in the night, trees sink deeply downward.
the sound of moonlight walking on black grass
magnifies the clear hard calls of a nightjar,
its soliloquy of ordered savagery, little intervals.
time, clinging on the wrist, ticks it by
but eyes, glued to the dark pages of night,
could not scan the source on the branch.

its insistence calls jab & jab so many times
to a silent ictus, so many times, ringing off the branch
in tiny sharp *tuks*, each lifting from the last

through the night, while the shadows of the trees
go past the edge of sleep & i sit awake,
if it's footfalls across the road, they should be
far away, sounding on the trees, an euphony
lodged on high, the starlit side of heaven.

These poems were previously published in *Man Snake Apple &
Other Poems*.

DR ARTHUR YAP is a senior lecturer in the Department of English at the National University of Singapore.

His first collection of poems, *Only Lines,* published in 1971 was awarded by the National Book Development Council of Singapore in 1976. His other works include *Common Place,* published in 1977; *Down the Line,* published in 1980, was awarded the NBDC Award in 1982 and *Man Snake Apple & Other Poems* is his latest collection of poems.

In 1983 he was awarded the Cultural Medallion in Singapore and the Southeast Asia Write Award in Bangkok. He was again awarded the NBDC Award in 1988.

Arthur has made seven solo exhibitions at the National Library and at the Alpha Gallery, Singapore from 1969-1977.

From Skoob Books Publishing Ltd,
London

ARTHUR YAP'S
Selected Poems

with an
Introduction by
DR. ANNE BREWSTER

Forthcoming 1995.

Skoob *PACIFICA* Series

MALACHI EDWIN
Review of Shirley G-l. Lim's
Nationalism and Literature
English-Language Writing from The Philippines and Singapore

Nationalism and Literature by Shirley Lim, Professor of Asian American Studies at the University of California, Santa Barbara, takes a critical view of two relatively literary new traditions in the English Language. As the sub-title suggests, *English-Language Writing from the Philippines and Singapore*, she gives an account of the development of literary traditions in two countries which have their own native literary traditions. It is worth noting that Shirley Lim has hyphenated *English-Language Writing* as it foregrounds the point that there are other literary traditions in these two nations. English-language writing in both the Philippines and Singapore is very much a twentieth century phenomenon, literary traditions very much in the process of establishing themselves in the world literary map.

In this book, Shirley Lim suggests that a profitable way of reading these writings (both for local and foreign readers) is to take a nationalistic and ethnocentric view. Nationalism and a foreign language for its cause seems rather contradictory. This however, as Lim illustrates, is not the case in these countries where the English-educated elite have resorted to use the language for the dual purpose of creative writing and nation building.

The nationalism of the writers in this study is a post-Independence phenomenon. The nationalism is not against colonial masters but is very much the writers' attempts at creating social and political consciousness in their readers, directed towards nation building. Yet, as Shirley Lim points out, the readership of these literary works in English is indeed very small, which among other factors has consequently affected the production of literary works in these two countries. These writers may do better writing in their native languages, one might argue. However, this may not be possible as, Lim also points out, many of the English-Language writers, "have lost fluency in their native languages and abandoned traditional ways for Western lifestyles."

As most critics on postcolonial writings in English, Lim calls for the reading of these works be based on their own literary traditions and not on purely Western critical practice. One may wonder why Lim chose Philippine and Singaporean literary traditions as companions in this volume. There are obvious differences in these societies in terms of politics, economics and cultural features. She states that her basis of comparison is the fact that these two are the only nations in this region to have a national policy of acceptance of English as an official language which has helped in the evolution of a literary tradition in English, a situation which would be envied very much by their neighbours, the Malaysian writers in English.

In *Nationalism and Literature*, Lim provides a comprehensive historical account of the development of the English-language literary traditions in these two countries, contextualising them in their respective societies. In the Philippines, the English-language writer is shown to be caught in a dilemma in his choice of language for his literary expression. There has been as shift towards the use of native languages and writing in English or Spanish goes against the grain of the present political trend. Not so in multi-racial and multi-cultural Singapore. English is perceived as a bridge language among the races and is accepted as a language for literary expression along with the local languages.

Lim in her discussion of the two literary traditions in English, she examines the work of two prolific writers from each tradition. Prose writer F.S. Jose and "multi-genre writer" Nick Joaquin for the Philippines and poets Edwin Thumboo and Arthur Yap for Singapore are discussed. The writers of the two countries again come from rather contrasting backgrounds, the Filipino writers are both with journalistic backgrounds whereas the Singaporeans are both from English-educated academic elite circles.

In F.S. Jose', which took thirty years in writing, Lim discusses the socio-political consciousness of a writer who she claims attempts to present the Filipino national history. His five-novel cycle, which she calls the Rosales quintology is set from the time of the Revolutionary 1890s to the Marcos Martial Law period in the 1970s.

In Jose's novels, Lim discusses the treatment of the themes of social justice, class conflict and nationalist struggles. She states that in order to appreciate Jose's achievement in the quintology the novels should be read as "an evolving discourse on Filipino national aspiration and identity".

Lim's study of Nick Joaquin novels illustrates the contrast between the styles these two writers. Lim provides a detailed discussion on Joaquin's two novels, *The Women Who Had Two Navels* (1972) and *Cave and Shadows* (1983). Joaquin emerges the more interesting as his concern is more for the individual and his psyche. Joaquin neither supports any social group or propounds any ideology. Much of his work revolves around his concern for Filipino cultural and national identity. This is reflected in his concern for the submergence of the Filipino-Hispanic identity by modern American influence. Of his work Lim states, "(H)is genius lies in his original synthesis of the Filipino-Spanish identity with the new English language".

In her discussion on Singapore writing in English, Lim discusses the work of two poets who are almost from two different periods in the history of the country. As such, Edwin Thumboo, the older poet is seen very much the forerunner to Arthur Yap. Thumboo is shown very much as a poet in a society in transition, a member of the postcolonial generation. His works reflect his attempts at departing from Western literary traditions and innovating a new Singaporean literary mindscape.

Lim provides an extensive study of Thumboo's three volumes of poetry, *Rib of Earth* (1956), *Gods Can Die* (1977) and *Ulysses by the Merlion* (1979). She traces his development as poet as she discourses his attempts at experimenting with local images. His poems are also seen in the light of personal and public poems. Lim states that the best of his public poems "is didactic, rooted in moral conviction rather than public dogma".

Lim's critique of Yap's four volumes of poems *Only Lines* (1971), *Commonplace* (1977), *down the line* (1980) and *Man Snake Apple* (1986) presents him as the more successful and exciting of the two Singaporean poets. This, however, is not to diminish Thumboo's contribution to the development of Singaporean poetry. Yap is shown to be able to capture in his poems "the possibilities of the English language used in Singapore". Lim sees this as Yap's ability to distinguish himself as a Singapore poet.

Yap is depicted both as a poet who is concerned with social issues and situations in Singapore and also a private poet. His satirical voice is said to "increase in sharpness with each book". Yap is seen to be critical of Singaporean social ideology whereas Thumboo is said to explain Singaporean state ideology.

Lim, in the concluding paragraph on her discussion of Yap's work, provides an interesting list of contrasts between the writing styles of Thumboo and Yap. This can be taken very much as fair evaluation of the two writers' works.

Nationalism and Literature on the whole is a valuable contributory volume to the study postcolonial writing in English. As a study it is well documented and researched. Almost a fifth of the book comprises notes and a selected bibliography. The chapters on Singaporean writings in English are highly recommended.

© Malachi Edwin 1994

Malachi Edwin is a Malaysian researching his Ph. D in South-East Asian literature at the University of Nottingham.

PART THREE

Other Literatures of

the Pacific Rim

HAN SUYIN
Picnic in Malaya

Excerpt from *TIGERS AND BUTTERFLIES*

When Maimunah rang me I thought at first that it would be about the mass meeting, because we were trying to hold a mass meeting for marriage reform and Maimunah had written to the police for a permit to hold the meeting.

"Come quick," she said, "Hasnah is very ill."

Hasnah is Maimunah's sister.

"Is it her baby coming?"

"No," she said, "the baby is not coming yet. Come quick."

I went in my Volkswagen to Maimunah's place. At the door was Kalsom, the little Chinese girl whom Maimunah has adopted. Kalsom is terribly spoilt, and I always tell Maimunah: "You are nicer to your little Chinese girl than to your own Malay sons." Maimunah laughs and gives Kalsom another hug, every time.

Kalsom screamed (she always screams, clatters, hurls herself, an ebullient fat little girl full of energy): "Mama, Mama, your friend has come!"

Inside the house, behind the screen, were women, about a score, including old ones with veils half-drawn, surrounding a weeping Hasnah with hair undone and her five children all weeping.

"What has happened?" I asked, but already I knew.

"Divorced," said Maimunah, "three *talaaqs* all at once, Doctor, and she knew nothing at all about it, nothing at all."

"How did it happen, and what about the children?"

"Ah," said Maimunah, "we are women, Doctor, so it happens and we cannot do anything."

The story was simple, so simple and so common story of Malay women in Malaya. Hasnah was happily married to Idris, and Idris had three other wives, two younger and healthier than Hasnah; but Hasnah had made up her mind about them, and there was no more than the usual small underground bickering between the women. It was Hasnah who had brought one of the wives and her little daughter, aged three, to me when they were ill with gonorrhea (caught from Idris, who had caught it from a prostitute) two years previously. Idris was now getting rich. Not only had he a good job in the government, but he dealt on the side in licences for transport, and he had bought a car and two houses in the name of his mother, so that the income tax man did not trouble him. Hasnah was very proud of her husband's business acumen, because many Malays were unable to make money, they did not know how to do business. "That's because his mother is Chinese," said Hasnah. In her mind, business acumen was an inherited trait from the Chinese side of Idris, and so a very good thing.

That morning, after a night of love, Idris had said to Hasnah: "Please go to your sister's house with the children. I have some business, and I will come round to pick you up."

At first Hasnah was puzzled. Idris was usually too busy to take her and the children out. Would he come to pick her up in the car, because of the children? She herself was six months pregnant, and with the usual anaemia became giddy at times, but she did not have the habit of asking questions. She dressed the children, and they sauntered off to the bus stop. They waited twenty minutes, and the bus came, and they all got on, paying 20 cents for herself and 10 cents for each child. Maimunah's house was about three miles away.

When Hasnah arrived Maimunah was busy with her sewing club. Maimunah is a born organizer, in fact she cannot stop organizing. Even jail for two years under the British had not stopped her. She had worked hard for *merdeka*, independence, as many Malay women had worked hard, believing independence would also bring them some measure of real rights, not paper rights, some true relief from the fearsome, man-made laws which had the sanction of religion and made it so easy for men to divorce and remarry, so easy for women to be thrown on the streets. "After *merdeka*, when they divorce us, they will have to pay for the children," they said. Maimunah had campaigned for women's rights. "After *merdeka*, there will be schools for the women, then we shall be educated, and if our men divorce us we shall be able to work for ourselves. We shall not have to become prostitutes to feed ourselves and our children."

But this had not happened for the poor women, though the women of the rich, the women of the upper class and the government officials' wives had gone to schools, and some of them even had jobs, and there were three women in parliament. For women like Hasnah and Maimunah there was no such protection.

So after *merdeka* and her release from jail, Maimunah organized sewing clubs to teach the girls to sew.

"You see, Doctor," she used to say to me when I visited her among the whir and tack of the sewing-machines, "if we women don't learn to work, we go on the streets. There are forty thousand prostitutes in my State. And what does the Religious Department do if they catch us? Put in jail, lah, and finished. And when come out, who is going to feed mother and children?"

It was through Maimunah that I began to understand the distress of the Malay woman. In the *kampongs,* the Malay villages, in times of flood, when the catch of fish was poor, when the paddy rice did not grow, to pay off debts (and all paddy planters were in debt), girls were married off at fourteen and fifteen, or sold to brothels.

"Divorce and marry, divorce and marry, Doctor," said Maimunah, laughing softly (she always laughed in sorrow, because she was polite and did not inflict a sad face upon the world, however bitter her heart became), "what else is there for us? In my *kampong* there is a girl of nineteen who has been married five times!"

That morning Hasnah came to Maimunah, sat for a while in the room below the stairs with the sewing-machines amid the girls sewing. But the children were restless, so she went to the inner room, behind the screen, to give them some sweets, and there the message came to her It was a letter from Idris, her husband, in which it said briefly that he had spoken the three *talaaqs,* by which she was irrevocably divorced.

When Hasnah read the message, brought by a boy who was a distant cousin of Idris and who hastily went away after thrusting the envelope in her hand, she could not believe it at first.

"My eyes are not good," she said to Maimunah, "a devil sits in front of them. Please read this from Idris, my husband."

"Allamah," cried Maimunah, "he has given you the three *talaaqs!* You are divorced. And you were not even present. Hasnah, what did you do wrong?"

Hasnah was too stunned to reply. She searched in her mind for something wrong she had done. Only last night Idris was with her...had she offended him in love-making? Had her breath, perhaps, been sour? Was it the child within her? She now felt, with terror, the child move, and beginning with a loud cry she wept, knocking her head against the wall, until her heavy hair fell from its bun on to her shoulders and back.

With the first sound of weeping automatically the women left the machines. The sewing girls, many of them married and divorced and remarried and redivorced again, and who knew without being told what had happened, crowded round Hasnah, asking: "*Apa?* what is it, why does she cry?"

"Three *talaaqs*," Maimunah answered.

And they whispered, looking at each other, round-eyed: "Three *talaaqs*? All at once? And not even in her presence?"

Some said: "What has she done of evil?"

Others said: "It happens…it was the same with me."

And still others said: "Allah's will."

And others ran to chafe Hasnah's hands, and wept with her and also for themselves, remembering their own pain.

"It is not fair," said a sturdy, tall girl with a slight hare-lip and big round eyes. She was a Sumatran and Minangkabau, where matriarchal tradition is strong. She had been to school somewhat, for two years, had been accused at one time of being a communist which is why she had lost her job in the welfare office and was now learning to sew because she had two children.

"It is Allah's will," said another, and Kalsom, the little Chinese girl, repeated, bouncing up and down: "Allah's will, Allah's will."

"No," said the girl from Sumatra, and her thick eyebrows came together. "It is not the Will of God. In other Islamic countries it is forbidden to give three *talaaqs* together. A man can only say: '*Talaaqs*, I divorce you,' once, clapping his hands, and the wife must be there to hear it. Then he must wait a month and for his wife to be unclean and clean again before the second time he claps his hands and says *talaaqs*. And once more a month, and another cleansing, before the third *talaaq*. To give three *talaaqs* together is not according to the Koran."

"Three *talaaqs* can never be taken back," said another. "It is unfair."

"But what has Hasnah done?" said others.

"I have a child," shrieked Hasnah. "It is Idris's child." And she wept till they thought she would die.

Meanwhile Maimunah had asked Fatimah's advice. Fatimah was match-maker, physician and midwife, and did not know her age so that she at times said forty and at others sixty. She applied herbs to Hasnah's temples, meanwhile counselled Maimunah: "Send that cousin of yours to Idris's house, quick, but let him stay outside and watch, and come back to report." So this was done.

It was time for the morning rice, and no one had thought of eating, there was too much sorrow; but the children clamoured for food, and Maimunah went to the kitchen to start the rice cooking. I sat with the women. The Sumatran girl said to me:

"In Indonesia now the husbands cannot be careless any more. They have to pay maintenance."

"My husband did not pay," said another, "and I had three children. He was in the police, and the government transferred him to Penang so he left me."

"How did you get your *talaaqs?*" asked the Sumatran girl.

"Post office," said the girl. "A letter, like Hasnah. I cannot read. The postman read it to me."

The children ate, the women talked, each one telling her own story, or rather the stories of her marriages. The divorce rate in Malaya is sixty per cent of the marriage rate, so there are many stories.

The cousin returned, a young man employed in the telecommunications who therefore owned a bicycle, which is why he had been selected. He spoke to Maimunah, standing on the other side of the screen. He had arrived to see Idris leave in the car with a tall young girl with curly hair, very *sombong* (proud), who used to work in a massage parlour. There are many massage parlours in Malaya, and their uses are obvious. He added that someone said Idris often went to this massage parlour. The back seat of the car had suitcases and parcels. Where they went, the cousin did not know, but "some people in the neighbourhood" said they knew Idris had had sick leave from a hospital doctor who was a relative, and that the certificate said Idris was suffering from typhoid and needed three weeks' sick leave. Idris had promised the hospital doctor to help him get a house from a Chinese merchant, hence the certificate. In effect, added the cousin, getting more loquacious, Idris had told some friends of his a few days ago that he was going to another job, in Kuala Lumpur, and that he would be leaving soon.

So now everyone understood why Hasnah had been divorced. Because Idris otherwise would have gone against the law, which says that a man can have no more than four wives at a time, and Idris had his quota. If he wanted a fifth, he had to divorce *one*. Now the older Number One wife was a rich woman with a fairly powerful family backing her; she lived for the greater part of the time at home with her own parents, her two sons were in England on government scholarships. Idris would never dare to repudiate her. Hasnah was not attractive now, five pregnancies had spoilt her teeth and her figure. The two younger wives would possibly join him later, in Kuala Lumpur, where he had gone to honeymoon with the new one.

Evening fell, and Hasnah stopped weeping from sheer tiredness, and by that time everyone in the *kampong* had added his piece to the story, and now Idris was rumoured to have gone from Kuala Lumpur by airplane to Hong Kong with his new bride to enjoy himself there.

"Just like the Sultan," said a neighbour, half admiring.

"When the Sultan of - took his twenty-fifth wife he went there for the honeymoon," corroborated another.

Others maintained he had gone to Singapore, where the sixth floor of a certain hotel was reserved for officials to enjoy themselves. Still others said no, it was Kuala Lumpur, because Idris, being a government official, had friends in Kuala Lumpur and the wedding would be celebrated there.

Hasnah went back to the house where the two younger wives, lids lowered, pretended not to see her, Maimunah and I went with her, since I had a car to convey them all, and Maimunah said sternly to one of the young wives: "Hasnah your sister was good to you. When you were ill with the dirty sickness she took you to the doctor to be cured. It was Idris who infected you, and also your little girl, and it was Hasnah who took her own money to pay for the doctor for you to be cured. Why did you not warn her?"

The young wife giggled and did not answer. She was an uneducated girl from a village, and whatever happened she only giggled, and never answered a word.

In the days that followed my Volkswagen was much used. I drove Hasnah, always with at least three children to cling to her, on necessary visits. The first one was to Idris's mother, a stout, powdered lady in flowered nylon, with gold pins in her false chignon and gold teeth gleaming in her mouth and gold bangles upon her arms. She believed in carrying all her cash upon herself, since one never knew when a man would clap his hands with: "*Talaaq talaaq talaaq,*" and out was the woman, to fend for herself. And since the law said that the woman would take with her, when divorced, the clothes on her back and the jewels on her body, and her dowry and property, Idris's mother had always, and wisely, invested in gold and, now that she was a widow, in real estate.

Consolidation had made her portly, the desire for hoarding traducing itself in her appetite as well. She received Hasnah coldly, but gave sweets to the children. "I shall look after my grandchildren," she announced. "You can leave them with me, Hasnah, when you go back to your *kampong.*"

Hasnah, who now wept as easily as she breathed, wept and said: "But I love my children. I do not wish to go back to the *kampong.*"

"Hasnah," said Idris's mother severely, "it is too late now. Hasnah and Idris are divorced, and it is best that Hasnah should marry again."

"Hasnah has a baby from Idris in her belly," said Maimunah. "To divorce her at this time is against the law."

Idris's mother looked round-eyed with anger at Maimunah. Then she spoke again in the third person. "Here is the crab that tells its young to walk straight. What does Maimunah know of the law, who has been, so I am told, in jail? I hear Maimunah is sub-versive." She pronounced it with weight, in English, soob-versiff.

"I went to jail under the British colonialists, yes," said Maimunah, "and I fought for *merdeka*, independence, while others went gazing at the sweet water." This she said because it was whispered that Idris's mother had had an illicit affair with a man from a village called Ayer Manis, "sweet water".

"Ah," said Idris's mother, looking into the air reflectively, "the turtle lays thousands of eggs and not a word says she; the hen calls the whole country to see her hatch one chick."

"Come, Hasnah," said Maimunah, "you can boil a stone, but you cannot make it tender." And after this parting shot Maimunah in great rage took Hasnah away.

The next visit was to the Kathi of the Religious Affairs Department. Hasnah and Maimunah had to wait some time, and

Hasnah, never strong in mind, in the dim corridor began to feel that truly she must have done something wrong. "It is no use, Maimunah," she wailed. "Let me die, that is all. Let Idris's mother take the children, I will die and the earth will be the lighter for it. It is Allah's will."

But Maimunah wanted to fight. "You must have maintenance at least until the child is born," she said.

The Kathi of the Religious Court (Divorces section) was a frail man with a fine Arab face under his white corded cap. He spoke sparingly, his cheeks were sunken and his eyes brilliant. When Maimunah had finished, he said:

"Idris has recorded divorce. He pleads unfaithfulness on the part of Hasnah his wife; hence gave her three *talaaqs*."

At this Hasnah threw her veil across her face and fainted. Maimunah and I carried her out. Then Maimunah returned to the Kathi. She came back pale with anger.

"It is no use," she said. "Idris has witnesses, he says. Now we must get a lawyer."

We went to the Indian lawyer, because he was cheaper than a Chinese or a European lawyer. He listened, and then he said that this was Religious Law, and in the state it was not against Religious Law for a husband to give three *talaaqs* at once to his wife, and it would be difficult if Idris had witnesses, even if witnesses did not tell the truth, and he was willing to take the case but five hundred dollars must be paid in advance.

"Five hundred dollars," said Maimunah desperately, "where can I get five hundred dollars?"

So I said I would lend them to her, and Maimunah said she would think about it, and the next day she came for the five hundred dollars for the lawyer to fight the case for Hasnah.

Hasnah went home, and now the rent was due, so Maimunah borrowed again for the rent; the other two wives disappeared. Maimunah asked Hasnah to come to live with her, but there was not room enough for six more people. Then Maimunah had another idea: she would speak to a Member of Parliament about this. She selected Che Marriamah, one of the three women members of parliament, and went up to Kuala Lumpur to speak to her, borrowing the train fare.

Meanwhile Hasnah moaned, and became persuaded that she had sinned. The habit of subservience was too strong. If Idris had said she had been unfaithful, perhaps it had been so, unknown to herself; she had been the victim of the demons, of evil spirits; perhaps she had unwittingly stepped upon someone's blood; perhaps a spell had been cast upon her...an incubus had come to her in the shape of Idris, hence she had been unfaithful without even knowing it.

So Hasnah hoped for death; did not die at once, managed first to deliver the child at six months, a puny two-pounder, at night, with old Fatimah helping, and died ten days later of an infection from a boil on Fatimah's finger; and I did not know, until told by Maimunah when she came back from Kuala Lumpur, that Hasnah was dead.

"Why did you not tell me?" I said to Maimunah. "Why did she not send word to me, I could have done something for her."

"Oh," said Maimunah, smiling with sorrow, "she had bothered you much already, she was so ashamed of being much trouble to you."

Then Maimunah told me about her visit to the woman member of parliament, or *parlimen* as it is called in Malaya. Che Marriamah had been very kind to her, asking her to sit and eat with her, but she could do so little to help. "Sister Maimunah," she said, "what can I do? Already the men in *parlimen* were so rude to me. When I get up and ask for schools for women, for education, and for protection for children, for reform for prostitutes and not jail, they clatter their desks and make a great noise and bang their briefcases and stamp their feet and go out and in, out and in...so that I have to shout to be heard. And they do this because I am a woman and they are men."

Che Marriamah had been to jail at the same time as Maimunah, and now she too had to fight hard, and, she felt, fruitlessly, for the women.

"They promised us everything when they wanted our votes, but now they do little or nothing because they are men." One day, she told Maimunah, she had said at the end of a speech: "You seem to have forgotten the women who voted for you." And one of the Ministers, getting up, had replied in a smooth, silky, arrogant way: "Now, how can we men forget women? Of course we *never* forget them, neither day...nor night." And all the honourable members of *parlimen* laughed at that sally, deeming it *so* witty.

"That is how it is," said Che Marriamah. "They will not move until we the women organize and force them to change."

"Then how about your mass meeting?" I asked Maimunah.

"Cannot, lah," said Maimunah. "The police asked me *why* I want to call mass meeting. Then they say cannot, it is subversive, because I have not registered our association, and it is subversive for more than five people to meet for a common purpose without notifying the police and without proper registration."

It was the day for the funeral. Maimunah borrowed two hundred dollars. It was a beautiful after-rain cool day, with a gusty breeze blowing from the sea at high tide, and burying was quickly over, and after it Maimunah and all the children and I went walking by the sea edge. Many people, European families with their children, had come to lie on the beach, to sun themselves and to eat food out of hampers. Maimunah was too modest to look at them because they lay with so few clothes, but she was always puzzled, she said, why they ate on the beach instead of in their houses.

"It is called a picnic," I said, "it is a habit to go out in the sun to a nice place and eat there. The children like it."

Maimunah decided, there and then, that the Friday after the next we should have a picnic for the children.

And so we did, all the girls and women of the sewing club, Maimunah and her children, and also Hasnah's children, and some neighbours and their wives and children. We went to a place by the sea. The girls sang, and the children played. Maimunah and the women cooked curry chicken, plantains and vegetables, and rice wrapped in leaves. Maimunah borrowed plates from me, and we ate with our fingers. The sun was hot and good, the wind blew, the tall girl from Sumatra began to sing. It rained a little, so that someone cried: "See, the frog croaks and the rain comes." And this made all of us laugh and laugh.

© Han Suyin, 1961

312

DUDLEY DE SOUZA
The Novels of F. Sionil Jose:
Protagonists in Spiritual Exile

Any examination of the fiction of Jose will inevitably have socio-political implications focusing around the question of exploitation and the sense of identity. In explaining the explicitly anti-Hispanic sentiment which is such a major component of his fiction, it would be necessary to understand the spiritual dilemma which recurringly afflicts the protagonists in his novels as it applies to the quintet comprising: *The Pretenders* (1962) *My Brother, My Executioner* (1973) *The Tree* (1978), *Mass* (1983) and *Po-on* (1984).

They constitute the backbone of Jose's achievement and they revolve around the realities - as he perceives them - of social injustice in the Philippines spanning a number of different generations.

Stated simply, the dilemma is this: in order to rise from poverty to power, wealth and all the trappings of success a brilliant or talented individual would have no other avenue except to cut his moorings with his people and join the exploitative class: the elite who have always been in power. He would, in other words, have to accept social injustice and join the oppressors. As Juan Puneta tells Pepito Samson in *Mass*:

The doors are wide open to those who are bright. [1]

It is only required that one should cut oneself off from one's own roots and be, like Antonio Samson in *The Pretenders*, a spiritual exile.

Before we examine the novels, it might be instructive to make a brief survey of the socio-historical context of the Philippines as a means of immediate access to the kind of literary exposition which Jose makes of the Filipino identity.

More than three hundred years of Spanish rule inevitably left a firm impression on the Filipino character - especially on religion, culture and social as well as economic institutions. And undeniably, the American regime that began at the beginning of this century also left its imprint on the life-style of the Filipino people through the education system, the form of government and popular culture. However, since national character - it would be generally agreed -

takes a long time stewing, it would be most likely that the Spanish regime has left a deeper impression on the Filipino soul.

However, the Spanish factor - in terms of a feudal structure with the conspicuous Spanish landlord - has always appeared an imposition on the indigenous Filipino in F. Sionil Jose's novel, as we shall show. What the Spanish regime made notorious was a feudal and decadent social order rooted in the fossilized *encomienda* [2] system.

This system originated in the commission of specific territory acquired by the Spanish, in the early years of conquest, to the charge of *encomienderos* who had the right to exact tribute from the inhabitants and to treat them as serfs. Although the system underwent transformation with the passage of time it remained basically exploitative, leading to widespread abuses like absentee landlordism and the transmission of indebtedness from generation to generation. Even after the departure of the Spanish government the exploitation maintained its momentum with the Filipino upper class moving into the vacuum created by the departure of the ruling elite. Thus, the revolutionary, peasant-based Hukbalahap movement rears its head in the fiction of Jose - especially in relation to *My Brother, My Executioner* (1973) where brother is pitted against brother on two sides of the same fence: the exploiter and the exploited, the landowner and the dispossessed.

Social problems in the writings of Jose are dealt with in literary terms i.e. through thematic contrasts, characterization, symbol and plot. Throughout his fiction, the underlying sense of social inequality is always present, from the picture of the peasantry turning away from the gates of the Asperri mansion while the master grinds his teeth at the image of his deformed successor in 'The Heirs' to the differences in the life-styles of Commander Victor, the guerilla leader and his half-brother Luis Asperri who lives on the Asperri estate (although not without qualms of conscience) in *My Brother, My Executioner*.

The polar positions in the structure of social inequality can be illustrated quite simply in diagrammatic terms thus:

The Exploiters	*The Exploited*
The Spanish or Basque Vascon in the time of the extension of Spanish colonization.	The Indios of the early years of Spanish conquest.

The half-Spanish landowner in modern times.	The peasantry and the slum-dwellers.
Foreigners like the Japanese, Chinese and American businessmen who are seen as partners of the local magnates.	The dispossessed Ilocanos.

Despite this disjunction between oppressors and victims, the key to the sense of conflict and tension in Jose's fiction is very often the internalization of these polar forces within a central character. This applies especially to the protagonists in the quintet. They belong to both camps and are exiles living in a limbo of uncertainty. Although written last, *Po-on* establishes the setting for the 'Rosales saga' - so-called because the protagonist (like the author himself) was born in Rosales. In *The Pretenders* (1966) Antonio Samson's father, a peasant rebel, was jailed for his part in an Ilocano revolt against unjust dispossession of land opened up by the Ilocano settlers. Nevertheless, Antonio has married into the camp of the dispossessors - the family of the industrial magnate and mestizo, Don Manuel Villa. In *My Brother, My Executioner*, Luis Asperri's mother with whom the protagonist identifies, is an Ilocano maid who had been wronged by his father, the wealthy Don Vicente Asperri. In *Tree* (1978) the narrator is the son of the Filipino sub-landlord managing Don Vicente's estate in the latter's absence. The father has sympathies with the workers in the household but has to hold the reigns according to the directives from Don Vicente. In *Tree*, however, the perspective is somewhat different since the boy protagonist is not fully aware of the implications of the social system he is part of - unlike the intellectuals who occupy centre stage in *The Pretenders* and *My Brother, My Executioner*. Consequently, the approach there is only mild compassion for the oppressed and an ironic understatement governing the presentation of social inequality in the narrative. The conflict and the tension are not within the protagonist himself: they are external events - viewed from a fairly safe distance.

In some respects, *Tree* antedates the other two novels. Although the publication date is 1978, it had appeared much earlier as the story entitled *The Balete Tree* which has been referred to before. The conception of the internalized conflict characteristic of the protagonists in the other two novels would thus appear to belong to a later stage of thematic evolution in the fiction of F. Sionil Jose. *Tree* could thus be seen as a throwback although the publication date is 1978.

In *Tree* the narrator is a mirror: he reflects the life going on around him and although he himself is touched at points in the story (eg in the circus girl episode or when he confronts his father's mistress) his responses reveal a humanism and a detachment that are somewhat surprisingly mature; more significantly, his position vis-à-vis his father and the issue of social injustice in the Filipino barrio also reveals a similar detachment: it is the distancing of one who is not fully involved in the proceedings. In other words, despite the emotional maturity of the narrator we remember that he is still too young to be aware of the extent or intensity of the social issues behind Tio Baldo's death or Old David's lament. It is as though we see more than the narrator sees as the novel unfolds: Uncle Berto who comes back from the United States, Padre Andong the parish priest. Tio Doro the school principal, Miss Santillan and Mr Sanchez who sing together...they all attest to the vivid life of the community around the narrator. They have the same right to be there - even if the episodes are humorous - as Tio Baldo's tragedy has. The narrator has reduced all episodes to the same level of significance simply because the other episodes do not serve as a justification for the existence of the Tio Baldo episode - they do not sub-serve; they exist as equals and are there for their own distinctive life. The theme of social equality is thus incidental to this novel; in the words of the narrator, *Tree* is

> ...a journey into the past - a hazardous trek through byways dim and forgotten - forgotten because that is how I chose to regard many things about this past. In moments of great lucidity, I see again people who - though they may no longer be around - are ever present still; I can almost hear their voices and reach out to touch them - my friends, cousins, uncles and aunts and, most of all, Father.[3]

The account is thus semi-autobiographical. It is a journey into childhood: a picture of life in Rosales - an enclosed segment of rural society under traditional, semi-feudal conditions (conditions originally rooted in the *encomienda* system although the system itself is not the central issue of the novel).

Towards the end of the novel, the narrator assumes a somewhat preachy tone, reminiscent of Bitfogel's outburst towards the end of *The Pretenders*. In *Tree*, this segment has the effect of making the narrator seem older than what he has projected himself to be all along (or is it that he has simply grown?). It summarizes the position of non-action that he has taken vis-a-vis the perception of social injustice around him:

> Who was Don Vicente, after all? I should not be angered when men in the highest places, sworn to serve this country as public servants, end up as millionaires in Pobres Park while using people's money in the name of beauty, the public good and all shallow shibboleths about discipline and nationalism that we have come to hear incessantly...But like my father, I have not done anything I could not because I am me; because I died long ago. [4]

The kind of spiritual death indicated here is obviously a death in terms of identity. He has rejected or rather become indifferent to the impulse to belong to the people around him. He has become part of the feudal and essentially foreign superstructure imposed on the Filipino people. In other words, apathy appears to be the root cause of his loss of identity and the heart of spiritual exile.

Although the attitude of the protagonist is significantly different in *Tree*, there are a number of major similarities in all three novels of Jose, thus establishing a shared context. Firstly, the setting - with minor variations here and there - is common to all three, although not restricted to only these works of Jose. An early extended image of Rosales actually appears in the short story entitled 'The Heirs' which is in the collection called *The God Stealer and Other Stories* (1968). Here, the genesis of Rosales is described. The place was originally inhabited by Ilocanos but the Vascon Don Jacinto Asperri sees it as a future family estate and annexes it without more ado:

> ...he drank in the wide and glorious scene and sighed, 'This is my land!' [5]

Rosales is used as the setting for the rich and decadent Asperri household in *My Brother, My Executioner* in the same manner as in 'The Heirs' - except that the characters are now situated in contemporary times.

In *The Pretenders*, there is also a Rosales although this time is not the base of the rich and exploitative; it is the poor who truly belong to the land where Emmy and Antonio Samson's son are staying.

In *Tree* Rosales again becomes the centre of the action and the land belongs to the rich absentee landlord Don Vicente Asperri who has left its management to the narrator's father, who behaves like a modified version of the Spanish landlord with a retinue of servants and farmhands.

There is also a sense of continuity in the retention of the Asperri family as a symbol of the decadent Spanish bourgeoisie in the Philippines although there is a wider variation here than in the use of the Rosales setting. Here, again, 'The Heirs' seems to be a prototype. In *My Brother, My Executioner* Luis Asperri is the son of Don Vicente Asperri by an Ilocano maid. Don Vicente appears again in *Tree* although here he is not in the foreground. In *The Pretenders*, deviation from the pattern is observable - partly, perhaps, because the story was conceived a little before 'The Heirs'. Here, the Villa family occupies the place accorded to the Asperris in the other novels. But the name is Spanish and the significance is similar. Don Manuel Villa, however, is a smooth-talking, self-aware and altogether more up-to-date version of Don Vicente, well-versed in the corruptibility of men:

> Don Manuel brought his forefinger to the right temple and gestured twice. 'It's all a matter of understanding what a man wants most. If you give him that, then he is yours to command...'[6]

While Don Vicente is the stereotypical image of the landed gentry in the Philippines wallowing coarsely in his wealth with seeming indifference to the condition of the peasantry, including that of his former lover (Luis' mother), Don Manuel is an urbane and conscious capitalist with a sort of philosophy. His argument proffered to the young Samson presents almost incontrovertible reasons for maintaining his line of action, or his course of corruption.

Most significantly, among these unifying characteristics in Jose's novels, there is a conspicuous thematic affinity in the quintet. The theme of betrayal pervades the series. This appears in the form of spiritual death as we have seen in the case of *Tree*, but more importantly, betrayal serves to underscore the tension produced by inner conflict in *The Pretenders, My Brother, My Executioner* and *Mass*.

In almost all the novels, the sense of the overwhelming odds of fighting against oppression is always conspicuous. This is especially so with *The Pretenders* where the protagonist commits suicide on the railway tracks - to a large extent the victim of his father-in-law's (a steel magnate's) oppressive role in Filipino society. Unfortunately, Tony Samson's position weakens towards the end. This is because his suicide is as much a case of opting out as an act of courage. His realization of his failure in both worlds - in that of the exploiters as well as the exploited - leads to the final act. Tony cannot be devoid of compassion in the manner of Don Manuel Villa yet he is unable to champion the cause of the poor with any degree of integrity: he is caught in the middle and decides not to continue the pretence of belonging to either side. His bourgeois wife takes a lover, his friends are bought over and his Ilocano lover rejects him just as he has turned his back on his Ilocano roots. Thus, the search for his roots is ironic, because he finds that his grandfather's name was Salvador (or Saviour), but as Samson, he has been shorn of his locks by a modern-day Delilah and has made unholy peace with the oppressors of the land. To some extent, *The Pretenders* can be characterized as an exposé of social injustice in Filipino society. Talent and ability are perverted to inglorious ends by the wealthy and powerful. Within this framework, Jose seems to place the true Filipino, the son of the soil or the Ilocano as the ultimate loser and all attempts at improving his lot either end in violence or come to nothing.

It is not until *My Brother, My Executioner* that we have some glimmering of a new dawn promising social justice with the imminent demise of the protagonist in the concluding chapter. Although sharing certain structural similarities with 'The Heirs', this novel has for its backdrop, a more immediate situation: the Hukbalahap uprising during the 1950s. This movement is of central significance to the novel because it symbolised a grass-roots reaction against social injustices perpetrated by the upper class Filipinos skilled in the arts of exploiting the rural masses - a skill inherited from the Spanish officials and friars who amassed vast tracts of property under the *encomienda* system. The Hukbalahap uprising, which began as peasant resistance to the Japanese during the Occupation years (1942-1945), reflects one of the central concerns of Jose's fiction: social injustice as a consequence of foreign exploitation of the Ilocano and dispossession of land which he had struggled to open up.

However, what distinguishes the novel from the prototype story 'The Heirs' is that now, the argument is more complicated. The novel centres on the perceptions of Luis Asperri who belongs to both camps. On his father's side he is with the exploiters; on his mother's, the exploited. There is some suggestion of this dilemma in 'The Heirs' with the depiction of the half-native child Antonio Asperri, but he is not the centre of interest in the story and we do not see him from the inside. With Luis we have an amalgamation of both identities: the identity of the upper class Spanish landlord and that of the peasant class Ilocano. More importantly, it is his consciousness that provides the focal point for the novel.

His father, Don Vicente Asperri is the archetypal Spanish landowner who plays approximately the same role as Don Felix Asperri in 'The Heirs'. In the novel, however, the portrait of the landowner is ameliorated by Don Vicente's genuine regard for his son and the awareness that what he has to do is done with the son's interest at heart. His cruelties are seen as necessary inhumanities, acts of self-defence against the actions of the guerillas led by Commander Victor - Luis' half-brother.

Despite this, however, what Don Vicente stands for is scrutinised by both his son Luis and Commander Victor. Luis is thus torn between alternatives - the extreme positions held by his blood relatives: on the one hand the outright rejection of reactionary Spanish feudalism and, on the other, the dismissal of the guerilla extremists in the name of an exploitative paternalism.

Like Antonio in 'The Heirs', Luis is the son of a servant girl who used to work in his father's household. In addition, the suggestion of Antonio's leanings towards culture and idealism are elaborated into Luis' incipient idealism and sense of justice which contrast markedly with the father's vulgar and cynical attitude towards emergent manhood and marriage.

The tension between the non-Filipino world of exploiters (Chinese shopkeepers are also aligned with Don Vicente) and the Ilocano

320

world of the exploited is symbolised in the two homes of Luis - with his father at Rosales and with his mother at Sipnget - where he feels he truly belongs:

> I am home. I am home. This is the place honoured in the mind and sanctified in the heart. Although he had been away, the sounds and smells were always with him, the aroma of the newly harvested grain, the grass fresh with dew, the mooing cattle...and, most of all, the tones of his language for there was in Ilocano, the aura and mystery of things left unsaid. [7]

There is thus an overpowering awareness of belonging to a specific ethnic identity. Despite this, however, there is the considerable material advantage posed by the world of the exploiters - and not only that, the social leverage gained could be turned to the benefit of the oppressed. Thus, although Luis sees that social justice would mean a re-allocation of his estate, it is a decision that he feels (not without guilt) should not be made too hastily. But Commander Victor and his rebels think otherwise and the home of Luis is visited with violence.

Significantly enough, the novel ends with Luis awaiting death in the doomed household. The forces of the oppressed are on the ascendant and violence is seen as the ultimate instrument of liberation. In the conclusion of 'The Heirs', the Indios wait patiently with their tithes at Don Felix's gates:

> He had told them to wait, these emasculated people who could go on waiting, living in servitude and at the mercy of his whims. [8]

In *Tree*, social justice is viewed from a distance - with a mild and relatively uninvolved compassion from a protagonist who confesses himself to being spiritually dead. In *The Pretenders*, the protagonist is very much involved, has compassion and searches for social justice: but the forces of corruption are too powerful and insidious. Thus, suicide appears to be the ultimate conclusion for Antonio Samson. But in *My Brother, My Executioner*, the fire of vengeance is strongly insistent and even those in between - who are 'neither fish nor flesh', who try to maintain an uneasy truce between both camps - are scorched. The people are no longer emasculated; they cannot go on living in servitude; they have lost their patience.

There is little doubt that *Mass* is the true culmination of the quintet despite the fact that, here and there, in *Tree*, for instance, the appearance of side-tracking into a cul-de-sac of passivity towards social injustice is clearly visible. *Mass* returns in a way, to the first volume in the series with the introduction, at the very beginning, of Antonio Samson's son, Pepe Samson:

> My name is Samson. I have long hair, but there is nothing symbolic or biblical about it; [9]

The link with the biblical Samson is however re-established and heightened. This Samson - as the tale unfolds - is the true inheritor of the name. There is a gradual development in the unfolding of the oppression of the masses culminating in an exposé of the real oppressors and the beginning of the final destruction of these exploiters: a breaking down of the pillars that uphold oppression through the gospel of violent yet cunning action.

The oppressors are no longer the Spanish landed gentry although there is enough of their blood in the veins of the *illustrados* of modern commerce who have replaced them. The real enemy Pepe realizes is the wealthy elite who will return to power no matter which figure-head holds the helm. As Juan Puneta explains:

> ...But the change comes from us, dictated by us. And as for the President - his interests are with us; he is one of us! Not with the masses - ha, the masses!...
> He likes to be surrounded by people who understand the impulses of power. Only the powerful know what these are. And the powerful are the rich. We will flock around him - pamper him, kow-tow to him and then, suffocate him! [10]

There is the implicit invitation to Pepe to join the elite, to be part of the oppressors just as his father had compromised through Carmen Villa. However, Pepe pulls a gun on him and the first killing of a violent revolutionary begins. He is the genuine nationalist aware of the conditions of oppression and unafraid of the necessary action to end it:

> Nationalism means us - for we are the nation and the vengeance we seek will never be satisfied till we have gotten measure for measure all that was stolen from us. [11]

Unlike his father Samson, he has decided to maintain faith with his people and so cannot be considered a spiritual exile.

His words appear to be prophetic in the light of events that have overtaken the Philippines. President Marcos was ousted in 1986 via the massive demonstration of the people's will - led by Cory Aquino who is now President. In this respect, *Mass* is very much rooted in the everyday reality of the Philippines, Jose has felt the pulse of the people. That is why it is difficult to agree without reservation when Shirley Lim states:

> Jose's stories in *Waywaya* direct us to a democratic, romantic, nationalistically committed path, a path which can easily become narrowly sociological in bent, or polemical, or fantastic. [12]

Truth sometimes appears to be stranger than fiction and in the case of *Mass*, truth finally appears to have caught up with fiction.

Jose's fiction has thus shown how spiritual exile was a condition of the dilemma that his protagonists found themselves in and one consequence was suicide - perhaps the ultimate expression of alienation - while the other was violent overthrow. There are, however, no easy solutions, as Jose is well aware. Having developed from a relatively simplistic position of splitting Filipino society into the two camps of alien exploiter and indigenous exploited, the author moves to the more convincing and dramatic portrayal of the Filipino as both inflictor and afflicted, oppressor and oppressed, exploiter and exploited - a progression which, perhaps, necessitates the existence of protagonists in spiritual exile.

Notes

1. *Mass* (manuscript), p.3.
2. A concise account of the system can be obtained from *A History of the Philippines: From Spanish Colonization to the Second World War* by Renato Constantino (New York Monthly Review Press, 1975), pp. 41-46.
3. *Tree*, p.1.
4. *Ibid.*, p.133.
5. *The God Stealer and Other Stories*, p.12.
6. *The Pretenders*, p.95.
7. *My Brother, My Executioner*, p.21.
8. *The God Stealer and Other Stories*, p.15.
9. *Mass*, p.1.

10. *Ibid.*, p.216.
11. *Ibid.*, p.218.
12. 'Dialectics of Form and National Consciousness in the Filipino Short Story.' (Unpublished paper).

© Dudley de Souza, 1993

This essay was first published in *A Sense of Exile* (ed. Bruce Bennett), with their kind permission.

F. SIONIL JOSE
The Marcos Years and After:
A Personal Essay

When President Marcos declared Martial Law in September 1972, our fragile institutions of freedom collapsed as he became a virtual dictator.

To paraphrase Dostoevsky, the outrage was that there was no outrage. The writers who were once the most raucous champions of freedom were either silent or quickly silenced. It is now possible to assess the impact of the Marcos regime on the creative arts and how the mythmakers and the shapers of a nation's soul have responded.

It must be remembered meanwhile that the Philippines is a one-city nation. Manila is not only the seat of government, it is also the hub of business, the residence of about 18% of the populace and the innovator of style. Where Manila goes, so does the Philippines.

I will concern myself with this Manila culture and those who shape it, including the generation of the sixties, which mounted the theatre of the streets, composed protest songs and wrote 'committed' literature. It is a generation born after World War II; it did not know how to sing the Star Spangled Banner the way I learned it in grade school. It has no memory of the euphoric days of the Liberation in 1945. Highly politicized, many in this generation have died for their beliefs.

It is this knowledge of their sacrifice that makes me hesitant to speak about what I went through during the Marcos years for, unlike them, I was not jailed or tortured and the harassment I was subjected to - which thousands who were opposed to Marcos also suffered - was nothing by comparison.

Literature, the noblest of the arts, was also the pauper of the arts in Mrs. Marcos's scheme of priorities. When she was asked why, she said that literature is elitist. This is no nonsense; I think that she and her husband were simply suspicious of writers - and justly so.

The first instrument of censorship in 1972 was the Army Office of Civil Relations which granted licences for new magazines and newspapers. It also imposed guidelines which were often arbitrary. Under these guidelines, the President, his family and the Armed

Forces could not be criticised, only praised. Before any manuscript was published, it had to be examined by the Army censors.

I was then publishing books in the humanities, and two which were already in their final blue print were proscribed. Bienvenido N. Santos's novel, *The Praying Man*, was banned outright because it portrayed a corrupt government official. The foremost Jesuit historian, the late Horacio de la Costa, had written a book on motifs in Philippine history; the censors objected to a line, 'the Army is a good servant, never a good master'. I thought it best not to release the book if even a single line was excised. Father de la Costa agreed, so his book, too, did not come out. Another history book, *The Propaganda Movement* by John Schumacher, S.J., almost failed to see print. The major who went over it objected to the title which, he said, was itself subversive. I argued that the book was about the Filipino propagandists in Spain in the 1880s who worked for reforms. It would have been another casualty of Martial Law, but the censor saw the light when I said that in the 1880s there was no radio, no television, no movies - how could anyone even compare the situation then with the Philippines in 1972?

A play by Nina Estrada Puyat which was already in page proof for my journal *Solidarity* was banned outright; it portrayed what was happening in the country, the corruption which Marcos said he would banish in his New Society.

In 1973, the functions of the Office of Civil Relations were taken over by a quasi-government body called the Media Advisory Council; it was run by a former newspaperman, Primitivo Mijares, one of the closest advisers to Marcos, and who has since mysteriously disappeared. The Media Advisory Council was hardly any improvement on the Army Office which banned and censored manuscripts just as wilfully. It banned my novel, *My Brother, My Executioner*, the official reason being there were many scenes in the book being enacted in many parts of the country, particularly in the Ilocos where the President came from - the burning of whole villages, pillaging by the Army. The book was about the Hukbalahap uprising in the early fifties - a full twenty years earlier.

The functions of the Council were finally taken over by the Publishers Association of the Philippines - another group closely identified with Marcos. It issued permits to publish - a duty zealously guarded by the body.

A few words about Philippine weeklies prior to 1972; in the absence of a well-developed publishing industry, it was the weeklies which regularly published fiction. Magazines like the *Sunday Times,* the *Philippines Free Press, This Week, Graphic* and others published quality fiction and poetry, and often serialized novels. Much of the fiction and poetry in the magazines was written by the country's leading writers; in the United States, these normally would be carried only in literary journals. The little literary publishing that was initiated by the late Alberto D. Benipayo was supplemented by magazine editors like Telly Albert Zuleuta, who serialized quality novels.

In the late seventies, the regime claimed there was a publishing boom, as evidenced in the appearance of several coffee-table books. But these can hardly be the vaunted proofs of a literary renaissance. Books are meant to be read, yet these volumes were not for reading. Printing and photographic marvels, they were 'safe' books, very expensive and well beyond the reach of most Filipinos. They reflected a shallow, elitist thinking so pervasive in our society. A book on jeepneys was bought by people who never rode in them.

The Cultural Center of the Philippines Awards for Literature was nothing compared to the unaccounted millions spent by the Marcos-directed Writers Union on the Afro-Asian Writers Conference in 1976 and its other plush projects. When a much smaller conference for ASEAN writers in 1979 was initiated and prepared by the Philippine Center of International PEN, its budget of US$27,000,000 from the ASEAN Cultural Fund was grabbed by the same literary rustlers who worked for the regime. The biggest literary award (70,000 pesos) for the English novel was discredited; it was administered by the presidential spokesman, Adrian Cristobal, who ladled it out to his coterie.

Literature declined because the magazines and newspapers which used to publish fiction and poetry were no longer around, and other outlets for literary work were pitifully limited. Nevertheless, there were areas where literary virtuosity and intellectual inquiry were still possible. I mention *WHO* magazine (closed in late 1984), the *Diliman Review* of the University of the Philippines, and the *Mr. & Ms. Magazine.*

I can understand the timidity of the magazine editors in the Marcos era. Shortly before Christmas 1979, G. Burce Bunao, managing editor of *Woman's Home Companion*, ran a couple of reprints from the American magazine, *Pageant*. The first was about American presidents, how most of them were 'mama's boys'. The second was about how American presidents, from Lincoln to Kennedy, were assassinated. Two weeks after the second article appeared, Bunao was out of a job.

At no other time was so much public money used in a cultural programme.

At no other time, too, has one single individual - Mrs. Marcos - been in a position to give direction to this programme. But when all is said and done, it is clear that all that money and energy did not spark a renaissance.

The assassination of Benigno Aquino Jr., on 21 August 1983 had an electric effect on Filipino apathy; many of the writers and artists who had been silenced by their own innate fears finally regained their courage, as did millions of people who, before the assassination, had taken passively every lie that Marcos and his wife dished out to them.

The Aquino murder also illustrated how the media were curtailed. The multitudes who attended the funeral were not shown on television or in the press. This censorship was soon remedied with the birth of courageous 'alternative' newspapers whose owners knew the great risks they were running.

Then, too, it was possible for my own novel, *Mass*, to be published. I wrote it in 1976; though it portrayed the conditions in the late sixties and shortly before the advent of Martial Law, it could not be published then and because it was also a frontal attack on Marcos and his regime. *My Brother, My Executioner*, banned in 1973, was published in the mid-seventies by New Day, but my publisher, who is as courageous as they come, said it was much too risky to do *Mass*. I agreed; I did not want to jeopardize the company.

My Dutch publisher heard about *Mass*; he liked it, and so it appeared first in Dutch in Holland in 1982 rather than in the original English. He then advanced me royalties so I could publish *Mass* in Manila.

I was not apprehensive; I knew the Marcos people had more important problems to attend to - the growing restiveness of the people, the continuous and massive demonstrations. Besides,

Filipinos do not really read novels, and I was not one to flatter myself by believing that 'the pen is mightier than the sword'.

For the artists then, what are the lessons of Martial Law? This much can now be said: Filipino creativity flourished despite - not because of - the Marcoses. Filipinos who read only the 'crony' press are not aware of it, but there was a lot of creative writing being done. The poets discovered how oral poetry can be more effective if recited in the native languages. The unpublishable entries to the Palanca Literary Contest also demonstrated the literary activity that could not see print.

It is now possible to identify those writers who lived in accordance with their convictions. This is important. All too often, we judge writers only by what they have written, not by how they lived according to their pronouncements.

It is a cliché, but it is true: we never really knew what freedom meant until we lost it. Still, there were many ways by which we got around censorship. Allegory was one of them. In this sense, censorship was not such a great problem except to the artist or writer with little imagination.

The February 'Revolution' which restored our freedom gave rise to more than a dozen new dailies in Manila and freed television from censorship. Now, the euphoria has given way to anxiety, for it seems the lessons of the past were not really learned. Perhaps this is due to the sudden unleashing of pent-up feelings, of energies that were chained, and ideas that could not be expressed.

The media, while free, must now be imbued with a deeper sense of responsibility, or else they will be plagued again by the licence and anarchy which Marcos gave as the reasons for his dictatorship.

We must also make some distinctions not so much for ourselves as for our friends abroad who supported us in our moment of need, particularly organizations like International PEN.

In the first days of Martial Law, many writers, particularly journalists, who had displeased Marcos and his wife were imprisoned. And certainly, all through the 12 years of Martial Law, several journalists were 'salvaged' - the term the regime coined for the assassination of those opposed to it. Indeed, we need time to cleanse our language of this double-speak.

By 1976, in spite of censorship and repression, no writer was actually imprisoned for his writing as all bona fide writers in jail were released. So-called writers and poets like Jose Maria Sison and Mila Aguilar were not in prison for their writing but for their political activities and 'Communist' affiliations.

A few exceptions were to come later in the eighties. Philippine PEN Board Members, Armando J. Malay and Salvador R. Gonzales ridiculed Marcos and his medals in *We Forum*, a courageous 'alternative' paper. They were jailed with a few others and *We Forum* was closed down.

The Philippine Centre of International PEN fought hardest against censorship and oppression all through the years of dictatorship. Its chairman, Salvador P. Lopez, proclaimed in 1974 that it was 'better to be silenced than to be silent', and as one of the first national figures to speak out against the Marcos dictatorship, he lost his presidency of the University of the Philippines.

No writer stands to be jailed today for expressing his view raucously. Taking advantage of such freedom, some of Manila's journalists have often attacked officials as well as private citizens. One member of PEN, Mauro Avena, who wrote about the Aquino assassination was charged with libel, with damages of more than 30 million pesos. Fortunately the men who filed the charge - General Ver and Ambassador Cojuangco - were forced to leave the country in February 1986 with their leader.

If, under Marcos, there was the tyranny of a dictatorship, what we will see now is the tyranny of an uninformed public opinion.

During the dark years of the Marcos regime, the writer had no choice but to be a revolutionary. Today, in being asked to be a mirror of his time, he became the enemy of all those crippling institutions which have, for centuries created a zombie culture and perpetuated injustice.

'Man can take on himself the denunciation of the world's total injustice,' said Albert Camus, 'and demand a total justice that he will be alone in creating. But he cannot affirm the total ugliness of the world. To create beauty, he must at the same time refuse the real and exalt certain of its aspects. Art questions the real but does not shun it...But there is perhaps a living transcendence promised us by beauty, which may make us love and prefer to any other our own limited and mortal world. Art thus brings us back to the origins of revolt, in the degree to

330

which it tries to give form to a value escaping in a perpetual becoming but which the artist senses and wishes to snatch from memory...'

Herein, I think, lies the clue to the longevity of artistic vision, if not the origin of that vision itself. Why have so many of our writers who bore so much promise in the thirties and forties stopped writing? Wallace Stegner who came to Manila in 1952 to conduct a workshop noted this after reading a chronological sampling of our English literature. Further, he said that most of our writers seem to have ignored the social issues that were festering then.

He could have added, too, that we also failed to strengthen our sense of identity and, in the end, were weak, perhaps unable to withstand the cultural confrontation with the West.

Much has been said about this inevitable clash. For the Filipino artist, it is a heart-wrenching process he must resolve if he is to banish his alienation from his own people. It is an act of killing his Western father, of immersion in his own culture no matter how primitive that culture may be and no matter how embarrassingly self-conscious the act of immersion will be.

All this does sound melodramatic and futile, but we must understand this hankering for a return to the womb of creation itself so that we may know what survival and renewal are from the stringent domination of a colonial past. Most of all, we have to secure that freedom of the mind without which we cannot even start to live. This is basic to the problem of change, and it is when we realize the necessity of this heroic step, and fulfil this profound psychological need, that all else falls into place, particularly for those among us who had nourishment from Western institutions.

But we are also pragmatic and having made this symbolic break, we must now proceed to learn from the past knowing only too well that the East-West clash has been going on since men and their ideas were transported on wheels or frail boats with nothing but the stars to guide them.

The transport of ideas had not been one-way. In the East weaker cultures were subdued by those in the region that were stronger and more aggressive. Archaeological diggings in the Philippines today reveal, for instance, the extent of our pre-Spanish trade with China and Thailand, how our ceramic art flourished, then was influenced and finally overwhelmed by the superior pottery of China.

By force of circumstance, most Filipinos have accepted, perhaps rather superficially, the Western rational view of life. We know, however, that the masses of our people are encrusted with superstition. We have a folk Catholicism different from that which is practised in Europe or in America. In the meantime, we are growing more aware of what has been flaunted so often as the Asian tradition and all that it connotes: complex religions, spirituality and the abnegation of the self. But these are not the only aspects of this tradition. In our part of the world, materialism has been pushed to its most sybaritic and corrupt limits and I suspect that some of those who practise self-denial, do so not because they have really rejected materialism but because they are incapable of coping with it.

Christianity is not based solely on a sense of guilt but like the other religions that flowered in Asia, it also carried with it a high degree of martyrdom and sacrifice. The monastic orders which spread Christianity to Asia in the 16th century were perhaps useful to Spain's or Portugal's imperial design but no one would deny them their high sense of duty. In those days, it required courage of the sternest kind, piety and faith to venture into the unknown, to brave the vicissitudes of the sea and the hostility of non-Christian peoples. Their sacrifice was not motivated only by the search for gold but also by faith.

They studied the flora and the fauna, taught the alphabet and in those three hundred years created the boundaries of our nation. It is well to remember these for there are those of us who knock down so called imported values with malicious facility without quite knowing them. Unfortunately, it was the exploitative values of the conquistador that seeped down to the bedrock of our culture.

As for Western concepts of the ego and individualism, as perhaps opposed to Asian concepts of harmony and hierarchy, I think we will find these in our part of the world, too diluted with native genius.

The artist knows that life is short and it is only with his good work that he can become part of history. Yet, history has little to teach the artist who is concerned not with his immortality alone but with change, with egalitarian ideals. History would tell him that the cause of freedom has always been demeaned. Even the Greeks who called themselves democrats and who pondered the

332

pre-requisites of self-rule, of utopia, had slaves whom they condemned to a life of burden and toil, whom they killed at will. Who would say that Greek literature flourished perhaps because they had the leisure to produce this literature? And in Asia, almost all the ancient monuments were built with the lash; the 'hydraulic society' of Asian despots was based on a hierarchy of values that emphasized absolute power.

All through history, too, tyrants have flourished. Still, man's search for freedom and the elusive meaning of life continues so that in the final analysis, the clash really is not between East and West but between those who seek freedom and those who deny it, between those who want to proscribe it and those who want to extend its boundaries. The clash continues, not between the old and the new but between those who want to brutalize humanity and those who want man to be free.

We have a saying that he who cannot look back to where he came from cannot reach his destination. It is perhaps only in this sense that the past has something to say to us. Like so many of our young, we want instant progress but we have been unwilling to pay the cost; we also overlook the fact that we live in an era that is not ours, that the lag between fact and vision is not just a matter of years but of generations.

In the West where the challenges to man's critical and creative spirit are more complex but less heroic, the artist and his work have taken on new dimensions. I am awed, even cowed, by the obscurantism and the deadly seriousness with which art and literature have been attended to. A poem can no longer be read for sheer music or pleasure - now it must be explicated. A novel must be read on many levels of meaning. In classes in literature, such archaic yardsticks as memorability or narrative tension are low-brow, unintellectual forms of success measurements.

I continue to be muddled by the many ephemeral trends which the artistic life in the post-technological society has taken and I often wonder whether or not these trends will endure when at times they question man's very value and existence. Is it possible after all that Oswald Spengler was right, that civilizations go through a cycle of growth and decay, that the decline of the West is already in process and that the creative genius of its artists has began to wither under the impact of dehumanizing technology and affluence? Is it true after all that the destructive impulse in the West is far stronger than the striving for life, that society has its own time bomb and that it is society which creates the artist and it is not the artist who creates society? The Club of Rome has come out with its formidable and portentous report on the limits of growth; Western man had ravaged his environment and threatened the existence of this planet. Because of his gross appetites and unlimited wants has Western man also reached the cul-de-sac of his artistic creativity?

The poison in the West need not be our food. I do not think that life is absurd or that we are headed towards mass perdition; the very act of living is a creative act. Always, as we go from day to day, we make our existence known, we assert ourselves above and beyond all the prisons that nature and the tyrannies of our time have imposed on us. This is not just an act of the artist but of man as well.

We have tended to disparage the Chinese cultural revolution and I state here that it is not my intention to suggest that we should ape the Chinese experience. But there is something salutary about the cultural revolution, some aspect of which were repeated in Cuba. The writers were sent home.

Let me end on a personal note. After an absence of many years I returned to my village unable to speak my native language. I had grown up in this village remembering what my forefathers had told me of Spanish oppression and their flight from the North, how they had cleared the virgin land only to be dispossessed by the *ilustrados* afterward. My mother, who was the single most important influence in my life, was God-fearing and hard working and she taught us, her children, those solid Ilocano virtues of patience without which we would not be able to endure the drudgery of the village.

I carried with me these poignant memories of boyhood, how I learned to read, how I wept over the fate of that hapless woman, Sisa, and her two sons, in Rizal's novel, *Noli*. I wandered in the prairies of Nebraska through the eyes of Willa Cather and at night when there was no kerosene for our lamp. I would walk to the far corner and under the electric street light, join that knight errant Don Quixote in his misadventures.

In 1939, I left this village to go to Manila to study with the help of a kindly uncle. I worked my way through college writing short stories for a living since that was the only thing I knew. I fell in love, got married, raised a family, and in time, travelled far. On occasion, I even dined with the mighty. But wherever I went, I always brought treasured memories of that village where I was born.

Like I said, I returned to it and to my profound dismay, saw that it had hardly changed, that my old friends had not even read what I had written. And seeing them, I asked myself why they were still poor and why I was comfortable.

My city friends asked me sometimes why my novels are sad. They are sad because memory has chained me to a past that was afflicted with injustice. Even now, as I look around me, the same injustices prevail. And I realize with sorrow and anger that my response to injustice has been inadequate, and that words are futile.

In writing as I have done, it was not my intention to present a bleak, human landscape. I have sought communion with any man in any village, hoping that I would be able to express the aspirations of those I have left behind, aspirations which they in their poverty and silence could not voice.

In returning to my village, I have left it forever, liberated myself from its deadening physical embrace. Of this I am sure but just the same, it is my fervent hope that, somehow, in my unhappy country I shall have touched another boy, just as Rizal, Cervantes and Cather had touched me when I was young, so that he would not leave his village as I had done.

This essay was first published in *A Sense of Exile* (ed. Bruce Bennett), with their kind permission.

Michael Wilding

Social Visions: Essays on Political Fiction

Maria Shevtsova

Theatre and Cultural Interaction

Zdenko Zlatar

The Epic Circle: Allegoresis and
the Western Epic Tradition from Home
to Tasso

Peter Hinton, ed.

Disasters: Image and Context

S.N. Mukherjee and J.O. Ward

Revolution as History

$25 each r.r.p.

Sydney
Studies

P.O. Box 575
Leichhardt 2040
Australia

PART FOUR

The Nobel Laureates

AS I PLEASE by **Salleh Ben Joned** (UK £6.99, USA $11.99)

"Anybody who wants to understand cultural politics today should read this book. Anybody who wants to understand Malaysia today should read this book. And anybody who wants an insight into the confrontations of East and West, of Islam and the secular or Christian world, should read this book!" Margaret Drabble

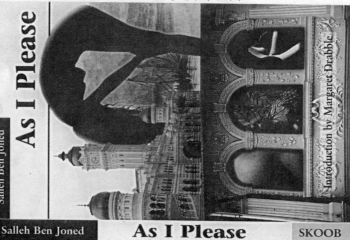

ON TONI MORRISON:
1993 Nobel Prizewinner for Literature
by
Amy M. Baker

There now resides among the hallowed ranks of Nobel literati the resonant voice of Afro-Americanism. The Swedish Academy has located Toni Morrison within the distinguished realm of those such as W.B. Yeats, Thomas Mann, Bertrand Russell, Samuel Beckett, and in doing so have conferred upon this granddaughter of Alabama slaves an honour worthy of her provocative and painfully honest oeuvre.

Growing up amidst the Great Depression in the small town of Lorain, Ohio, Morrison developed a dramatic sense of the tragic that later manifested itself in her writing. Born Chloe Anthony Wofford in 1931, her penchant for literary expression demanded a vehicle and she later received her Master's in American Literature from Cornell University. Upon divorce from Jamaican architect Harold Morrison, she moved to New York City where she worked as a book editor for Random House to subsidize her own writing career and the raising of her two sons. It was her third novel, *Song of Solomon* (1977), that catapulted her into wide acclaim by securing for her The National Book Critics Circle Award, and with her fifth, *Beloved* (1988), came a Pulitzer Prize. During this period she occupied academic posts at Texas Southern, Howard, and Yale Universities. Since 1989, Morrison has held a Professorship at Princeton where she teaches literature and creative writing. Most recently her talent has been recognised by the French government with their prestigious award for excellence in the arts, The Commander of Arts and Letters.

Scholars worldwide, however, lament the fact that the original manuscripts from her first six novels were destroyed in a Christmas Day fire in 1993. Apart from being a devastating and personal loss, Morrison had planned to donate her working papers to Harlem's Schomburg Center for Research in Black Culture. Such original writing is extremely valuable to historians and students of literature in the opportunity it gives them to scrutinise the genesis and evolution of a literary work.

As well as documenting the travesties of her cultural past within the genre of literature, Morrison is also unabashedly political. Her vociferous defense of Anita Hill, and consequent condemnation of then Supreme Court Justice nominee Clarence Thomas, confirmed her role as the articulate spokesperson of a dissatisfied feminist, black American. Her efforts culminated in the editing of *Race-ing Justice, En-gendering Power: Essays on Anita Hill, Clarence Thomas, and the Construction of Social Reality* (1993), a collection of academic essays examining the sexual scandal that rocked America, black and white alike, and made one reassess the limits of racial solidarity.

While politics is a profound part of the social comment which is her writing, Morrison's forte lies in the application and employment of lyrical prose and mythical characterisation. Such a style, however, has led many a critic to accuse her of creating personalities who are unnecessarily hyperbolic - who function as absurd caricatures, and hence de-legitimise the black message. Characters such as Sula, the witch girl in an isolated black community, who delights in the burning alive of her own mother (*Sula*, 1973), or Sethe, the mother who kills her children to free them from their predestined life as slaves *(Beloved)*, or Joe, the married man who shot his young lover because of his confused overabundance of feelings (*Jazz*, 1992) all lead the less discerning reading to censure Morrison for an overextended use of metaphor. The diametrical worlds of Pecola Breedlove (*The Bluest Eye*, 1970) and Jadine (*Tar Baby*, 1981) illustrate to what a robust extent Morrison's character development is informed by a perspicacious awareness of the spectrum that is reality. Her detractors, however, have heralded such eclecticism as the chicanery of an author who uses obvious melodrama instead of scholarly rigour. But shocking her readers into an intellectual submission to or engagement with her philosophy is not Morrison's design; her project is much more subtle. The nascent stages of her writing career were defined through a need to fill a void - a void whose existence gave birth to an acutely sensed disadvantage. Black literature had, hitherto, been a pedagogic discourse for *white* ears; a way to *teach* whites about blacks. This left the blacks bereft of any literature with which they could learn about *themselves*. Enter Toni Morrison. Morrison's corpus encapsulates the black experience in a language derived from the black tradition, and hence a language of emasculation, bereavement, and asperity. Morrison is not afraid to employ such language, nor is she ashamed that it is the language that *must* be her medium. The African heritage, *her* heritage, beseeches authentic expression.

In *Playing in the Dark, Whiteness and the Literary Imagination* Toni Morrison brings the genius of a master writer to this personal inquiry into the significance of African-Americans in the American literary imagination. Her goal, she states at the outset, is to "put forth an argument for extending the study of American literature...draw a map, so to speak, of a critical geography and use that map to open as much space for discovery, intellectual adventure, and close exploration as did the original charting of the New World - without the mandate for conquest."

She ponders the effect that living in a historically racialized society has had on American writing in the nineteenth and twentieth centuries. Professor Morrison argues that race has become a metaphor, a way of referring to forces, events, and forms of social decay, economic division, and human panic. Her compelling point is that the central characteristics of American literature - individualism, masculinity, the insistence upon innocence coupled to an obsession with figurations of death and hell - are responses to a dark and abiding Africanist presence.

Through her investigation of black characters, narrative strategies, and idiom in the fiction of white American writers, Morrison provides a daring perspective that is sure to alter conventional notions about American literature. She considers Willa Cather and the impact of race on concept and plot; turns to Poe, Hawthorne, and Melville to examine the black force that figures so significantly in the literature of early America; and discusses the implications of the Africanist presence at the heart of *Huckleberry Finn*. A final chapter on Ernest Hemingway is a brilliant exposition of the racial subtext that glimmers beneath the surface plots of his fiction.

Written with the artistic vision that has earned her a preeminent place in modern letters, *Playing in the Dark* will be avidly read by Morrison admirers as well as by students, critics, and scholars of American literature.

Blacks *too* are mystified by the tumult that is their history. They *too* need to develop a cerebra; involvement with the events,

341

emotions, and ideas - however unfriendly or unattractive - that so invade (albeit in varying degrees) every black psyche; ergo Morrison's almost lurid characters. Language is integral to her prose, but the author realises that language only reaches full emotional capacity when embodied by a fantastic character. Morrison's heroes and her language compliment each other, are developed for one another, and hence synthesize into a whole that communicates the black story in a disquieting but utterly profound way.

Morrison states this conception with a more political emphasis in her introduction to *Race-ing Justice, En-gendering Power*, "...if the language of one's own culture is lost, one may be forced to describe that culture in the language of the rescuing one [the *white* one]...Minus one's own idiom it is possible to cry and decry victimization...and one is obliged to cooperate in the reinforcement of cliché, the erasure of difference, the denial of history...and the sentimentalization and trivialization of the torture black people have suffered...because without one's own idiom, there is no other language to speak."

This new breed of literary communication has set Toni Morrison apart from other Black Americans writing within this particular movement, but such a literary style is not only admirable *within* the tradition. Such an estimation has been confirmed, not least by the Swedish Academy, hence reassuring us that Morrison is not just a fine Afro-American author, or an accomplished female novelist, but a sterling *littérateur*.

Amy M. Baker is an American postgraduate student at the London School of Economics. She is researching for her Ph. D on the works of Nietzsche.

TONI MORRISON
Nobel Lecture, 1993

"Once upon a time there was an old woman. Blind but wise." Or was it an old man? A guru, perhaps. Or a griot soothing restless children. I have heard this story, or one exactly like it, in the lore of several cultures.

"Once upon a time there was an old woman. Blind. Wise."

In the version I know the woman is the daughter of slaves, black, American, and lives alone in a small house outside of town. Her reputation for wisdom is without peer and without question. Among her people she is both the law and its transgression. The honour she is paid and the awe in which she is held reach beyond her neighbourhood to places far away; to the city where the intelligence of rural prophets is the source of much amusement.

One day the woman is visited by some young people who seem to be bent on disproving her clairvoyance and showing her up for the fraud they believe she is. Their plan is simple: they enter her house and ask the one question the answer to which rides solely on her difference from them, a difference they regard as a profound disability: her blindness. They stand before her, and one of them says, "Old woman, I hold in my hand a bird. Tell me whether it is living or dead."

She does not answer, and the question is repeated. "Is the bird I am holding living or dead?"

Still she doesn't answer. She is blind and cannot see her visitors, let alone what is in their hands. She does not know their color, gender or homeland. She only knows their motive.

The old woman's silence is so long, the young people have trouble holding their laughter.

Finally she speaks and her voice is soft but stern. "I don't know", she says. "I don't know whether the bird you are holding is dead or alive, but what I do know is that it is in your hands. It is in your hands."

Her answer can be taken to mean: if it is dead, you have either found it that way or you have killed it. If it is alive, you can still kill it. Whether it is to stay alive, it is your decision. Whatever the case, it is your responsibility.

For parading their power and her helplessness, the young visitors are reprimanded, told they are responsible not only for the act of mockery but also for the small bundle of life sacrificed to achieve its aims. The blind woman shifts attention away from assertions of power to the instrument through which that power is exercised.

Speculation on what (other than its own frail body) that bird-in-the-hand might signify has always been attractive to me, but especially so now, thinking as I have been, about the work I do that has brought me to this company. So I choose to read the bird as language and the woman as a practiced writer. She is worried about how the language she dreams in, given to her at birth, is handled, put into service, even withheld from her for certain nefarious purposes. Being a writer she thinks of language partly as a system, partly as a living thing over which one has control, but mostly as agency - as an act with consequences. So the question the children put to her: "Is it living or dead?" is not unreal because she thinks of language as susceptible to death, erasure; certainly imperiled and salvageable only by an effort of the will. She believes that if the bird in the hands of her visitors is dead the custodians are responsible for the corpse. For her a dead language is not only one no longer spoken or written, it is unyielding language content to admire its own paralysis. Like statist language, censored and censoring. Ruthless in its policing duties, it has no desire or purpose other than maintaining the free range of its own narcotic narcissism, its own exclusivity and dominance. However, moribund, it is not without effect for it actively thwarts the intellect, stalls conscience, suppresses human potential. Unreceptive to interrogation, it cannot form or tolerate new ideas, shape other thoughts, tell another story, fill baffling silences. Official language smithered to sanction ignorance and preserve privilege is a suit of armour, polished to shocking glitter, a husk from which the knight departed long ago. Yet there it is: dumb, predatory, sentimental. Exciting reverence in schoolchildren, providing shelter for despots, summoning false memories of stability, harmony among the public.

She is convinced that when language dies, out of carelessness, disuse, and absence of esteem, indifference or killed by fiat, not only she herself, but all users and makers are accountable for its demise. In her country children have bitten their tongues off and use bullets instead to iterate the voice of speechlessness, of disabled

344

and disabling language, of language adults have abandoned altogether as a device for grappling with meaning, providing guidance, or expressing love. But she knows tongue-suicide is not only the choice of children. It is common among the infantile heads of state and power merchants whose evacuated language leaves them with no access to what is left of their human instincts for they speak only to those who obey, or in order to force obedience.

The systematic looting of language can be recognized by the tendency of its users to forgo its nuanced, complex, mid-wifery properties for menace and subjugation. Oppressive language does more than represent violence; it is violence; does more than represent the limits of knowledge; it limits knowledge. Whether it is obscuring state language or the faux-language of mindless media; whether it is the proud but calcified language of the academy or the commodity driven language of science; whether it is the malign language of law-without-ethics, or language designed for the estrangement of minorities, hiding its racist plunder in its literary cheek - it must be rejected, altered and exposed. It is the language that drinks blood, laps vulnerabilities, tucks its fascist boots under crinolines of respectability and patriotism as it moves relentlessly toward the bottom line and the bottomed-out mind. Sexist language, racist language, theistic language - all are typical of the policing languages of mastery, and cannot, do not permit new knowledge or encourage the mutual exchange of ideas.

The old woman is keenly aware that no intellectual mercenary, nor insatiable dictator, no paid-for politician or demagogue; no counterfeit journalist would be persuaded by her thoughts. There is and will be rousing language to keep citizens armed and arming; slaughtered and slaughtering in the malls, courthouses, post offices, playgrounds, bedrooms and boulevards; stirring, memorializing language to mask the pity and waste of needless death. There will be more diplomatic language to countenance rape, torture, assassination. There is and will be more seductive, mutant language designed to throttle women, to pack their throats like paté-producing geese with their own unsayable, transgressive words; there will be more of the language of surveillance disguised as research; of politics and history calculated to render the suffering of millions mute; language glamorized to thrill the dissatisfied and bereft into assaulting their neighbors; arrogant pseudo-empirical language crafted to lock creative people into cages of inferiority and hopelessness.

Underneath the eloquence, the glamour, the scholarly associations, however, stirring or seductive, the heart of such language is languishing, or perhaps not beating at all - if the bird is already dead.

She has thought about what could have been the intellectual history of any discipline if it had not insisted upon, or been forced into, the waste of time and life that rationalizations for and representations of dominance required - lethal discourses of exclusion blocking access to cognition for both the excluder and the excluded.

The conventional wisdom of the Tower of Babel story is that the collapse was a misfortune. That it was the distraction, or the weight of many languages that precipitated the tower's failed architecture. That one monolithic language would have expedited the building and heaven would have been reached. Whose heaven, she wonders? And what kind? Perhaps the achievement of Paradise was premature, a little hasty if no one could take the time to understand other languages, other views, other narratives. Had they, the heaven they imagined might have been found at their feet. Complicated, demanding yes, but a view of heaven as life; not heaven as post-life.

She would not want to leave her young visitors with the impression that language should be forced to stay alive merely to be. The vitality of language lies in its ability to limn the actual, imagined and possible lives of its speakers, readers, writers. Although its poise is sometimes in displacing experience it is not a substitute for it. It arcs toward the place where meaning may lie. When a President of the United States thought about the graveyard his country had become, and said "The world will little note nor long remember what we say here. But it will never forget what they did here." His simple words are exhilarating in their life-sustaining properties because they refused to encapsulate the reality of 600,000 dead men in a cataclysmic race war. Refusing to monumentalize, disdaining the "final word", the precise "summing up", acknowledging their "poor power to add or detract", his words signal deference to the uncapturability of the life it mourns. It is the deference that moves her, that recognition that language can never live up to life once and for all. Nor should it. Language can never "pin down" slavery, genocide, war. Nor should it yearn for the arrogance to be able to do so. Its force, its felicity is in its reach toward the ineffable.

Be it grand or slender, burrowing, blasting, or refusing to sanctify; whether it laughs out loud or is a cry without an alphabet, the choice word, the chosen silence, unmolested language surges toward knowledge, not its destruction. But who does not know of literature banned because it is interrogative; discredited because it is critical; erased because alternate? And how many are outraged by the thought of a self-ravaged tongue?

Word-work is sublime, she thinks, because it is generative; it makes meaning that secures our difference, our human difference - the way in which we are like no other life.

We die. That may be the meaning of life. But we do language. That may be the measure of our lives.

"Once upon a time,....." visitors ask an old woman a question. Who are they, these children? What did they make of that encounter? What did they hear in those final words: "The bird is in your hands"? A sentence that gestures toward possibility or one that drops a latch? Perhaps what the children heard was "It's not my problem. I am old, female, black, blind. What wisdom I have now is in knowing I can not help you. The future of language is yours."

They stand there. Suppose nothing was in their hands? Suppose the visit was only a ruse, a trick to get to be spoken to, taken seriously as they have not been before? A chance to interrupt, to violate the adult world, its miasma of discourse about them, for them, but never to them? Urgent questions are at stake, including the one they have asked: "Is the bird we hold living or dead?" Perhaps the question meant: "Could some one tell us what is life? What is death?" No trick at all; no silliness. A straightforward question worthy of the attention of a wise one. An old one. And if the old and wise who have lived life and faced death cannot describe either, who can?

But she does not; she keeps her secret; her good opinion of herself; her gnomic pronouncements; her art without commitment. She keeps her distance, enforces it and retreats into the singularity of isolation, in sophisticated, privileged space.

Nothing, no word follows her declarations of transfer. That silence is deep, deeper than the meaning available in the words she has spoken. It shivers, this silence, and the children, annoyed, fill it with language invented on the spot.

"Is there no speech," they ask her, "no words you can give us that helps us break through your dossier of failures? Through the education you have just given us that is no education at all because we are paying close attention to what you have done as well as to what you have said? To the barrier you have erected between generosity and wisdom?

"We have no bird in our hands, living or dead. We have only you and our important question. Is the nothing in our hands something you could not bear to contemplate, to even guess? Don't you remember being young when language was magic without meaning? When what you could say, could not mean? When the invisible was what imagination strove to see? When questions and demands for answers burned so brightly you trembled with fury at not knowing?

"Do we have to begin consciousness with a battle heroines and heroes like you have already fought and lost leaving us with nothing in our hands except what you have imagined is there? Your answer is artful, but its artiness embarrasses us and ought to embarrass you. Your answer is indecent in its self-congratulation. A made-for-television script that makes no sense if there is nothing in our hands.

"Why didn't you reach out, touch us with your soft fingers, delay the sound bite, the lesson, until you knew who we were? Did you so despise our trick, our modus operandi you could not see that we were baffled about how to get your attention? We are young. Unripe. We have heard all our short lives that we have to be responsible. What could that possibly mean in the catastrophe this word has become; where, as a poet said, "nothing needs to be exposed since it is already barefaced." Our inheritance is an affront. You want us to have your old, blank eyes and see only cruelty and mediocrity. Do you think we are stupid enough to perjure ourselves again and again with the fiction of nationhood? How dare you talk to us of duty when we stand waist deep in the toxin of your past?

"You trivialize us and trivialize the bird that is not in our hands. Is there no context for our lives? No song, no literature, no poem full of vitamins, no history connected to experience that you can pass along to help us start strong? You are an adult. The old one,

348

the wise one. Stop thinking about saving your face. Think of our lives and tell us your particularized world. Make up a story. Narrative is radical, creating us at the very moment it is being created. We will not blame you if your reach exceeds your grasp; if love so ignites your words they go down in flames and nothing is left but their scald. Or if, with the reticence of a surgeon's hands, your words suture only the places where blood might flow. We know you can never do it properly - once and for all. Passion is never enough; neither is skill. But try. For our sake and yours forget your name in the street; tell us what the world has been to you in the dark places and in the light. Don't tell us what to believe, what to fear. Show us belief's wide skirt and the stitch that unravels fear's caul. You, old woman, blessed with blindness, can speak the language that tells us what only language can: how to see without pictures. Language alone protects us from the scariness of things with no names. Language alone is meditation.

"Tell us what it is to be a woman so that we may know what it is to be a man. What moves at the margin. What it is to have no home on this place. To be set adrift from the one you knew. What it is to live at the edge of towns that cannot bear your company.

"Tell us about ships turned away from the shorelines at Easter, placenta in a field. Tell us about a wagonload of slaves, how they sang so softly their breath was indistinguishable from the falling snow. How they knew from the hunch of the nearest shoulder that the next stop would be their last. How, with hands prayered in their sex they thought of heat, then suns. Lifting their faces, as though this was there for the taking. Turning as though there for the taking. They stop at an inn. The driver and his mate go in with the lamp leaving them humming in the dark. The horse's void steams into the snow beneath its hooves and its hiss and melt is the envy of the freezing slaves.

"The inn door opens: a girl and a boy step away from its light. They climb into the wagon bed. The boy will have a gun in three years, but now he carries a lamp and a jug of warm cider. They pass it from mouth to mouth. The girl offers bread, pieces of meat and something more: a glance into the eyes of the one she serves. One helping for each man, two for each woman. And a look. They look back. The next stop will be their last. But not this one. This one is warmed."

It's quiet again when the children finish speaking, until the woman breaks into the silence.

"Finally", she says, "I trust you now. I trust you with the bird that is not in your hands because you have truly caught it. Look. How lovely it is, this thing we have done - together."

© THE NOBEL FOUNDATION, 1993.
With the kind permission of the Nobel Foundation.

Bibliography

* Middleton, David L. *TM: An Annotated Bibliography*. NY: Garland, 1987.

Books

The Bluest Eye. NY & c: Holt, Rinehart & Winston, 1970. Novel.
Sula. NY: Knopf, 1974. Novel.
Song of Solomon. NY: Knopf, 1977. Novel.
Tar Baby. NY: Knopf, 1981. Novel.
Beloved. NY: Knopf, 1987. Novel.
Jazz. NY: Knopf, 1992. Novel.
Playing in the Dark: Whiteness and the Literary Imagination. Cambridge, Mass & London: Harvard U P, 1992. Lectures.

Other

Race-ing Justice, En-gendering Power: Essays on Anita Hill, Clarence Thomas, and the Construction of Social Reality, ed. with intro. by TM. NY: Pantheon, 1992.

Interviews

BOOK SECTIONS

Koenen, Anne. "'The One Out of Sequence': An Interview With TM, New York, April 1980." *History and Tradition in Afro-*

American Culture, ed. Günter H Lenz (Frankfurt, Germany: Campus Verlag, 1984), 207-221.

McCluskey, Audrey T. "A Conversation With TM." *Women in the Arts* (Bloomington: Women's Studies Program, Indiana U, 1986), 82-88.

Parker, Bettye J. "Complexity: TM's Women - An Interview Essay." *Sturdy Black Bridges,* ed. Roseann P. Bell, Parker & Beverly Guy-Sheftall (Garden City, NY: Anchor/Doubleday, 1979), 251-257.

Ruas, Charles. "TM." *Conversations With American Writers* (NY: Knopf, 1985), 215-243.

Stepto, Robert B. "'Intimate Things in Place': A Conversation With TM," *Chant of Saints,* ed. Michael S. Harper & Stepto (Urbana: U Illinois P, 1979), 213-229.

Tate, Claudia. "TM." *Black Women Writers at Work* (NY: Continuum, 1983), 117-131.

ARTICLES

Bakerman, Jane. "The Seams Can't Show: An Interview With TM." *Black American Literature Forum,* 12 (Summer 1978), 56-60.

Darling, Marsha. "In the Realm of Responsibility: A Con-versation With TM." *Women's Review of Books,* 5 (Mar 1988), 5-6.

Dowling, Colette. "The Song of TM." *New York Times Magazine* (20 May 1979), 40-42, 48, 52, 54, 56, 58.

LeClair, Thomas. "'The Language Must Not Sweat,'" *New Republic,* 184 (21 Mar 1981), 25-29.

McKay, Nellie. "An Interview With TM." *Contemporary Literature,* 24 (Winter 1983), 413-429.

Naylor, Gloria & TM. "A Conversation." *Southern Review,* 21 (Summer 1985), 567-593.

Watkins, Mel. "Talk With TM." *New York Times Book Review* (11 Sep 1977), 48, 50.

Wilson, Judith. "A Conversation With TM." *Essence,* 12 (Jul 1981), 84-86, 128, 130, 133-134.

Critical Studies

BOOKS

Butler-Evans, Elliott. *Race, Gender, and Desire: Narrative Strategies in the Fiction of Toni Cade Bambara, TM, and Alice Walker*. Philadelphia: Temple U P, 1989.

Holloway, Karla F C & Stephanie A Demetrakopoulos. *New Dimensions of Spirituality: A Biracial and Bicultural Reading of the Novels of TM*. NY: Greenwood, 1987.

Jones, Bessie W & Audrey L Vinson. *The World of TM: Explorations in Literary Criticism*. Dubuque, Iowa: Kendall/Hunt, 1985.

Mbalia, Doreatha D. *TM's Developing Class Consciousness*. Selinsgrove, Pa: Susquehanna U P/London: Associated U Presses, 1991.

*Mobley, Marilyn Sanders. *Folk Roots and Mythic Wings in Sarah Orne Jewett and TM: The Cultural Function of Narrative*. Baton Rouge: Louisiana State U P, 1991.

Otten, Terry. *The Crime of Innocence in the Fiction of TM*. Columbia: U Missouri P, 1989.

*Rigney, Barbara Hill. *The Voices of TM*. Columbus: Ohio State U P, 1991.

*Samuels, Wilfred D. *TM*. Boston: Twayne, 1990.

COLLECTIONS OF ESSAYS

*Bloom, Harold, ed. *TM*. NY: Chelsea House, 1990.
*McKay, Nellie, ed. *Critical Essays on TM*. Boston: Hall, 1988.

SPECIAL JOURNALS

Callaloo, 19 (Summmer 1990), 471-525. TM Section.
Texas Studies in Literature and Language, 33 (Spring 1991), 89-123. TM

JEAN-PAUL SARTRE
1905-1979
1964 Nobel Prizewinner for Literature

«for his work which, rich in ideas and filled with the spirit of freedom and the quest for truth, has exerted a far-reaching influence on our age»

Address
by Anders Österling, Member of the Swedish Academy

This year the Nobel Prize in Literature has been granted by the Swedish Academy to the French writer Jean-Paul Sartre "for his work which, rich in ideas and filled with the spirit of freedom and the quest for truth, has exerted a far-reaching influence on our age."

It will be recalled that the laureate has made it known that he did not wish to accept the Prize. The fact that he has declined this distinction does not in the least modify the validity of the award. Under the circumstances, however, the Academy can only state that the presentation of the Prize cannot take place.

Refusal

In a public announcement, printed in *Le Figaro* of October 23, 1964, Mr. Sartre expressed his regret that his refusal of the Prize had given rise to scandal, and wished it to be known that, unaware of the irrevocability of the Swedish Academy's decisions, he had sought by letter to prevent their choice falling upon him. In this letter, he specified that his refusal was not meant to slight the Swedish Academy but rather based on personal and objective reasons of his own.

As to personal reasons, Mr. Sartre pointed out that due to his conception of the writer's task he had always declined official honours and thus his present act was not unprecedented. He had similarly refused membership in the Legion of Honour and had not desired to enter the Collège de France, and he would refuse the Lenin Prize if it were offered to him. He stated that a writer's accepting such an honour would be to associate his personal commitments with the awarding institution, and that, above all, a writer should not allow himself to be turned into an institution.

Among his objective reasons, Mr. Sartre listed his belief that interchange between East and West must take place between men and between cultures without the intervention of institutions. Furthermore, since the conferment of past Prizes did not, in his opinion, represent equally writers of all ideologies and nations, he felt that his acceptance might be undesirably and unjustly interpreted.

Mr. Sartre closed his remarks with a message of affection for the Swedish public.

At the banquet, S. Friberg, Rector of the Caroline Institute, made the following remarks: "Mr. Sartre found himself unable to accept this year's Prize in Literature. There is always discussion about this Prize, which every one considers himself capable of judging, or which he does not understand and consequently criticizes. But I believe that Nobel would have had a great understanding of this year's choice. The betterment of the world is the dream of every generation, and this applies particularly to the true poet and scientist. This was Nobel's dream. This is one measure of the scientist's significance. And this is the source and strength of Sartre's inspiration. As an author and philosopher, Sartre has been a central figure in postwar literary and intellectual discussion - admired, debated, criticized. His explosive production, in its entirety, has the impress of a message; it has been sustained by a profoundly serious endeavour to improve the reader, the world at large. The philosophy, which his writings have served, has been hailed by youth as a liberation. Sartre's existentialism may be understood in the sense that the degree of happiness which an individual can hope to attain is governed by his willingness to take his stand in accordance with his ethos and to accept the consequences thereof; this is a more austere interpretation of a philosophy admirably expressed by Nobel's contemporary, Ralph Waldo Emerson: 'Nothing is at last sacred but the integrity of your own mind.'

The quality of human life depends not only on external conditions but also on individual happiness. In our age of standardization and complex social systems, awareness of the meaning of life for the individual has perhaps not been lost, but it has certainly been dulled;

and it is as urgent for us today as it was in Nobel's time to uphold the ideals which were his."

Biography

Jean-Paul Sartre (1905-1979), born in Paris, studied at the École Normale Supérieure from 1924 to 1929 and became Professor of Philosophy at Le Havre in 1931. With the help of a stipend from the Institut Français he studied in Berlin (1932) the philosophies of Edmund Husserl and Martin Heidegger. After further teaching at Le Havre, and then in Laon, he taught at the Lycée Pasteur in Paris from 1937 to 1939. Since the end of the Second World War, Sartre has been living as an independent writer.

Sartre is one of those writers for whom a determined philosophical position is the centre of their artistic being. Although drawn from many sources, for example, Husserl's idea of a free, fully intentional consciousness and Heidegger's existentialism, the existentialism Sartre formulated and popularized is profoundly original. Its popularity and that of its author reached a climax in the forties, and Sartre's theoretical writings as well as his novels and plays constitute one of the main inspirational sources of modern literature. In his philosophical view atheism is taken for granted; the "loss of God" is not mourned. Man is condemned to freedom, a freedom from all authority, which may seek to evade, distort, and deny but which he will have to face if he is to become a moral being. The meaning of man's life is not established before his existence. Once the terrible freedom is acknowledged, man has to make this meaning himself, has to commit himself to a role in this world, has to commit his freedom. And this attempt to make oneself is futile without the "solidarity" of others.

The conclusions a writer must draw from this position were set forth in "Qu'est-ce que la littérature?" (1948) [What Is Literature?]: literature is no longer an activity for itself, nor primarily descriptive of characters and situations, but is concerned with human freedom and its (and the author's) commitment. Literature is committed; artistic creation is a moral activity.

While the publication of his early, largely psychological studies, *L'Imagination* (1936), *Esquisse d'une théorie des émotions* (1939) [Outline of a Theory of the Emotions], and *L'Imaginaire:*

psychologie phénoménologique de l'imagination (1940) [The Psychology of Imagination], remained relatively unnoticed, Sartre's first novel, *La Nausée* (1938) [*Nausea*], and the collection of stories *Le Mur* (1938) [*Intimacy*] brought him immediate recognition and success. They dramatically express Sartre's early existentialist themes of alienation and commitment, and of salvation through art.

His central philosophical work, *L'Etre et le néant* (1943) [*Being and Nothingness*], is a massive structuralization of his concept of being, from which much of modern existentialism derives. The existentialist humanism which Sartre propagates in his popular essay *L'Existentialisme est un humanisme* (1946) [*Existentialism is a Humanism*] can be glimpsed in the series of novels, *Les Chemins de la Liberté* (1945-49) [*The Roads to Freedom*].

Sartre is perhaps best known as a playwright. In *Les Mouches* (1943) [*The Flies*], the young killer's committed freedom is pitted against the powerless Jupiter, while in *Huis Clos* (1947) [*No Exit*] hell emerges as the togetherness of people.

Sartre has engaged extensively in literary criticism and has written studies on Baudelaire (1947) and Jean Genet (1952). A biography of his childhood, *Les Mots* [*The Words*], appeared in 1964.

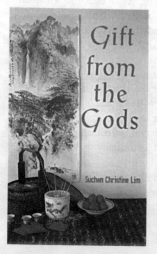

Gift from the Gods

Suchen Christine Lim

GRAHAM BRASH PTE. LTD.
32 GUL DRIVE
SINGAPORE 2262
TEL: 65-861 1336
FAX: 65-861 4815
P'bk.
ISBN 9971-49-222-9

356

JEAN PAUL SARTRE
Politics and Literature:
The Writer and His Language

There is something deeply narcissistic about poetry, then?
There is something deeply narcissistic about poetry but it passes
naturally through the other person. In prose, on the other hand,
there is an element of narcissism but it is dominated by a need to
communicate. It is more mediatized, that is to say it is transcended
in the movement towards the other person - in whom, incidentally,
you are also going to engender narcissism: your words will please
him precisely because they throw him back on himself. This is what
I call 'resonance'. Reading by resonance is one of the most
widespread forms of reading and one of the most regrettable in so
far as it is that and nothing else. I mean the reader who, coming
across a particular sentence - say a sentence which lies quite outside
the general intention of the work or which is perhaps intended as a
jumping-off point to something else - the reader who suddenly feels
himself resonate at that point is immediately turned in upon himself
and away from the communication aimed at by the work as a whole.
But this resonance is nevertheless essential, on condition that it be
kept within certain limits, both by the reader and by the writer.

*So the narcissism of poetry is simply a multiple narcissism, affecting
not the author alone but also the reader. The reader's attitude to
poetry is analogous to that of the poet as he writes. Wouldn't this
mean that communication was as it were ruled out, since from
both points of view the object of poetry would be a kind of self-
satisfaction?*
This is what I believe poetry is all about - or at least has been since
Romanticism.

*Does this imply a negative, depreciatory judgement on your part
with regard to poetry?*
Negative? No, merely descriptive.

*But as soon as you introduce the idea of narcissism, the idea of
non-communication, or the idea of an aesthetic Grand Mediator*

between consciousness to define poetry, there is a certain negative implication. How, in view of this, do you see the salvation of poetry? I think it's extremely useful. The salvation of poetry lies in the fact that there is also prose; it lies in the fact of their being mutually complementary. In this sense prose is continually having to rediscover and re-establish itself as against poetry. Poetry is that which is transcended or dominated in prose, real prose I mean, i.e. that inner structure of words which throws us back upon ourselves, upon history, upon narcissism, and at the same time upon the practico-inert which takes on things one never intended to invest in it. In this respect prose is the going beyond poetry. But you could also say that poetry is the true recovery of what is for all of us a moment of solitude which can always be 'gone beyond' but to which we have to return, the moment when words mirror for us the monster of solitude that we are, but do so gently, with a certain complicity - that is what you are giving the reader. So it is a different kind of communication by narcissism: the reader is there only to resurrect the author in the deepest quality of his being, and this he can only do by himself becoming narcissistic and putting himself in the author's place.

So one would uphold the distinction you have always maintained between prose and poetry by saying that basically they both stand in a certain relationship to communication, i.e. to the other person, but that in the one case this relationship as it were the reverse of what it is in the other. Neither activity is wholly exempt from communication, but whereas the one as it were swims against the current of communication - in order to restore to its depth - prose on the other hand seeks to overcome the separation or, to put it more simply, to establish communication. It remains perhaps to understand the import of this twofold communication, so rich in comparison with the banal kind of communication which is effected by way of neutral or neutralized significations. You said earlier, in distinguishing literary communication from ordinary communication, that the former consisted in more than the simple communication of significations, i.e. that communication per se was not enough to define literary prose. What, then, is left of 'communication' in the essence of the literary phenomenon?
That kind of communication is not enough because what

distinguishes prose is the fact that there is always an overflow, above and beyond mere signification. One might even say that everything overflows the banks of signification, and it is this 'everything' that forms the basis of communication, or at least of communication in depth. For example, if you ask me: 'What street am I in?' and I tell you what street you are in, a whole series of tacitly understood implications passes between us which if we cared to go into them in detail would bring in the whole world. In fact we remain on a strictly practical level where language confines itself to imparting information. But if language is to become true communication it must reflect at each moment our positions in the world, both respectively and comparatively. And this is something it only does in writing, in the writing of prose. Poetry is the breathing space, the moment in which one recollects oneself. As I said, this moment seems to me to be indispensable. I do not at all accept the idea that absolute communication would involve no moments of narcissistic solitude. There is this movement of expansion and contraction, dilation and retraction.

So there are two kinds of communication in depth, as it were: that which is effected by prose and which is so to speak prospective, and that effected by poetry, which is more retrospective. Does this in your view correspond to an anthropological structure? What I mean is, could one regard the movement of prospection - and hence prose - as being bound up with history, or becoming, or action, i.e. with commitment, whereas the movement of retrospection represents a more strictly reflective attitude in the sense that reflection or thought is more static in its very content, that is to say represents ultimately a kind of falling back on a structure which in turn cannot be 'gone beyond' - the former constituting the future anthropological structure, and the latter - that which is engendered or revealed by poetry - constituting the ontological structure from which one sets out? Does that express your view?

That seems to me definitely so and it effectively stresses the fact that you do after all have externalization of internalization and internalization of externalization. You might call it the moment of interiority. And in the case of poetry we can say that this moment becomes a stasis. But it is absolutely indispensable, rather like a kind of brief halt enabling one to go back to the phenomenon of interiority without ever losing sight of the phenomenon of externalization.

Does this moment fulfil an ethical function, as you see it?
Yes, in so far as for me the concrete universal must always imply a kind of self-awareness that is other than conceptual, a kind of self-awareness that is awareness of Wish, awareness of History. Take awareness of Wish, for example. As I see it, a wish necessarily utilizes the force of need, but whereas need is a simple requirement - the need to eat, and to eat no matter what so long as it is edible - wish is on the level of Epicurus' titillation, i.e. I need to eat this rather than that. As soon as I want to eat this rather than that, the thing I want to eat inevitably refers me back to the universe. Because basically if I detest oysters but love lobster, or *vice versa*, it is always for a reason which goes beyond oysters or lobsters themselves; there are certain relationships to life, relationships to whole hosts of things, which refer us back to ourselves at the same time as referring us back to the universe. Strictly speaking, then, this wish is not directly related to articulation, as Lacan says. It is not something capable of articulation. My language is incapable of designating my deep-seated wish, hence another non-positive theory of non-communication - that one can never, except through vague approximations set in perspective, furnish by means of language an equivalent for the phenomenon of desire - whereas I maintain that one does furnish precisely such an equivalent in poetry and in that going beyond the kernel of meaning through signification which is prose. Particularly in poetry, though, one furnishes this equivalent through the use of words not in so far as these are uttered for their own sake but in so far as the level below articulation is at work in their very reality, i.e. in so far as the density of the word in fact refers us back precisely to what has insinuated itself into it without having produced it. There is no deliberate expression of wish. Articulation is not designed to express wish, but the wish insinuates itself into the articulation of it.

It's an attractive answer but I wonder whether in fact it is exempt from the pessimism of psycho-analytical theory. When you say that poetry succeeds in expressing wish, there I agree with you. But then wouldn't psycho-analytical theory also agree in saying that

360

words can at a pinch express wish but that in no case can they master or control it; that is to say that poetry can reflect it, but it is reflection which, by virtue of poetry's characteristic complacency, remains wholly bound up with the dramaturgy of desire, whereas what you were suggesting just now was in the nature of a possible dialectical - and hence progressive - relationship between what is concealed in poetry and what is aimed at in prose, since prose is bound up with the future and is thus prospective, while poetry, being retrospective, is consequently elemental. In this sense one could, potentially and in the long run, envisage a possibility not so much of reconciliation as of a mutual - and hence modifying - placing in perspective of ontological solitude with equally ontological communication. In view of what you have just said, does this possibility still obtain?

But there's no difference! I don't think poetry is ever going to be a catharsis in itself; rather it reveals man to himself through meaning. There is meaning there. After all the poet is not the same as a man who is dreaming; the conscious intention of the poet's awareness lies very far above the material infrastructure of the dreamer's. Hence there is something there, something which is objectivied in what I might call this almost silent relationship of the words one to another, and it is this something which strictly speaking makes the poem. But there has to be this moment before you can have the moment of prose.

It's a kind of two fold process, then, the one aspect being perhaps comparable to what Freud called the death instinct, i.e. this moment of desire or of meditation on desire which poetry succeeds in mastering with its own resources, that is to say without going beyond it but simply by testifying to it, and the second being like the life instinct, namely prose, though this can never completely emancipate itself from poetry.

A very good thing too, because it is precisely this that gives it its true meaning, in other words furnishes the concrete universal. You utilize your desires, you utilize the way the world is for you in order to go beyond these things to something else: that is the depth and density of the word. That is why I think there is nothing that cannot be said.

It's perhaps in this respect too that prose alone can be effective - and I mean 'effective' in the sense that it can bring about direct change in things and not merely change through lucidity. Poetry may show man what he is, may actually be his lucidity and awake in him areas of darkness of which he is not yet in control, whereas the power of prose lies in its superior effectiveness - superior to the mere presence of literary potential - which comes from giving man the possibility of a real coming to grips with the world. In this sense, as far as you are concerned, poetry can have nothing to do with the criteria of commitment.

We're talking about a particular kind of poetry here, namely modern poetry. There are of course other kinds - the poetry of the Spartan Tyrtaeus, for example, which was in effect a summons to war, consisting of heroic chants, etc., and there was a stream of rhetorical poetry running right through the nineteenth century, even with Romanticism. These were obviously something quite different. What we are talking about here is the poetry of today, which came slowly into being through the Romantic period and emerged fully with Nerval and Baudelaire. In this kind of poetry I think that the poetic moment is in fact always a pause. And to begin with it was very often a pause of self-pity, of complacency with self seen as wish, as desire. It is the moment when desire objectifies itself through words, but above and beyond their articulation. Take one of Baudelaire's prose-poems: he loves clouds, which signifies that he loves a certain kind of beyond, he expresses his dissatisfaction, etc., all of which is on an abstract level, but when he writes: '*Les nuages, les merveilleux nuages*' the position of '*merveilleux*' and the repetition of '*nuages*' give rise to something else, and that something else is something of him or of us.

You were saying earlier that philosophy represents as it were the complete, diametrical opposite of prose, and hence a fortiori of poetry. How do you see this kind of purity of conceptual communication, again in relation to the ordinary, common-place prose of communication which we have succeeded in distinguishing from literary prose but which we ought also to distinguish from philosophical prose - in so far as this prose of ordinary communication can be regarded as being weak, over-simplified, and too pure as compared with the affective impact of literary

362

language? Do you see the question? Because it may turn out to be necessary to do the opposite of what we were doing a moment ago, namely to show that this ordinary, everyday prose is itself too highly charged or pre-charged...

Well, what I would say is this: we all know, don't we, what this everyday prose is. It has nothing to do with philosophical prose at all, because curiously enough the most difficult language of all in a way is the language that is most concerned to communicate, namely philosophy. Take Hegel. If you read a sentence of Hegel's without knowing something of what Hegel was talking about you will not understand it. This is another problem. Because as I see it the point of philosophy - which is neither that of anthropology nor that of any kind of science of man, nor is it even that of history - is to come as close as possible, by means of conceptual approximation, to the level of the concrete universal as given us in prose. In fact literary prose seems to me to be the still immediate, not yet self-aware, totality, and philosophy ought to be powered by the ambition to attain that awareness while disposing only of concepts. Its aim is thus to forge concepts which grow steadily and cumulatively weightier until we finally have as it were a model of that which yields itself up directly to prose. One might cite a profound and true remark of Rousseau's in his *Confessions*, for example, as the ideal to be achieved conceptually when one is philosophizing. For example, he was with Mme de Warens; he often went off on his own for quite extended journeys but always came back to her. He wasn't happy. It was then that he became disaffected. He wrote: 'I was where I was, and went where I went, never further.' What he meant was: 'I was on a lead.' But you see the meaning that gives to his signification. You see how a sentence like that refers us to a whole host of things. It's a perfectly simple sentence. 'I was where I was...' There was no transcendence. And why was there no transcendence? Because of this immanent relationship with Mme de Warens. He could pretend there was transcendence, but wherever he went he was never anywhere but where he was. Or else there were just little transcendences, on loan. He was allowed to visit such and such a town: he went, and he came back. 'I was where I was, and went where I went, never further.' Turning the sentence round, what it meant was: 'When I am free, free to wander as I will, I always go further than I travel.' What does that mean - to 'go further than one travels'? That is when you have true transcendence. The sentence refers us to freedom, to immanence, to transcendence, to a whole host of things, And furthermore to the relationship that lay behind it, the love relationship between two people.

Could one say that every philosophy is as it were the logics of a phenomenology of existence, with the paradox that usually this distinction, so central to philosophy, appears as the distinction between abstract and concrete? In Hegel's philosophy, phenomenology is the concrete of which logic is the abstract; logic, on this basis, can put into few words what phenomenology says in many. Here, though, it's the other way round, because it appears that the phenomenology of existence - i.e. the sentence as it stands in Rousseau's Confessions *and the whole experience it covers - has to be minted in philosophical language of much greater length and complexity than the simplicity of the actual sentence.*
Yes, certainly it does, because you have to rediscover that sentence and give it a foundation. That's the problem.

The paradox I wish to point out, though, is this: why is it that the foundation may turn out to be more prolix than the thing itself?
Precisely because philosophy has to reject meaning. It has to reject it because it must search for it. Desire is expressible but, as we have seen, indirectly, as meaning through words. That is the density of words. But in the same way one can say that experience, in the sense in which it is written in prose, is incapable of articulation for philosophy from the word go precisely because philosophy is a matter of borrowing and inventing concepts which progressively, through a kind of dialectic, bring us to a broader awareness of ourselves on the experimental level. Ultimately philosophy is always designed to cancel itself out. I don't mean cancel itself out in the sense in which Marx said there would come a day when there would be no philosophy. But the necessity of philosophy being the acquisition of awareness, the moment one could say that a man was totally aware of all he was saying and all he felt when he said: 'I was where I was, and went where I went, never further,' - as Rousseau was not - in other words if at that moment he could preserve the concrete density of experience as expressed in literary prose while at the same time being aware of it conceptually, that

would mean that he had not only defined his relationship to the other person and his relationship to himself but gone beyond that to something else. What this amounts to is that philosophy must continually be destroying itself and being reborn. Philosophy is thought in so far as thought is invariably already the dead moment of praxis since, by the time it occurs, praxis is already framed. To put it another way, philosophy comes after, while none the less constantly looking forward. It must not allow itself to dispose of anything other than concepts, i.e. words. Yet even so what counts in philosophy's favour is the fact that those words are not completely defined. The ambiguity of the philosophical word does after all offer something which can be used to go further. It can be used in order to mystify, as Heidegger often does, but it can also be used for the purposes of prospecting, as he uses it also.

A
SENSE
OF
EXILE

Essays in the Literature
of the
Asia Pacific Region

"We are all exiles, who will not rest, but will dream, and travel, seeking an alternative reality, a better future."

Ee Tiang Hong

edited by
BRUCE BENNETT
Associate Editor
SUSAN MILLER

The Centre for Studies in Australian Literature
The University of Western Australia

In Print

True Tales of British India *edited by Michael Wise.*
Unlike most previous books on the British Raj, *True Tales of British India* allows the men and women of British India to speak for themselves. To compile this collection, Michael Wise has painstakingly trawled through published and unpublished reminiscences, letters, diaries and histories, to provide a graphic insight into the Indian Mutiny, the humdrum life of the memsahib and such bizarre topics as Oriental magic and ropetricks. Pieces by Winston Churchill, Rudyard Kipling, Mark Twain and Aldous Huxley are included, beside numerous less well known chroniclers of this fascinating period. *ISBN 1 873047 06 1, 304pp, pb £11.95.* **Publication March 1993**

In Print Publishing Ltd
9 Beaufort Terrace
Brighton BN2 2SU, UK

Tel: 0273 682836
Fax: 0273 620958

The Puppeteer's Wayang: A Selection of Modern Malaysian Poetry *edited and introduced by Muhammad Haji Salleh.* This collection, a copublication project between In Print and Dewan Bahasa dan Pustaka of Malaysia, contains the best of modern Malaysian poetry. In subject matter, the poems range from a woman's place in society to studies of modern alienation, from Islam to civil rights. Nineteen poets are represented and their work reveals a fascinating blend of influences and innovations. A substantial introductory essay by Muhammad Haji Salleh, himself one of the country's leading poets, relates the work of the contemporary poets to traditional Malaysian literature and shows how forms have been adapted to give modern Malaysian poetry an individual and urgent voice. *ISBN 1 873 047 11 8, xxxiv + 124pp, pb £6.95.* **Published December 1992**

PART FIVE

Literary Features

Discover
MALAYSIA
With
Maybank

The Official Bank For
Visit Malaysia 1994

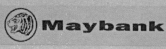

V.S. NAIPAUL
Among the Believers
An Islamic Journey

I

First Conversations with Shafi:
The Journey Out of Paradise

It was from India or the Indo-Pakistan subcontinent that religion went to Southeast Asia. Hinduism and Buddhism went first. They quickened the great civilizations of Cambodia and Java, whose monuments - Angkor, Borobudur - are among the wonders of the world. These Indian religions, we are told, were spread not by armies or colonists, but by merchants and priests. And that was the kind of Indian traveller who, after Islam had come to the subcontinent, began in the fourteenth or fifteenth century to take Islam to Indonesia and Malaysia.

Islam went to Southeast Asia as another religion of India. There was no Arab invasion, as in Sind; no systematic slaughter of the local warrior caste, no planting of Arab military colonies; no sharing out of loot, no sending back of treasure and slaves to a caliph in Iraq or Syria; no tribute, no taxes on unbelievers. There was no calamity, no overnight abrogation of a settled world order. Islam spread as an idea - a Prophet, a divine revelation, heaven and hell, a divinely sanctioned code - and mingled with older ideas. To purify that mixed religion the Islamic missionaries now come; and it is still from the subcontinent - and especially from Pakistan - that the most passionate missionaries come.

They do not bring news of military rule, the remittance economy, the loss of law, the tragedy of the Bihari Muslims now wanted neither by Bangladesh nor by Pakistan. These events are separate from Islam, and these men bring news only of Islam and the enemies of Islam. They offer passion, and it is the special passion of the Muslims of the subcontinent: the passion of people who, in spite of Pakistan, feel themselves a threatened minority; the passion of people who - with their view of history as a "pleasant tale of conquest" - feel they have ceased to be conquerors; and the passion, above all, of Muslims who feel themselves on the margin of the true Muslim world. The Persian distance from Arabia created the Shia faith, and the Persian conviction that they are Islamically purer than the Arabs. The Indian Muslim distance from Arabia is greater than the Persian; and their passion is as fierce or fiercer.

Every Muslim is a missionary for Islam: that was the idea of the brotherhood assembled in the waterlogged desert of the Punjab. And after four days of tent life, of mass prayers, the simple men go out intoxicated by their vision of a world about to change. Some go to Malaysia; they have been going for years; and now their passion finds a response.

There are a few Hinduized architectural remains in the far north, but no great Indianized civilization grew in Malaysia, as in Java or Cambodia. The land (though touched on the coast by Europeans) was more or less bypassed and left to the Malays until the last century.

The stories of Joseph Conrad give an impression of the remoter places of the Malay Archipelago a hundred years ago: European coasting vessels, occasionally in competition with Arabs, men of the pure faith; European trading or administrative settlements on the edge of the sea or the river, with the forest at their backs. Chinese peasants and labourers taking root wherever they can; Malay sultans and rajas, warriors with their courts; and, in the background, simpler Malays, people of river and forest, half Muslims, half animist.

Separate, colliding worlds: the world of Europeans, pushing on to the "outer edge of darkness," the closed tribal world of Malays: it was one of Conrad's themes. And in Malaysia today the Islamic revolutionaries, the young men who reject, are the descendants of those people in the background, the people of river and forest. In Malaysia they have been the last to emerge; and they have emerged after the colonial cycle, after independence, after money.

There is now in Malaysia more than coconuts and rattan to be picked up at the landing stages. Malaysia produces many precious things: tin, rubber, palm oil, oil. Malaysia is rich. Money, going down, has created a whole educated generation of village people and drawn them into the civilization that once appeared to be only on the outer edge of darkness but is now universal.

These young people do not always like what they find. Some have studied abroad, done technical subjects; but not many of them really know where they have been. In Australia, England, or the United States they still look for the manners and customs of home; their time abroad sours them, throws them back more deeply into themselves. They cannot go back to the village. They are young, but the life of their childhood has changed.

And they also grow to understand that in the last hundred years, while they or their parents slept, their country - a new idea: a composite of kingdoms and sultanates - was colonially remade; that the rich Malaysia of today grows on colonial foundations and is a British-Chinese creation. The British developed the mines and the plantations. They brought in Chinese (the diligent, rootless peasants of a century back), and a lesser number of Indians, to do the work the Malays couldn't do. Now the British no longer rule. But the Malays are only half the population.

The Chinese have advanced; it is their energy and talent that keep the place going. The Chinese are shut out from political power. Malays rule; the country is officially Muslim, with Muslim personal laws; sexual relations between Muslims and non-Muslims are illegal, and there is a kind of prying religious police; legal discriminations against non-Muslims are outrageous. But the Malays who rule are established, or of old or royal families who crossed over into the new world some generations ago.

The new men of the villages, who feel they have already lost so much, find their path blocked at every turn. Money, development, education have weakened them only to the knowledge that the world is not like their village, that the world is not their own. Their rage - the rage of pastoral people with limited skills, limited money, and a limited grasp of the world - is comprehensive. Now they have a weapon: Islam. It is their way of getting even with the world. It serves their grief, their feeling of inadequacy, their social rage and racial hate.

This Islam is more than the old religion of their village. The Islam the missionaries bring is a religion of impending change and triumph; it comes as part of a world movement. In *Readings in Islam*, a local missionary magazine, it can be read that the West, in the eyes even of its philosophers, is eating itself up with its materialism and greed. The true believer, with his thoughts on the

371

afterlife, lives for higher ideals. For a nonbeliever, with no faith in the afterlife, life is a round of pleasure. "He spends the major part of his wealth on ostentatious living and demonstrates his pomp and show by wearing of silk and brocade and using vessels of gold and silver."

Silk, brocade, gold and silver? Can that truly be said in a city like Kuala Lumpur? But this is theology. It refers to a *hadith* or tradition about the Prophet. Hudhaifa one day asked for water and a Persian priest gave him water in a silver vessel. Hudhaifa rebuked the Persian; Hudhaifa had with his own ears heard the Prophet say that nonbelievers used gold and silver vessels and wore silk and brocade.

The new Islam comes like this, and to the new men of the village it comes as an alternative kind of learning and truth, full of scholarly apparatus. It is passion without a constructive programme. The materialist world is to be pulled down first; the Islamic state will come later - as in Iran, as in Pakistan.

And the message that starts in Pakistan doesn't stop in Malaysia. It travels to Indonesia - 120 million people to Malaysia's 12 million, poorer, more heterogeneous, more fragile, with a recent history of pogroms and mass killings. There the new Islamic movement among the young is seen by its enemies as nihilism; they call it "the Malaysian disease." So the Islamic passion of Pakistan, with its own special roots, converts and converts again, feeding other distresses. And the promise of political calamity spreads as good news.

Malaysia steams. In the rain season in the mornings the clouds build up. In the afternoon it pours, the blue-green hills vanish, and afterwards the clouds linger in the rifts in the mountains, like smoke. Creepers race up the steel guy ropes of telegraph poles; they overwhelm dying coconut branches even before the branches fall off; they cover dying trees or trees that cannot resist and create odd effects of topiary. Rain and sun and steam do not speak here of decay, of tropical lassitude; they speak of vigour, of rich things growing fast, of money.

The old colonial town of Kuala Lumpur, the Malaysian capital, still survives in parts. Old tile-roofed private dwellings, originally British; the rows of narrow two-storey Chinese shop-houses, the shops downstairs, the pavement pillared, the pillars supporting the projecting upper storey; Malay kampongs or villages - modest but attractive houses of weathered timber and corrugated iron brown-red with rust - in areas reserved for Malays at the time of the foundation of the town; near the railway station, the official British buildings: the Victorian-Gothic-Mogul law courts, domes and arches and staircase towers.

That colonial town has been left behind by the new residential developments, the skyscrapers of the new city, the Korean-built highways that lead in from the airport, first through plantations (Western Malaysia from the air is dark with forest, but it is an ordered forest, with trees in rows, and the white steam rises in pillars like smoke from chimneys), and then past the factories and the assembly plants of international companies.

In public gardens and in other places in this new town can be seen young village Malays dressed as Arabs, with turbans and gowns. The Arab dress - so far from Pakistan, so far from Arabia - is their political badge. In the university there are girls who do not only wear the veil, but in the heat also wear gloves and socks. Different groups wear different colours. The veil is more than the veil; it is a mask of aggression. Not like the matter locks of the Ras Tafarian in Jamaica, a man dulled by a marginal life that has endured for generations; not like the gear of the middle-class hippie, who wishes only to drop out; these are the clothes of uprooted village people who wish to pull down what is not theirs and then take over. Because an unacknowledged part of the fantasy is that the world goes on, runs itself, has only to be inherited.

Shafi worked for the Muslim cause. He didn't wear Arab clothes. But he understood the young men who did. Shafi had come to Kuala Lumpur from a village in the north. The disturbance of the move was still with him.

Shafi said: "When I was in the village the atmosphere is entirely different. You come out of the village. You see all the bright lights, you begin to sense the materialistic civilization around you. And I forgot about my religion and my commitments - in the sense that you had to pray. But not to the extent of going out and doing nasty things like taking girls and drinking and gambling and drugs. I didn't lose my faith. I simply forgot to pray, forgot responsibilities. Just losing myself. I got nothing firm in my framework. I just floating around, and didn't know my direction."

I said, "Where did you live when you came to Kuala Lumpur?"

He didn't give a straight answer. At this early stage in our conversation concreteness didn't come easily to him. He said, "I was living in a suburb where I am exposed to materialistic civilization to which I had never been exposed before. Boys and girls can go out together. You are free from family control. You are free from society who normally criticize you in a village when you do something bad. You take a goat, a cow, a buffalo - somewhere where the goat is being tied up all the time - and you release that goat in a bunch of other animals: the goat would just roam anywhere he want to go without any strings."

"Is that bad for the goat?"

"I think the goat would be very happy to roam free. But for me I don't think that would be good. If goat had brains, I would want to say, 'Why do you want to roam about when you are tied and being fed by your master and looked after? Why do you want to roam about?'"

I said, "But I want to roam about."

"What do you mean by being free? Freedom for me is not something that you can roam anywhere you want. Freedom must be within the definition of a certain framework. Because I don't think we are able to run around and get everything. That freedom means nothing. You must really frame yourself where you want to go and what you want to do."

"But didn't you know what you wanted to do when you came to Kuala Lumpur?"

"The primary aim was education. That was a framework. But the conflict of this freedom and the primary aim is there, and I consider this is the problem I faced and many of my friends face."

"Other people in other countries face the same problem."

Shafi said, "Do they face the same restrictions of family life as I do?"

"What restrictions?"

"Religious restrictions. You have that frame with you. Religious tradition, family life, the society, the village community. Then you come into the city, where people are running, people are free. The values contradict.

"You see, in the village where I was brought up we have the bare minimum. We have rice to eat, house to live. We didn't go begging. In the city you can buy a lunch at ten dollars [Malaysian dollars, $2.20 to the American]. Or in a stall you can have a lunch for fifty cents. That excess of nine-fifty which the city dwellers spend will be spent by us on other purposes. To us, with our framework and tradition and religion, that is excessiveness.

"Sometimes my wife feels that we should go back to the village, and I also feel the same. Not running away from the modern world, but trying to live a simpler, more meaningful life than coming to the city, where you have lots of waste and lots of things that is not real probably. You are not honest to yourself if you can spend fifty cents and keep yourself from hunger, but instead spend ten dollars.

"I will tell you about waste. Recently the government built a skating rink. After three months they demolished it because a highway going to be built over it. They are building big roads and highways across the villages. And whose lorries are passing by to collect the produce of the poor and to dump the products that is manufactured by the rich at an exorbitant price - colour TVs, refrigerators, air conditioners, transistor radios?"

"Don't people want those things?"

"In the end they are going to use the colour TVs - which the people enjoy - to advertise products to draw people into wasteful living."

"Village life - wouldn't you say it is dull for most people?"

"The village? It's simple. It's devoid of - what shall I say? - wastefulness. You shouldn't waste. You don't have to rush for things. My point about going back to the kampong is to stay with the community and not run away from development. The society is well knit. If someone passed away there is an alarm in the kampong, where most of us would know who passed away and when he is going to be buried, what is the cause of death, and what happened to the next of kin - are they around? It's not polluted in the village. Physical pollution, mental, social."

"Social pollution?"

"Something that contradicts our customs and traditions. A man cannot walk with a woman who doesn't belong to his family in the kampong. It is forbidden."

"Why is it wrong?"

"The very essence of human respect and dignity comes from an honourable relationship of man and woman. You must have a law to protect the unit of your society. You need your family to be protected. When the girls come from the villages to KL they don't want to be protected by the law."

Shafi was thirty-two. He was small and slender, with glasses, a sloping forehead, and a thin beard. He had at one time set up as a building contractor. But he hadn't succeeded; and he had given up that and all other business to work full-time for the Muslim youth movement called ABIM. ABIM was the most important and the most organized Muslim youth group in Malaysia; and Shafi venerated the leader, Anwar Ibrahim, who was a man of his own age.

Anwar Ibrahim's story was remarkable. He came from the more developed west coast of Malaysia, and was a generation or two ahead of Shafi. His grandfather ran a little village restaurant; his father was a male nurse in a hospital; Anwar himself had gone to a British-founded college for the sons of local princes or sultans. Anwar had to pass an entrance examination; the boys of royal blood didn't have to.

The British had pledged not to dishonour the Muslim religion of the sultans, and in the college they were scrupulous about that pledge. But Anwar thought that religion as practised in the college was only a matter of ritual, with no great meaning. So, with the help of a British teacher (who late became a Muslim convert), Anwar began to study Islam; and he grew to understand the value of discipline, unity, and submission to God's will. By the time he was sixteen he was making speeches about Islam in the villages; he was a fiery orator. Out of that schoolboy activity his movement had developed, and it was now highly organized, with a building in Kuala Lumpur, offices, staff, even a school.

He was in touch with Muslim movements abroad - in Indonesia, Bangladesh, Pakistan. He had been to Iran and met Ayatollah Khomeini; that had added to his reputation locally. For Anwar Ibrahim, Islam was the energizer and purifier that was needed in Malaysia; true Islam awakened people, especially Malays, and at the same time it saved them from the corruption of the racialist politics of Malaysia, the shabbiness of the money culture and easy Western imitation.

His office in ABIM - with staff in outer cubicles, with typewriters and filing cabinets - was like the office of a modest business executive: modern tools and modern organization to serve the Islamic puritan cause. He was small and slight, slighter than Shafi, and even more boyish in appearance. He was attractive; and it added to his attractiveness that in spite of his great local authority he gave the impression of a man still learning, still thinking things out. His grand view of Islam gave him a security that not all of his followers had; and travel had added to his vision. He disapproved of the "faddishness" of some Malaysian Muslim groups, their religious and political simplicities. He admitted that he had not yet thought through the economic side of things; he said he was still only at "the conscientization stage." I got the impression that he genuinely believed that an Islamic economic system was something he might one day bring over from a place like Pakistan.

I would have liked to talk more with Anwar. It occurred to me, after our first meeting in the ABIM office, that I should travel about Malaysia with him and see the country through his eyes. He was willing, but it didn't work out. He was busy, at the centre of all the ABIM activity; he was constantly on the move, by car and plane; he was in demand as an orator. When the second of our arrangements fell through, he sent Shafi to see me at the Holiday Inn, where I was staying.

It was only because of Anwar's recommendation that Shafi, when he came, opened himself to me. And even as it was, Shafi was diffident about putting himself forward, of appearing as a spokesman, of derogating from the dignity of the leader.

"I am not the leader," Shafi said with a laugh, when we sat in the Gardenia coffee shop. "I'm only a general."

It wasn't easy to talk with Shafi in the beginning. He spoke the abstractions of the movement, and abstractions made his language awkward. He dodged concrete detail, not because he was secretive, but because he was used only to answering questions about the faith and the movement, and not about himself.

He said he didn't like places like the Holiday Inn. I thought this was an exaggeration until he began to talk about the wastefulness of city life. And I never became reconciled to the difference between the man who was talking to me - intelligent, self-possessed, scholarly-looking - and the slack village life he said he came out of and longed to go back to.

He wanted to go back, to have again a sense of the fitness and wholeness of things; and I could see how for him Islam was the perfect vehicle. But Shafi - a professional man, an organizer - had been made by the world he rejected; that was the world that had released his intelligence. It would not have been easy for him to separate the part of himself that was purely traditional or instinctive from the part for which he alone was responsible. And his village had changed; and Malaysia had changed; and the world had changed.

It was of that changed and urgent world that, not long after Shafi left me, I heard the Malaysian foreign minister speak at a seminar at the university. The minister wore a flowered shirt: that was the only touch of traditional colour. He - and the Indian official from his ministry - spoke of the discussions at the recent Non-aligned Conference in Havana; he spoke of the disturbance on the northern borders: Thailand, Cambodia, Vietnam. Foreign ambassadors were present. The two men from the Chinese embassy, in short-sleeved grey safari suits, made notes, holding their pens straight up in the Chinese calligrapher's way. Afterwards big cars took some of the ambassadors away. It wasn't only the rich local Chinese and the builders of highways and the manufacturers of colour TV sets that had altered the world.

It was to another kind of old life that later, at dinner at the house of a distinguished Indian lawyer, the talk turned. James Puthucheary, the lawyer, had once been active in colonial politics in Malaysia and Singapore. He said, "I've been jailed by the British, the Singaporeans and the Malaysians. The only people who jailed me in such a way that it was possible to be friendly with them afterwards were the British." The British colonial secretary - in rank just below the governor - came to see him in jail one day. Before he came into the cell he said, "Mr. Puthucheary, do you mind me coming into your room?" Afterwards, Puthucheary said, they "both went down in the world." The colonial secretary retired and went into business; Puthucheary completed the studies he had begun in jail and became a lawyer. "We used to meet and play bridge."

It was an elegant and educational middle-class gathering, conscious, in addition, of its racial variety: Malays, Chinese, Indians. There were many cars in the drive and on the lawn. Old battles, old rules; and it might have been said that - with the help of the money of Malaysia - these men had just arrived at dignity. The world had moved fast for them. But already what had been won was being undermined by the grief and rage of the people not represented there, the people of river and forest who had stood outside the awakening of colonial days, and whose sons now made the first generation of educated village Malays. For them the world had moved even faster.

It was possible in the morning to read the newspaper with greater understanding. *Shares worth $15m offered to bumiputras*. A *bumiputra* (the word was Sanskrit, pre-Islamic) was a "son of the soil," a Malay; and Malays were to be given loans to buy the shares reserved for them. This was how the government discriminated in their favour, seeking to bring them up economically to the level of the Chinese. The method was ineffectual; it had only created a favoured class of Malay "front men." It was against this kind of racialism that Anwar Ibrahim and ABIM campaigned, setting up against it a vision of a purer Islamic way.

Mandatory Islamic studies welcome, says Abim: Islam was to be a compulsory subject for Muslims in schools. *Rahman: Don't neglect spiritual growth*: that was a government man, as Muslim as anyone else. *Hear the call from across the desert sands*: that was a feature article, for this special day, the Festival of Sacrifice, by a well-known columnist, a good, lyrical piece about family memories of the pilgrimage to Mecca.

Only half the population was Muslim; but everyone had to make his obeisance to Islam. The pressures came from below: a movement of purification and cleansing, but also a racial movement. It made for a general nervousness. It made people hide from the visitor for fear that they might be betrayed. It led - oddly, in this land of rain and steam and forest - to the atmosphere of the ideological state.

Shafi came in the morning, dressed in formal Malay clothes for the religious holiday, the Festival of Sacrifice. He wore a pale-orange tunic and trousers (this part of the Malay costume copied from the Chinese), with gold studs in the tunic; he had a sarong around his middle like a slack cummerbund (the sarong was the original Malay dress, and Shafi's had been woven for him, in pastel stripes, by his mother); and he had a black velvet cap that folded flat (the cap was the Indian part of the Malay costume). He looked princely. With a knife at his side he might have been a raja of a hundred years before, standing on a riverbank, with his own court. But he had driven up in his car, and we were in the lobby of the Holiday Inn.

He said, "Did you read what I said last night? Did you like it?"

"I liked what you said about your family unit."

"Do you want to ask more?" He was eager, open. The effort at autobiography, my interest in the details of his life, had excited him.

"Yes. But I know your philosophy, the ideas of your movement. I want something more personal."

We went from the lobby to the Gardenia coffee shop, passing the bar on one side, where at night in near-darkness couples sat and "The Old Timers" - Indians and Malays or perhaps only Malays - sang amplified pop songs. In the coffee shop we sat next to the window, over-looking the small oval pool with its ancillary little oval pool for children. Everybody there was white this morning.

I said, "What do you think about that?"

He had grown a little tense, waiting for the personal questions. He turned and looked at the people around the little pool, showing me his profile, the smooth brown Malay skin, the slope of his forehead, his glasses, the dip of his nose-bridge, the knob of his snub nose, his beard. He looked hard; his face grew serious.

He said, "I don't know what I think. They are foreign to us, that's all. They don't belong to our culture."

"You wouldn't like to be with them?"

"No. But the water's quite cooling. We have the same clear water in the village. More natural environment. You would see the riverbed. You would see the plants, creepers by the side, on the bank."

Across the pool was a woman in her forties in a black bathing suit. She was white, untanned, soft-bodied but still with a fair shape, and her legs were drawn up awkwardly rather than provocatively on the white plastic straps of the easy chair. Below us was a younger woman in blue, smaller, firmer, lying on her belly. Both might have aroused desire in a sexually active man.

I said, "Do you think those white women are pretty?"

He looked at them one after the other, with the same serious expression: he was trying hard to find out what he thought.

He said, "We don't have a sense of comparing."

"But white men and others find Malay women pretty."

380

"I have heard that. But is it true? Is that really what they feel?"

And in the coffee shop, with the Malay waitresses in long green dresses pinned with their Holiday Inn identity badges ("Beautiful and Homely"), we talked of the village. It was not easy for Shafi, though the effort of thought and memory excited him. The narratives that came out was shaped by my questions.

"I know every corner of my village. We used to go bird-hunting, catching some fish. Either in trousers or sarong. In the trousers, the pockets loaded with pebbles. We used those pebbles to catapult birds. We would go out about ten a.m. in the school holidays or much earlier in the fasting month. And returning about lunchtime with the whole pocket of pebbles gone and returning without any reward. Sometimes we diverted to collecting rubber seeds. We would each put some seeds in a section of bamboo, put the bamboo on supports about four inches above the ground, and try to knock it down from a distance. The boy who knocked it down got all the stakes.

"One of the other activities in childhood was to read Koran, even without knowing the meaning of the verses. We were told by our parents to do it. We were just obeying them."

I said, "Don't you think that's a bad intellectual start?"

"You're right. But it's more than that when you read Koran. We were told from various sources about reading Koran. Each time you read will bring you some goodness in life. I do feel that."

"Like magic, then?"

"It is above magic in this case. It is not written by human being. Magic is operated by human being, whereas Koran is above that. The other book we had is text written by a few well-known leaders in the village. Religious texts, mainly dealing with teachings. They were printed in the town. On how to pray, on keeping yourself clean. Physically clean. If you have water you wash in water. If you don't have water you're allowed to used other things. Stones, wood, bark, leaves, paper. But not bones of animal which is not slaughtered. Basic hygiene.

"You should choose, if you don't have a proper toilet, a secluded place where nobody would see you, and not in the flowing stream where people are using the same source of water supply, and not under a house, and not any place where the faeces will give offence to the public. It is a holy teaching and it is applicable in our life. So

I took it as something we've got to follow. This was when we were not more than twelve years old."

"Was there a book like that in every house in the village?"

"Each of those who attended the course would be given the book. Part One and Part Two and Part Three. The book was written by the mullah of the mosque. My impression is that he had a big cabinet by the wall, about ten feet long and ten feet high, filled up with these printed books. He gave one free first. But if you lose that you got to buy. There were teaching sessions every Friday afternoon and Saturday morning at the mosque. For the children, from nine to fifteen, sixteen."

"Did the books have anything about masturbation or sex?"

"Basically it was teaching about cleanliness. That was one part. The other part was how to pray. What sort of water is allowed for you to use for your ablutions before praying. You must use clean water. Clean water is defined mostly as running water in a stream. The volume of water will have to be a minimum of twenty or thirty gallons. Then you can say it is clean. You mustn't see any dirt, smell any dirt, or touch any dirt. Unless these conditions are met, then the water is dirty.

"If you didn't attend one teaching session without valid reasons you would be punished. And this punishment by the mullah would be acceptable to the parents. In addition there were the Friday-morning teachings by the head of the elders in the village. This was for everybody, and not only children. They taught worldly and heavenly things then. Human relations. Elders and the young, men and women. Cleanliness, prayers. During this Friday-morning teaching they referred to Koran and translation and this encouraged people to read Koran and translations. Later, every day we have to go to Koran reading, morning and afternoon.

"My village is in Kota Bharu. In the northeast. The people in my village I would consider quite enterprising. They do this cloth-weaving - my mother did this sarong I'm wearing. Not many of them are working in the government. Some of them own plantations, rice fields, coconut plantations. They get the people from the village to do the work.

"There were about two thousand people in the village at that time. Everybody had a house of their own, on their own land or the land of a relative or the land that belongs to the religious department of the government. They build their own houses. Nobody squats. And if I can remember, nobody begs. There is no beggar in our village. I would say it was quite a prosperous village. One man and his family had to leave because the land their house was on was sold. They went to another village, and when we asked them later how they were getting on they said nothing can be compared to this village. In the village they could find work easier.

"In the village there were no pollutions of yellow cultures, yellow literatures. A school where you learned to read and write, that's all. In Malay."

I said, "But if you have such a simple life you can't have intellectual pursuits?"

"Intellectual pursuits were nothing. I will give you an instance. There were not many young people who went out of the village for higher education. The only people who went out were the family of the mullahs. They only went for religious education, not secular education. They went to Mecca. The whole of the mullah's family went to Mecca. One of them had a relative there.

"There were no foreigners in our village. But adjacent to our village is a Chinese village. They were different, that's all. They ate pork, and we say the pig is dirty. They looked different. We didn't think they were ugly. They had small eyes and fairer skin. They're a lot dirtier than us. Their backyards stink. Waste water from the backyard stinks. They kept pigs, and the pigsties stink. And whenever the pigs broke loose out of the compound into our village, then the young boys will stone them. And any stray dogs from the Chinese village will be stoned. Because it's taboo to a Muslim to have dogs and pigs. But there were no village fights."

"Were the Chinese rich?"

"At that time they were not rich. In education they were very strict with their children. After dinner they will see the child attend or recite their schoolbooks aloud, in the kitchen or in the front room."

"But you were strict, too? But with religious education only."

"With us religious education is compulsory. Almost every young Muslim has to know it. It's a duty. With us the human value was being emphasized more than the religious value."

"But you fell behind intellectually."

"Yes, we fell behind intellectually. I would say further - in terms of pursuit for material and secular education we fell behind. But in terms of being more human, more responsible persons, being more reasonable in our conduct or way of life, I think that we are a lot better than them. Morally we are a lot better than them."

"But you weren't technically equipped."

"No, we weren't technically equipped. One of our mullahs in the village faced this problem. He started a coconut-oil-mill-processing, as well as soap-making. And that was unsuccessful. Why? I consider he don't have the technical know-how as well as the managerial ability. I wasn't allowed to go to his factory, so I can't say more.

"But we never thought about it, technical learning. I remember one instance. When they started to build a bridge across the river in Kota Bharu, the few of the mullahs and *hajis* [Muslims who had made the pilgrimage to Mecca] were shocked. And they said, 'How on earth could they build such a huge structure across the river?' When they were doing the filling work - this very much shocked them.

"Basically we are good persons, but not technologically equipped, for reasons that we are self-sufficient. We don't need skyscrapers, the big lift, the road. We don't need technology."

I said, "Are you sure?"

"I don't think so. When we were in the village we saw a calendar with a picture of a twenty-five-storey building in Singapore, and we were astonished with that. This was in 1957. In the village we feel we don't need that sort of development. The realization of the need for all these things comes from the experiences on the visits we made out of Kota Bharu, to Kuala Lumpur and elsewhere."

"How did you get that calendar?"

"A few of our relatives went for *haj* [the pilgrimage to Mecca] through Singapore, and they brought back that calendar. Singapore was a busy town - which they expressed in this way: when they sleep in a hotel they felt as if cars are passing by at the end of the bed. That bothered them in their sleep. I can remember only two or three cars in the village. The same person who described Singapore described the village now as more like Singapore - the sound of the car passing at the back of the bed."

"You don't think the old village life is gone forever?"

"No, it should be there. We need good basic amenities. We need good bus service, good school."

This vision of simplicity! But it required a bus - a road - road-making - machinery.

I said, "What was your school like?"

"In the village we had an earth floor and when it rained it was always flooded. And we didn't have electricity."

But in that simple school the new world had broken in, lifting Shafi without his knowing it out of purely village ways. There was the scout movement. It was part of the British system, but to Shafi it would have appeared only as part of the life of his village school. There was a scout camp-craft competition in Malaysia in 1963. It was to take part in that competition that, at the age of fifteen and as a member of his school scout troop, Shafi left Kota Bharu and came to the British-Chinese city of Kuala Lumpur for the first time. After sixteen years the nervousness and upheaval of that journey were still close to him. It showed in his language.

"We came in by train. One day and one night. We expected that. We looked forward. We were adventurous. We were in a group. On the journey we were searching for similarities. For instance, good Malay restaurants - we had them in Kota Bharu. We couldn't find. It was difficult for us to eat; for us we have to take Muslim food.

"When we left we could see a village scene. Towards the evening we see rubber estates and jungles and at night most of it is jungle. But in the morning, on approach to KL, we realized that we are passing by a Chinese community, Chinese neighbourhood, which is quite familiar to us, and we realized the pessimism we faced about the problems of having good Muslim food and not being able to meet more Malays. We were seeing more Chinese and Indians. Quite difficult for us to communicate. Because we don't know them. For us it's easier to talk to a Malay who knows us. It was a shock, but not an upset. Because we expected that. But we were not in the least frightened.

"We had some ideas of certain landmarks in KL, so we get around easily. But we felt we were nowhere. We were lost in the huge community. Each time we go around, out of ten people we could hardly see a Malay. We had expected that. But we were in a group and we didn't bother with them very much. We were staying right in the middle of a non-Muslim, non-Malay community, and that was the difficulty we had. We knew that there were Malay kampongs scattered about the town. But we stayed where we were because of the competition."

Shafi was tired. The exercise of memory had exhausted him. And he was nagged by the inconsistency - as it had come out in our conversation - between his longing for the purity of village life and his recognition of the backwardness of Malays. Deep down he felt - he knew - that there was no inconsistency, no flaw; but he couldn't find the words to express that.

It was now one o'clock. Too late for Shafi to take me to his brothers, which was part of his plan for me for this festival day. Because of the festival the big Holiday Inn Friday buffet lunch had been laid out here in the coffee shop rather than in the enclosed, mirrored room on the upper floor, where on normal Fridays (for non-Muslims, or Muslims not observing the sabbath) there was a fashion show, with music. The hotel depressed Shafi because it was alien, wasteful, full of strangers without belief and indifferent to the rules: I could see it now with his eyes. We walked past the bar, dark even in daylight. On the other side of the corridor were show-cases of Selangor Pewter - locally made decorative objects on show in every hotel, every souvenir shop, advertised in every local brochure, every magazine.

It was strange to think of books being written and published in Shafi's village, books of rules like those written in Iran by ayatollahs like Khomeini and Shariatmadari, copies of which were to be found in the houses of their followers, who could consult them without shame on the most intimate matters to find out what was permitted by the Koran and approved Islamic tradition, and what was not permitted. The simple life was a rigid life. It had rules for everything; and everyone had to learn the rules.

In Pakistan the fundamentalists believed that to follow the right rules was to bring about again the purity of the early Islamic way: the reorganization of the world would follow automatically on the rediscovery of the true faith. Shafi's grief and passion, in multi-racial Malaysia, were more immediate; and I felt that for him the wish to re-establish the rules was also a wish to re-create the security of his childhood, the Malay village life he had lost.

Some grief like that touches most of us. It is what, as individuals, responsible for ourselves, we constantly have to accommodate ourselves to. Shafi, in his own eyes, was the first man expelled from paradise. He blamed the world; he shifted the whole burden of that accommodation onto Islam.

This thought came later. That afternoon, after Shafi had left me, I was full of his mood. In the bar that evening I at last had the Holiday Inn's complimentary drink, "Tropical Aura." The Old Timers dinned away; the drink tasted of tinned pineapple juice. Later, in the coffee shop - again - I had an omelette. It wasn't good. But the young Malay waiter was punctilious and helpful. And I thought, looking at him laying the next table carefully, trying to do the right thing, "He is like Shafi, I must remember."

THE JOURNEY CONTINUES IN SKOOB PACIFICA ANTHOLOGY NO,3 : EXILED IN PARADISE

VIKRAM SETH
From Heaven Lake
Travels through Sinkiang and Tibet

2
Heaven Lake

In the eastern provinces of China there is today little space for solitude or contemplation. In Nanjing, the city I live in for most of the year, there are Ming tombs outside the town itself, where, if I am willing to bicycle from the university, I can gain some sense of quiet: the wooded paths, with acorns and chestnuts strewn across the ground, the layers of leaf mould, the sunlight spraying through the branches of the *wutung* trees. The crowds visit the Ming tombs or the mausoleum of Sun Yat Sen, but the forest between these monuments, on the slopes of the Purple Gold Mountain (Zi jin shan) is deserted but for the occasional farmboy gathering acorns for fodder, the scratch and scamper of a squirrel ('pine-rat' in Chinese) or the startling chack of a magpie, an oversized version of its European counterpart. Here one can lie in the spring and autumn, and also in the summer, when the city-dwellers are gasping in the humid trap of the 'third furnace of the Yangtse' (the outer two being Chongqing and Wuhan); the cooling canopy of leaves blunts the virulence of the heat.

Such refuges are rare in the eastern provinces, though, and their margins closely defined. The road, the observatory, the farms with their overpowering odour of pig manure, the well-visited historical monuments on either side of the wood, combine to curb the freedom of the wanderer. There are few places where poets like Tao Yuanming or Wang Wei would feel at ease today. Even where such still centres exist, more inaccessible perhaps, less amenable to blind construction and defacement, there are too many human impositions: calligraphy carved into a precipice as you turn a bend on a bamboo raft, or a red pavilion capping a peak of fern and pine.

But the western provinces are less oppressed by the charge of population and settlement. The day after we leave Turfan and arrive at Urumqi, I find an area of such natural beauty that I could live here, content, for a year. This is the region of Tian Chi, or Heaven

Lake, a few hours by bus from Urumqi. It is not that this area is not geographically circumscribed (this time by desert rather than by tillage), but that its area is larger, so that one can wander for a day, for days, and not exhaust its limits. Again, it is not that man does not impinge on it, but that the unconscious ornamentation of hut and flock does not abrade its spirit or form.

It was initially John's idea to go to Heaven Lake. After we left Turfan, we discovered that he had forgotten to take with him his travel pass and residence permit - both essential documents. Since we too are heading for Urumqi, we bring them for him. When, after a short train journey, we arrive at the hotel there, we see him seated on the stone steps like one of the flanking lions at the entrance to buildings all over China, a disconsolate but anticipatory expression on his face. He cheers up considerably when he gets his pass back, and begins to talk about dinner. This is not the first important object that he has left of late: he lost a pair of shoes earlier on in his travels - he left them behind on a train - and had since had to make do with slippers. There are even some who, having heard him apostrophising a mop as the head of Genghis Khan, believe that he has lost his mind. The two things that John seems incapable of losing are his good humour and his appetite. His continuing leanness complements a permanent hungry look. The large amounts of food he compresses inside himself are converted into a wiry energy remarkable in one so thin. After he cheerfully climbed Mount Emei in Sichuan in a few hours in midwinter ('trotted up' would be how he would put it), I began to wonder if he was immune to exhaustion in the way that some people are born physiologically immune to pain.

Dinner over, we return to our room and talk about travel plans. After visiting Heaven Lake, John plans to go further into Xinjiang. I discover that he met a Uighur family on the train to Xinjiang, who had adopted him, as indeed everyone who meets John is tempted to do. He responded by falling quickly and passionately in love with the daughter, another not infrequent occurrence. Now John wants to go to their home town, Kuche, yet further west. If he cannot get a pass, though, he will have to think of something else; he cannot jeopardise their good standing with the authorities by visiting them without permission. I mention that I now have a pass to Lhasa, and would much prefer hitch-hiking through western

China to flying - if it is feasible. John also wants to go to Tibet; a policeman he has met on a train has offered him a possible lift from the railhead of Liuyuan all the way to Lhasa by jeep. Since Liuyuan, not far from here, is the starting-point for one of the routes that cross Qinghai, I ask if I can join him. John thinks it will be possible; this pleases me, as I have no idea how to set about getting a lift into Tibet and also because John would make, I think, an ideal travelling partner, with his practical manner and his sound core of madness.

Whilst in Urumqi, John mentions that he is interested in going to Heaven Lake, and, if he likes it, staying there for three or four days; for my part I am not eager to be shown further ruins by the local branch of the Foreign Affairs Office. The teachers from the university mention that they, too, will be making a day-trip to Heaven Lake, and describe the alternative delights on offer to the group: horse races and a visit to a Kazakh hut. But I am certain that I want to leave them for a few days, and in a little convulsion of flexibility, they agree.

The public bus from Urumqi to Heaven Lake leaves at eight the next morning; however, our hotel is a considerable distance outside the city, and there are no buses that could get us to the city centre in time. We stand on a deserted firing range at dawn, a forlorn knot of three - Ann, a friend of John's, is going to Heaven Lake for a day - gazing from the top of a mound at the long and trafficless road into town. Around seven o'clock we get a lift in a transport company truck, but this takes us just a couple of miles down the road. One further lift and a bus journey later we are in the city centre, but it is 8.05. Resigning ourselves to a day's delay, we decide not to go to the bus depot and instead to buy breakfast, when suddenly we see a bus with the sign 'Heaven Lake' bearing down on us. We try desperately to flag it down; the driver, catching sight of this unkempt trio, slams on the brakes.

We sit in the last row but one, bumped about but free of stares. The bus rolls out of the drab grid of the city, and we are soon in open countryside, with fields of sunflowers as far as the eye can see, their heads all facing us. Where there is no water, the land reverts to desert. While still on level ground we see in the distance the tall range of Mount Bogda, our destination, abrupt like a shining prism laid horizontally on the desert surface. It is over 5,000 metres high, and the peaks are under permanent snow, in powerful contrast to the flat desert all around. Heaven Lake lies part of the way up this range, about 2,000 metres above sea-level, at the foot of one of the higher snow-peaks.

As the bus climbs, the sky, brilliant before, grows overcast. I have brought nothing warm to wear; it is all down at the hotel in Urumqi. Rain begins to fall. The man behind me is eating overpoweringly smelly goats' cheese. The bus window leaks inhospitably but reveals a beautiful view. We have passed quickly from desert through arable land to pasture, and the ground is now green with grass, the slopes dark with pine. A few cattle drink at a clear steam flowing past moss-covered stones: it is a Constable landscape. The stream changes into a white torrent, and as we climb higher I wish more and more that I had brought with me something warmer than the pair of shorts that have served me so well in the desert. The stream (which, we are told, rises in Heaven Lake) disappears, and we continue our slow ascent. About noon we arrive at Heaven Lake, and look for a place to stay at the foot, which is the resort area. We get a room in a small cottage, and I am happy to note that there are thick quilts on the beds.

Standing outside the cottage we survey our surroundings. Heaven Lake is long, sardine-shaped and fed by snowmelt from a stream at its head. The lake is an intense blue, surrounded on all sides by green mountain walls, dotted with distant sheep. At the head of the lake, beyond the delta of the in-flowing stream, is a massive snow-capped peak which dominates the vista; it is part of a series of peaks that culminate, a little out of view, in Mount Bogda itself.

For those who live in the resort cottages there is a small mess-hall by the shore. We eat here sometimes, and sometimes buy food from the vendors outside, who sell kebab and *naan* until the last buses leave. The kebabs, cooked on skewers over charcoal braziers, are particularly good; highly spiced and well-done. Horses' milk is available too from the local Kazakh herdsmen, but I decline this. I am so affected by the cold that Mr Cao, the relaxed young man who runs the mess, lends me a spare pair of trousers, several sizes too large but more than comfortable. Once I am warm again, I feel a pre-dinner spurt of energy - dinner will be long in coming - and I ask him whether the lake is good for swimming in.

'Swimming?' Mr Cao says. 'You aren't thinking of swimming, are you?'

391

'I thought I might,' I confess. 'What's the water like?'

He doesn't answer me immediately, turning instead to examine some receipts with exaggerated interest.

I look at the water again, inviting and smooth, just begging a body to slice through it, to luxuriate in its clear depths. I untie my shoelaces. This little mess will serve as a changing room; after all, I have just changed into a pair of trousers here.

Mr Cao, with great offhandedness, addresses the air. 'People are often drowned here,' he says. After a pause, he continues. 'When was the last one?' This question is directed at the cook, who is preparing a tray of *mantou* (squat white steamed breadrolls), and who now appears, wiping his doughy hand across his forehead. 'Was it the Beijing athlete?' asks Mr Cao.

'Yes, yes, it was the Beijing athlete.'

'The Beijing athlete?' I quaver. The placidity of this water must be deceptive.

'Yes, I think so,' says Mr Cao to the cook. 'He'd swim across the lake and back every day...'

'Every day,' repeats the cook.

'And then one day he swam to the other side, and had just started on his way back when he simply disappeared. Drowned.'

'Drowned,' tolls the cook.

'Drowned? The Beijing athlete?' I ask, anxiously.

'Yes,' says Mr Cao. 'He was from an athletics college in Beijing. Or was it Tianjin?'

'Beijing,' says the cook, with authority.

'But...how did this happen?' I blurt out.

Mr Cao has gone back to his receipts. He looks up at the cook, who says, in a lugubrious tone, 'Well, no one knows. He might have had a heart attack.'

'Or he might have got cramp,' suggests Mr Cao.

'Or maybe the water was too cold,' adds the cook.

'Or maybe it was a current under the surface. No one knows. His body was never found.'

'Never found,' mutters the cook as he heads back for the kitchen.

I retie my shoelaces.

Later, however, temptation overcomes caution; I take a short dip, keeping close to the shore. The water is clean and extremely cold, and I splash around for a few minutes before emerging blue and refreshed. John and I walk around the foot of the lake looking for the point where it flows out into the stream that we drove along this morning. We find it, eventually, and it is spectacular, the more so since the sky is now in the last multicoloured spasms of sunset. The stream plunges downwards in a series of cataracts through the pines, into a small round blue pool, almost completely enclosed by forested slopes. The pool is probably about thirty metres across; the stream that we assume must flow out from it cannot be seen - which is odd, because the whole pool seems to be visible.

We spend several days at Heaven Lake wandering around, though John's slippers severely hinder him. The day John is leaving, we go down to the small ice-blue serendipitous pool with a picnic lunch provided by Mr Cao (bread, dry cooked meat, peanuts, tomatoes and oranges). We are completely cut off from the world. It drizzles and is brilliantly sunny by turns. We make a fire in the lee of a rock, swim nude without fear of upsetting chance tourists, sun ourselves or shiver before the fire as the weather alternates, eat, drink and are merry. The pool, it seems, flows out in one hammering vertical plunge through a narrow slit in its steep enclosing walls, then churns through a sluice of rock into a gorge-like stream bed. It is this stream that we saw tamely channelled through pasture and a field a few miles below, finally disappearing into the sand and heat of the desert around.

John leaves ('trundles along', in his phrase) by the afternoon bus. We have agreed to meet in about two weeks to begin our journey to Tibet. I will miss his Monty Python banter which exaggerates (and thus defuses) the irritations and inefficiencies of travelling. When I get back to our room I find that he has left a dictionary behind.

I decide to stay an extra day or two at Heaven Lake, so much do I like this place. I spend them roaming around by the head of the lake, watching herdsmen cross the stream delta with cattle and horses; walking towards the snowline; or reading Confucius' *Analects*. I lie on a rock by the shore, and read very slowly, pausing to digest it with segments of orange. I find the sage himself somewhat stodgy until, among the strictures and dicta, the condemnations of improprieties and impieties, I come across a passage where he is talking to his disciples:

When Tzu-lu, Tseng Hsi, Jan Yu and Kung-hsi Hua were seated in attendance, the Master said, 'Do not feel constrained simply because I am a little older than you are. Now you are in the habit of saying, "My abilities are not appreciated," but if someone did appreciate your abilities, do tell me how you would go about things.'

Tzu-lu promptly answered, 'If I were to administer a state of a thousand chariots, situated between powerful neighbours, troubled by armed invasions and by repeated famines, I could, within three years, give the people courage and a sense of direction.'

The Master smiled at him.

'Ch'iu, what about you?'

'If I were to administer an area measuring sixty or seventy *li* square, or even fifty or sixty *li* square, I could, within three years, bring the size of the population up to an adequate level. As to the rites and music, I would leave that to abler gentlemen.'

'Ch'ih, how about you?'

'I do not say that I have the ability, but I am ready to learn. On ceremonial occasions in the ancestral temple or in diplomatic gatherings, I should like to assist as a minor official in charge of protocol, properly dressed in my ceremonial cap and robes.'

'Tien, how about you?'

After a few dying notes came the final chord, and then he stood up from his lute. 'I differ from the other three in my choice.'

The Master said, 'What harm is there in that? After all, each man is stating what he has set his heart upon.'

'In late spring, after the spring clothes have been newly made, I should like, together with five or six adults and six or seven boys, to go bathing in the River Yi and enjoy the breeze on the Rain Altar, and then go home chanting poetry.'

The Master sighed and said, 'I am all in favour of Tien.'

I walk back along the shore by boulders and juniper bushes. The round Kazakh tents squat at the head of the valley in a grassy clearing among pines. Pieces of driftwood lie among the pebbles on the shore. In places, a white cottony blossom lies thickly on the ground, making it slippery underfoot. It is now drizzling.

At the resort area I find that the Nanjing University group has come to Heaven Lake for a few hours. We return together to Urumqi. The next morning we are given an hour or so of 'free activity' before we board the train eastwards. I am walking briskly towards

394

the Urumqi mosque when I notice a pedlar selling sheepskin jackets on the pavement. He glances quickly at my shoes to confirm that I am a foreigner, and doubles the price I have just heard him offer to a passer-by. We haggle for a few minutes until I bring out some 'funny money' (foreign exchange certificates denominated in Chinese currency, issued to foreigners in lieu of ordinary currency by the Bank of China); then his eyes glow with interest and I am able to get a good deal on the purchase. He, too, is satisfied, for with these certificates he can buy fancy goods in the so-called 'Friendship Stores' - goods that are more expensive, and sometimes unavailable, elsewhere.

I am still hurrying to the mosque when a dark, narrow shop, with caps of all kinds displayed by its doorway, catches my eye. I stop: I will need a cap to protect myself in Tibet from the rays of the sun. The interior of the shop is dingy. A sewing machine is clattering anciently away. Moons of cloth, strips of plastic, bobbins of thread, circles of cardboard lie on the floor, or on shelves, or hang from nails in the door. An old, bespectacled, bearded man, sharp-featured and dark, sits inside the shop talking in Uighur to a boy of about twelve. When I enter, he addresses me in Uighur. I shrug my shoulders. He repeats his sentence, but louder this time.

'I don't understand,' I say in Chinese.

He understands this, but not much more, in Chinese. 'Hussain!' he calls out in a thin and authoritarian voice.

Hussain, who must have learned Chinese at school, asks me what I want.

'A cap. Maybe one of those,' I say, pointing at blue cloth caps hanging by the door. 'How much are these?'

The boy speaks to the old man, who holds up three fingers.

'Three yuan. Are you travelling through here? Where are you from?'

'Yes,' I answer, as I try on a couple for size. 'I'm from India. This one fits. I'll buy this one.' I take out a five yuan note.

'Yindu!' exclaims the boy. He exchanges a few excited words with the old man, who peers at me over his spectacles in annoyed disbelief. The boy runs out of the shop.

'Yes, Yindu. Hindustan,' I say, hoping to convince the old man. In a flash of inspiration, I pull out my pen and write 'Hindustan' on the palm of my hand, in Urdu.

The old man readjusts his spectacles, catches hold of my wrist tightly and peers at the writing. Urdu and Uighur share the Arabic script; as he reads it his face lights up.

'Ah, Hindustan! Hindustan!' This is followed by a smiling salvo of Uighur. He hands me three yuan in change.

'But the cap costs three yuan,' I say, handing him back the extra yuan, and raising three fingers.

He refuses to take it, and I refuse to do him out of a yuan. Suddenly, with an exasperated gesture, he grabs the cap from off my head and begins to rip it apart. I am horrified. What is he doing? What have I done? Have I insulted him by refusing his gift? Fifteen young boys suddenly appear at the door with Hussain at their head. They gather at the open entrance in a jigsaw of heads and gaze unblinkingly at the man from India. They are all speaking at once, and I am even more concerned and confused than before.

The old man shouts 'Hussain!' There is silence in the shop. He then fires rapid sentences off at me, which the boy translates.

'My father says he will make the stitching firmer for you because you will be travelling a long way.'

With a few strong pulls of the needle and a few minutes at the sewing machine, the old man, now intent on his work and paying me not the slightest attention, stretches and stitches the cap into a tougher form. With a restrained smile, and a faint snort of satisfaction, he stands up to put it back on my head, gently, and adjusts it to the correct angle. He says a few more words, but I am too moved by his kindness to think of asking Hussain for a translation. As I nudge past the fifteen spectators at the door, I turn to say 'salaam aleikum', knowing that he will understand this.

He repeats the words, and I walk back into the street.

I have rejoined the school trip; our next journey is by train to Xian. The train eastwards is leaving soon. I get on, having decided to return for a short while to Nanjing and Beijing in order to complete formalities, to pack appropriately for the journey to Tibet, and to see Xian, the ancient capital of China. There is some frustration in all this. I could see Xian next year; but a passport, a Nepalese visa, a cell for the light-meter of my camera and money for further travel force me to make this eastward diversion. As the train passes through Liuyuan I chew a little helplessly over the fact that I will be travelling for more than a week, merely to return to this point in order to continue my journey south.

3

An Eastward Loop

Xian reminds me irresistibly of Delhi. It is, I think, the broad streets, the dryness, the shop-fronts with their small canopies leaning out over the pavements, the bicycle-riding white-shirted population - it is too hot to wear the otherwise ubiquitous thin blue cotton jackets - and, most of all, the city wall, the presence of history. The only other place where I have had a similar sense of *déjà vu* is Shanghai. There the intolerable density of population, the sluggish river crammed with boats and sewage, and the vestiges of British commercial architecture combine to create an atmosphere evocative of Calcutta. Beijing and Nanjing, the two cities I know best, remind me of nothing but themselves.

Xian lies on the site of Changan, the capital of China during one of the most brilliant of its periodic flourishings of culture. There is almost too much to see here, and since I have rejoined the group, I see it all: museums, including the 'forest of steles', one of the most famous collections of calligraphic inscriptions; sites of prehistoric settlements; the pool where the emperor Ming Huang first set eyes on Yang Gui Fei, the courtesan who disrupted the Tang empire and cost him his throne; the site of the tomb of the Empress Wu in the dry hills a few hours outside the city; but, most remarkable of all, the vast underground labyrinth where Qin Shi Huang was buried, with its thousands of soldiers and horses, life-size in clay, testimony to the megalomania of the first great unifier of China, and to the skill of artisans over two thousand years ago.

I should have known that this hectic tourism would inevitably exhaust me. One evening, in search of a haven among the bus horns and bicycle bells, I walk through a maze of alleys to the Grand Mosque of Xian. It is late, almost the time for prayer, and I stand outside the entrance to the first courtyard until the gatekeeper roughly asks me what I want. There follows a short and aggressive interrogation, after which I am allowed into the courtyard. I sit and watch the white-capped, white-clad believers pass through a gateway into the second courtyard, and from there into the eaved prayer-

397

hall. The imam, also in a white turban, has a word or two with the man watching the gate before he goes in to lead the prayers.

I sit in the courtyard, imbibing the evening calm, the beauty of the place. There is a pomegranate tree, a small pavilion, a few stone tablets with Chinese and Arabic inscriptions. Arabic inscriptions cover the entranceways into the courtyards, and on the platform where the main hall stands are ceramic basins filled with mossy stones.

When the service is over, I walk to the entrance of the main hall. It is of an austere simplicity; the one concession to comfort is a large threadbare rug spread over the floor. I do not enter, as a few worshippers are still on their knees inside.

A casually dressed young man with a high-boned, sensitive face approaches me while I'm still standing under the eaves. 'Excuse me, which country are you from?' he asks, hesitantly.

'India.'

'I saw you wandering about the courtyards. I felt a bit embarrassed about the way the gatekeeper treated you.'

'Oh, that was nothing.'

'He's a bit abrupt, that's all.'

'Yes. I wasn't annoyed. This is a beautiful mosque.'

'You know, I've been watching you for a while, while you've been taking photographs. You have a very respectful attitude.'

I burst out laughing. 'Really? Well, really, I didn't think...This is such a beautiful place; peaceful, calm. Do you work here?'

'No, not yet. I'm learning Arabic from one of the imams.'

'This place is interesting - half Arabic in style, half Chinese. The inscriptions too, some in Chinese, some in Arabic. That, for instance,' I say, pointing to the inscription across an arch, 'you could find in any mosque in the world. But this,' I gesture towards the small pavilions in the courtyard, 'you wouldn't see outside China.'

On the arch, carved in Arabic, is the fundamental credo of Islam: 'There is no God but God, and Mohammed is his prophet.' The first half of the inscription is especially striking, with its repeated vertical strokes of 'laam' and 'alif'. 'Can you read Arabic?' asks the young man. 'Are you Muslim?'

'Well, I can read the script, very slowly, but I don't understand the language. I only know what that means because I've seen it so

398

often before. And I'm not Muslim. But one tenth of the people of India are, and some of our languages use that script.'

By now it is almost dark. We stroll towards the deserted courtyard where repairs are going on. 'What happened to this place during the Cultural Revolution? The mosques in Nanjing, I know, were closed down. In some places the imams were sent to prison.'

He looks uncomfortable. 'This place, too, was closed down and fell into disrepair. We've re-opened sections of it just recently.'

'Was there any destruction?'

'Yes, there was some. This part of the city is Muslim, though, and the lanes are narrow. The people banded together, and prevented the Red Guards from doing much harm.'

'But did services continue at all during that period?'

'No. The imams were ordered not to hold services.'

I decide not to ask any more questions; we carry on walking. He talks about the wall structure and Chinese roofs, comments on the absence of cupolas. Suddenly he turns towards me and says, 'There were some services. But they were in private homes. You know, that is where women normally pray, at home. So it was not so difficult to arrange things, though of course they had to be held secretly. The whole flavour of our life changed during those years. We could hardly even eat meat, because none of the meat sold in the shops had been slaughtered in the prescribed manner. It was considered a vestige of feudal thought for us to maintain the custom.'

'Things are better now, I suppose?'

'Yes, better. But once something like that has happened...No, it's better now. Maybe it'll stay this way.'

We talk for a while of interesting but more neutral matters, and he asks me to have dinner at his house. I would greatly like to, but I already have a dinner appointment.

'When do you leave Xian?' he asks.

'Tomorrow.'

'If you're in Xian again...'

'I'll ask for you at the mosque.'

'No. Let me give you my address.' The young man scribbles on the back of an old bus ticket. He waits at the bus stop with me - I tell him it's not necessary, but he smiles if off - until the bus comes. Later I discover that my dinner date has been called off. I feel a pang of regret that I had not spent the evening in the congenial

399

company that had been offered to me with so much openness and goodwill.

Returning to Nanjing has for me the flavour of a minor homecoming: my room, my friends, familiar sights. But the moist heat of the city, which even the trees lining the main roads barely lessen, is conducive to stupor rather than to carrying out the enormous number of errands I have to cram into one day. I rummage about my room for my passport, a few clothes, three or four books; cadge a new cell for my camera's light-meter from a friend; cash a cheque for a few hundred yuan; buy a ticket for Beijing; and examine my mail.

Everyone who returns after an absence of a month to the place where he lives, knows, as he opens his mailbox, a uniquely bitter-sweet mixture of anticipation and apprehension. There is no letter from Stanford about my research, but then there are no unpaid bills either. At least my family has not forgotten me. I read their letter with a twinge of conscience: they are expecting me to be home by the 25th of August, on a flight from Hong Kong. I write a cryptic note, saying that I'm going to try to return 'by a more interesting route'. I cannot say more, since it is an open secret that foreigners' mail is read in China. I hope that they will not be too worried if I am not on the scheduled plane. I mention that I will be home by the end of August at the latest.

For all the enthusiasm with which I am undertaking this journey, I am conscious that I know almost nothing about Tibet. My understanding of what I see will lack the counterpoint of expectation, of a previous comprehension, however fragmentary. I have always wanted to go to Tibet, yet I know that this is largely due to the glamour surrounding the unknown. About Tibetan religion I know very little; and I will have to learn about the climate and geography at first hand. I have no Tibetan friends. A picture of the Potala, Tibetan dancers seen in Darjeeling, an article or two in the newspapers about the Dalai Lama, chance remarks made since my childhood: it is of scraps such as these that my idea of Tibet is composed. And in one sense my purpose is not to travel in Tibet, but merely to pass through it: 'coming home', as I write to my parents, 'by a more interesting route.'

Perhaps, I tell myself, this journey will be wasted on me unless I make a concentrated effort to read about Tibet. I envisage a crash course on the subject: a book on Tibetan history, one on Tibetan religion, a reading of the relevant section of Nagel's *Encyclopaedia-Guide: China*. But books, even if I were able to obtain them here, are heavy to carry, and it is too late to sit down and read them. Time has become an important constraint. Besides, I tell myself optimistically, the freshness of the vision may compensate for the ignorance of the viewer. I have only one day in Nanjing and a lot to do. I can't spend the time hunting for books. The few paperbacks I pack are those I have wanted to read during my year in China but have not read for lack of time. They include the *Lao Tzu* and the *Chuang Tzu*: Chinese, not Tibetan, classics.

I continue packing. Sleeping bag? Too bulky, I decide. My small orange backpack? It could be useful; if I don't need it I can easily pack it away into another bag. A few research materials? Yes, I can look them over when I get to India. It occurs to me that my spectacles are badly scratched. I decide to get a new pair, in case my present ones get lost or deteriorate any further. Time is probably too short now, but in any case I can try. My bike has a puncture, and I realise with a pang that I will have to make the sweaty journey to the opticians on foot. But the time I get there I am in a kind of a daze.

> Below the broadleafed planes the sweltering street
> Contorts and shimmers in the miraging heat
> That like a melting lens now damps now swells
> The shrill cicada-choir of bicycle bells.

The kindly old man in charge of the shop gives me a glass of water and a fifteen-minute eye-test. I am lucky; the vision is the same in both eyes, and a pair of ready-made spectacles is in standard stock. He moulds the frame over a candle and fits it to my face again and again until he is satisfied. The whole thing comes to less than 10 yuan, including thirty cents for the test. (A yuan is a little more than half a US dollar.) Elated by how pleasantly and quickly all this has gone, I walk out into the concussive heat of the street.

It is my last evening in Nanjing, and I go out with Claire - she has not yet left for France - to the Shuang Men Lou Hotel for dinner. I wear Chinese clothes, as I have during much of the summer, but now that I have had my hair cut and have Chinese spectacles, the guard at the gate challenges me.

'Stop, comrade.'

I keep on walking. He runs up to me and holds me by the shoulder. 'Didn't you hear me? What unit are you from? You can't go in there.' It is dark, so he cannot see my features too well. Claire walks up to me, and we smile. The guard looks abashed, but I am pleased that with my loss of hair and gain of spectacles I do not now appear too emphatically un-Chinese. If I need to stress my foreignness I will fiddle with the knobs on my digital watch.

For this last supper in Nanjing I have bought a bottle of Californian red wine at the Friendship Store: Paul Masson's Rubion, incomparably better than the second-rate French, Spanish and Italian wines of similar price available there. But the price has just gone up and, disgruntled, I go on to expatiate on the increased demand for wine, general inflation, yuan-dollar exchange-rates and mark-up percentages for luxury goods. Claire looks on with a bemused expression and probably wonders why I have bought the bottle at all. But it all seems worthwhile as we drink the lovely well-analysed liquid. Nostalgia for the Golden State, and particularly San Francisco, pours over me in pacific waves, and even Claire, through the mesh of her French loyalties, admits that perhaps the Californians can produce wines after a fashion.

Increasingly of late, and particularly when I drink, I find my thoughts drawn into the past rather than impelled into the future. I recall drinking sherry in California and dreaming of my earlier students days in England, where I ate *dalmoth* and dreamed of Delhi. What is the purpose, I wonder, of all this restlessness? I sometimes seem to myself to wander around the world merely accumulating material for future nostalgias.

I have been to Beijing twice before; once in the October cold when the hills near the Great Wall were covered with the reds of autumn, and once in the spring when there were violent dust storms; but this time it is just as much of a furnace as Nanjing. I enjoy a leisurely two days there. One of my friends tells me that what I propose to do is 'a damn foolish idea, Jesus, you must be mad,' but most of them are encouraging if pessimistic about my chances of getting through to Lhasa. The main purpose of my visit to Beijing is to get a visa for Nepal. The Nepalese Embassy tells me that Indian citizens do not require a visa for Nepal. The only document I will need in order to leave China is an exit visa; this I already have, and it specifies no particular place of exit. I convince myself that to exit from Tibet will be just as valid as to fly out from Shanghai. I am to discover that I am wrong.

When I set out from Beijing for Lanzhou I feel a surge of optimism, despite the gloomy predictions of my friends. At last I am moving back towards the deserts of the northwest. The best way to preserve this mood is not to think more than a couple of days ahead. As for the trip to Lhasa, there is John's friend, the policeman, and if that doesn't work out, something else, I tell myself, is bound to turn up.

The journey to Lanzhou is by train, first diesel and then steam. The route runs along the Great Wall, then the northern grasslands, and finally along the Yellow River, the railway line hugging the wall of hill above. It is pleasant to be travelling by myself. I can stare out of the window for hours, watching the river turn silver towards evening, and the green irrigated corridor surrounding it grow narrower as we move up-river. Or I can talk to my fellow-travellers, many of whom will never have met a foreigner before. Once you get past the inevitable questions (nationality, age, occupation, salary, cost of watch, what do you think of China, etc.), conversations broaden out into more interesting channels: politics, art, the recent floods, Sino-Indian relations, the price of watermelons in different places. Discussions meander on as station follows station, interrupted only by meals and broadcasts on the loud-speakers. In general, unless you are talking to a political cadre, people show a frankness and a curiosity that I had not expected when I first came to China. Train journeys are the best of all. Chinese rarely get to travel - apart from Sundays, workers get only eight days off in the year - and there is usually a sense of euphoria in escaping from one's work-unit, if only for a short time. Besides, a conversation with a foreigner whom you will probably never see again triggers no signal for caution. Finally, it is true that the Chinese policy towards foreigners is very slow, if irregularly, becoming more liberal.

I say irregularly, because from time to time the *People's Daily* thunders out against the corrupting influence of foreigners, their music and clothes and sexual morality, their lack of seriousness and their exploitative intentions. China is to learn foreign science and technology, not foreign habits and mores. But contact cannot be as aseptic as all that. The Chinese students in the US, Canada, Japan and Europe - and there are thousands of them - will not return home unaffected by their general experiences. Nor will foreign students in China refrain from contact with their Chinese classmates. The lapses into paranoia that the official line sometimes suffers from, and that universities have to follow, cannot but harm the much-acclaimed cause of international friendship. One's attitudes towards a place are only partly determined by the greatness of its history, or the magnificence of its scenery. When I think of China, I think first of my friends and only then of Qin Shi Huang's tomb.

Lanzhou is a brown-earthed dreary city stretched out along the upper course of the Yellow River. I buy some travel-sickness pills, repair my watch-strap, and get a small black travelling bag to go with my Chinese clothes and spectacles. I take a bus for a few stops, hoping to see something of interest in Lanzhou, but give it up as pointless: 'There is no there there.'

But Lanzhou merely embodies more completely what is present to a greater or lesser degree in all Chinese cities: a stupefying architectural sameness, based on a stupefyingly ugly set of models. Street of standard shop-cuboid follows street of standard shop-cuboid. There is no basic variation in the design of workers' flats, government offices, parks, bookstores or even streetlamps. The difference in street architecture between, say, Beijing and Guangzhou (Canton) is far less marked than the difference in the climate would lead one to expect. In the countryside, as one passes by train from province to province, sometimes even from county to county, the houses change: the building materials, the shape of the doorways, the eaves of the roofs, the style of the walls and courtyards, the number of windows, everything changes along with climate and terrain.

But this harmony with nature is absent in the stodgy and conformist architecture of the cities. (Even the names of streets repeat themselves from city to city; the bookstores all have the same name and there is invariably a Sun Yat Sen Park to visit.) However, the older parts of the cities, the lanes and alleys, are their one saving grace: here the style varies both among and within cities, as concessions are made to climate and individual taste.

Almost all modern construction is undertaken by the government: it requires much less thought and expense if the same designs can be implemented everywhere. To be innovative or individual or eccentric is to risk criticism.

Nor is it just in architecture that this monotony makes itself felt. The clothes people wear are similar in style and colour (deed blue, and greens and greys). There is little contrast or brightness to meet the eye as one looks down the street. And in the evening everything closes down by eight o'clock. With the exception of a few all-night eateries intended for night-shift workers, and - recently - one or two catering to the foreign tourist trade, you cannot get a meal in a restaurant after 6.30 pm. At night, a pall of tedium settles over the city. Almost everyone is at home, and has to get up at six o'clock in the morning to go to work.

Some cities do show a few signs of individualism: the tea and coffee shops of Kunming, the gardens of Suzhou, Xian's great city wall, or the plane trees of Nanjing compensate to some extent for the identicality of their main streets. Moreover, it is only in the cities that one will find good restaurants, movie theatres, playhouses, exhibitions and museums. But for all this, the first impression one gets is of a wearisome physical predictability; and Lanzhou is a paradigm of this unloveliness.

John is staying at the Lanzhou Hotel. He has shaved off all his hair against the heat, and looks worn out. He has been unwell since we last met - mainly stomach troubles and exhaustion. He was not able to get permission to go to Kuche, and has spent the last week in Urumqi. He is clearly too tired to try for Tibet; he plans now to continue on to Loyang, and from there to Hong Kong and eventually England. I return his dictionary to him. We talk late into the night and the following day share a parting apple. Though it is clear that he has made the right decision, I am filled with a sense of regret.

As I am about to board the train for Liuyuan, my final destination by rail, I feel a hand on my shoulder. I turn around to face a middle-aged depressed-looking man with a wheedling voice. He asks me a number of questions in an interrogatory manner, and from the way the platform attendants defer to him, I assume that he is a plainclothes policeman. After an officious, offensive and unhurried examination of my travel pass, interspersed with insinuating and adenoidal queries, he lets me onto the train only seconds before it is due to pull out.

I am upset, but say nothing as I clamber into the carriage. My luggage is pushed on after me. A young man sitting opposite me, who has watched this scene, offers me a cigarette. He lights up himself, then offers his pack around to the other travellers near us. I don't usually smoke - I smoked perhaps one cigarette a year before I came to China - but I have learned in the villages where I carried out my research that a cigarette refused may be taken as a slight. In fact, a 555 or a Kent, exchanged for a Peacock or a Double Happiness, is a quick way to break the ice with people you have just met. At one time I was smoking, with no enjoyment and with some discomfort, more than a pack a day. The Chinese smoke more than any other people I have met; the men, that is: it is not considered appropriate for a woman to enjoy a cigarette; dissolute women in movies may be identified by their inexpert but determined puffing.

The young man is an engineer, one of a group of engineers and technicians who are on their way to install some radio equipment near the Soviet border. We talk, share food, play cards. The carriage contains travellers of different nationalities: Han, Uighur, Kazakh, Mongolian. There are young people, returning resentfully to their far-flung outposts after a rare visit home to Shanghai. 'We have been sent to New Zealand for life,' says one bitter young man. 'We could just as well be on the moon.' 'New Zealand' or Xin-xi-lan, is an acronym for Xin-jiang, Xi-zang (Tibet) and Lan-zhou. To be posted to any of these places, is, for most Han people, to be condemned to an uncomfortable and barbarous limbo.

Two members of a women's tennis team, returning to Urumqi after a successful tournament in Beijing, take out a pack of cards and give the men a drubbing. An older woman talks about the grain supply organisation she works for, and about the drought and near-famine which have struck large parts of China this year. Counterpointing her story, rain comes down in sheets outside the window, and the semi-desert ravines swirl with the waters of a flash-flood. As the train jolts on, her six-year-old son draws our attention to the more spectacular torrents, and tells me to take photographs, laughing half gleefully half ruefully whenever a tree or telegraph pole ruins my shot. His mother warns him not to 'disturb Uncle'.

My camera is examined - it is a Nikon on which I spent the last of my savings - and disappointment expressed when it is discovered that it is not a Polaroid. All foreigners are expected to have cameras that develop photographs instantly. My watch, a present from my father after two watchless years, and full of superfluous gimmickry - chime, stopwatch, alarm, etc. - is passed from hand to hand and much admired. I am asked whether I have 'established house', i.e. got married yet, and anxiety is expressed when I say that, although I'm twenty-nine, I haven't. My family photograph is taken out, and I am asked to explain my mother's *tika* and my father's *kurta*, not to mention my sister's cut-off jeans. It is decided that the 1962 border conflict between India and China was 'just an unfortunate incident, the fault of governments, not of peoples, and anyway a very short period of hostility when looked at in the perspective of such a long friendship.' The Russians are denounced, Raj Kapoor praised, the trial of the Gang of Four cautiously skirted around, the government system of job allocation debated. What job will I be allocated when I return home? When I tell them that I will look for one myself, this arouses a good deal of amazement and interest. When I critically examine the Indian birth control programme, I am asked, with some incredulity, how I can possibly criticise my country's official line.

I spend a comfortable night on the middle bunk (Chinese sleepers are three-tiered in the 'hard sleeper' class), and wake up to the strains of radio music blaring out on the loudspeaker system. This is one of the banes of railway travel in China. In general, however, train journeys are comfortable compared to those in India, and one is provided with a continuous supply of drinkable hot water, which the Chinese imbibe in extraordinary quantities, with or without tea.

At five in the afternoon of the second day, the train stops at Liuyuan, which is as far as it will take me in the direction I want to go. I get off and look around. Liuyuan is a dusty, treeless, godforsaken depot, its main street merging with the road to Lhasa, now 1,800 kilometres away. But as I look down the empty street, it comes home to me that I don't have the faintest idea about how to get a lift. Enquiries reveal that the possible contact John had mentioned is nowhere to be found.

THE JOURNEY CONTINUES IN SKOOB PACIFICA
ANTHOLOGY NO.3: EXILED IN PARADISE